We Also Make Policy

Celebrating
30 Years of Publishing
in India

We Also Make Policy

AN INSIDER'S
ACCOUNT OF HOW THE FINANCE
MINISTRY FUNCTIONS

Subhash Chandra Garg

FORMER FINANCE SECRETARY

HarperCollins *Publishers* India

First published in India by HarperCollins *Publishers* 2023
4th Floor, Tower A, Building No. 10, DLF Cyber City,
DLF Phase II, Gurugram, Haryana – 122002
www.harpercollins.co.in

2 4 6 8 10 9 7 5 3 1

P-ISBN: 978-93-5699-471-3
E-ISBN: 978-93-5699-470-6

Typeset in 11/15 Classical Garamond at
Manipal Technologies Limited, Manipal

Printed and bound at
Thomson Press (India) Ltd

To Anjali, my wife, soulmate and collaborator.

To Arun Jaitley, legal and financial stalwart who was finance minister during much of my tenure in the Department of Economic Affairs.

To the ministers, officers and staff in the Department of Economic Affairs, Ministry of Finance, Ministry of Power, Prime Minister's Office and other ministries and departments of the government whom I worked and interacted with during 2017–19.

Contents

SECTION III
INSTITUTIONAL ISSUES

SECTION IV
GOVERNMENT OF INDIA BUDGETS

SECTION V
VOLUNTARY RETIREMENT

A Note on Data and References

THIS BOOK IS, BY ITS VERY NATURE, A NARRATIVE, BUT USES DATA AND references from the Budget documents published by the Government of India, the National Accounts Statistics, and minutes and documents publicly available.

At places, my posts on Twitter have been used, which have been specifically referenced. Newspaper reports have been used to draw some conclusions and references. These have been generally referred to wherever it has been considered necessary.

No part of any secret or confidential government document has been used in the book.

Prologue

A Confluence of Circumstances Landed Me the Job

MORE THAN MERIT, RELEVANT EXPERIENCE OR TRACK RECORD, IT WAS the confluence of circumstances that landed me the job of secretary, economic affairs in the Ministry of Finance, Government of India in July 2017.

Some years ago in 2012, the United Progressive Alliance (UPA) government had decided to appoint officers of the rank of senior joint secretaries and newly promoted additional secretaries as executive directors in multilateral bodies like the World Bank and Asian Development Bank (ADB), in place of retired or shortly retiring secretaries. These jobs pay dollar salaries besides providing the opportunity to work at a board-level position in global developmental and financial institutions.

I was considered to have the required relevant experience and was shortlisted for the position of executive director in ADB in 2013. Finance ministry mandarins at that time thought I lacked the diplomatic skills necessary and denied me the job. I had no complaints, but in 2014 the new government perhaps thought that I had been unfairly treated by the outgoing government.

The Bharatiya Janata Party (BJP)-led National Democratic Alliance (NDA) government assumed power in May 2014. Very shortly thereafter, in September, the government had to choose a candidate for the position of executive director in the World Bank. I had moved to Rajasthan from a cabinet secretariat position in Delhi to head the finance department in the Vasundhara Raje government in December 2013. I was fully engrossed in my job and had no expectation of any change for at least two more years.

In a curious sequence of developments, I got to be chosen as India's executive director in the World Bank by the Narendra Modi government. I happened to be the youngest executive director India sent to the World Bank in many decades. I had six years of service left in the Indian Administrative Services (IAS) from the day I joined the World Bank.

I landed in Washington DC on 31 October 2014 to assume my responsibilities as executive director in the World Bank, elected from a constituency which, though the voting power was predominantly held by India, also represented three other important nations—Bangladesh, Sri Lanka and Bhutan.

A rationale adduced for the decision to send younger officers to the World Bank and other multilateral institutions was that such officers—equipped as they would be after serving in global development finance institutions—would have a better skill set and experience to deal with macro-economic policy issues such as growth, development, poverty alleviation, global financial flows and the like. The government could post such adequately equipped and experienced officers in the finance and other economic ministries and departments as secretaries. The Department of Economic Affairs (DEA), also the administrative department of the multilateral development institutions, was the most proximate department to use the services of such officers.

The government appointed me secretary, DEA, in June 2017, curtailing my World Bank tenure by about four months and making me the first officer appointed as secretary, economic affairs after having served as executive director in the World Bank. Most of the times it had been the other way around—a secretary in the Ministry of Finance going to World Bank as executive director on a post-retirement sinecure.

There was no possibility of my appointment as executive director, World Bank, and secretary, economic affairs if the NDA government had not come to power in 2014. Though I checked all the boxes of the criterion prescribed for the job of executive director, World Bank, it was quite an unusual coincidence that the Modi government decided to pull me out of Rajasthan. It was also not in any ordained order of things that I was chosen for the job of secretary, economic affairs. My successor as executive director also had three years of service left, when she completed her tenure in the World Bank but was not posted in the Ministry of Finance as secretary. The government thereafter stopped the practice of sending younger officers to the World Bank.

Whether it was the result of coincidences or an engineered confluence of circumstances or a merit-based selection, I considered myself fully qualified for the job in the World Bank and as secretary, DEA. I felt no sense of undue gratitude to anyone. I was determined to do a thoroughly professional job, serving the larger public interest.

DEA Offers Unparalleled Economic Policy Engagement

DEA in the Ministry of Finance is the economic policy powerhouse of the government and is in charge of the government's monetary policy. It is the government which formulated policy and rules for inflation targeting in 2015 and decided upon the inflation target of 4 per cent with a tolerance of 2 per cent plus/minus. DEA decides, as government, on all currency-related matters, working with the Reserve Bank of India (RBI). It also prints the bulk of the bank notes and the minting of all coins in its 100 per cent-owned public-sector enterprise, the Security Printing & Minting Corporation of India Ltd.

The budget is the formal and the principal responsibility of DEA. The secretary, expenditure, finalizes departmental expenditure estimates and the secretary, revenue, primarily writes what is known as part B of the budget speech relating to tax proposals. The budget speech, non-tax receipts, deficits and borrowings, etc., are all finalized by DEA. Almost all the fourteen budget documents are prepared, finalized, printed and distributed to the law makers by DEA. DEA also processes the presentation of demands for grants to Parliament and gets the appropriation law and other necessary matters approved from the Parliament and the President.

The responsibility for institutionalization and development of capital markets is entrusted to DEA, while the Securities Exchange Board of India (SEBI) is the regulator of capital markets. The appointment of the SEBI chairman and SEBI's whole-time and other board members is managed by DEA. DEA is represented on the SEBI Board as well. There are numerous provisions in the Securities Contracts (Regulation) Act (SCRA), 1956, and other capital market laws which confer significant policy responsibility on the government, which is exercised through DEA. DEA also administers all these laws.

Economic policy is ever evolving and DEA gets to work for and develop all the new emerging areas of economic and financial policy. Infrastructure finance has seen massive development in the last three decades. Public private partnerships (PPPs) and new instruments of infrastructure financing like Infrastructure Investment Trusts (InvITs) and Real Estate Investment Trusts (REITs) have all been incubated in DEA. The scheme of viability gap funding (VGF), developed and administered by DEA, helped mainstream infrastructure construction in the country. DEA also helped set up National Infrastructure Investment Fund (NIIF), the largest sovereign fund of India. DEA secretary sits as the chairperson of the NIIF. Policy and new legislations for insolvency (the Insolvency and Bankruptcy Code or IBC), Fugitive Economic Offenders Act, 2018, and many other legislations, were all developed and formally enacted in DEA. Many of these legislations were later passed to other ministries and departments for administration.

DEA is represented on the major economic and financial policymaking bodies and organizations. It is also a member of RBI and SEBI Boards. The DEA secretary sits on the Digital Communications Commission (formerly known as the Telecom Commission). Most economic policy committees and structures headed by the principal secretary to the Prime Minister (PM) and the cabinet secretary have the DEA secretary as its representative. DEA is the nodal department for matters connected with the Comptroller and Accountant General (CAG) and Finance Commissions. All the important examinations and deliberations in the disinvestment department and many other economic departments are undertaken with DEA duly represented therein.

DEA is the one department which has the closest ringside view of, and the most intense participation in, most of the economic and financial policy formulation and development in the government. The episodes and narrative in the book reflect several facets of economic policymaking in India.

DEA: India's Economic Policy Interface with the World

There are three principal ways in which India engages with the rest of the world in the sphere of economic and financial policymaking—through ownership and participation in multilateral institutions like the World Bank, ADB and the International Monetary Fund (IMF); through the exchange of views and development of global agreements and coordination via multilateral forums like the G20; and by entering into and administering bilateral investment treaties and other economic policy instruments/forums.

India has been a major shareholder in the World Bank, IMF and ADB. DEA is the administrative department concerned with these institutions. All these institutions have resident boards. DEA handles all matters, including ownership stakes, and agenda items that come up for consideration and approval in their boards. In the last two decades, India has played a significant role in the development of new multilateral financial institutions in the world as well. Two of these—Asian Infrastructure Investment Bank (AIIB) and New Development

Bank (NDB)—deserve special mention in this regard. India is the second largest shareholder in the AIIB. In NDB, sponsored by all the five members of the five-nation grouping (Brazil, Russia, India, China and South Africa) BRICS, India had an equal 20 per cent share at its formation.

India is an important member of the G20, the global economic and financial sector policy coordination body. The G20 has no permanent secretariat and its presidency rotates amongst the members from year to year. This year in 2023, India is holding the G20 Presidency. There are many other global and regional bodies under the aegis of the United Nations (UN), the Commonwealth, and the South Asian Association for Regional Cooperation (SAARC), which are tasked with the coordination of global economic and development policies. DEA represents India in all these forums. The Organization for Economic Cooperation and Development (OECD) has emerged as the global think tank. India, though, has only limited engagement with the OECD.

The most important instrument of bilateral engagement is the bilateral investment promotion agreement (BIPA), also referred to as bilateral investment treaty (BIT). As of 2023, India has concluded investment agreements with more than sixty countries. As the investor state disputes settlement (ISDS) became messier, India decided in 2015 to rescind/lapse these bilateral investment agreements. These were intended to be replaced with new bilateral treaties reflecting a more appropriate investment framework. This work is still in progress.

India has numerous bilateral engagement forums with all the significant countries as well. These forums provide opportunities to DEA to negotiate the best investment terms for India and sort out many other economic and financial policy and cooperation issues.

DEA is known more for its external engagements, though its responsibilities in the domestic sphere are far more significant and important. There are interesting chapters in this book which reflect the width and depth of India's economic policy, development and investment engagement with the rest of the world and the multilateral institutions.

Three Finance Ministers Enriched My Policy Experience

I spent two years in DEA. Normally, a secretary would not encounter three finance ministers in such a time period.

Arun Jaitley was the finance minister when I joined the department in July 2017. He used his legal brilliance, persuasive approach and deeper understanding of the compulsions and chemistry of political parties and his colleague ministers to forge a consensus and make agreements, to find solutions for difficult economic and fiscal issues. He could accomplish a nearly impossible consensus on the Goods and Services Tax (GST), which, after unanimous enactment all over the country, had come into effect on 1 July 2017, two weeks before I stepped into the corner room in North Block. Arun Jaitley had also pulled through the enactment of the IBC a few months earlier. The GST and IBC laws are still our biggest showpieces of economic reform fiscal federalism and resolution of non-performing loans in the banking system. It felt great to ride on the reform momentum generated by Arun Jaitley despite some pullback on account of the demonetization misadventure.

Arun Jaitley's approach provided a highly conducive setting for me to get engaged in running the department and engage in a big way in economic policymaking and institution building. Arun Jaitley concerned himself with only the broadest aspects of policymaking and left all the nitty-gritty to his secretaries. He was also quite comfortable with entrusting much of the job of writing his budget speeches to the secretary, economic affairs. It was always satisfying to see him making only a few changes to the budget speech and other drafts I would submit to him. He also recognized the reality and accepted it quite willingly that the PM's office (PMO) played quite an intense role in crafting the economic agenda and finalizing the budgets. He would intervene only when he found the evolving policy to not be in the larger national interest. The PM listened to him and respected his judgement. The PM also entrusted him the tough task of forging consensus on difficult policy issues. Being a very senior minister with an unparalleled ability to speak convincingly in

Parliament and respected by almost every political party, Arun Jaitley could have his way whenever he felt it necessary to push.

I spent most of my time in DEA with Arun Jaitley. Consequently, most episodes in this book reflect my shared policy understanding with him and his policy preferences. There were occasional differences as well. On some issues I preferred to be overruled, which he did not mind doing, while respecting our difference in opinion and positions.

Piyush Goyal was never a full-fledged finance minister. In the two-year period that I cover in this book, he was formally appointed finance minister for some months when Arun Jaitley had to go to the US for medical treatment and also convalesce in isolation in Delhi. He was, however, required to consult Arun Jaitley, which allowed us to continue to deal with him. Piyush Goyal had to be drafted hurriedly to present the Budget 2019–20 (interim) on 1 February 2019; only a few days earlier Arun Jaitley had to rush again to the US for medical reasons. Piyush Goyal knew the world of finance and business much better than any other minister in the government. He perhaps considered himself entitled to be arrogant about it. He had an abrasive style of functioning, which sometimes led to friction with secretaries and other senior officers.

Barring a few instances of serious disagreement, which I have recounted in this book, I must say Piyush Goyal was generally quite respectful to me. He perhaps believed that I too had some understanding of business and finance.

I had the shortest overlap with Nirmala Sitharaman lasting fifty-five days in all. Those eight weeks turned out to be quite eventful and, in some sense, even dramatic. Nirmala Sitharaman is a feisty person and considers offence as the best way to put the person facing her, in his or her place. Having heard from other colleague-secretaries about how she used to make sure that even the services chiefs knew who the boss was, I was quite prepared to be addressed as Mr Secretary in her typical officious way, and leave the files with her personal secretaries for her decision. It was a far cry from the time when Arun Jaitley would call secretaries to discuss important files and issues and dispose them off then and there without the presence of his personal staff.

Nirmala Sitharaman is the first full-time female finance minister of India. She also has formal qualifications in economics. Unfortunately, she has far less familiarity with economic policymaking, financial systems, the financial sector, and public financial and budgetary management, as compared to the predecessors she took over from. This is not unusual though. There have been finance ministers who grew very quickly in the job and used their political and instinctive judgements fabulously well to prove to be quite effective and successful. I had hoped that would be the case with Nirmala Sitharaman as well.

Unfortunately, she started with certain biases against me. It was apparent from the first time I called on her on the day she assumed office on 31 May 2019. I have described many interactions with her, most of them policy-related, which reflected these biases. Perhaps there was some problem with personal chemistry as well.

RBI, SEBI and Other Institutions Have Massive Influence on Policymaking

RBI has evolved into one of the most powerful central banks in the world and has more functions than any other central bank globally.

Besides the core work of monetary policy and currency management, RBI is also the regulator of banks and non-banks. Besides being the banker of the government, RBI also manages the debt and borrowing of the government. India is unique in this, as the world over the treasury or the ministry of finance raises and manages government debt and borrowing.

RBI is the machine which is designed to generate super-profits. It has zero cost liabilities and its assets yield market returns. Over the years, it has retained considerable amounts from its surplus to create a big pool of other equity. While its official equity capital is only Rs 5 crore (which indicates that RBI needs no capital for discharging its functions), its accumulated reserves and other equity exceeded Rs 13.5 lakh crore at the end of financial year 2021–22. Sharing of the annual surplus between the government and RBI has been a big bone of contention for many years. The Bimal Jalan committee, one of many committees, was also appointed to find a solution to this problem.

Urjit Patel, an eminent economist, was the governor at RBI when I took over. Other than the secretary, financial services, the secretary, economic affairs, is also a member of RBI's central board. Viral Acharya, another eminent economist, was a deputy governor. It was rare that RBI would have two eminent economists as governor and the senior deputy governor. While this had its advantages, it did create problems between RBI and the Ministry of Finance.

DEA has a very intense engagement with RBI on monetary policy matters, including constitution of monetary policy committee and establishment of inflation targeting framework, currency management, borrowing framework and issuance of government securities, treasury bills and other instruments for managing debt and cash of the government, issues connected with foreign exchange management law and many others. The Department of Financial Services, however, is the administrative department for RBI in the government. DEA is both the administrative department and policy counterpart for SEBI. DEA plays a much more significant role in what goes on in the SEBI board agenda and the decisions made therein. In terms of relative seniority, while the governor of RBI is treated equivalent to a minister of state in the government, chairman, SEBI, is considered equivalent to the secretary, economic affairs.

There have been resignations of the RBI governors, but Urjit Patel's resignation in 2018 over policy differences was a rare event in the history of RBI, taking place after 1957 when Governor Benegal Rama Rau had resigned. There are chapters in this book which describe these policy and coordination conflicts, including the fiery speech by Viral Acharya on the subject of independence of central banks, the resignation of Urjit Patel as governor and the big issue of the time—the economic capital framework and distribution of RBI surplus. All these are described at good length in the book.

Ajay Tyagi remained the chairman of SEBI during my entire stay in DEA. I made it a point to attend all of SEBI's board meetings, unlike the practice earlier when secretary, economic affairs did not find time to attend many meetings. Instead, views of DEA were communicated in writing, with the expectation that the board decisions would be drafted in line with DEA's views. The practice of attending the board meetings and thrashing out issues then and there smoothened out the finalization of SEBI board minutes. Policy interactions and conflicts with SEBI during this period do come up in a couple of chapters in this book.

The Life Insurance Corporation (LIC) is a behemoth with the assets under its management exceeding the total assets under management of the entire mutual fund industry. The LIC management, however, lacked the governance structures and modern skills and experience for investment management. It took over majority stake in the IDBI Bank during the time I was on its board. I describe the story of this takeover in one of the chapters.

Secretary, DEA, engages with many other government organizations and committees. Interaction with the PMO on economic policy is the most intense and meaty. This engagement waxes and wanes depending upon who the principal secretary to the PM and who the secretary, economic affairs, are. During my time in DEA, this indeed was quite intense and extensive. There were hardly any days when I did not attend one or more meetings in the PMO or have a telephonic conversation. I was even involved in subjects and matters normally not in the scope of economic affairs. There were two equally strong stalwarts in the PMO—Nripendra Misra and Dr P.K. Mishra. This book recounts my numerous interactions with these pillars of strength in the PMO and the consequences thereof.

The NITI Aayog was the other fulcrum where economic policy and programme issues were thrashed out. Rajiv Kumar, vice-chairman and Amitabh Kant, chief executive officer, led many of these discussions. The physical limitations of this book prevent me from including many of these issues. I do recount some significant ones, however.

There are many economic and infrastructure ministries and departments of the government with which DEA engages on policy and programme issues. The Department of Telecommunications, with the Telecom (later Digital Communications) Commission as its highest policymaking body, the Department for Promotion of

Industry and Internal Trade (DPIIT), the Department of Commerce, the Ministry of Electronics and Information Technology and numerous others. With them, there was another mode of engagement as well. Whenever these ministries and departments wanted any major policy decision from the cabinet, or the cabinet committee on an economic affairs, the draft cabinet note would invariably land up in DEA, providing us an excellent opportunity for suggesting an alteration of approach and course corrections, if necessary. DEA could stop proposals for royalty terrorism or enactment of highly restrictive data and e-commerce laws, using its persuasive power of making comments on cabinet notes. These are described in this book.

Officers Working with You Have a Significant Impact on Your Outputs

I had the benefit of working with quite a few highly qualified and experienced officers in DEA.

Dinesh Sharma, my batchmate and special secretary, was a big pillar of strength and never minced words, always calling a spade a spade. Additional secretary M.M. Kutty, later special secretary in DEA and secretary in the Ministry of Petroleum and Natural Gas, was another person with considerable gravitas. He was instrumental in helping me to successfully organize the annual meeting of AIIB in Mumbai. K. Rajaraman, currently telecom secretary, and Samir Khare, currently India's executive director in ADB, were also highly accomplished officers and provided excellent support.

Many joint secretaries who worked with me offered varied experiences. Govind Mohan, currently secretary in the Ministry of Culture, was outstanding, bringing to work his massive experience in the Ministry of Finance and as a minister in the Indian embassy in the US. He also provided excellent support in developing the international economic relations division, which I set up for streamlining India's increasing engagement with the economic and financial policy coordinating bodies in the world—the G20, OECD, Paris Club and so on.

Kumar V. Pratap, who handled the difficult infrastructure division, was very knowledgeable in the infrastructure space and hardworking as well. His examination of the subject was always quite complete and convincing, but his tendency to get stuck in the narrow straitjacket of agreements signed, and qualifications and other criterion prescribed for the sector, prevented him from thinking and accepting offbeat solutions to real difficulties. He enjoyed full freedom to express his views but had to be overruled sometimes with detailed speaking orders. There are chapters in this book which bring out such major policy episodes.

A.M. Bajaj handled the capital markets division very well. He was also instrumental in seeing through the reforms in stamp duty law and also in the enactment of the International Financial Services Centre Authority Act, 2019, which enabled the creation of India's first international finance centre in GIFT City Ahmedabad. I saw to it that he was elevated to be a member of SEBI Board. Shashank provided quality services in dealing with the RBI agenda and was particularly helpful in handling the economic capital framework committee work and also making the case for government throwing out the IL&FS board.

There were some, who despite being quite energetic and also eminently qualified, would bind themselves in knots causing unnecessary disruptions and delays in making decisions. Prashant Goyal did two budgets with me. He was quite meticulous and hardworking. He also contributed significantly to the consolidation and streamlining of many small savings-related laws into one and also bringing amendments to the Fiscal Responsibility and Budget Management (FRBM) Act, 2003. He would, however, come up with ideas which would make sense only superficially. Another officer, Anurag Agarwal, well-meaning but a loner and always suspicious of others' motives, shut down the currency mints to send a message to RBI over its not lifting the minted coins, leading to a personnel crisis. Anurag Agarwal was the only officer for whom I asked for a transfer, in my entire service life.

There were competent directors, deputy secretaries, under-secretaries and section officers who provided excellent services.

There is a tradition in the department for a comprehensive brief to be provided to secretary, economic affairs for all his meetings and engagements of the day. I would read the briefs very carefully to help me fully prepare.

A True and Fair Account

I think it serves the larger public interest if a truthful and fair account of what goes on inside North Block, regarding formulating and determining economic policy of the country, is presented. I have attempted to provide a true and fair account in this book.

As it is a true account, it names the ministers, officers and other public functionaries involved and the positions taken by them. It also brings this up to provide a background to what was finally announced to the public. Obviously, I have rendered this account as I saw and understood events. Certain interactions might have taken place when I was not present or not involved. Instead of surmising about these, I have generally chosen to ignore them.

It is not an account to show someone in a poor light or better light or to blow my own trumpet. I have recounted quite a few episodes where I just did not succeed. I hope the dramatis personae will take it in the right spirit. I will certainly be grateful if any of these people point out aspects that had a bearing on the final decision that I might have missed out or not presented accurately.

I have tried to update the narrative wherever I felt it necessary contextually, up to 13 July 2023 when I sign this off.

SECTION I

ON INDUCTION AS SECRETARY, ECONOMIC AFFAIRS

1

The Prime Minister Mentions Two Priorities

A Call for an Early Return

FINANCE MINISTER ARUN JAITLEY, AND INDIA'S GOVERNOR FOR THE World Bank, visited Washington DC along with Shaktikanta Das, secretary, economic affairs, and India's alternate governor for the Bank, for the Spring Meetings of the World Bank and International Monetary Fund (IMF) in April 2017; they stayed for four days. Shaktikanta Das was to retire on 31 May after completing three months of extension. In one of our conversations in my room, Jaitley asked me about my remaining tenure in the Bank, years of service left and other related information. My three-year tenure was due to expire only at the end of October 2017—over six months away. There was, however, nothing mentioned about any future postings for me. I did not ask about it either.

Sometime in the later part of May 2017, P.K. Mishra, additional principal secretary to the Prime Minister (PM), called me while I was travelling in the United States (US). He asked for certain details and dropped a hint that I was being considered for a secretary-level posting in India. When he asked if I had any objection to returning prior to completing my tenure in the World Bank, I confirmed that I did not. He said nothing more.

Shaktikanta Das retired, as expected, on 31 May and the charge of his position was given to Tapan Ray, a Gujarat-cadre Indian Administrative Service (IAS) officer and secretary, Ministry of Corporate Affairs, who was due to retire at the end of September 2017. Tapan Ray started operating from the office of the Department of Economic Affairs (DEA) and became a regular member of Indian delegations for international meetings, including the G20 Heads of State meeting in Germany in June 2017. This created the impression that he would continue holding the charge until the end of September.

During a visit to India in mid-June 2017, I called on Finance Minister Arun Jaitley, as was the norm. I wanted clarity on whether I would be required to return before the completion of my tenure as that had a considerable bearing on housing and other issues in Washington DC. Arun Jaitley only indicated that there were four names under consideration, including mine, for the post of secretary, economic affairs. I returned to the US without much greater clarity.

However, on 22 June, orders appointing me as secretary, DEA, were issued by the Government of India. I bid adieu to the World Bank, Washington, DC and the US on 10 July, taking the direct Air India flight from Washington, DC, and joined work at North Block in New Delhi on 12 July 2017.

The PM's Two Priorities

Prime Minister Narendra Modi was kind enough to give me time for a meeting soon after my return. In general, I felt that he viewed foreign postings in somewhat lower esteem, believing that there was a fat salary and no work in such assignments whereas domestic postings, both in the states and at the Centre, involved considerable work.

Though he was quite welcoming in his attitude towards me, he did not miss the opportunity to tell me it was time for me to return to hard work again!

In our ten minutes together, he discussed his broader assessment of the economy, the policy issues at the forefront and the rollout of the Goods and Services Tax (GST). He underlined two major issues for me to attend to. First, he expressed his keenness to promote digital payments. Second, he wanted India to shift to a calendar-year budgeting for the Government of India in place of the financial year (April–March) format.

Digitalization of payments was unquestionably a key policy priority for a country where cash payments constituted more than 95 per cent of all payments. Cash payments were also associated with black money, tax evasion and corruption. I assured the PM that I would do everything possible to work to promote digital payments.

I was not sure about the merits of shifting the ongoing financial year format (April–March), to the calendar year. In our meeting, I told the PM that the world had mixed practices regarding the financial year. I further noted that India also had two 'new years': one in March and the other in October. However, I assured him that I would examine the matter expeditiously and get it decided.

Prime Minister Modi told me to feel free to come to him whenever necessary. I expressed my gratitude to him for being so generous and accommodative. The meeting left me with the feeling that I would have a highly productive and satisfying tenure in the government.

In Addition, Electoral Bonds Were Everybody's Priority

At the time, Ashok Lavasa was functioning as finance secretary besides shouldering the responsibilities of expenditure secretary. During our first interactions after I joined DEA, he mentioned electoral bonds as the top issue to attend to. He underscored a sense of feeling in the Prime Minister's Office (PMO) and Ministry of Finance that DEA was not progressing fast enough in the matter. In addition, he pointed out the urgency of setting up the next Finance Commission and some discussions that had taken place in the Group of Secretaries, chaired by him, on the matter.

When I called on Nripendra Misra, principal secretary to the PM, he also highlighted the need to attend to the electoral bonds issue urgently. I had met Misra in the past three years on most of the occasions I travelled to Delhi on my Bank-related functions. There was a very large difference between his IAS batch and mine. He had served in DEA as joint secretary, under the secretaries whom he would call 'the stalwarts of the service'. I probably appeared to him as an upstart. He advised me to ensure that the intent of the government with regard to electoral bonds must be fully implemented and DEA officers should not be allowed to dilute or delay the matter.

My interactions with Finance Minister Arun Jaitley were more intense, as he would come to attend the IMF–World Bank meetings twice a year and we spent considerable time together in briefings and meetings. He was an extremely nice and polite person besides being intellectually astute. During our first interaction after I returned, he gave me a detailed background of the electoral bond scheme, the reasons why he had brought it in, and why it was a better alternative to the situation prevailing in the country.

I will discuss the electoral bond matter in a subsequent chapter.

Promoting Digital Payments

Most reforms in the financial sector have been incubated in DEA. Therefore, transforming the system of payments from cash to a digital system was by default entrusted to DEA. However, digital payments use IT networks and applications. They also involve considerable security issues. The Ministry of Electronics and Information Technology (MEITY) had an important role to play in promoting digital payments and was also implementing the Digital India programme.

The cabinet took a number of decisions to promote digital payments in the country in its meeting on 24 February 2016. Besides mandating government departments to accept all payments and make salaries and other payments in digital modes, it entrusted responsibilities related to legislative, regulatory, promotional and other measures to different departments.

MEITY was tasked with the responsibility to promote digital payments by subsidizing merchant discount rate (MDR) charges to make digital payments as costless as cash payments were presumed to be. After an announcement was made to this effect in Budget 2017–18 and other necessary measures were taken, MEITY came out with a comprehensive scheme to subsidize MDR charges on debit cards/BHIM (Bharat Interface for Money), UPI (Unified Payment Interface) and other digital payments. The work relating to the promotion of digital payments by providing incentive was thereafter not handled by DEA but by MEITY.

The cabinet decided to divide legislative, regulatory and other governance reforms for facilitating the transition to digital payments in short-term and long-term measures. For unclear reasons, the work of taking short-term measures was entrusted to the Department of Investment and Public Asset Management (DIPAM), perhaps because (then) Secretary Niraj Gupta had taken considerable interest and initiative in digital payments. A task force was constituted by the cabinet secretariat headed by the cabinet secretary for implementation of decisions taken on 24 February 2016.

DEA was essentially entrusted with the long-term measures primarily because the Payments and Settlement Systems (PSS) Act, which regulates the system of payments in the country, was administered by DEA. It constituted a committee to review the framework related to digital payments on 23 August 2016, which was headed by Ratan Watal, a former finance secretary who was working as a principal advisor in NITI Aayog.

The committee headed by the cabinet secretary was regularly reviewing the progress of the implementation of these decisions. After I looked into the background, after my first meeting with the PM, I realized the high priority he had accorded to the promotion of digital payments in India.

Digital payments are essentially payments made by transferring deposits from one bank account or wallet to another, unlike cash payments which are made by transferring cash. Deposits are held by banks, with only a limited amount of deposits/cash allowed to be kept in wallets by the Reserve Bank of India (RBI). Most payments are instantaneous and, therefore, the settlement of purchase and sales takes place instantaneously the moment the cash gets transferred. Many purchases and sales take place where settlement takes place with a lag, such as the purchase of shares in the stock market, which are settled after two days.

The cash payment system does not require any systemic infrastructure, unlike payments by deposit transfers. Payments by issuance of cheques require a system of cheque clearance, the settlement of share purchases requires formation of settlement corporations to guarantee settlements, and so on. The PSS Act 2007 was designed to take care of payments by non-digital modes.

Digital payment infrastructure is quite different. It requires embedding of technological applications to allow depositors to make payments. It also requires creation of market infrastructure that permits instant transfer of funds from the account of one depositor to another seamlessly to complete the payment/settlement. The digital payment system is quite different to the physical payment system, even from the cheque system.

Though the Ratan Watal Committee did not fully comprehend the challenge of transforming the non-digital payment system by deposit transfers in the country, it made a far-reaching recommendation to substantially modify the PSS Act to liberalize the participants in the payment system (by including non-banking financial companies [NBFCs], fintechs and others, besides banks), streamline the system of payment infrastructure by registering and licensing payment system operators (and payment system infrastructure operators) and creating an independent Payment Regulatory Board (PRB).

A Weak PRB Was Created by Finance Act, 2017

The PSS Act, 2007 did not provide for a PRB. RBI created such a board as a committee of its central board. This internal PRB was headed by the RBI governor and essentially comprised RBI officials with two members of the central board also made members of the RBI PRB. This board functioned virtually as a department or extension of RBI.

The recommendations of the Ratan Watal Committee were given a complete go-by when the Finance Act 2017 designated RBI as the authority for the regulation and supervision of the payment system under the PSS Act, 2007. The Finance Act also created a PRB and laid down that RBI would exercise its powers, perform the necessary functions and discharge duties under the PSS Act through this board. The board was to consist of the RBI governor, the RBI deputy governor in charge of payment and settlement systems, one officer of RBI nominated by the central board of RBI and three people nominated by the Central government.

In my understanding, this caused considerable resentment among the members of the Watal Committee, who felt that the entire thrust of their report to create an independent regulatory system for payments to give impetus to digital payments was undermined by creating a board that was no better than the internal PRB functioning in RBI for some time.[1] The only difference this amendment would make was that RBI would get some advice from the three people nominated by the Central government. This would hardly inspire any confidence in the technology companies building the requisite infrastructure and applications to transform the system into a digital payment system and the new fintech companies that would act as disruptors.

The opposition to this amendment resulted in it not being notified by the government, and the creation of another group in DEA to draft a new PSS Act that could meet the aspiration of making India a digital payment country.

This DEA group had drafted a new PSS Act and submitted its report on file. It was at this stage that I entered DEA as secretary.

Overhauling the Draft PSS Act

To implement Prime Minister Modi's two priorities, I reviewed the new draft PSS Act. It proposed bringing provisions relating to what digital payments were, some provisions relating to

---

1 'Inter-Ministerial Committee for Finalisation of Amendments of the PSS Act, 2007', https://dea.gov.in/sites/default/files/Payment%20 and%20settlement.pdf

recognizing digital payment infrastructure operators and other digital payment system participants, and some other incidental provisions. However, it retained the PRB formulation enacted by the Finance Act 2017 unchanged.

I called a meeting that was attended by most members of the Ratan Watal Committee and an executive director of RBI. Ratan Watal, Neeraj Gupta and A.B. Pandey (then chairperson, Unique Identification Authority of India [UIDAI]), all expressed that the draft PSS Act was nowhere near the transformational modifications the Watal Committee wanted and that were necessary to fast-track digital payments in India.

Upon my recommendations, Finance Minister Arun Jaitley constituted an inter-ministerial committee, which I headed, comprising only the concerned departments and organizations: MEITY, Department of Financial Services (DFS), Law, RBI and UIDAI. I thought these were the principal players and if we could develop a shared understanding, the task of creating a facilitative and robust payment regulatory system in the country would become a reality.

There were four clear departures we wanted to make from the existing system: first, the payment space be opened to non-banks and banks, and non-banks be treated with the same regulatory brush; second, the payment system be opened massively to the technological innovation sweeping the world in the form of the fintech revolution, with a highly facilitative system that encouraged testing of innovation through a robust sandbox system; third, payment infrastructure entities be regulated more closely than other payment system participants; and finally, as RBI had a systemic bias towards banks, which it regulated, the payment regulator be an independent regulator with significant presence of the government and RBI.

The committee could achieve a good deal of consensus on all the four major issues. It drafted a report as well as a new comprehensive PSS Bill. The report was signed by all the committee's members, including Ganesh Kumar, the executive director of RBI who was its representative.

The report was submitted to the finance minister and a copy was placed on the DEA website for general information in August 2018.

RBI 'Wakes Up' to Issue a Dissent Note

After the signed committee report had been placed in the public domain, RBI revisited the matter. Ganesh Kumar had represented RBI in all the meetings. The specific formulation of the independent PRB was arrived at after a round of consultations with him. The proposed PRB was to be headed by an eminent central banker with long experience in managing payment and settlement systems. The government was not proposed to be kept in the majority.

However, RBI did a complete turnaround after the report was signed and released. It questioned the very need to overhaul the PSS system, and sent a dissent note to DEA after the release of the report. We pointed out that all these issues had been discussed by the committee and the proposed bill was finalized after comprehensive clause-by-clause reading with the full participation of RBI.

Under Urjit Patel, RBI had a habit of making complete about turns. It had done so on the electoral bond issue. It was doing the same in this case. It had also developed a habit of taking unilateral decisions, like ordering complete data localization for participation in the payment system.

We humbly pointed out to RBI that the report was unanimous. If there was any dissent, it should have been made before the report was finalized. We would have gladly included the dissent note as part of the report and provided a rejoinder to the points raised by RBI.

However, claiming inaccurately that its representative had submitted a dissent note on certain recommendations of the committee, RBI posted a dissent note on its website by way of a press release on 19 October 2018.[2]

The 2007 PSS Law Remains Unamended

The government has still not notified the PRB as created by the Finance Act 2017.

---

2   'Reserve Bank of India releases Dissent Note on Inter-Ministerial Committee for finalization of Amendments to PSS Act', Reserve Bank of India, 19 October 2018, https://www.rbi.org.in/scripts/FS_PressRelease.aspx?prid=45287&fn=9

The government did not take any action on the recommendations of the inter-ministerial group that I headed. These recommendations had the potential to transform the payment architecture, infrastructure and institutional arrangements in the country.

Though RBI is acting upon some of the recommendations made, India still has not institutionalized a good experimental regulatory sandbox. Recently, in a paper issued by RBI, it proposed opening up the payment space to NBFCs and other private entities.

A number of operational decisions made and the spread of faster digital payments have made digital payments as convenient and costless as cash payments are; the best measure being the institutionalization and adoption of UPI that has digitally integrated deposits in all deposit accounts in all banks and facilitates their instant transfer from one account to another. However, the institutional and regulatory reforms that can make digitalization of payments and delivery of credit more comprehensive, all-pervasive and secure, which was perhaps the PM's intent in mentioning this as one of his top two priorities, are still to get fully rooted in India.

Change Fiscal Year to Calendar Year

India has seen annual budgets being presented on 28 February since Independence, though the time of presentation was changed from 5 p.m. to 11 a.m. in 1999. However, the presentation of the budget on 28 February delays its approval by Parliament to April/May of the financial year for which it has been presented. In India, the first quarter of the financial year, from April to June, is the most productive period to carry out development work and undertake capital expenditure. The late approval of the budget affects the extent and flow of the government's development expenditure.

Primarily motivated by the desire to productively utilize every day of the new financial year, right from the first day of April, Prime Minister Modi decided to advance the budget presentation from 28 February to 1 February. The Budget 2017–18 was the first one to be presented on 1 February.

The PM appeared keen on the financial year beginning from 1 January, if not 1 November coinciding with Diwali. For millennia, the kharif crop has been the principal crop of India, harvested around the time of Diwali. With agriculture contributing the majority of the gross domestic product (GDP) and people's income for thousands of years, the Indian psyche and customs treat Diwali as the beginning of the new year. Internationally, a good majority of countries treat the calendar year as the financial year.

Bibek Debroy, then member of NITI Aayog, was the most vocal proponent of changing the financial year from 1 January to 31 December. He produced a paper bringing out the history of the financial year and the deliberations that had taken place several times in the past to change the financial year. The PM noted this and expressed that he was in favour of considering a change in India's financial year at the full meeting of the NITI Aayog in early 2016.

The Shankar Acharya Committee Report Made No Specific Recommendation

The government appointed a committee under noted economist and former Chief Economic Advisor (CEA) Shankar Acharya to delve further into this question. The Shankar Acharya Committee had submitted its report to the finance minister in December 2016. The report was under examination in the Budget Division of DEA when I joined the government in July 2017.

The Shankar Acharya Committee included several heavyweights, including former Cabinet Secretary K.M. Chandrasekhar and the last NITI Aayog Vice-Chairperson Rajiv Kumar. The government never publicly released the committee's report.

The committee conducted a very dispassionate examination of the subject. It catalogued both the pros and cons of switching over to 1 November or 1 January as the beginning of the financial year.

As Prime Minister Modi had mentioned this as one of his top two priorities, I got into the matter very quickly. The Budget Division had prepared a lengthy presentation on the subject, essentially summarizing the conclusions of the Shankar Acharya Committee.

I carefully examined the proposal. The fact base had materially changed from the situation prevailing for millennia. Agricultural production was no longer the most significant component of GDP;

in fact, agricultural production, including animal husbandry value addition, made up only about 15–16 per cent of GVA. Moreover, kharif was no longer the primary agricultural season. Rabi constituted about 60 per cent of India's crop production. The vicissitudes of kharif production had also decreased with the expansion of irrigation and the spread of new crop technology. Agricultural production no longer generated the same kind of impact on India's GDP, people's income and government finances.

Technical development in terms of estimating GDP and income and compiling fiscal estimates and accounts had also ensured that information was available on a quarterly and monthly basis. It was much easier to simply club the quarterly numbers to generate the economic, financial and fiscal performance data for the calendar year or any other configuration. In fact, the government was releasing its financial information on a month-to-month basis.

An element of procedural disruption also had to be considered, as any change in the financial year would have required changes in a number of laws and systems. It was also expected, though not necessary, that most business entities would also change to the new financial year if the government shifted to the calendar year.

Both dates, 1 November and 1 January, suffered from another difficulty in India's context. With Diwali falling between 16 October and 15 November, it was expected to cause considerable administrative difficulty to compile budget documents and numbers on account of large staff unavailability owing to the festive season. December also suffered from this problem.

The compilation of global practices also suggested that the calendar year was not a universal practice; a large number of countries still followed 1 April or other dates—such as 1 July and 1 October—as the commencement of the new financial year.

Thus, the arguments in favour of a change to the calendar year were few, except for some emotional attachment to the tradition of Diwali being the commencement of the new financial year. Even in India, many businesses traditionally started their financial year from the Chaitya month, which falls in March–April.

Government Does Not Proceed Further

I made a presentation before Finance Minister Arun Jaitley. He had probably come to the same opinion as us. He advised that the PMO be taken in confidence. I informed senior officials at the PMO about the conclusions we had reached and offered to make the presentation before the PM. I was asked to wait till they discussed it with him.

The presentation was never scheduled. The matter died a slow death. At one stage, A.K. Sharma, then joint secretary in the PMO, spoke to me about the matter. When I provided all the reasons and rationale for continuing with the status quo—almost no economic or financial advantage of making the switch and the unnecessary disruption it would cause to government, businesses and people—he agreed. This was more of an informal chat but I assume he spoke to the PM about it, which probably explained why the matter was not followed up.

An unstarred question (unstarred questions are not taken up for oral answer in the question hour; a written reply is sufficient) was asked in the Lok Sabha on 15 July 2019 on the subject. I was still secretary, DEA. The question was whether the government had decided to change the commencement of the financial year from January instead of April and, if so, the details thereof and whether it had taken the views of the states before implementing the change.

The reply furnished by the government was that no such decision had been made. This made it evident that the government had decided to maintain a status quo as far as the financial year was concerned. The government also responded, in typical parliamentary language, that the question of consulting the states before implementing the decision did not arise, which also indirectly confirmed that the government had not undertaken any consultation with the states.

This reply affirmed the unsaid fact that the government had decided not to go in for any change in the financial year. This does not mean that this would be the last time such a proposal would be pushed. But it certainly confirmed that the case for shifting the financial year was quite weak and was not on the table.

2

Nix This Economic Survey

Partly because of the budget presentation being shifted to 1 February in 2017 and partly on account of Arvind Subramanian's contempt for the traditional survey (which he would call backward looking, only recording what went up and what went down), the finance minister presented an analytical and thematic *Economic Survey* for the year 2016–17 at the commencement of the Budget session in January 2017. The preface noted, 'This year's Survey is different in coming in just one volume. The detailed review of the year gone by that was covered by the companion volume will now appear later in the year as a standalone document.'[3]

The companion volume (termed Volume II), which reviews the economy, is mostly fact-based and has a well-drilled schedule and system of compilation. It should have been relatively easier to complete and present Volume II in January as well. As this was not done, the time for presenting it to Parliament was in the next session— the monsoon session—which was convened from 17 July 2017.

---

3   Department of Economic Affairs (January 2017), *Economic Survey 2016–17*, New Delhi: Ministry of Finance, Government of India.

Chief Economic Advisor Arvind Subramanian decided to use the occasion of presenting Volume II in the monsoon session as another opportunity to present one more thematic *Economic Survey* during the year. He drafted a comprehensive first chapter, 'State of the Economy: An Analytical Overview', divided in three sections: 'Analytical Review of Recent Developments', 'Outlook and Policies for 2017–18' and 'Review of Developments in 2016–17'. He focused all his energies and creativity on the first two sections of this chapter.

The *Economic Survey* is, in its authorship and ownership, the product of the CEA. However, it is presented as a government document by the finance minister who lays it before both Houses of Parliament. The survey is formally approved on file in DEA with the CEA routing the file for approval of the finance minister through secretary, DEA, who is formally the administrative head of DEA, of which the Economic Division, headed by the CEA, is a part.

I joined the department on 12 July 2017. It had been decided earlier that Volume II of the *Economic Survey* would be presented in the later part of the monsoon session. A couple of days after I joined the department, Arvind personally handed over the file to me for consideration and submission to the finance minister.

A day before, additional private secretary (APS) to the PM, P.K. Mishra told me that there was considerable discomfort about the draft of the survey Arvind Subramanian was likely to present. He said the surveys Arvind Subramanian was presenting were not really economic surveys, as they were understood to be, but more akin to personal research documents. He believed Arvind Subramanian was free to publish these papers as his research contributions, but not as official government documents that ended up criticizing the government unfairly and casting institutions like RBI in a poor light. He wanted me to go through the document thoroughly to ensure it contained no such thing.

For his part, Finance Minister Arun Jaitley generally supported Arvind's approach to the survey and was prepared to live with his take on the economy, which he described as 'constructive criticism'.

I had been associated with DEA for many years and had closely followed past surveys. I found such lack of confidence in the PMO about Volume II of the *Economic Survey*, which was only supposed to be a review of the economy, quite unprecedented. I decided to read through the draft carefully despite not even being a week old in the job and going through an international and institutional transition.

First Reading Hinted at Difficulties Ahead

I read the overview chapter carefully and glanced through the rest of the document. The overview was the meat of the matter. Some of the controversial issues taken up in the chapter were further detailed in two of the review chapters.

Arvind writes with flourish. His language is penetrative and impactful. To drill a point home, he sometimes over-emphasizes, though. Most of the points he made might have appeared critical but were based on facts. Arvind is also enamoured with himself, his findings and his language! Thus, he sometimes neglected to ascertain the fairness of the conclusions drawn and also failed to realize that the same point could have been made in a manner that was less caustic and less hurtful to others.

I marked all the areas where some moderation or use of an alternative formulation could convey the same meaning and message in a non-controversial manner. I also found a few controversial areas that appeared unnecessary, unsupported by facts or unfairly criticized the government or RBI. Arvind and I discussed these areas. While he was quite open to write/adopt alternative formulations for most of the changes I suggested, he was inflexible on some controversial matters.

One of these was Arvind's conclusion that RBI had been consistently wrong about forward inflation forecasts, which imparted unnecessary bias for the adoption of a tight money policy, leading to very high real interest rates in the economy. Others related to his pessimistic forecast about growth, his overkill for the three Rs (Recognition, Recapitalization and Resolution) approach (recognition of the non-performing or bad loans of banks, recapitalizing the banks for loss of capital on account of recognition of provisions and losses on bad loans and recovering the bad loans through resolution of defaulting debtors through bankruptcy and other legal venues available), for stabilizing the banking sector, which also included the use of RBI's reserves for bank recapitalization, and his insistence on including the contents of a note of dissent he had submitted to the Fiscal Responsibility and Budget Management (FRBM) law review committee headed by N.K. Singh as the right policy prescription.

We held a few more rounds of discussions and also took the matter to Arun Jaitley. Finally, I was able to persuade Arvind to leave out the FRBM dissent note and improve his GDP forecast. However, he was not prepared to tone down his conclusions about RBI's inflation forecasts and the use of RBI reserves for recapitalizing banks. The facts were on Arvind's side on both these issues, so I decided to persuade P.K. Mishra to accept these formulations as they were.

P.K. Mishra's Disagreement Led to a Widening of the Examiners' Net

Arvind and I went to see P.K. Mishra, Arvind quite unhappily as he found this an 'inquisition'. But he agreed to come along at my request. I tried to reason with P.K. Mishra to drop his objection to the two RBI-related matters. It appeared he had passed on the draft to RBI, which had pointed out two quarters where its forecast had proved to be quite accurate. Arvind's conclusion that RBI had consistently failed in its inflation forecast was thus not fully correct. I suggested alternatives like 'generally failed' or 'was inaccurate in a majority of quarters', which also failed to pass muster with Arvind.

This meeting led to a hardening of positions. The day before our meeting, P.K. Mishra had passed on a copy of the draft survey to the cabinet secretariat as well as to Brajendra Navnit, joint secretary in the PMO, for a look. The cabinet secretary involved Joint Secretary Girdhar Armane, who looked at the document more as a government handout. He found some more areas that needed to be modified. I told Girdhar that the language and conclusions in the survey were the prerogative of the CEA and that we had no business to second-guess or rewrite the survey.

P.K. Mishra convened a meeting in the cabinet secretariat. In the meantime, Arvind was getting increasingly restless. At one stage, he told me he would rather leave the government than see his survey mauled in such a manner. I did not take him along to the meeting with the cabinet secretary.

Cabinet Secretary P.K. Sinha, more influenced by Girdhar's findings, was also quite sceptical about the draft. We discussed the main issues I had identified. I proposed further moderation of RBI-related issues. P.K. Mishra appeared to be somewhat more accommodative that day, whereas P.K. Sinha started line-by-line reading and formulating alternative language, including deleting portions he thought were 'unnecessary'. After some time, the exercise appeared to be going nowhere. I did a little bit of plain speaking. P.K. Mishra also realized the approach adopted by the cabinet secretariat was not appropriate. The meeting ended without any positive or negative outcome.

'Don't Present Economic Survey'

The DFS had convened a meeting in the Committee Room of North Block on asset reconstruction company (ARC) related issues, which Finance Minister Arun Jaitley was chairing. Anjali Duggal, secretary, DFS, had invited me to the meeting as well.

At one stage, Arun Jaitley received a call that he went out of the room to receive. After a minute or so, he called me outside to tell me that the PMO had called to tell him not to present Volume II of the *Economic Survey* in the monsoon session. He appeared a bit concerned, though not excessively ruffled.

After the meeting, we reconvened in his room. Arun Jaitley summarized the issue again. I told him about the unacceptable approach of the cabinet secretariat and the need to bring balance in the PMO about content connected with RBI. I also told him that Arvind, though quite unhappy, had been forthcoming in incorporating many suggestions.

Arun Jaitley spoke to Nripendra Misra, principal secretary to the PM, who understood Arvind better. I had another discussion with P.K. Mishra. After this, the cabinet secretariat's involvement with the draft survey ended.

In the evening, I received a sealed envelope from P.K. Mishra's office that contained specific suggestions/changes to be made to the draft survey. I went through those fifteen to twenty suggestions. I found some acceptable; the others not. I told P.K. Mishra I had incorporated some, but all the modifications suggested could not be accommodated.

The RBI bugbear—the inflation forecast being consistently wrong—was retained and partially modified, without specifically naming RBI. The survey said that research indicated that consumer price inflation undershot professional forecasts fairly consistently over the past five years or so, globally as well as in the advanced economies. In the Indian context, evidence seemed to be pointing to the same conclusion—though the errors have been on both sides over a longer time horizon. The graph on consumer price inflation (CPI)-RBI Forecast and Actual was retained.

Volume II of the *Economic Survey* was presented in the monsoon session of Parliament in August 2017. Like other surveys produced by Arvind Subramanian, this edition was also quite well received.

Finalizing Survey 2017–18 Was Contentious As Well

The discomfort of the PMO regarding Volume II of the *Economic Survey* for 2016–17 spilled over to the *Economic Survey* for 2017–18 as well. P.K. Mishra asked me to ensure no theme was selected that was critical of the government or RBI.

Arvind and I discussed the matter. I told him two things would need to be done for the 2017–18 survey. First, the entire survey—thematic, review and data tables—would have to be brought together as one volume and be presented before Budget 2018–19. Second, the subject selections for thematic part should be made in the next two to three months (well before October) and we should have a discussion with Finance Minister Arun Jaitley about themes to be finally selected for inclusion.

Arvind relished thematic part of the *Economic Survey*, which was what really mattered in his judgement. He was reluctant about both my asks. We had a meeting with the finance minister. Realizing there

were no good grounds to split the survey for that year, Arvind agreed
to present the entire *Economic Survey* together, though still split in
two volumes. That was fine with me, as long as the two volumes
were placed in Parliament together.

Arvind had prepared a list of tentative subjects for the meeting
with the finance minister. There were eleven themes he had chosen
to highlight, including a chapter on the overview of the economy.
His selection of themes appeared quite brilliant and most of themes
were breaking new ground in research and analysis of data, which
was increasingly getting available in ever greater depth, like GST
data.

However, there were two themes I found problematic. One
related to the new method of GDP measurement based on corporate
data filed by companies with the registrar of companies. Arvind had
discovered a large disconnect between GDP growth coming out
of this corporate data and the traditional way of measuring GDP
using the index of industrial production (IIP) and other metrics.
He had produced a paper on the matter. The findings, though
not very strongly supported by data, confirmed what some people
were alleging as the deliberate overestimation of the growth rate.
The other theme related to critical examination of the economic
impact of some judicial pronouncements, such as the Supreme Court
judgement in the matter of selling liquor along the highways and
some environmental laws.

The paper on GDP measurement was still to be discussed
with the National Statistical Organization (NSO) and it was, in
my understanding, poor judgement to put such conclusions in an
official document like the *Economic Survey*. Arvind was passionate
about his research and findings but oblivious of the impact of such
research on the government and public mind. I asked for this theme
to be dropped. Arun Jaitley also felt that subject was not worth
pursuing in the *Economic Survey*. It was agreed that Arvind's
paper would be shared with NSO and internally pursued in the
government. If there was some deficiency in the new methodology,
which by the way was not India's design but internationally
accepted practice, it would be modified. Arvind was not happy but

agreed to drop this theme. He later on published his entire paper in his book, *Of Counsel*.[4]

Arun Jaitley suggested a reorientation of the piece on judicial pronouncements. He agreed that it may prove counterproductive to point fingers at the judiciary and that such battles needed to be fought in the courts. Instead, he suggested that the survey pursue the non-controversial but significant theme of delays caused by the enormous pendency in the courts, the reasons for it, and how it was impacting the ease of doing business. This was also finally accepted by Arvind.

With this agreement on the single survey and themes for thematic volume, I briefed P.K. Mishra. He did not have any serious arguments against any of themes selected, but was generally unhappy about the *Economic Survey* pursuing and publishing such personalized and controversial research. I took this as a go-ahead, though the caveat he made—that the *Economic Survey*, when ready, would have to be scrutinized in the PMO to ensure that it did not contain any unfair criticism of the government—was expected to cause some problems.

PMO Did Have Its Views

Arvind hated the PMO's interference in the production of the survey. However, he and I developed a reasonably good understanding and mutual respect. He found himself unable to negotiate the drafts with the PMO and cabinet secretariat. We agreed that Arvind would share with me thematic volume chapter by chapter as soon as he finished with them.

I did read through all the chapters carefully. Every chapter was well grounded in data and enriched by Arvind's eloquence. It was a delight to read these chapters. There were, however, quite a few major conclusions drawn by him that reflected relatively poor judgement and biases. We would have free and frank discussions on these identified areas. I found Arvind reasonable enough to agree

4 Arvind Subramanian, *Of Counsel: The Challenges of the Modi-Jaitley Economy* (New Delhi: Viking, 2018).

to drop or modify his conclusions in such matters. For instance, the findings on the impact of climate on agriculture or some conclusions about the results of perceived preference for sons in the context of gender equality, were not really worth publishing.

When the complete draft was ready, incorporating many modifications I had suggested, I shared the same with the PMO and the cabinet secretariat. Arvind found this scrutiny difficult to stomach. Very soon, some evidence emerged that the PMO had shared the draft with RBI this time as well and its objections/comments were essentially echoing RBI's discomfort. At one stage, Arvind became desperate. He told Arun Jaitley he had some family issues to deal with and would therefore like to leave (some months before his term was to expire). We persuaded him to stay on and later accept a year's extension.

I argued with the PMO on every point it objected to and defended. This time, they could not point out anything serious and unnecessary that my scrutiny had not taken care of. After some to and fro, P.K. Mishra decided to leave the matter to me.

The *Economic Survey* for 2017–18,[5] was placed in Parliament in one go, two days before the presentation of Budget 2018–19 as per normal practice. This edition of the survey was also a hit. In fact, most of the cost of the survey was covered by the sale of its copies on Amazon and other media.

The government's discomfort with the thematic part of the *Economic Survey*, initiated by Arvind Subramanian in 2015, finally led to its discontinuance in 2021–22.

---

5   Department of Economic Affairs (January 2018), *Economic Survey 2017–18*, Volumes I and II, New Delhi: Ministry of Finance, Government of India.

SECTION II

POLICY DECISIONS THAT IGNITED CONTROVERSIES

3

Untrustworthy Electoral Bonds

IT WAS AROUND 1.30 A.M. ON 31 JANUARY–1 FEBRUARY 2017 IN Washington DC when Finance Minister Arun Jaitley read paragraph 164 of his Budget Speech, proposing electoral bonds to bring 'transparency in electoral funding'. Fighting sleep, I heard him say: 'Even seventy years after Independence, the country has not been able to evolve a transparent method of funding political parties, which is vital to the system of free and fair elections.'[6]

Arun Jaitley referred to the two 'reforms' made in the past: exemption granted from tax if companies made a donation by transparently disclosing the same in their accounts; and, reporting of all donations received in cash in excess of ₹20,000 by political parties to the Election Commission (EC). Arun Jaitley opined in his Budget Speech that the situation had 'only marginally improved' after these measures, as 'political parties continue to receive most of their funds through anonymous donations, which are shown in cash'.

---

6 'Budget 2018–2019 Speech of Arun Jaitley Minister of Finance February 1, 2018', available at: https://www.indiabudget.gov.in/budget2018-2019/ub2018-19/bs/bs.pdf

Noting that donors 'expressed reluctance in donating by cheque or other transparent methods as it would disclose their identity and entail adverse consequence' as the primary reason for companies not making donations to political parties by expensing them on companies they control, Arun Jaitley proposed 'electoral bonds' issued in accordance with a 'scheme that the Government of India would frame'. These electoral bonds could be purchased by donors from 'authorized banks against cheque and digital payments only'. These electoral bonds would be 'redeemable only in the designated account of a registered political party' and 'redeemable within the prescribed time limit from issuance of bond'. He also limited cash donations to a maximum amount of ₹2,000 from one person.

The Finance Bill presented along with the Budget proposed specific changes in the RBI Act and Income Tax Act for institutionalizing electoral bonds. The RBI Act 1934 was amended to empower the Central government to 'authorize any scheduled bank to issue electoral bond'. An electoral bond was defined to mean 'a bond issued by any scheduled bank under the scheme' notified by the Central government. The Income Tax Act amendment allowed contributions made through electoral bonds as admissible for deduction under Section 88GGB, like other company donations, without the requirement of mentioning the party in the accounts of the company.

The first impression I got from this announcement in Budget 2017–18 was that a devious way had been designed for funnelling company donations to the ruling party, though my confidence in Arun Jaitley's sagacity suggested that this might actually not be the case.

Arun Jaitley Explained the System of Political Funding

Arun Jaitley had been the treasurer of the Bharatiya Janata Party (BJP) for many years. When I called on him, after joining DEA in July 2017, five months after the electoral bond announcement had been made, the matter of electoral bonds was uppermost in his mind.

DEA was the department responsible to frame 'the scheme' to be notified by the Central government under the powers assumed under the RBI Act.

The announcement had created considerable controversy in the country. Fearing that the scheme would divert all corporate political funding to the ruling party, the Opposition in general opposed the electoral bond scheme. The RBI bureaucracy found the electoral bonds akin to bearer bonds, which could be misused for money laundering. The EC also felt that the scheme was a non-transparent way of funding. All this weighed on Arun Jaitley's mind, when I met him.

He was convinced that the scheme announced by him in the Budget was much more transparent, more equitable and was most necessary to transform the financial management of political parties. He began by explaining the state of funding received by political parties, saying that even a party like the BJP received 90 per cent of its funding in cash. Parties had to break the donation received in cash in bulk, into multiple donations of less than ₹20,000 each to ensure they were not required to report the actual donors to the EC. Most of this bulk donation came from companies.

The promoters of these companies would buy cash by siphoning money from their companies. The prevalent system encouraged money laundering and the formation of shadowy shell companies to hide transactions, he went on to explain. Political parties, saddled with so much cash, found it difficult to keep track of it and had to make most payments from the hoard received. They usually did not have enough money in their bank accounts to make payments by cheque.

The system he had devised was, he recognized, not the best and most transparent, but was better than any other prevalent system. Companies would be able to make donations from their accounts without the need to search for cash. There would be transparent accounting in companies. The only compromise made in the scheme was that companies/their sponsors would not be required to disclose which party they had made contributions to. This would, he argued, build confidence in companies as no one would know whom they had given donations to. He also said other political parties had supported the scheme in private but were not courageous enough to do so in public.

I was fairly convinced by his arguments that the electoral bonds were an improvement over then existing arrangements.

Electoral Bonds: An Improvement to Existing Arrangements

The reading of all available papers in the Budget Division, which handled the matter, and the session with Arun Jaitley, convinced me that the electoral bond scheme was better than existing arrangements and, therefore, I decided to push the scheme through.

A meeting was convened with RBI and a representative from the EC in July.

The Reserve Bank of India's principal concern at that time was to ensure that the electoral bonds were not akin to bearer bonds. This could be done by ensuring that the bonds did not get transferred from one party to another and that the window of holding the bonds was small enough to allow the donor to buy the bonds lawfully and against full 'know your customer' (KYC) norms, donate them to political parties and for political parties to deposit these bonds in designated bank accounts. We toyed with the idea of keeping the bonds valid for only seven days but that was found to be grossly inadequate for this entire cycle of events to be completed. We settled for fifteen days. The features of the bonds developed, ensured they would not work like bearer bonds, and RBI was reasonably satisfied.

The EC representative did not want to be party to any decision, as the EC was in principle against electoral bonds. Nonetheless, we discussed the features that would make the bonds least unpalatable. One major issue was to ensure that every serious political party had equal opportunity to receive the bonds. The EC registered political parties and recognized them as national and state parties. There were more than 2,500 registered parties as registration was very simple and almost anyone could register a political party. Nationally recognized parties were only five to six, whereas state-recognized parties were about fifty to sixty.

If electoral bond funding was allowed to every registered party, the system could become prone to misuse and blackmail. Moreover, it would be difficult to manage the electoral bond issuance and management system. Further, as a great majority of these parties were not politically significant, it did not appear advisable as it would become an avenue for funding individuals or groups rather than parties. If funding were to be restricted to only recognized parties, only a few political parties would be able to avail of the facility. After mulling over some permutations and combinations, we arrived at the cut-off of 1 per cent of votes obtained in the last election, nationally or in the state, as the identifier of eligibility.

After firming up the key features of the electoral bond scheme, I submitted the file to the finance minister in the first week of August 2017 to approve the scheme. He approved the file with the instruction that it be discussed with the PMO.

Government Approves the Framework of Electoral Bonds

As the matter was urgent, a meeting took place in August chaired by Prime Minister Modi. Prior to the meeting, I spoke to the RBI top brass. They were mostly on board. Some other issues—four quarterly opening of bond sale windows, with one additional window in case of general elections being held—were decided in the meeting, which we incorporated in the draft of the scheme.

We considered the matter wrapped up. The Budget Division wrote to RBI to provide the draft of notification to be issued in this regard, incorporating the key features of the scheme as approved by the government. It was not necessary that RBI provide the draft of the scheme, as it was the Central government that had been conferred the power to authorize the scheduled banks to issue electoral bonds. Yet, this was done as it was a common and long-standing practice for RBI and the Central government to consult each other before exercising the powers conferred by the law on all important issues.

Election Commission Had to Be Convinced Again

One of the election commissioners, O.P. Rawat, made a statement in public that was critical of the electoral bond scheme. He referred to the EC's letter to the law ministry in this regard, which he said was not responded to. He further stated that he suspected the scheme would encourage political funding by shell companies.

When the features of the electoral bond scheme were being finalized in August–September 2017, Finance Minister Arun Jaitley had advised me to meet the full EC (all the commissioners) to explain the scheme and secure its concurrence, if possible. The appointment of Sunil Arora as an election commissioner was expected to help bring balance to the approach of the EC.

I had a meeting with the full EC. I recorded a note after the meeting that I submitted to Finance Minister Jaitley; I also sent a copy to Nripendra Misra, principal secretary to the PM. This note is now publicly available, having been obtained by RTI enthusiasts and published in newspapers and other online publications.

I explained the features of the electoral bond scheme, as determined by then, and compared the same with the system of cash funding of political parties. I told the EC that there was no change in the information it received. Earlier, it received information about the cash donations received in total by a political party; now it would get the same information about the donations received in the form of electoral bonds. In terms of the transparent use of company funds to make political donations, bonds would be issued only in a fully KYC-compliant manner by the banks. Buyers/donors would be able to buy the bonds only from their fully KYC-compliant account in a bank or by presenting the account payee cheque of a KYC-compliant bank customer. The practice of using shell companies was more prevalent in the cash donation system and there was no likelihood of shell companies being used for making political donations by electoral bonds.

Nevertheless, O.P. Rawat continued to object. His objections were not convincing. Finally, he realized he was flogging a dead horse. Sunil Arora was quite pragmatic. He asked for some information and thereafter was generally supportive of the view that it was for the government to take a decision on the matter. Chief Election Commissioner (CEC) Achal Kumar Joti also appeared quite convinced about the transparency of the scheme but he felt the eligibility of parties receiving minimum 1 per cent was unduly restrictive. It was a little amusing. While the EC had an objection to the scheme in principle, here was a CEC who wanted to make it more liberal and made available to all registered parties on the grounds of equity.

I explained the soundness of using 1 per cent votes in the last elections as a cut-off for identifying serious political parties, when transparency in political funding was the principal electoral reform needed in the country. While he seemed to agree, he asked me to note his suggestion and inform the government to find ways to make the scheme more equitable.

After this meeting, the EC remained silent on the matter until a petition was filed in 2018 in the Supreme Court by the Communist Party of India (CPI). The EC then filed an affidavit in court objecting to the electoral bond scheme. By this time, however, the scheme had been fully implemented.

Urjit Patel's Complete About-Turn

The key features of the electoral bond scheme were approved at the highest level of the government in late August/early September, with RBI on board. The bonds were to be issued as physical bonds by scheduled banks authorized by the government.

Governor of RBI, Urjit Patel, for reasons best known to him, wrote to Finance Minister Arun Jaitley sometime in the middle of September questioning the issuances of bonds by anybody/bank other than RBI. Equating the bonds as currency, he wanted RBI to issue the bonds as it was the monopoly issuer of currency. This was a shocking ask. The RBI Act had been amended, which provided for the government-authorized scheduled banks to issue electoral bonds. By making this proposal, he was questioning the law of the land.

The second suggestion was a bigger shocker. Urjit Patel proposed that the bonds be issued in digital, not physical mode. This implied that potential donors would have to apply digitally to RBI to buy electoral bonds; and RBI—after completing the entire process of KYC and collecting funds from the buyer's bank account—would issue a digital bond that the buyer would digitally transfer to a political party. Finally, the political party would collect the proceeds of the bond digitally by going through the banks. Every political party would know who had contributed, and so would the EC and RBI. This would kill the most important feature that Arun Jaitley wanted to build in—the anonymity of the donor vis-à-vis political parties.

These two proposals from RBI worried the government. In a meeting called by Arun Jaitley, which Urjit Patel attended along with his deputies, Patel was combative and confrontational. He told Arun Jaitley that he could have objected to this provision in the Finance Bill (amendment of the RBI Act to allow electoral bonds) like his predecessor Raghuram Rajan had done earlier. Rajan had objected to the proposal in the Finance Bill 2015, that the government take over the issuance of government bonds from RBI, and had made the government roll it back. Arun Jaitley kept his cool and tried to explain the pith and substance of the electoral bonds to Urjit Patel.

Considerable correspondence took place between RBI and the government thereafter on the issue. We also discovered that Urjit Patel had used the mechanism of the Committee of Central Board (CCB), the meetings of which were never attended by most RBI and government directors. He had proposed the issuance of the electoral bonds as digital bonds by RBI in one of the CCB meetings. The CCB, being almost an internal body of RBI, went along with this suggestion.

More discussion took place, involving the PMO as well. After this ping-pong went on for about three to four weeks, one day I saw in one of the CCB minutes: 'If the government decides to issue electoral bonds in script through SBI (State Bank of India), the Bank (RBI) should let it be.'

RBI, under Urjit Patel, never furnished its comments on the draft electoral bond scheme or provided its formal consent to electoral bond issuance. We took the minutes of CCB as the consent of RBI and proceeded ahead.

The Law Ministry Introduces Its Own Complications

Once RBI's googly (issuance of electoral bonds only in digital mode and that too only by RBI) was negotiated without any loss of wicket, the government decided to use only SBI as the authorized bank to manage the electoral bond scheme. The draft of the scheme was shared with the SBI top management. SBI designated one of its managing directors to finalize the scheme. After a few meetings, a draft acceptable to both the government and SBI was developed. SBI wanted to start with a few branches and gradually expand the network of issuing branches. This was also accepted.

The scheme required the Ministry of Law's concurrence before being notified by DEA. Its job was essentially twofold: first and foremost to ensure that the draft of the notification met the standards of good legal drafting; and, second, to check its constitutionality. The formulation of the scheme and its key features were not the concern of the Ministry of Law. This was the job of the concerned administrative ministry/department.

We had expected the ministry to vet the proposed notification in a routine manner, the way hundreds of other notifications are cleared. This was not a new law, nor were the rules being framed under any particular law. The fundamental features of the electoral bond scheme had been mentioned in the Budget announcement and the relevant laws had been amended to allow bringing in electoral bonds.

The Ministry of Law proposed numerous amendments of drafting nature. This was not a problem. We discussed all of these and jointly agreed to modify the draft scheme wherever the suggestions were found to be in order. The ministry had a few substantive issues as well. The most important related to questioning the rationale for the 1 per cent vote share cut-off.

Noting that a registered political party required 6 per cent of the votes to get the status of a 'recognized political party' by the EC, the ministry asked that only the recognized parties be made eligible for receiving electoral bonds. We argued that this would be highly restrictive as there were only a few parties (less than ten) recognized nationally and in the states (about fifty). This qualification would make a bulk of the political parties ineligible to receive political funding. The ministry then made an about turn. Taking shelter under the elections laws which make every 'registered' political party entitled to accept political donations voluntarily offered to it, it suggested that every registered party (in excess of 2,750) be made eligible. It seemed they had got EC fever.

I went through with the ministry officials the discussions I had with the EC a few weeks earlier. Eventually, we were able to persuade the Ministry of Law to treat the matter as a 'policy matter' and not a legal issue, to be decided by DEA. Finally, we had their concurrence to the issuance of the electoral bond scheme.

Electoral Bonds Finally Notified in January 2018

The tortuous journey of bringing electoral bonds to life finally got over by the end of the calendar year 2017. The scheme was notified on 2 January 2018. A new system of political funding did get institutionalized in the country.

The electoral bonds were challenged in the Supreme Court by the Association for Democratic Reforms (ADR), even before the scheme was notified.

The Department of Economic Affairs, the administrative department, had to defend the government and the scheme. Based on the rationale and logical briefs prepared by DEA, cleared with the legally astute Finance Minister Arun Jaitley, the Attorney General (AG) presented the government's case effectively. The court did not grant any stay.

After the scheme was notified, we could implement it. It envisaged opening up the sale of bonds for a period of ten days once every quarter in the calendar year, and for an additional period of thirty days before the national general election, and an additional thirty days in the specific state when assembly election would take place.

Though there was demand from the PMO to be a little flexible about the number of days for opening the sale of bonds in the initial years, in 2018 we resisted the same and stuck to the limit. When the general elections for the Lok Sabha were ordered in 2019, there was a suggestion that the period of sale be increased to the entire campaign period. We succeeded in limiting it to forty-five days, which made the total period of sale exceed the time specified (thirty plus ten days) in the scheme by five days.

The Supreme Court, in the ADR case, passed an interim order on 12 April 2019, in the middle of the elections, and reduced the forty-five days to forty days, bringing the total period for which bond sale was opened in calendar year 2019 (until June) to fifty days (ten days each for the January–March and April–June quarters and thirty days for general elections). This was a welcome decision. We immediately notified a revised calendar implementing the order and bringing it in line with the scheme.

Purity of Election Funding

The most contentious aspect of the electoral bond scheme was the anonymity of the donation made (which company or person donated which specific electoral bond(s) to which party).

The scheme was framed to ensure that this information could not become available to anyone. The Supreme Court was also concerned about this key issue in the ADR case and wanted to understand the same comprehensively. However, the interim order noted above asked political parties to furnish this information to the EC in a sealed envelope. Rejecting the apprehensions loosely aired from time to time and argued in the ADR petition that electoral bonds could be sold to someone for cash, be bought by foreigners, or promote use of black money, the Supreme Court again refused to grant any stay on the operation of the scheme in April 2021.

The ADR publishes data on the electoral bonds issued. A total of about 14,000 electoral bonds for a total amount of over ₹7,200 crore were purchased from March 2018 to April 2021. Quarterly electoral bond sale ranged between ₹82 crore in July 2018 to ₹974 crore in

April 2021. The bulk of contribution through electoral bonds came during the 2019 general elections, when bonds worth ₹937 crore, ₹2,742 crore and ₹4,681 crore were sold in March, April and May 2019, respectively.

Today the scheme has become quite stabilized (though the legal challenge in the Supreme Court is still to be finally decided), having been operational for over five years. While the ruling party, the BJP, did get the bulk of donations through electoral bonds (a little over 75 per cent of all contributions), other national and prominent state parties have also got political contributions by way of electoral bonds.

The electoral bond scheme has made its contribution to cleaning up cash financing of elections. It has drastically reduced the contribution received by political parties in cash.

4

Unusual Terms for the Fifteenth Finance Commission

THE FIFTEENTH FINANCE COMMISSION (XV FC) WAS CONSTITUTED by the President of India on 27 November 2017 under the chairpersonship of N.K. Singh, a veteran of public administration and fiscal management. The work relating to the constitution of the finance commissions (FCs) is handled by the Budget Division of DEA. While the principal terms of reference (ToRs)—distribution of Union taxes between the Union and the states, principles for governing grants-in-aid of the revenue of states from the Union, and measures needed to augment states' resources for supplementing the resources of panchayats and municipalities—are defined in the Constitution [Article 280 and Article 280 (3) (c)], any other matter referred to the FC by the President in the interest of sound finance allows the Central government to include additional ToRs. The Centre also chooses the chairperson and other members of the FC.

Finance Commissions are required to be constituted every five years and typically provide their recommendations for a five-year period. They are usually given a period of twenty-four to thirty months to complete their deliberations. The XV FC was expected to be constituted by the month of September 2017 for it to provide its report by the end of calendar year 2019. The XV FC's recommendations were to be put into effect from 1 April 2020.

Finance Minister Arun Jaitley had formed a committee of officers, chaired by Expenditure Secretary Ashok Lavasa, to formulate the ToRs of the XV FC. The secretary, economic affairs, was a member. The group's work was convened and facilitated by the joint secretary, Budget. When I joined DEA in July 2017, the group had held one meeting to discuss the broader formulation of the ToRs prepared by the Budget Division and had given some directions to reformulate some of the proposals. As there was not much time to constitute the XV FC, I realized we needed to put the finalization of the ToRs on a fast track. Simultaneously, the chairperson and members had to be selected in consultation with the finance minister and the PMO.

I had worked closely in the implementation of the XI FC and played a part in designing some of the key recommendations of the XII FC and implementing these briskly (more elaborately described in the chapter on state finances in the forthcoming book *Steely Resolve*). I had worked at the fiscal federal policy level, both at the Centre (as joint secretary, state finances) and in the state (as finance and principal finance secretary in Rajasthan). Thus, I was keen to play a constructive and impartial role in the determination of the ToRs of the XV FC. The implementation of GST and the need to bring down the general public debt had underlined the imperative to bring significant changes in the architecture of fiscal federal finance. The ToRs of the XV FC definitely needed to have a somewhat different orientation than the ToRs of previous FCs.

Finalizing and Proposing Standard ToRs with a Few Departures

Another round of meeting chaired by Ashok Lavasa in September 2017 brought the ToRs closer to their final shape. We made three major departures from the past.

One, we wanted to make the latest census population data (Census 2011) for use by the XV FC wherever it wanted to use the population of states as a factor. The fiscal needs of the states are best represented by their current population, not the 1971 population.

Second, we wanted the FC to recommend the share of taxes for Union Territories (UTs) with legislature, separate accounts and a separate consolidated fund. Article 280 mandates the division of the proceeds of Union taxes between the Union and the states. The UTs of Delhi and Puducherry, at that time, were effectively closer to being states than UTs.

Third, we wanted to propose that the XV FC consider doing away with the system of revenue deficit grants, which had developed over the years to take care of the gap that remained in any state's requirement of fiscal resources and availability of post-tax devolution resources. The need for revenue deficit grants represented fiscal unviability of the state, which needed other structural solutions. Filling these structural gaps by devolving additional Central taxes as grants was not a sustainable and systemic solution.

Ashok Lavasa retired at the end of October. He was replaced by Ajay Jha. Jha had worked as secretary to the XIV FC. Revenue Secretary Hasmukh Adhia took over as chair of the group. Some discussions took place with the Prime Minister's Economic Advisory Council. The draft ToRs stayed more or less along the lines of what I had proposed at the end of September.

These ToRs were approved by the finance minister and in early November, duly forwarded to the PMO (APS P.K. Mishra) for further consideration, along with a draft cabinet note, as ToRs are required to be approved by the cabinet before being submitted to the President for approval.

I went to Singapore with Finance Minister Arun Jaitley for bilateral meetings with the Singapore government and to participate in the Fintech Festival taking place from 15–17 November 2017.

A Desperate Call from the Joint Secretary (Budget)

We had just landed in Singapore and were on our way to the hotel when Prashant Goyal, joint secretary, Budget, called. He sounded exasperated and informed us that the file had come back from the PMO, with a note proposing almost a complete recasting of the proposed ToRs. The constitution of the XV FC was already late and the list of changes the PMO proposed virtually amounted to going back to the beginning of the exercise. Anyway, I asked him not to panic, and to send me the communication received from the PMO by email.

The communication appeared to be a compilation from three different sources. It was not collated into one integrated set of expected ToRs. Later, we found one was a compilation by Brajendra Navnit of internal points suggested by different joint secretaries in the PMO, another was from N.K. Singh, the future chairperson of the XV FC, and the third was a set of instructions from the PM himself on his expectations from the XV FC.

A closer analysis revealed three types of suggestions. There were some suggestions that emanated from the impression that GST was turning out to be a losing proposition for the Central government (states were assured of a 14 per cent annual increase, with the Centre expected to bear all risks of future rate reductions or bad economic performance). Another set of suggestions emanated from the desire to integrate investments and expenditures by states with national objectives and priorities. Finally, with the underlying assumption that the states were spendthrifts, there were suggestions to control their borrowings and expenditures.

While it was apparent that the changes had been suggested with honest intentions to improve fiscal management, the basic thrust of the communication went beyond the fundamental architecture of India's fiscal federal system and the role of the FC. The FC was the instrument to transfer a share of Central taxes to states without any conditions attached to the transfers, whereas the communication virtually treated states as subordinate entities that needed to be disciplined and integrated into national development planning. I found that Article 280 (3)(c), which permitted the President to suggest additional ToRs in the interest of sound finance, was being massively overstretched.

Deep Dive with the PMO on the Suggested Changes

We prepared a detailed point-by-point commentary on all the suggestions received from the PMO, stating our understanding of what they meant, their real implications in terms of the FC's work and how best to build them into the draft ToRs we had prepared, if the suggestions were worth incorporating. A round of discussions took place with P.K. Mishra, with Navneet joining in.

There were a number of suggestions on the nature of expectations from the states for good fiscal behaviour. The way the FC had always structured its ToRs was to state the three constitutional mandates as specific ToRs. 'The interest of sound finance' was served by building in suggestions for review of specified aspects of public finance like indebtedness, fiscal deficits, need for fiscal consolidation, state of public-sector enterprises, etc. Further, wherever the Government of India wanted the FC to be nudged towards making recommendations for sound financial practices, the ToRs mandated it to keep in mind certain considerations while making its recommendations.

I proposed an additional method to take on board as many of the suggestions as could be accepted. I suggested building an additional type of ToR that could provide states additional financial resources (over and above their share in Union taxes) if they managed their finances and affairs well on specified expected outcomes. This seemed to work.

Another characteristic of this communication was that the onus for everything was completely on the states. If these suggestions were incorporated in toto, the ToRs of the XV FC would have become completely lopsided.

Besides GST, the Government of India wanted to undo the excess of XIV FC that had recommended a 42 per cent share to states from Central government taxes. The suggestions were in the form of virtual directions to the XIV FC to find a solution to these matters. After considerable discussions on GST, we agreed on the formulation incorporated in the official ToRs of the XV FC. This formulation talked of the XV FC having regard to the 'impact on the GST, including payment of compensation for possible loss of revenues for five years, and abolition of a number of cesses, earmarking thereof for compensation and other structural reforms programme, on the finances of the Centre and the states'.

Likewise, the XV FC was expected to take into consideration only 'the impact on the fiscal situation of the Union Government of substantially enhanced tax devolution to states following the recommendations of the 14th Finance Commission'. This formulation did not amount to any new mandate to the FC. The FC, in any case, had to study the implications and impact of the GST and the XIV FC devolution formula on finances. On my insistence, the ToRs as finalized required the XV FC to assess the impact on the finances of both the Centre and the states.

There was an expectation to provide additional resources for the expenditure responsibilities of the Central government. The FCs had always been expected to study, in particular, the demand of the Centre's responsibilities on defence, internal security, etc. We agreed to include some newer types of expenditures, like climate change.

There was also an expectation that a provision be made for financing the flagship programmes of the Government of India and also what was being conceptualized as a development package for New India 2022. We incorporated these as part of the ToR on the impact of enhanced tax devolution by adding, 'coupled with the continuing imperative of the national development programme including New India 2022'. In any case, after abolition of the distinction between plan expenditure and non-plan expenditure, the XV FC was expected to take into account needs for both development and non-development expenditure, which was the original and real intent of Article 280.

We built a similar ToR to take care of the state governments. This ToR required the FC to keep in mind 'the demand of the resources of the state governments, particularly on account of financing socioeconomic development and critical expenditure, assets maintenance expenditure, balanced regional development and impact of the debt and liabilities of their utilities'.

Making States Fall in Line

The asks relating to disciplining the states to be fiscally responsible, and directing their expenditures towards what was considered to be the 'right' type of expenditures, were more difficult to build into the ToRs, without compromising the sanctity and independence of the FC as a neutral federal institution.

One expectation was that the FC should control populist expenditure by states, particularly such expenditures unleashed before the elections. While the intention was quite understandable, defining populist expenditure would have been impossible for anyone. In any case, the fiscal authority, whether the Centre or the states, has full competence to incur any expenditure on the extensive responsibilities it has been entrusted with under the Constitution, subject only to the approval of the concerned legislature. Moreover, the FC was not in a position at all to define ex-ante any 'populist' expenditure to be incurred by the states in future elections and estimate these. If the FC were to undertake an exercise of identifying such expenditures based on past accounts, it was likely to get completely lost. Moreover, we thought, to be fair, it would be equally good to reward the avoidance of populist expenditure instead of only punishing states for incurring such expenditure.

For this and other such suggestions, I proposed a workable compromise. Taking a cue from the fiscal reform and debt consolidation and relief facilities, which were designed to incentivize states based on predetermined measurable performance indicators, I suggested that the government create a ToR that provides incentives to the states for 'good behaviour'.

This idea appeared to strike the right balance between the expectation of good behaviour without impinging on the freedom of states to incur expenditures on the heads they wanted. Those states that choose to willingly participate in this endeavour would be rewarded with additional grants from the Centre as per the scheme recommended by the independent FC.

All such good behaviour—efforts made by states to expand the tax net under GST, eliminating losses in the power sector, adoption of the direct benefit transfer (DBT) system for fiscal transfers, progress in adoption of ease of doing business (EODB) and progress made in sanitation, among others—were identified as areas for the XV FC to 'consider proposing measurable performance-based incentives for states, at appropriate level of government'.

There was an expected adverse impact of moving over to the 2011 population as the base for the FC's recommendations wherever population was a factor. To reward the good work done by many states, especially southern states, 'efforts and progress made in moving towards replacement rate of population growth' was identified as a specific area for the XV FC to design performance-based incentives.

This device passed muster. The finally agreed ToRs of the XV FC were unusual but fair. There was no ostensible bias against the states or any attempt to treat them as the Centre's subordinate entities. The cabinet approved the ToRs. After the President's approval, the ToRs, along with the constitution of the XV FC, were notified on 2 December 2017.

Needless Controversy over Change of Reference Year for Population

Every FC's ToRs lead to some adverse comments by fiscal economists and the states. The ToRs of the XV FC also faced criticism. This was understandable, as many economists rightly observed some elements of partisanship in the attitude of the Centre. However, the FCs have invariably been fair and impartial in their interpretation of the ToRs and treating the states equally and equitably. We had expected the same from the XV FC.

One ToR, however, invited shrill controversy. Southern states Andhra Pradesh, Kerala and Karnataka, and UT Puducherry—all ruled by opposition parties at that time—opposed the change from 1971 to 2011 as the base year for the population as a factor in the FC's recommendations. They argued this would lead to major losses for them. Their principal argument was that the population was one of the largest factors/weightages in determining the relative share of states in the total quantum of Central taxes devolved. They had done enormous work over the prior five decades to control population and to bring population growth to the replacement rate. They rightly pointed out that the northern states were laggard in this endeavour and a change in the reference year of population would reward the laggards and punish their good work.

While the issue flagged by the southern states had considerable validity, the persistence to maintain the 1971 population to determine the share of states was fiscally counterproductive. The whole objective of the FC was to determine the right amount of Central taxes to be devolved to the states as a group and then distribute it among states to meet the gap in their fiscal needs to provide a minimum and common standard of services all over the country. This required the FC to direct resources towards poorer and more populous states, which meant lesser overall resources for less populous states and lesser per capita resources to relatively richer states.

I explained the rationale of moving to the 2011 population, at the same time emphasizing the other ToR that specifically asked the XV FC to incentivize states that had made progress towards replacement rate of population growth. The TV channels conducted debates on the issue, questions were raised in Parliament and much was written in the newspapers. Quite a few representations were also received from chief ministers and other public personalities. We responded to them all. Finally, Finance Minister Arun Jaitley also wrote a blog post explaining the dimensions and rationale of this decision.

It took some time but slowly the issue lost its appeal. After the XV FC furnished its recommendation, no southern state complained about the adverse impact of this change of reference year.

Furnishing Government Memorandum to XV FC Proved Trickier

The Finance Ministry submits a memorandum to the Finance Commission. Some ministries/departments also do so, but only on matters concerning their respective ministry/department.

Sometime in the summer of 2018, the cabinet secretary wanted to discuss the strategy for furnishing the government's memorandum to the XV FC. I told him that it was the Ministry of Finance that assessed resources and fiscal demands, had all the information relating to the implementation of previous FC recommendations, and submitted the government's memorandum. Further, the government was expected to comment on all the ToRs of the FC besides providing all the necessary financial data. This memorandum was under preparation in the ministry and would be submitted to the XV FC after the approval of the finance minister.

The cabinet secretary had something different in mind. He was of the view that every ministry/department of the government should submit a memorandum to the FC and ask for resources for its schemes. Some ministries/departments that dealt with major flagship schemes and social issues had submitted memorandums in the past, but each ministry/department submitting its memorandum was likely to overwhelm the system. There was also the major risk of the Ministry of Finance memorandum and departmental memorandums talking at cross purposes.

However, as Cabinet Secretary Sinha was quite keen to initiate this exercise, it was decided that over eighty ministries/departments of the Government of India would be clubbed into ten strategic groups; each group would come up with a common memorandum for submission to the FC.

I had very little hope of anything meaningful coming out of this exercise. Noting that these groups would need some thematic anchor, joint secretary, Budget (by that time, Arvind Srivastava) and I made a presentation before these ten groups. We used two ToRs of the XV FC to channel their energies: first, the imperative of the national development programmes, including New India 2022; and, second, the requirement for the XV FC to suggest a measurable and monitorable programme around ten specified areas, which pretty much covered the work allocation of most of the ministries/departments, to incentivize the states.

This exercise went on for many months. Nothing coherent came out of it. At one stage, I suggested the fundamental restructuring of the system of centrally-sponsored schemes (CSS). The cabinet secretary invited Chairperson N.K. Singh to a few of these meetings. Finally, I proposed submitting the Government of India memorandum to the XV FC in two parts: one, to make a case for financing national development programmes; and, two, the part related to resources and ToRs.

After several rounds of discussions with the cabinet secretary and finance minister, the government finalized its two-part memorandum. I shared it with the XV FC before the formal approval of the government as the election process came in the way of its formal submission; the cabinet secretariat had agreed to our draft. The Government of India had submitted only a cursory memorandum to the XIV FC, that too only after the new government had taken office after elections in 2014. The 2019 memorandum, available on the FC website, is a very detailed two-part memorandum.

The Government Amends ToRs for Defence Financing

The Press Information Bureau (PIB) issued a release on 17 July 2019 about an amendment in the XV FC ToRs to address serious concerns regarding the allocation of adequate, secure and non-lapsable funds for the defence and internal security of India.

Nirmala Sitharaman, the new finance minister, who had earlier been defence minister, gave me a note sometime before the Budget that proposed creation of a non-lapsable fund to meet defence expenditure, for inclusion in the Budget speech. The creation of non-lapsable funds at a time of heavy fiscal deficits made no fiscal sense. Moreover, whatever non-lapsable funds the government created, fiscal expenditures would always be incurred by providing the same in the budget of the department concerned and from the Consolidated Fund of India (CFI). This made the entire exercise of creating a non-lapsable fund meaningless as it only meant creating a few more accounting entries, rather than the actual administration of any non-lapsable outside the government.

I advised against the creation of such a fund and explained the same to the defence secretary and other officials. While Nirmala Sitharaman did not pursue this matter for the Budget thereafter, another note landed on my table from her office a few days later, asking to refer the matter to the XV FC by amending its ToRs.

The ToRs given to XV FC included taking into account the demands of defence and internal security expenditures, while assessing the expenditure needs of the Central government. The FCs recommended division of Central taxes between the Centre and the states, not setting apart some Central taxes for any specific expenditure or creating a fund for them. The proposed additional ToR did not fit in the scheme of things for the FC at all. I explained the entire matter to Nripendra Misra, principal secretary to the PM, as the reference had come through the PMO. While he understood, he said the decision had already been taken and the matter would have to be referred to the XV FC. My relationship with Nirmala Sitharaman had become quite strained during the Budget.

I noted the inappropriateness of making this additional reference to the XV FC. Knowing that my view would not be accepted, I couched the language in terms of the FC examining 'whether a separate mechanism for funding defence and internal security ought to be set up and if so how such a mechanism could be operationalized'. This made the additional ToR advisory in nature. The XV FC, as expected, did not recommend any non-lapsable fund for defence or internal security.

XV FC Generally Stayed Clear of Controversy

The XV FC stayed clear of the controversy generated by its unusual terms. It did assign 12.5 per cent weight to the demographic performance criterion—efforts and progress made in moving towards replacement rate of population growth—for determining inter-se shares of the states in total devolution. This protected devolution shares to a good extent for the states of Tamil Nadu, Karnataka and others that had done well in controlling population growth.

The XV FC did not recommend any specific measurable performance-based incentive grants for incentivizing states not to undertake populist expenditures or achievements in implementation of flagship schemes of the Government of India, promoting savings by adoption of direct benefit transfers, progress made in promoting EODB, etc. Instead, it brought back the older practice of giving sector-specific and recommended grants, building-in the element of performance measurement, which had to be there in any case, and recommended a total of under ₹3 lakh crore of grants for 'performance-based incentives and grants'. These grants are for education, health, agriculture, roads, aspirational districts, faster disposal of court cases, statistics, administrative reforms and the usual other heads that state governments spend their resources on.

On the defence non-lapsable fund, the XV FC opted for a sterile optical solution, which has no real meaning. By recommending that the Government of India might create a non-lapsable Modernization Fund for Defence and Internal Security (MFDIS) in the public account of Government of India to cover the gap between 'projected budgetary requirements' and 'budget allocation for defence and internal security', the XV FC left it to the Government of India to fend for its inability to find budget allocations for defence departments.

It is ironic to recommend that if the government did not have resources to allocate a budget for the projected demand, it could meet it by transferring budgetary resources to the public account! It must have been quite difficult for the XV FC and Chairman N.K. Singh to reject an unreasonable and constitutionally impermissible demand in a forthright manner. That possibly explains why this was done in a roundabout way.

5

ATMs Run Dry: Consequence of Demonetization Misadventure?

CURRENCY IS THE LIFEBLOOD OF ECONOMY, TRADE AND EXCHANGE. IT IS the core sovereign function. Governments minted, issued and managed currency in times of metal currency. When fiat money—paper currency—took over, the sovereign entrusted the function of currency issuance and management to the central banks. The Reserve Bank of India became India's currency issuer and manager when it was nationalized in 1949.

Currency notes, legally called bank notes in India, are issued by RBI. They are printed in the two note printing presses owned by the Government of India in Nashik and Devas and one note printing press owned by RBI in Mysuru. The government presses are now part of the Security Printing and Minting Corporation of India Ltd (SPMCIL) and RBI-owned press is housed in its subsidiary, Bhartiya Reserve Bank Note Mudran Pvt. Ltd (BRBNMPL).

The two companies print the notes in the number of the denomination, which is generally determined by RBI. After printing, the notes are handed over to RBI, which holds the notes with the presses, its regional offices and the specified custody branches of banks. Once notes are issued to the banks from these custody branches, they are considered to be in circulation. Bank notes in circulation minus the bank notes held by bank branches, make up the currency with the public.

Banks release notes to the public directly through their branches and, increasingly now, through ATM machines. These machines are configured to hold a certain amount of currency in three or four dockets that can handle specified notes as the dimensions of different notes—₹100, ₹500 and ₹2,000—differ.

In March and April 2018, many ATMs became inoperative on account of a note shortage. People could not withdraw notes when they went to the ATM machines. The problem was more acute in certain states like Telangana, Andhra Pradesh, Karnataka and Madhya Pradesh, though most states felt some shortage of supply. Newspaper headlines screamed: 'ATMs running dry'; opposition parties, media commentators and many others blamed the government for mismanagement. Many attributed this to the demonetization undertaken back in 2016. Some speculated that the government was doing it deliberately.

Currency management is the exclusive work of RBI, but when things go wrong people blame the government. I had to hold a press conference in the middle of April to discuss the situation and to apprise them, what the government and RBI were doing to manage it, and how it was only a matter of a few weeks before normalcy would return.

Why did things come to such a pass?

No More Printing of ₹2,000 Notes

Reserve Bank of India Deputy Governor B.P. Kanungo, in charge of currency management, came to see me sometime in early August 2017. By then, the currency in circulation had crossed ₹15 lakh crore (it had been more than ₹17.5 lakh crore at the end of October 2016 before ₹500 and ₹1,000 notes were demonetized in November 2016). There was no shortage of currency felt in the country and it was widely believed that the Indian public had learnt to live with a lower proportion of currency to GDP, as digital payments had also expanded in the meantime.

In the aftermath of demonetization, all three currency presses had been made to work 24×7 (all three shifts) to print the ₹2,000 notes (exclusively printed in the RBI Mysuru press), new ₹500 notes, old ₹100 notes, and the ₹200 note, which was about to make its debut.

A few days before Kanungo met me, there was a discussion on the economy with Prime Minister Modi at a select gathering where the subject of demonetization and the ₹2,000 currency note had cropped up. The PM indicated his resolve to remove the ₹2,000 note from circulation as soon as the situation permitted.

I had given some thought to the use of the ₹2,000 note. Based on common experience, including my own, it appeared to me that the note was not really useful for day-to-day transactions. Usually, shopkeepers and other service providers would refuse to accept it as they did not have the change to return. Noting the PM's preference as well as the common experience of the lack of utility of the ₹2,000 note, it was quite natural for me to bring it up in my discussion with Kanungo.

Kanungo wanted to stop running the note printing presses in 24×7 mode. He had made a careful assessment of the existing quantum of notes in circulation, in RBI custody and with the banks. He also had calculations regarding how much the note supply would be every month if the presses were switched to a two-shift mode. I found no reason to disagree with his proposals. We agreed that from the first of next month, note-printing work could move to two shifts.

I checked with him whether he had heard anything regarding the ₹2,000 note. He informed me that notes of ₹2,000 amounting to ₹7 lakh crore had already been printed, making up as much as 50 per cent of the total notes in circulation at the time. He indicated that RBI was considering stopping production of any more ₹2,000 notes.

I thought this was the best way to begin their eventual phase-out. We agreed that the production of ₹2,000 notes be stopped for the time being, until a final decision was taken.

Later, I learnt that RBI had already stopped the production of ₹2,000 notes in July 2017.

Defending the Government on the First Anniversary of Demonetization

Demonetization was a shock event. Currency circulation had returned to near normalcy by the time its first anniversary arrived on 8 November 2017. All emergency measures and temporary restrictions imposed in its wake had also been fully rolled back. Yet, the wounds of the public were fresh and there was a widespread perception that the government could be put on the mat or at least embarrassed by keeping the bogey of demonetization alive. Though the Uttar Pradesh elections earlier in the year had dented the efficacy of demonetization as a weapon for the Opposition, the subject was still very much alive on 8 November 2017.

Nripendra Misra, principal secretary to the PM, convened a meeting to discuss the strategy for 8 November. It was decided that the PIB would release a full-page advertisement on DEA's account and that DEA would provide the material for it. He also asked me to speak to the press on the day and defend the government. A schedule of interviews with some friendly business and popular TV channels was also arranged.

I went about preparing myself on the subject, besides collecting the relevant information from the Coins and Currency Division (CCD) of DEA, which handles currency-related matters. There was clear evidence that counterfeit notes had gone out of the system as they were essentially of the [old] ₹500, and the ₹1,000 denominations, which were no longer legal tender. There was also good evidence that the disappearance of counterfeit currency probably explained the drastic reduction in the incidence of stone-pelting in Jammu & Kashmir. The currency in circulation was still about ₹1 lakh crore lesser than the currency in circulation at the time of demonetization, which indicated a good reduction in the cash to GDP ratio. There was also good evidence that digital payments had notably increased.

In the meantime, the fact that almost all the [old] ₹500, and the ₹1,000 bank notes in circulation at the time of demonetization came back to RBI had become common knowledge. Barring only about

₹10,000 crore worth of notes, the entire ₹16.44 lakh crore worth of demonetized currency had come back to RBI. This did surprise RBI and the government but it was an undeniable fact. In its annual report released in August 2017, RBI had quietly reported this data—in a small font in a footnote.

A few journalists asked pointed questions about the ₹2,000 note and the likelihood of it being demonetized. Without confirming or denying the stoppage of its printing, I argued for its functional inadvisability for India in terms of its value as a transaction currency. There were many questions relating to the supposed failure of demonetization on account of almost the entire demonetized currency coming back. I explained that the assertion 'some portion of the currency will not come back to land windfall gains to the government' was never the stated objective of the government at any stage of the demonetization decision-making process. Journalists persisted that the government had estimated ₹5 lakh crore worth of currency not coming back; I insisted that these might have been individual officers' opinions, but not those of the government, at least in any official document.

I had seen the cabinet note on demonetization. There was no mention in the note that demonetization was intended to generate any windfall profit for the government by demonetized notes not returning to the system. The journalists cited the advocate general's remarks in the Supreme Court. However, those were essentially made in his personal capacity.

Although I was able to defend the government's move satisfactorily, in retrospect, I have to say the move was not a clear success. Poor planning and implementation had made many people suffer. At the end of the day on 8 November, I tweeted that it was high time to put the demonetization episode behind us and move on.

A Joint Secretary Locks Up Coin Mints

Anurag Agarwal, an IAS officer of Punjab cadre, joined DEA as joint secretary in September 2017. Considering his technical background and relative seniority, I placed him in charge of CCD, which was always considered a sensitive division. A quiet officer by nature, he was also appointed sometime later as chairman and managing director (CMD) of SPMCIL.

On 10 January 2018, I saw a news item from Kolkata in *The Economic Times*, saying the Government of India mint in the city had stopped minting coins. I was worried as I had no prior information about any such decision taken by the government. More enquiries revealed that on the orders of Anurag Agarwal, boards had been put up in all four mints that production of coins had been stopped.

When I questioned Agarwal, he informed me that he had to stop the minting of coins as RBI had not been lifting coins for some time. Further enquiries revealed that RBI's own coffers and the coffers of banks for storing coins were all full and RBI had informally advised SPMCIL to slow down minting. Agarwal, who said he wanted to send a message to RBI, had taken a hasty decision without assessing how long the mints would be closed and how the unions would react. It was clear we were going to have a major industrial action and public relations problem on our hands.

I briefed Finance Minister Arun Jaitley. He was also surprised and wondered how a joint secretary could make such a decision without consulting the secretary and minister. He said he would not have made such a decision himself without taking the PMO in confidence. I also briefed the PMO about the matter.

As expected, the unions landed before noon and demanded an immediate roll back of the decision. In the time before the union representatives arrived, after discussing the matter threadbare, I asked Agarwal to remove all the notice boards from the gates of the mints, open one shift in the mints from the next morning and convene a meeting with RBI the next day to decide the course of action regarding further minting of coins. When the unions demanded lifting the ban on the production of coins, I told them that production would resume the next day but the programme, shifts for coin minting and related issues would have to undergo a major change as it was not sustainable to keep minting billions of coins without their demand.

The storm created by a poorly thought-out decision blew over.

Agarwal was also instrumental in brewing another crisis. He headed a committee with representation from RBI, all the currency presses and two corporations on procurement matters. The printing of notes involves the procurement of very sensitive and costly inks, papers, security features and other goods and services from outside, as well as coordination of production within the two organizations.

Sometime in November 2017, the contract with the supplier of one of the critical types of ink was about to expire. The issue had been flagged by RBI at the meeting of the procurement coordination committee headed by Agarwal. It had invited tenders for supply, but the security vetting of the bidders was taking time (the security clearance granted by the Ministry of Home Affairs was an elaborate and time-consuming process). Fearing that the security clearance would not be available in time, RBI wanted the procurement committee to extend the contract of the existing supplier for some time.

Without realizing the implications, Anurag decided not to agree to RBI's suggestion. He also chose not to bring the matter to the notice of his additional secretary or to my attention. This decision contributed to the crisis of the ATMs running dry that India faced in the winter of 2017-18.

Indian Dependence on Foreign Currency Security Features Creates Issues

Not even two months into my job in DEA, I received a file from the Department of Personnel and Training (DoPT), which processes cases of departmental enquiry against IAS officers, asking for confirmation of the chargesheet it intended to serve on Arvind Mayaram, who had served as secretary of DEA for a little over two years during 2012–14. The DoPT was in a hurry as the chargesheet had to be served before the expiry of three years from his date of retirement, which was in October 2017.

Arvind Mayaram had been a senior officer in the service and also from my cadre, Rajasthan. He had been somewhat prejudiced against me; I have recounted some instances of this type in the forthcoming book *Steely Resolve* in connection with my World Bank posting. However, I bore no grudges or ill-will against him and, as always, I was determined to examine the matter fairly and without any bias. Within a few hours of the file landing in my office, Arvind Mayaram called and asked if he could come over to explain the matter. I requested him not to take the trouble and assured him that I would examine the matter entirely on its merits.

The accusation against him related to the extension of the contract of British firm De La Rue, which was a major printer of currency notes and producer/supplier of currency note security features. When India wanted to strengthen the security features of its bank notes, it concluded a contract with De La Rue to supply 'colour shift ink' on a proprietary basis, believing the firm owned the proprietary technology. The initial contract was for five years; after 2010, it was extended twice for a year each, pending the decision to determine new security features to be either domestically developed or acquired from external companies.

The work on identifying new security features did not lead to identification and finalization of the new security features until 2012. In a somewhat unusual manner Arvind Mayaram extended the supply contract of De La Rue for three years at a stretch, without taking the approval of the finance minister on file, despite a note existing on file from the finance minister not to extend the contract beyond 2012.

Arvind Mayaram had recorded a speaking order. Noting that the desired security features had not been developed and extending the contract by a year was not very efficient, he decided to extend it for a three-year period. One could interpret this decision as administratively efficient as it rendered it unnecessary to process the file again and again. However, the Coin and Currency Division (CCD) had seen similar decisions taken on extraneous considerations, which gave rise to the suspicion of an ulterior motive in this case. Approving an extension for an unusually long period of three years, without the finance minister's approval was certainly a major irregularity.

Another development had aggravated the situation. In 2016, the leaked Panama Papers revealed that De La Rue had paid money to

Indian officials to conclude a matter relating to defective supplies to Indian currency presses. Though it perhaps did not relate directly to the matter at hand, this revelation had made officials in the CCD even more wary of dealing with anything concerning De La Rue.

I presented the facts in a note to the finance minister. Arun Jaitley generally hated to take or recommend disciplinary action against any officer. However, he was possibly miffed at Arvind Mayaram's public criticism of the demonetization decision, which, in Jaitley's judgement, Mayaram should have understood better than others. On merit, too, he found the irregularity of a three-year extension without the finance minister's approval too stark to be glossed over. He approved the chargesheet, which was sent to DoPT. It was served to Arvind Mayaram before the expiry of the three-year-deadline.

Rajiv Mehrishi, another senior officer from the Rajasthan cadre, who succeeded Arvind Mayaram as secretary, DEA, and finance secretary, had ordered faster identification of security features. This was done, albeit not with full due diligence. He ordered tenders to be called but the tendering of security features was tortuously slow. This process was still midway when I joined DEA, about two years after Rajiv Mehrishi left in August 2015.

After the Panama controversy came to the fore, as proposed by the CCD, the finance minister had approved the suspension of De La Rue in early 2016 until CBI had enquired into the matter. This meant Indian currency presses could not buy anything from De La Rue until the CBI enquiry was over. As this hurt the interests of a British firm, the British government took up the matter with the finance minister. The British ambassador came to see me as well and explained how unfairly De La Rue had been treated. When Arun Jaitley travelled to Peru for the spring meetings of the IMF and World Bank in April 2018, the British chancellor raised the matter with him and asked for fair treatment. The director general (DG) of the British treasury also raised the same issue in a meeting with me.

CBI seemed in no hurry to take any action. It was over one-and-a-half years since the CBI enquiry had been ordered and we couldn't continue to use it as an excuse. CBI had not even registered a preliminary report. On the other hand, the British side claimed it had supplied all the papers relating to the reference in the leaked Panama Papers. There was indeed a complaint about one lot of supply for which corrective action had been taken. It contended there was no gratification paid to anyone.

I tried to expedite the matter with CBI and called its joint director for a meeting, and reviewed the status. After constant follow-up, CBI decided to register a preliminary enquiry after about two years of reference. It might not have been based on good evidence and, in that sense, might have been unfair, but it provided a clearer path of action. We told the British that De La Rue would stay suspended.

When the matter was raised by the British ambassador and my counterpart, the director general (DG), I had wanted the determination of facts on an expeditious basis. I recorded this on the references received and also on file. Anurag Agarwal, who was an ever suspicious officer, thought that I was trying to help De La Rue. He did not say anything until he was in DEA. As soon as he was moved out, he engineered a spate of complaints against me and Govind Mohan (another joint secretary in DEA who was handling investments and international economic relations and was also assisting me in the Fintech Committee). Anurag Agarwal suspected Govind was behind my asking for his lateral transfer from DEA. Principal Secretary Nripendra Misra showed me two or three such complaints. I smiled and apprised him of the facts.

Though nothing came of these complaints, it surprised me to see the conspiracy theories officers like Anurag Agarwal believed in.

ATMs Run Dry

In the middle of March 2018, Nripendra Misra convened a meeting at the behest of DFS Secretary Rajiv Kumar, to discuss the currency situation. Reports had started emerging on the shortage of currency notes in some parts of the country. Rajiv had a detailed statement about the status of printed notes with the presses and in the custody of banks. He had characterized the level of notes in the reserve as very low and told Nripendra Misra that if something was not done urgently, the situation could get out of hand.

Anurag Agarwal's poor sense of judgement had brought us considerable embarrassment in the coin mints case. My enquiries a few weeks before this meeting was convened had brought out the folly of his decision-making in the case of the critical ink for note printing. I decided enough was enough. On my persistent requests to the cabinet secretary and APS to the PM, the government had laterally transferred Anurag Agarwal out of DEA in the middle of March 2018. Only a few days earlier, I had given the charge of CCD to Prashant Goyal, joint secretary, Budget, who had also wanted to move out of the Budget Division.

The amount of currency in circulation follows a pattern in India. There are two busy seasons in a calendar year when currency in circulation expands: during March–May and during September–November. During these periods, currency usually expanded on an average of about ₹20–30,000 crore per month in the years preceding demonetization. From the months of June and December, the currency in circulation actually dipped below the levels prevailing in preceding months. On average, currency expanded by about ₹1.75 to 2 lakh crore per calendar year in the two to three years prior to demonetization. Based on this prevailing pattern we could reasonably model the currency pattern, once supply normalized after demonetization.

In the meeting with Principal Secretary Nripendra Misra, I accepted that currency notes in stock were lower than historical levels, but the stock was still enough for three to four months; therefore, there was no need to panic. Instead, we could plan to ramp up production to make sure stock levels reached about twice the normal level in six to eight months. I suggested we could liberally use the existing stock to increase the currency in circulation to meet the demand.

Nripendra Misra, drawing from his experience of working as joint secretary, CCD, in DEA many years back, felt that we were lax in monitoring the currency-note situation as tightly as his secretary did and he would have done. However, he directed that all immediate steps be taken to ramp up production and ordered the constitution of a committee under my chairpersonship with DG Kanungo and DFS Secretary Rajiv Kumar as members to monitor the situation closely and take all measures to increase supply and improve the distribution network.

We met almost every three to four days for a few weeks and sorted out the ink and other procurement-related issues. The denominational shift in the printing of notes was revised with the printing of the ₹500 note—the largest effective denominational note—being made the workhorse. The presses were ordered to shut production of smaller denomination notes. Fortunately, there was an adequate number of ₹100 notes, though these were also going to be soon replaced with the new ₹100 note. Only the ₹200 note was the other note printed in sizeable quantities.

The PM Calls from Abroad

In the first week of April, when the currency distribution shortage was at its peak (though not a crisis in my judgement), Prime Minister Modi also got worried. Arun Jaitley had just taken some weeks off for his medical treatment. The PM was travelling.

Someone in the PM's staff called me and connected me directly to him. While he sounded confident and assured as always, he expressed his concern at the currency shortage. He did not want people to suffer and wanted normalcy to be restored as soon as possible. He said to me, 'Subhashji, you are Arun Jaitley and Piyush Goyal for me at this moment. Make sure the currency situation gets resolved immediately.'

It was assuring to see the PM place so much confidence in me. I explained the situation as it stood and assured him that the shortage of currency notes in ATMs in some states would be completely over in three to five weeks and that we would soon build surplus stocks to ensure India did not face a shortage again.

Our reorganized production programme for printing notes got underway very soon. Much higher production was reported daily from the presses.

I called a press conference. Currency printing and the state of currency notes in reserve are generally a black box for the media and public. I decided to explain the basics to people through the press conference. I told the media there was an unusual spurt in currency demand in March–April 2018. From the usual average ₹20,000 crore increase a month during this period, currency demand had increased by ₹45,000 crore in the first two weeks of April 2018. Despite this spurt, we had adequate currency stocks of over ₹2 lakh crore. The shortage of currency experienced in some parts of the country was largely because of distributional problems caused by a massive spurt in demand in these areas.

Assuring the media that we were ramping up production of ₹500 notes from ₹500 crore a day in March, to ₹2,500 crore a day, I informed them that the total increase in currency supply would be over ₹75,000 crore a month. I further added that though currency demand usually tapered off from the month of June, the government would be well prepared to meet any demand in those lean months as well.

These statements were carried in all news channels and newspapers. I think they assured the public considerably. There is always an extra demand for currency or any other goods or services if people in general feel there is a shortage. The moment there is an assurance that there is no shortage, this extra demand falls.

While April saw a record increase in currency circulation of about ₹80,000 crore, additional net demand fell to about ₹25,000 crore in May and to less than ₹15,000 crore in June 2018. In July 2018, the currency in circulation contracted by about ₹30,000 crore, mirroring the normal pattern.

The currency shortage, which some people dramatized as a crisis, painting pictures of ATMs running dry, blew over by the end of April 2018.

Did Raghuram Rajan Question Demonetization?

In July 2019, member of Parliament (MP) Kumar Ketkar gave notice of a question classified by the Lok Sabha Secretariat as an unstarred question. He asked for the details of the note prepared by former RBI Governor Raghuram Rajan on demonetization 'in which he has shared his opinion'. The question further asked the details of the concept note prepared by either the PMO, finance minister or RBI on demonetization and its expected benefits.

Rajan had been telling the media from time to time that he had warned the government that demonetization was not a wise move. He never shared with the media any copy of the note that he might have prepared or shared with the PMO or finance minister. At one stage, he said he had left a note with the PMO.

This was a dicey question.

Prashant Goyal confirmed, after searching through the available records of the CCD, that there was no such note of Raghuram Rajan in their division. A reference from Prashant Goyal to RBI and the PMO elicited no response. On taking up the matter with RBI on phone, the concerned chief general manager (CGM) told Prashant Goyal that RBI would be sending information to me in a sealed envelope.

This made the situation trickier. I did not know what they would send me and why they would send anything to me directly and confidentially in a sealed envelope, instead of responding to the parliamentary question in the standard official manner.

Principal Secretary Nripendra Misra called me on the phone to check how the ministry was thinking of responding to the question. He informally told me that there might have been some paper from Rajan but that it did not exist any longer in the PMO. When I reminded him that we had a reference to the PMO to inform us of the factual information in this regard, he said that the PMO would respond by saying there was no such concept note on record with it.

The sealed envelope from RBI arrived. It did not carry a copy of any concept note or any other note from Raghuram Rajan on his views or advice on any demonetization proposal, general or specific. It only had a copy of a note recorded by the CGM who had accompanied Raghuram Rajan on a visit to the PMO where the supposed note from Rajan was discussed. RBI note only said that he (the CGM) had recorded the gist of the discussion in the meeting, which was seen by the governor who then asked the CGM to keep this recorded note in his personal custody.

After a year had passed, the concerned CGM passed on the note to the division concerned in RBI to keep it confidentially. This note was neither here nor there. It did indicate that demonetization was discussed in the PMO, but did not have the contents of the proposal. I decided to send the hot potato back to the sender of the sealed envelope in RBI. I kept no copy of what was received. Nothing was taken on record in DEA.

I drafted the answer to the question, read it out to Nripendra Misra who, somewhat unwillingly, agreed. The reply the government officially furnished to the Lok Sabha for question number 2573 answered on 16 July 2019 read:

> Does not arise as no Note from Shri Raghuram Rajan on demonetisation was received in the Ministry of Finance. RBI made a detailed proposal (which is not a Concept Note), which was considered in its Central Board Meeting held on 8.11.2016 and passed a resolution to recommend withdrawal of the legal tender of banknotes in the denomination of ₹500 and ₹1,000.

We did not speak for the PMO and RBI in the Reply, as the PMO only said it was not available in their record and RBI did not officially respond. The note in the sealed envelope that my office received from RBI CGM also did not say that anything was furnished to the Ministry of Finance.

Whenever ₹2,000 Notes Are to Be Phased Out

The ₹2,000 note was introduced along with the demonetization of ₹1,000 and ₹500 notes to relieve the distress caused by the sudden disappearance of 86 per cent of the currency in circulation. It was ironical to use ₹2,000 to remonetize when ₹1,000 and ₹500 notes were being demonetized on the grounds of being easier to use for storing black money. It was quite natural to expect that the

₹2,000 note would be either demonetized or withdrawn as soon as possible.

As noted earlier, the PM had expressed unease with the continuance of the ₹2,000 note and very much wanted these withdrawn. There was, however, no government decision to phase out the ₹2,000 note. Nor was any time frame indicated. The possibility of such a decision at some point of time had to be kept in mind. I thought we should be ready, just in case.

The basic equation in the case of the ₹2,000 note was simple. These notes were not printed after July 2017, barring a small batch in March–April 2018. In all, notes of a total value of ₹7 lakh crore were printed. There was no firm data but estimates suggested that ₹2,000 notes worth about ₹3–4 lakh crore had probably been hidden away, as this denomination was the most convenient for anyone who wanted to stock up value in currency.

As the effective value of ₹2,000 notes in circulation dwindled, banks started removing them from ATMs and replacing the ₹2,000 dockets/trays with ₹500 trays. There was a net inflow to banks of ₹2,000, which started returning these notes to RBI. Some notes got soiled or damaged as well.

In 2018, we estimated, in case the ₹2,000 note was to be phased out, we would need ₹7 lakh crore worth of ₹500 denomination notes to replace all the notes in circulation (assuming everyone deposited/ exchanged their ₹2,000 notes, which was quite likely considering the demonetization experience). Therefore, we decided to keep printing a greater number of ₹500 notes to build up stocks of ₹8–9 lakh crore. This process was substantially over by the time I left the Ministry of Finance.

The government informed the Parliament in 2020 that no decision to demonetize or phase out the ₹2000 note had been taken. Currency demand increased massively after Covid-19 struck. Notes in circulation were worth ₹23.2 lakh crore at the end of February 2020 and increased to more than ₹28.3 lakh crore at the end of March 2021—an increase of over ₹5 lakh crore in thirteen months.

I would like to believe that the extra ₹500 notes printed during 2018–19 served their purpose. The country faced no currency shortage during the pandemic, despite the sharp increase in demand, thanks to well-stocked coffers.

As per the annual report of RBI, only 21,420 lakh ₹2000 notes, with a total value of ₹4.28 lakh crore, were in circulation as on 31 March 2022. This made up only a little less than 14 per cent of the total currency in circulation, of ₹31.06 lakh crore on that day. By 31 March 2023, the number of ₹2,000 notes in circulation had come down to 18,111 lakh, with a total value of ₹3.62 lakh crore, accounting for only 10.8 per cent of the total currency (₹33.48 lakh crore) in circulation.

The ₹2,000 notes were finally 'withdrawn' on 20 May 2023. By this time, ₹2,000 notes valued at more than ₹3 lakh crore had already returned to RBI (presumably destroyed as well). RBI, which issued the withdrawal press release, as the move did not amount to demonetization, has given time until 30 September 2023 for the holders to deposit or exchange these notes. The ₹2000 notes continue to remain legal tender. It is quite certain that all of the outstanding ₹2000 notes will come back to RBI much before the September deadline.

With that the story of the ₹2000 note will become a page in history in India's currency management.

6

Wooing Farmers

THE GOVERNMENT TOOK SEVERAL INITIATIVES FOR AGRICULTURE AND farmers during the two years I served in the Department of Economic Affairs (2017–19). Most of these initiatives were announced through the three Budgets presented during this period.

These initiatives, though quite major in their reach and impact, remained within the existing agriculture system developed to spread green revolution technologies in the country. In my judgement, this approach was well past its time. There was too much government in agriculture, with programmes subsidizing everything from agriculture inputs to purchase of crops. However, the farming community was too big a vote bank to take chances with. Consequently, the government essentially went along, with more populist programmes.

In this chapter, I will discuss what went behind the formulation, announcement and implementation of two major agriculture and farmer-related initiatives taken during this period: giving minimum 50 per cent profit to farmers through the revamped minimum support price (MSP) system; and, provision of ₹6,000 per farming household per year as direct income support.

New MSP Regime: Minimum 50 Per Cent Profit for All Crops

The MSP system in India was introduced in the mid-1960s to incentivize farmers to undertake production of green revolution crops—wheat and rice—by assuring full procurement of their produce at remunerative prices. The Commission of Agriculture Costs and Prices (CACP) was established in 1965[7] to recommend MSPs for various crops, to be finally determined by the Union cabinet. The CACP has developed a comprehensive methodology to work out MSPs based on: actual cash costs incurred by farmers (called A2 costs); imputed cost of family labour (FL); and all other imputed costs like notional rent of land and notional interest on the fixed investment made (termed C2 costs, which includes A2 and FL costs).

By the turn of the century, the MSP system had been extended to almost all kharif and rabi field crops, and covered twenty-three crops.[8]

In 1965 the government also created the Food Corporation of India (FCI), to establish a national system of procurement of food crops—primarily wheat and rice—and for the distribution of procured grains. Over the years, the procurement of wheat and rice took firm root in the green revolution states of Punjab, Haryana, western Uttar Pradesh, northern and eastern Rajasthan and Andhra Pradesh. Later, governments in states like Madhya Pradesh and Chhattisgarh also provided additional incentives to establish an attractive system of wheat and rice procurement.

As MSP became the lynchpin of the food and agriculture system in the country, the government came under constant pressure to keep increasing the MSP of various crops. Eventually, these MSPs, especially for wheat and rice, were much higher than international prices and the domestic market price during many years, which free play of the forces of demand and supply would determine in ordinary course. In the case of wheat, for instance, the higher-than-market-price MSP led farmers to sell all their crops to the government,

---

7   Commission for Agricultural Costs & Prices, Ministry of Agriculture & Farmers Welfare, Government of India, https://cacp.dacnet.nic.in/content.aspx?pid=32

8   Ibid.

which ended up buying 40–50 per cent of the total wheat produced in the country. The high MSPs also made Indian farmers produce much more wheat and rice than their consumption demanded.

While the MSP strategy successfully converted India from a food-deficit country to a food-surplus country, it also meant that, for the past many years, FCI has had to carry much larger stocks of wheat and rice in its warehouses; with the government sometimes forced to subsidize export. Overall, the government now spends enormous fiscal resources—over ₹2 lakh crore a year—in subsidies to keep the MSP system going.

Besides farmers, many other interests have piggy-backed onto the MSPs. Many kinds of charges leviable on agriculture produce, traded in the agriculture produce markets (APMCs)—such as weighing costs, traders' commission, APMC charges and mandi fees payable—are payable on MSP-based procurement in APMCs and other declared markets. Some state governments have started collecting additional taxes/cesses from the procurement made by FCI, such as Punjab and Haryana's infrastructure cess.

All these charges, termed procurement incidentals by FCI, add up materially to the MSP cost of procurement. The FCI further incurs distribution costs in: transporting procured produce from the markets to its warehouses; and on storage in procurement; and distribution centres. The economic cost to FCI thus includes basic prices paid to farmers (MSP), procurement incidentals and distribution costs.

This economic cost to FCI was about 150 per cent of the basic pooled procurement cost. For financial year 2016–17, FCI's pooled cost of procurement of wheat was ₹1,467 per quintal, whereas its economic cost was ₹2,197 per quintal. In addition, FCI incurred an annual cost of ₹525 per quintal as carrying cost of buffer stock. For the nation, the wheat procured under the MSP system cost ₹2,722 per quintal in 2016–17. The farmers got only 54 per cent of the economic cost as MSP. In June 2017, the all-India monthly average price of wheat was around ₹1,700 per quintal, higher than the MSP. International prices were only ₹1,300 per quintal, which was lower than the MSP. The market prices of wheat in India thus hovered around the MSPs.

A comparison of the MSPs, economic costs, total cost to FCI/ nation, domestic market prices and international prices explains eloquently the economics and politics of the MSP system, benefits to farmers and cost to the country.

BJP's Promise to Implement Swaminathan Commission's Recommendation

The election manifesto of the Bhartiya Janata Party (BJP), which led the ruling National Democratic Alliance (NDA) after the elections in 2014, promised to: 'take steps to enhance profitability in agriculture, by ensuring a minimum of 50 per cent profits over the cost of production, cheaper agriculture inputs and credit; introducing latest technologies for farming and high-yielding seeds and linking MGNREGA [the Mahatma Gandhi National Rural Employment Guarantee Act, 2005] to agriculture.'

The promise to provide 'a minimum of 50 per cent profits over the cost of production', emanated from the recommendation made by the National Commission on Farmers, headed by noted agricultural scientist M.S. Swaminathan, in 2006. The Swaminathan Commission suggested that MSPs be fixed at a price 'at least 50 per cent more than the weighted average cost of production'.

As mentioned above, CACP considers three weighted costs of production while recommending MSPs: A2 (actual cash costs incurred by farmers), FL (imputed cost of family labour), and C2 (all other imputed costs like notional rent of land and notional interest on the fixed investment made, including A2 and FL costs). The Swaminathan Commission did not specify which weighted average cost was to be taken into account while building a 50 per cent margin of profit for farmers. Farmers' leaders undoubtedly have always wanted C2 costs to be taken into account.

I had looked at this issue when I served a group of ministers constituted by the Prime Minister's Advisory Council on Trade and Investment in 2011, while working as joint secretary in the Department of Agriculture. This ministerial group had also recommended that the government consider moving towards the goal of fixing MSPs at least 50 per cent higher than the A2 plus FL cost. The government had not implemented this promise in the manifesto in the years 2014–18. Instead, it had focused its attention on doubling farmer income by 2022, which incidentally was not an explicit promise in the 2014 manifesto.

Nripendra Misra Presents a Fait Accompli

In the first fortnight of January 2018, a couple of weeks before the presentation of Budget 2018–19, Nripendra Misra, principal secretary to the PM, convened a meeting in his chamber. He had a paper with the basic numbers for all crops then under MSP—their MSPs, their cost (A2 plus FL), profit element in the MSP (MSP minus cost), and percentage of profit over the cost. There was another sheet that calculated MSPs with at least 50 per cent profit over cost (wherever the profits were less than 50 per cent, they were raised to 50 per cent with the rest unchanged).

He said the decision to provide minimum 50 per cent profit over the cost of cultivation of crops was to be announced in the 2018–19 Budget.

This directive came as a surprise. There were many other subjects relating to agriculture under discussion for inclusion in the Budget, but this was not one of them. The papers with the principal secretary did not have firm estimates of what this decision would cost the government. I asked that I be allowed to work out the financial implications. Raising the MSP further for certain crops would have marketing implications, including on export. I quickly remembered how Thailand had gone out of the rice export business a couple of years earlier when it had raised the support price for rice excessively; which, incidentally, established India as the largest rice exporter.

Chief Economic Advisor Arvind Subramanian and his team made some quick calculations after collecting data of procurement made in the past. There was also a likelihood of procurement at MSP going up further, but we ignored that for the time being. Most crops with an MSP with less than 50 per cent profit over cost were kharif crops. The minimum bill came to about ₹35,000 crore, with rice alone likely to cost an additional ₹12,000 crore.

There was also a big issue regarding the ability of the government to honour its commitment. Many crops like pearl-millet, etc., were not suitable to procurement and storage. Government organizations did not have the capacity to procure and market the likely quantity that would be procured at the increased MSP. There were implications for inflation, particularly for crops in which India was deficient, such as pulses and oilseeds. Increased prices could increase importers' profits. Moreover, no one had undertaken any exercise to understand the impact of this decision on crop diversification.

We flagged these issues, but as a decision had been taken, it was included in the Budget speech.

MSP Policy Gets Reset in Budget 2018–19

Budget 2018–19 had quite a few announcements for farmers and agriculture, the MSP announcement being the star. Finance Minister Arun Jaitley, focusing his announcement on kharif crop MSPs with lower than 50 per cent profits, announced that the government had decided to 'keep MSP for all unannounced crops of kharif to at least one-and-a-half times of their production cost'. He underscored the government's commitment to the party's manifesto.

Making it clear that the government intended to follow through, Arun Jaitley declared that increasing MSP was not adequate and it was more important that farmers get the full benefit of the announced MSP. He committed that the government would either purchase the crops at MSP or 'work in a manner to provide MSP for farmers through some other mechanism' that would be foolproof.

This Budget announcement received the largest coverage after the presentation and generated an enormous amount of comments and questions. Many senior economic and political commentators criticized the announcement and its negative implications on prices, fiscal deficit and the surfeit of production it would generate, as with MSPs in the case of wheat and rice.

Defending on Principles of Inter-crop Equity

India's crop land is not expanding. In fact, from the 1970s, there has been some, albeit minor, reduction in total land under crops on account of industrialization, infrastructure and urbanization.

As Arun Jaitley pointed out, except probably for safflower, the MSPs for all the rabi crops (wheat, barley, gram, etc.) carried more than a 50 per cent profit element over cost. It was the kharif crops (paddy, jowar, ragi, moong, groundnut, etc.) that did not have the 50 per cent profit element, with some being only marginally above their cost of production.

There was inter-crop inequity in the MSP system (cereals like wheat and rice were procured but not barley, millets, etc.: oilseeds and pulses were procured but in much smaller quantities). This inequity was further accentuated in terms of seasonal crops reflected in the fact that kharif crops, except paddy/rice, were seldom procured.

The acreage under kharif crops, being dependent upon the monsoon, meant areas were more or less fixed for crops. There was very little likelihood of crop diversification taking place. Moreover, when all the crops were likely to generate 50 per cent profit over cost for farmers, it was unlikely that farmers would shift crops simply because some crops had higher profits than others. The moment the inter-se advantage between crops in terms of surplus/profit generation for farmers ceases, the MSP also ceases to be a driver for farmers to grow any particular crop.

Therefore, I argued in my post-Budget interviews that the new system of MSP would not distort farmers' incentives to grow any particular crop. In fact, it would remove or at least reduce that distortion. For fiscal implication and inflation, my arguments were more informed by the fact that the first procurements that would be impacted by the MSP announcement would be for crops that came after September 2018. Further, as I did not expect production of any crop (supply) reducing on account of the MSP decision or any impact on demand, there was unlikely to be any inflationary implications, except for some cost-induced price increase. This would need to be watched.

There was expected bickering over whether the 50 per cent profit would be over A2, A2 plus FL or C2. We made it clear that it was A2 plus FL, based on the information supplied by the Ministry of Agriculture. This ebbed the enthusiasm of some farmers' organizations, but that was understandable.

Implementation Mechanism Dilutes the Punch

Making institutional arrangements for implementing the decision was critical for the credibility of the government. The financial bill of the decision also depended on the implementation of the decision. While the expenditure secretary was primarily concerned with expenditure implications, I was also particularly keen to fix this.

Sometime before the presentation of Budget 2018–19, the government had stepped up procurement of kharif crops. Pulses and oilseeds, the primary crops of kharif, other than rice, were procured by the National Agricultural Cooperative Marketing Federation of India (NAFED), and not FCI. As it had very weak finances, NAFED needed to borrow funds for procurement. Banks gave it funds only after the government's guarantee, which was issued by DEA. The stepped-up procurement had led to the guarantee amount going up sharply from levels of about ₹10,000 crore to over ₹25,000 crore. Requests for further guarantees were pending. The implementation of increased MSP was likely to further exacerbate the situation.

Madhya Pradesh had experimented with a price difference payment scheme for some crops, to complement the MSP system. This system operated through market participants. They were to buy the crop in the market at market price, with the government paying the farmer the difference between the MSP and market price. In principle, this system looked simpler, involved far lesser funds and was more market-oriented than the FCI/NAFED system of procuring at full MSP and stocking the crops in their godowns. However, there were considerable risks of fake sales taking place, hence Madhya Pradesh was experimenting with safeguards as well. Amitabh Jain, an officer from the state in the PMO, led this effort.

Rajiv Kumar, vice-chairman of NITI Aayog, which was entrusted the task of designing the 'foolproof' system, came up with a market-oriented but more complicated system of traders working as procurement and storage agents.

Several rounds of discussions took place in the PMO to select and firm up the institutional mechanism. The fiscal implications critically depended on the quantity of crops procured and the difference between the total cost of procurement/storage (economic cost plus buffer stock cost in case of FCI) and the prices at which procured stocks got sold.

Several rounds of discussions in the PMO—on finalizing the institutional mechanism to buy all the crops offered at MSP or paying the difference to the farmers between the MSP and market prices—did not lead to any commonly accepted mechanism. Prime Minister Modi himself chaired a few meetings where presentations were made on the alternatives being considered.

The tried and tested system of FCI/NAFED was the costliest. If it were to be expanded to procure all the crops offered at MSP prices, it would also require considerable expansion of procurement, storage and distribution infrastructure and human resources. Different cost implications were worked out on the assumption of the proportion of crop expected to be procured. The Madhya Pradesh alternative was generally taken to be too risky and highly prone to misuse. The alternative presented by Rajiv Kumar did not get much traction either, on account of the complications involved.

One day, after quite a few meetings, the PM posed a simple question to the effect—if at any time in the past, all the crop that should have been procured at MSP, had not been procured; why would it be necessary to do so now? I thought this poser was intended to suggest to stick to the tried and tested procurement system even if all the crops—for which 50 per cent profit over cost had been promised—might not really get procured.

This poser decided the matter. The government went with the tried and tested method of procuring crops through FCI and NAFED. The system of crop procurement at MSP, with minimum 50 per cent profit over the cost of growing crops, continues to be operated after the Budget announcement in 2018–19 much the same way as it did before—MSPs do have a 50 per cent profit element but procurement of crops other than wheat and rice remains limited.

PM-KISAN: Basic Income Support to Farmers?

In addition to the MSPs with minimum 50 per cent profit over cost of cultivation, as explained above, the 2018–19 Budget had announced two other major initiatives in agriculture policy: the Operations Greens scheme to transform the farm-to-fork ecosystem for horticultural crops; and a flurry of funds for agriculture infrastructure investments.

Like the MSP scheme, other initiatives also limped along. The Operations Greens scheme was entrusted to the Ministry of Food Processing for implementation. There was no Varghese Kurian (the 'Father of the White Revolution in India') in the ministry to organize the transformation of the total production-distribution-consumption chain of horticulture crops in a scientific but commercially sound manner. The scheme drifted and has ended up as yet another scheme to fund small investments in sporadic food-processing facilities. The infrastructure funds were, in any case, not intended for a quick rollout.

The situation of farmers, in fact, was worsening in 2018–19. Thanks to the excessive imports of pulses a year before, the bumper production of most crops, and indifferent procurement at MSP prices, food prices fell to lower levels. In 2018–19, food inflation turned out to be only 0.7 per cent as against general inflation of 3.4 per cent. Lower food inflation translated into lower price realization for farmers. Instead of moving towards doubling, their income was declining. Farmers were in distress.

Some states started implementing direct income transfer schemes for farmers. The Telangana government implemented the Rythu Bandhu scheme in May 2018, which provided ₹10,000 per acre per year (₹5,000 per acre for two seasons) income support to all farmers, including tenant farmers, in the state. The Odisha government also came out with a scheme named Krushak Assistance for Livelihood and Income Augmentation (KALIA) in October 2018 that promised ₹5,000 cash support for five agricultural seasons, amounting to ₹25,000, to every small and marginal farm family. Some more states were contemplating such income-support schemes for farmers.

The Central government also wanted to take up additional measures to support farmers. The Department of Agriculture developed an income-support scheme sometime in December that looked more like the Telangana scheme.

Ever since my stints in the agriculture domain in Rajasthan and at the Centre, I have believed that the farm sector needed structural reforms to increase production and improve the lot of farmers. The government needed to do away with input subsidies to usher in more productive and appropriate use of inputs. The electricity subsidy needed to go if the use of water was to be rationalized and a shift towards less water-guzzling crops, engineered. Fertilizer subsidies needed to go, to bring about more balanced and economical use of nutrients. Likewise, MSPs needed to be replaced by free-market prices, supported by a good functional system of futures and options, for farmers to get good commercial returns for their produce.

When the Department of Agriculture was working on the contours of the farmer income-support scheme, I worked on an alternative income-support scheme. With the help of officers in the Economic Division, I worked out the per-hectare incidence of input subsidies (of both the Centre and states) and the higher cost of procurement and distribution of MSP crops (over and above market prices) by both FCI and NAFED. The exercise revealed that the Centre and states were spending over ₹3 lakh crore on such subsidies and support for the net cropped area of 140 million hectares in India. This worked out to a little over ₹20,000 per hectare. Most farmers did not earn a profit of ₹20,000 from a hectare of agricultural land in the country.

During the previous Budget presentation, I had proposed the replacement of the subsidized fertilizer scheme with an income-transfer scheme. Nripendra Misra had found the suggestion atrocious. When I had repeated the same suggestion at the meeting with Prime Minister Modi, Nripendra Misra had shot back, saying it would lead to political suicide. I was comforted by the PM's reaction when he asked Nripendra Misra to leave political matters to him.

Perhaps because of this background, I was not involved with the consideration of the scheme formulated by the Department of Agriculture. There was a minister's committee headed by Arun Jaitley, which was serviced by the Department of Expenditure. Feeling strongly that the opportunity to reform the agriculture sector should not be allowed to go waste, I made a presentation before the finance minister proposing a basic reform: eliminate the MSP and replace all input subsidies with a blockbuster farmer income-support scheme that could also engender freedom from agriculture, enabling farmers to move into higher, value-added skills.

Arun Jaitley found my proposals worthy of consideration. Aware of the political economy and that the general elections were only a few months away, he asked me to make my presentation before Nripendra Misra and, if he agreed, then before the PM. Nripendra Misra looked at the presentation and asked me to stay away from any discussion on the farmer income-support scheme. He said I would be given the paragraphs on the scheme to include in the Budget speech which I should include without any modification.

Close to the day of the Budget, when Piyush Goyal had been put in charge of the Ministry of Finance, he disclosed the basic features of the income-support scheme at a meeting of the ministry's secretaries. It envisaged providing income support to about twelve crore farmers. India did not have twelve crore farmers. It had approximately that number of operational farm holdings. The farm holdings did not equal the number of farmers. The socioeconomic Census undertaken in 2011 had counted under eight crore farmers. The proposed scheme also envisaged a fresh round of enrolment of farmers, whereas family-wise data was already available in the Census.

I told Piyush Goyal about this basic discrepancy in numbers and the likely administrative waste of time in undertaking fresh enrolment, which also had serious implications of miscarriage and corruption. He understood and took it up with the PM and the PMO. It was possibly acknowledged that there were flaws in the scheme. However, instead of going back to the drawing board, it was decided to go ahead with the scheme and have a committee under the cabinet secretary to look into these plumbing issues later.

The government took an unprecedented step. Interim Budgets do not normally announce new schemes. The interim Budget presented by Piyush Goyal on 1 February 2019 not only announced the new farmer income-support scheme, but also made it applicable for the outgoing financial year 2018–19; thus one instalment would be delivered before the close of the year.

The Budget announcement said:

> To provide an assured income support to small and marginal farmers, our government is launching a historic programme, namely Pradhan Mantri Kisan Samman Nidhi (PM-KISAN). Under this programme, vulnerable landholding farmer families, having cultivable land up to 2 hectare, will be provided direct income support at the rate of ₹6,000 per year. This income support will be transferred directly into the bank accounts of beneficiary farmers, in three equal instalments of ₹2,000 each. This programme will be funded by Government of India. Around 12 crore small and marginal farmer families are expected to benefit from this. The programme would be made effective from 1 December 2018 and the first instalment for the period up to 31 March 2019 would be paid during this year itself. This programme will entail an annual expenditure of ₹75,000 crore.

The scheme was quickly formulated and approved before the elections were announced in early March 2019. The first instalment was disbursed to 3.16 crore farmers. The government could raise the disbursement to about 9 crore farmers in 2019–20. In 2020–21, the number ranged between 10.23 and 10.5 crore. After exceeding 11 crore in 2021–22, the number of farmers suddenly fell to less than 9 crore for the second instalment of 2022–23 and further to about 8.5 crore in the latest instalment disbursed in March 2023. The numbers—first rising massively and then falling dramatically— are indeed baffling.

7

Foreign Direct Investment without FIPB

FOREIGN DIRECT INVESTMENT OR FDI IS A CAPITAL ACCOUNT MATTER subject to government control under the Foreign Exchange Management Act, or FEMA. DEA is the administrative department for FEMA. Considerable powers of managing capital account transactions have been delegated to RBI. The policy relating to FDI has been allocated to the Department of Industrial Promotion and Policy (DIPP) since the first liberalization of FDI policy was undertaken in 1991.

Two routes for permitting FDI have evolved over the years: the government route and the automatic route. Under the automatic route, FDI can be brought into the country by filing the relevant declarations and papers with an authorized foreign exchange dealer, while FDI flows under the government route require government approval.

The Foreign Investment Promotion Board (FIPB) was constituted in 1991, initially in the PMO, but transferred to DEA. Until the middle of 2017, it functioned under the administrative control of DEA, headed by secretary, DEA. All cases requiring government approval were considered and decided upon by FIPB.

FIPB Work Gets Disoriented

On 5 June 2017, a month before I arrived, DEA issued an office memorandum abolishing FIPB. The government abolished FIPB, but not all the government route approvals required for FDI by this order. In place of FIPB, FDI cases were to be considered and approvals provided by the concerned administrative ministries/departments. In all, eleven ministries/departments were assigned specific areas for consideration of FDI proposals. DEA was left with cases relating to financial services not regulated, or regulated by more than one regulator, or where there was a doubt about who the concerned regulator was. In addition, cases relating to foreign investment in core investment companies and investment companies also remained with DEA.

Most of the residual and miscellaneous work was transferred to DIPP, including cases relating to FDI by non-residents, export-oriented units or issue of equity shares for import of capital goods. The FIPB portal created by DEA was transferred to DIPP. Over 4,500 files in the FIPB secretariat with DEA were transferred to the respective ministries/departments, along with pending cases in courts and other adjudicatory forums. DIPP was made the reference and nodal department for FDI. It was provided that no department/ministry would reject an FDI proposal without making a reference to DIPP. DIPP renamed the portal: Foreign Investment Facilitation Portal (FIFP).

A quarterly joint review arrangement was envisaged. This quarterly joint review committee was co-chaired by secretary, DEA, and secretary, DIPP.

The FIPB secretariat in DEA had organized the FDI government approval process quite systematically. The inherent nature of the process—which required circulation of FDI proposals to the concerned ministries, besides the mandatory consultation with DIPP and the Ministry of Home Affairs (MHA)—meant processing the proposals took a certain minimum time. FIPB had established efficient working processes and a timetable to process cases and issue approvals.

Processing FDI approval required a certain understanding of FEMA, foreign investment policy and rules, functioning of the capital account convertibility system, financial markets, international capital flows, functioning of banking and capital markets and companies and other regulatory legislation. There are important security considerations involved as well.

The transfer of pending cases, about sixty at that time, to administrative ministries/departments, brought the approval process to a grinding halt. Most departments (the Ministry of Mines for FDI in mining cases, the Ministry of Information and Broadcasting for FDI in digital news and other FDI cases, the Department of Telecommunication for FDI in telecom, and so on) found the cases too complex and contentious to deal with. They did not have the appropriate skills, experience and understanding to deal with these cases.

In the first joint review meeting that I co-chaired with DIPP Secretary Ramesh Abhishek, it was apparent that nothing had moved, except, in the case of DIPP and DEA; DIPP had disposed of most of the cases and DEA also disposed of more than twenty cases with only two pending. Pendency of cases in telecom, broadcasting and home affairs had risen to much higher levels than earlier. There were many cases pending for more than a year. While their inability to deal with the cases was the real reason for delay, the primary justification offered by most of them was complications arising out of security clearance-related issues.

MHA's Additional Comments Bog Down Admin Departments

Certain FDI proposals required security clearance from MHA. For instance, investments in broadcasting, telecommunications, satellites, private security agencies, defence, civil aviation and mining required such clearance. In 2017–18, FDI proposals that came under the automatic route from 'countries of concern'—Pakistan and Bangladesh—also required security clearance.

Most of the pendency in the first review meeting was found to be concentrated in departments where FDI proposals required security clearance. In many cases, MHA had provided security clearance without any conditions; and in some, with conditions. While the security clearance was available, the departments were unable to move further. When probed a little further, they cited comments (not conditions) made by the MHA examiners and, sometimes, additional information noted in the communication, which created problems for them.

In some cases, MHA noted that there were criminal and tax-related cases pending against some directors, or there were allegations that the company or its directors were involved in money laundering or round-tripping of money, or that the company or its directors were named in controversial documents like the Panama Papers and the like. None of the additional information provided, or comments made, affected the security clearance and therefore MHA granted it. However, the existence of such information on record created enormous doubts in the minds of the officers handling the FDI cases. They feared they might be taken to task later for permitting suspicious FDIs.

In my view, all such observations/comments/information were to be simply ignored. Ramesh agreed in principle, but was not that sure. I suggested that DIPP issue a clarificatory circular and after analysing each such observation/comment and giving its reasons, ask the department/ministry concerned to ignore such comments and not allow them to come in the way of clearing FDI proposals. This was agreed to. I extensively amended the draft minutes received from DIPP to incorporate this solution as DIPP draft only made a cursory reference to it.

After a few days, Nripendra Misra, principal secretary in the PMO, reviewed the progress of the disposal of FDI cases. He was the principal architect of the proposal to abolish FIPB. In the review meeting, he wondered whether the abolition of FIPB was the right thing to do. I suggested we needed to make the new system work. He also concurred with the proposed mode of disposing of the additional and unnecessary comments of MHA received along with the security clearance. Thereafter, DIPP issued the circular.

FIPB Went but Not the Examination for CBI Prosecution

After the abolition of FIPB and transfer of all cases, including the closed files, to respective ministries/departments, DEA had no original files with it. Yet, when the Central Bureau of Investigation (CBI) sought permission to prosecute former Finance Minister P. Chidambaram and the officers who had processed the INX Media FDI approval by FIPB, the DoPT (which is the administrative department of CBI), insisted that DEA not only provide comments on the facts and conclusions reached by CBI, but also offer its views and its opinion on granting prosecution sanction for the former minister as well as the officers.

This insistence was despite the rules that prosecution sanctions for ministers were processed by MHA, prosecution sanctions for IAS officers by the DoPT, and the FDI policy had always been with DIPP.

There was another such matter concerning the Aircel–Maxis case. The accusation in the Aircel–Maxis case was that the minister Chidambaram approved the investment recommended by FIPB without having the competence to do so, while the officers, including former DEA Secretary Ashok Chawla (at that time, additional secretary in DEA), processed the case either under pressure from the minister or in collusion with him.

The FIPB note presented by the division back then had noted the face value of shares for which FDI was brought in at less than ₹600 crore. The total amount of investment brought in was separately mentioned as $800 million. The total investment brought in at the exchange rates prevailing at the time (around ₹45 to a dollar) made the total investment flow exceed ₹3,500 crore. FIPB took note only of the face value and recommended the transaction for approval of the finance minister, who as per the cabinet's mandate, had powers to approve total investment up to ₹600 crore. All the officers from the joint secretary to secretary, had either simply signed the note sheet or recommended approval of the FIPB recommendation.

There were some other allegations regarding corruption or money laundering against the minister, but DEA's views and opinion were sought basically regarding approval of the transaction without having the authority thereof. Proposals of investment above ₹600 crore went to the Cabinet Committee on Economic Affairs (CCEA).

After comprehensive examination of the photocopied files (the originals had gone to the Department of Telecom), I wondered what crime the officers had committed. FIPB was empowered to recommend the transaction, whether it was for ₹3,500 crore or less than ₹600 crore. No case sent to CCEA regarding approval of the FIPB recommendations, was ever questioned or rejected. If, in this case, FIPB had recommended approval of the same number of shares for a total consideration of $800 million and the minister had sent it to CCEA, the transaction would have still been approved. Was it a criminal conspiracy or just a procedural lapse? DEA's comments were provided on these lines.

The INX Media case was more complex and the evidence of criminal negligence or collusion stronger. The investment was proposed for INX Media and INX News. The investment proposed for the companies had come to India, though FIBP had approved only the INX Media investment in the first place. The investment in INX News was approved much later in a clandestine manner to regularize the irregularity. There was more credible information relating to the payment of a bribe to Chidambaram's son Karti, connected with these investments.

The Department of Economic Affairs supported the prosecution of Chidambaram in this case, as well as charges of criminal negligence on two of the five officers involved. There was unnecessary collateral damage to two officers, especially Prabodh Saxena, who had handled the file in the first week of his arrival in the division. We suggested no action against these two officers.

Start-ups Become Unintended Victims of Angel Tax Excess

Start-ups, nursed by FDI inflows from off-shore venture capital funds, had begun playing a significant role in India's growth story in the twenty-first century. By 2015, though far behind the US and China, India had become the third largest start-up eco-system in the world. Animal spirits were so vividly evident in the start-up ventures set up by young risk-taking and mostly techno-entrepreneurs. At the same time rouge business operators in stock exchanges were devising clever modes to launder their ill-gotten money. Petty stocks were being pumped up to skyrocketing valuations and shell companies were being set up to do shady businesses under cover and to convert their black money into white.

The government, perhaps fully unaware of its implications on the start-up eco-system, inserted Section 56(2)(viib) in the Income Tax Act through the Finance Act 2012, to catch generation and laundering of unaccounted money effected through subscription of shares of closely held companies, at a value which is higher than the fair market value (FMV) of shares issued. This tax—levied on the start-up for investment by its capital investors (the angels)—has come to be known as the notorious 'angel tax'.

Determination of the FMV proved the trickiest part for start-ups. The law provided that the FMV of the shares be determined in accordance with the method prescribed by the Income Tax Department. At that time the method that was approved was the book value method (net asset value or NAV) or as substantiated by the company to the satisfaction of the Assessing Officer, based on the value, on the date of issue of shares, of its assets, including intangible assets being goodwill, know-how, patents, copyrights, trademarks, licences, franchises or any other business or commercial rights of similar nature, whichever is higher.

The start-ups, already hassled and struggling to set-up their difficult and risky ventures, were completely flummoxed by the requirement of determining FMV when they issued their capital. Many start-ups received notices from the Income Tax Department and ran to the government for succour.

Nripendra Misra convened a meeting. Ramesh Abhishek defended then current regime. His department (then DIPP) was in charge of start-ups. DIPP registered start-ups, though on a dicey criterion, which did not distinguish between real tech-start-ups and routine MSMEs. Start-ups receiving capital from SEBI-registered venture capital funds and foreign investors, were exempt from the angel tax. A government notification had also exempted start-ups with an annual turnover of less than ₹25 crore.

After spending some time in understanding the crux of the issue, including reviewing presentations from start-up protagonists like Mohan Das Pai and others, I concluded that the FMV business for start-ups did not make any sense and that tech start-ups were not the vehicles that were being used for laundering money. In the meeting, I therefore, argued that there was no point in tinkering with the DIPP notification (Ramesh Abhishek had proposed to increase the turnover limit and do some tweaking of registration criterion); rather, the entire tech start-up eco-system had to be excluded from the reach of Section 56(2)(viib)/ angel tax.

Nripendra Misra showed some initial interest in what I proposed. However, the system had large departmental interests and designs. Income Tax Department proposed to drop the notices and evolve better methods of FMV determination. Finally, turnover limit was raised to ₹100 crore, income tax notices were withdrawn and two more methods of FMV determination were prescribed. It brought some relief, but Indian start-up investors continued to suffer.

As of January 2023, more than 80 per cent of start-up funding came from foreign investors However, in Budget 2023–24, Finance Minister Nirmala Sitharaman decided to withdraw exemption to foreign investment from angel tax in start-up capital raising.

Not all foreign investors in start-ups are SEBI-registered virtual currency (VC) entities. Start-ups are also facing a funding winter as foreign investment in start-ups has even otherwise dried up. This measure has revived the ghost of angel tax. The government has again tried to find patchwork solutions. It is still not prepared to dump the entire angel tax ecosystem. The angle tax pain lives on.

Government Finally Has a Unified Regulator for International Finance City

India had been desiring to set up an international finance city for quite some time. The Mistry Committee appointed in 2005 recommended setting up an international finance city in Mumbai, with an ambitious finance reform agenda, in place of an international finance centre which the government's terms of reference had asked for. No action was taken thereon.

After Prime Minister Narendra Modi assumed power in 2014, the centre of gravity shifted to Gujarat. In April 2015 the government decided to set up an International Financial Services Centre (IFSC) in Gujarat International Finance Tech-city (GIFT) in Gandhinagar. GIFT was established in 2008, when Narendra Modi was chief minister of Gujarat. Soon after, the process of transferring financial functions to IFSC started with GIFT city authorities playing the role of facilitators. The necessity of establishing a unified regulator was felt for the financial services transacted in IFSC, as all financial services—savings, loans, equity, bonds, insurance etc.—are tightly regulated by powerful regulators such as RBI, SEBI and IRDA.

The Capital Markets Division in DEA, responsible for the subject, had entrusted the task of formulating a law for the establishment of a unified regulator, to the Indira Gandhi Institute of Development Research (IGIDR), Mumbai. GIFT city authorities were quite at their wits end, struggling with financial sector regulators in their desire to see financial services providers set up their shops in IFSC. The IGIDR was taking its own time and it had its own woolly ideas about the unified regulator. I entered in the Department at this juncture.

A thorough review in a series of meetings, with the Capital Markets Division (Shashank first and then Bajaj) suggested that there were serious pitfalls in the structure of the unified regulator proposed in the IGIDR draft law itself. I thought of a simpler structure which would identify specific financial products, financial services and financial institutions for transfer to IFSC and would confer exclusive regulatory authority on IFSC thereafter to the exclusion of sector regulators like RBI, SEBI and others. I thought such a practical structure would work the best and prevent friction caused by overlapping authority. The IGIDR structure was based more on principles in place of any specified structure.

As IGIDR was not quite willing to redraft the proposed unified authority bill (the International Financial Services Centres Authority Bill) in line with our requirement, I decided to do away with their services and DEA assumed full responsibility for preparation of the Bill.

Bajaj and his team rose to the occasion and soon readied a Draft Bill, building-in the basic structure and directions I had provided. There were a few further rounds of fine-tuning until we finalized the Draft and were satisfied about it. After obtaining the approval of the finance minister, we circulated it to the law ministry and other concerned ministries. The consultation process was quickly completed and the cabinet happily approved the Bill without any changes.

The International Financial Services Centres Authority (IFSCA) Bill, 2019 was introduced in the Rajya Sabha by acting Finance Minister Piyush Goyal, on 12 February 2019, as we did not want the Bill to lapse with the Lok Sabha elections round the corner. The Bill was referred to the Standing Committee on 22 February. Consideration of passing the budget did not allow the Bill to be taken up in the Budget Session held in July–August 2019. I left the finance ministry on 24 July. The Standing Committee report also came in much after the elections.

The Bill was taken up for consideration in Parliament in November 2019, almost in the same form in which we had drafted it. It was passed in December 2019. The International Financial Services Centres Authority Act, 2019 was published in Gazette of India on 19 December 2019. India had its unified regulator for IFSC.

I felt quite happy when the IFSCA authority was established in 2020 and my batchmate Injeti Srinivas was appointed as its first Chairperson. The IFSC GIFT City has grown into a good international financial centre, thanks to numerous tax concessions granted by the government over last three years and functions/services transferred to it. Bonds are being issued and listed in IFSC. A couple of equity stock exchanges have been set up. Many banks have established their branches and offices there. Other financial services providers are also trooping in.

8

Royalty Terrorism and E-Commerce Misadventure

Abortive Attempt to Roll Back Royalty Liberalization

INDIA LIBERALIZED ITS HIGHLY RESTRICTIVE REGIME ON PAYMENT OF ROYALTIES on foreign technology imports/agreements and payment of royalties on brand and trademark use (without involvement of technology transfer) in a two-stage reform process, first in 1991 and then in 2009.

In 1991, India allowed royalty payment up to $2 million in lumpsum or payment of 5 per cent on domestic sales and 8 per cent on exports, in case of foreign technology agreements on automatic approval basis. For use of brands/trademarks without technology transfer, payment of royalty up to 2 per cent on exports and 1 per cent on domestic sales was permitted under the automatic approval route. Payment of royalties higher than these limits required specific approval of the Government of India. Such cases were considered by the Project Approval Board (PAB) located in DIPP.

The government completely liberalized payment of royalty for both technology transfers and non-technology transfers in 2009. Press Note 8 issued in 2009 permitted payments for royalty and lumpsum fee for transfer of technology and payments for use of trademark/brand name on the automatic route, which did away with the need to obtain specific approval of the government. All payments of royalties were only subject to foreign exchange rules, which treated payment of royalties as current account transactions.

These liberalized regulations aided the technological transformation of India's industry substantially, turning the country into a producer of good quality machinery and consumption products. Payment of royalties, however, increased substantially in the process. Reserve Bank of India statistics for 'charges for the use of intellectual property' for the year 2016–17 recorded net payments of $5 billion, which grew to $6 billion the following year. With regard to overall imports, however, gross royalty payments of $5.7 billion in 2016–17 were only a little over 1 per cent of the total imports of $536 billion.

Worried by excessive payment of royalties from India, DIPP initiated moves to roll back liberalization in royalty payments in 2017.

The DIPP Proposal a 'Royalty Terrorism'?

Some time in November–December 2018, DIPP circulated a draft cabinet note proposing a cap on royalty payments, restricting royalty payments to foreign technology and other intellectual property service providers. All three departments of the Ministry of Finance— DEA, revenue and expenditure—were separately consulted.

Clearly, DIPP was concerned with rising royalty payments. It found that some companies in the IT sector were paying as high as 80–90 per cent of total revenues as royalty payments. It used data from the Revenue Department (which was company-specific) to support its claim that, in many cases, royalty payments exceeded 5 per cent. Its proposal was to go back to the pre-2009 regime and place separate limits of 4 per cent on technology transfers and 2 per cent on the use of intellectual property (without technology transfer).

We were horrified at the proposal. In terms of policy, this was going back to the control era and the government substituting its judgement for the commercial judgement of the business parties involved: the technology supplier and the technology recipient.

The administration of such a regime would have required companies coming back to the government/DIPP whenever they wanted to pay higher royalty. Moreover, what constituted total sales and what constituted royalty payments were also a matter of immense dispute—in another context, dispute relating to determination of adjusted gross revenue (AGR) had upended the telecom sector.

On FDI, the government was moving towards increased liberalization (except in the e-commerce and retail sectors). The proposal relating to capping royalties appeared to be moving in the reverse direction.

In the era of digital technology, competitive advantage was all about the development and assimilation of Industry 4.0 and digital technology in Indian companies. Several global digital technology companies were establishing technology and research and development (R&D) centres here in India. Any regime that restricted full and free flow of technology would hurt the country's industrialization and digitalization.

Therefore, we opposed the proposals very strongly. Tax terrorism was very much in the air on account of the retrospective tax policy. We dubbed the proposal as 'royalty terrorism'. Finance Minister Arun Jaitley endorsed this view.

PMO Meeting Kills the Proposal

DIPP's views on the royalty issue were, perhaps, shared by the PMO. After it received DEA's comments, duly endorsed by the finance minister, it hurriedly convened a meeting chaired by Nripendra Misra, principal secretary to the PM. All the departments of the Ministry of Finance were present. CEA Arvind Subramanian was also present. DIPP Secretary Ramesh Abhishek made the presentation.

Ramesh Abhishek argued his case passionately, pointing out the rising payment of royalties using data from the current account and the Income Tax Department, Indian subsidiaries or substantially-owned companies being forced into higher payment of royalties, and a disconnect between the real advantages of technology supplied and royalty payments made.

Arvind and I stood our ground and argued that there was no justification to bring back such a subjective regime and micromanage businesses. Somewhat discordant voices came from the Departments of Expenditure and Revenue. While the Department of Expenditure's views were more proforma, the Department of Revenue looked at the issue from a narrow revenue angle. Royalties were covered under most double tax avoidance agreements (DTAAs) and only a low rate of 10 per cent was chargeable on royalty payment income of foreigners. I guessed their rationale was that if the amount going as royalty were reduced, the remaining profits could be taxed at a higher rate.

Discussions generated a certain amount of heat. DEA was accused by Ramesh Abhishek of talking in contradictory terms—while DEA opposed DIPP proposal so strongly, calling it royalty terrorism, on the other hand, SEBI, under DEA, was formulating regulations to put a cap on royalty payments paid without shareholder agreement.

I had only a very vague memory of what SEBI was doing in this matter. Some quick SMSing and a Google search refreshed my memory and I underlined the difference. While DIPP had proposed a ban on royalty payment, SEBI's proposal was only intended to improve corporate governance by making higher royalty payments subject to shareholders' concurrence.

The DIPP proposal got shelved after this meeting.

Suzuki Gets Royalty Burden Off Its Back

Reference by Ramesh Abhishek related to SEBI capping the royalty payments impacted Suzuki Motors the most. The case soon cropped up.

The corporate governance reform committee, set up by SEBI in 2017 and chaired by Uday Kotak, had suggested a cap on royalty payments of 5 per cent of sales unless the shareholders approved higher payment under a special resolution procedure. SEBI initiated a move to introduce this cap on the payment of royalties.

Some Indian companies with substantial foreign ownership stake, like Maruti Suzuki, Colgate, Nestle, etc., were likely to be impacted by SEBI's regulatory cap.

Uday Kotak Committee: 5 Per Cent Cap on 'Majority of Minority' Basis

The Uday Kotak Committee was established to make recommendations for improving standards of corporate governance of listed companies in India. It submitted its report in October 2017.

Primarily motivated by the necessity to improve disclosures to shareholders, the committee felt that companies with high royalty payout levels and in excess of 5 per cent of consolidated revenues, must take shareholder approval. To ensure that this approval was granted only by shareholders that were not related parties to the payment of royalty, the committee further recommended that in such cases of payment of royalties, shareholders should approve the transaction by a majority of minority basis (passed by majority of the non-promoter shareholders by excluding promoters from such voting).

This required interested parties not to vote on such transactions. In the case of Maruti Suzuki, it meant that Suzuki, the recipient of royalties from Maruti, could not vote on the matter concerning the royalty payment. Many other proposals of the Uday Kotak Committee—separation of the post of CMD, age limits, increase in number and proportion of independent directors—had generated considerable controversy and public interest. The royalty matter also attracted attention but it was limited to only a few companies.

To take a more considered and pragmatic view on the recommendations of the committee, the PMO constituted an inter-ministerial group [IMG] under my chairpersonship, with SEBI

Chairman Tyagi and Corporate Affairs Secretary Srinivas as the other two members.

The IMG devoted considerable time on the contentious recommendations of the Kotak committee and came up with more pragmatic solutions. The issue of a cap on royalty payments did not receive close attention. The Ministry of Corporate Affairs had proposed a lower limit of 2 per cent in its submissions before the Uday Kotak Committee.

As the move was seen to improve the standards of corporate governance and the only requirement was the approval of the shareholders (the ultimate owners) if the payment of royalties exceeded 2 per cent of consolidated sales, the IMG decided to recommend placing the cap at 2 per cent, instead of the 5 per cent recommended by the Kotak committee. The SEBI team's analysis that there were only a handful of impacted parties, further convinced the IMG about the desirability of the move. I did not pay much attention to the issue at that stage.

Worried, Suzuki Raises Objections

After the IMG recommendations were made, the SEBI Board considered the matter sometime in January 2019 and amended the listing obligations and disclosure regulations to make 'majority of minority' approval necessary for payment of royalties in excess of 2 per cent of annual consolidated turnover of the listed entity. These regulations were to come into effect from 1 April 2019.

Maruti paid around 4.5 per cent of consolidated turnover as royalty to its promoter parent Suzuki. The 2 per cent cap got Maruti and its patriarch Osamu Suzuki worried. Chairman of Maruti Suzuki India, R.C. Bhargava, called me. I was surprised that Maruti was so worried. It was only getting a shareholders' resolution passed. No other multinational or Indian company appeared as concerned. I dismissed the matter.

Osamu Suzuki escalated matters and got the Japan government involved. For Kenji Hiramatsu, the Japanese ambassador to India, this became a key issue. He went to Nripendra Misra, who had no sympathy for high payment of royalty. Kenji met me a couple of times. Osamu Suzuki and almost the entire Maruti Board came to see me. It was becoming a diplomatic issue between India and Japan.

I tried to understand why Maruti Suzuki had such a big problem when no one else seemed disturbed. Apparently, the Maruti management and Suzuki wanted to avoid taking the matter to their general body meetings for optical reasons. They suspected some public-interest shareholders would make a big show of such a proposal in the general body meeting. While such shareholders would not be able to defeat the proposal, the bad publicity it would generate would spoil the image of Maruti.

With the passage of time, the realization was also growing on me that there was hardly any gain accruing to India by persisting with the 2 per cent proposal. It was absolutely unlikely that any such proposal would be rejected by shareholders of any company. The number of listed companies impacted was also quite small. The 2 per cent regulation was not tax terrorism, but it certainly generated bad publicity for the country. It was also becoming a thorn in the India–Japan economic relationship.

SEBI Postpones the Rule for Three Months

I went to Nripendra Misra, after sounding out Arun Jaitley, who had independently heard the Japanese out and concluded that it was no good to expose companies like Maruti to what he termed 'jholawalas'. However, Nripendra Misra made clear his lack of sympathy for foreigners taking away fat profits in the name of royalties, adversely impacting other shareholders and the government. His first reaction was not to do anything.

I presented a holistic picture and argued that going back to the 5 per cent rule recommended by the Uday Kotak Committee was the right solution. He asked me to re-consult the corporate affairs secretary and the chairman of the Securities and Exchange Board of India (SEBI).

The Ministry of Corporate Affairs was the prime mover of the 2 per cent cap proposal. In the meeting, after I gave both of them the complete background of the case, I asked the secretary, corporate affairs, for a reasoned rationale of the 2 per cent cap originally suggested by his department and whether any study of the cost and benefit of this proposal had been done. He could not produce any study but felt the rationale for going back to 5 per cent was also weak and that it would make the government and SEBI look silly to modify the proposal even before it came into effect. The SEBI chairman was quite unconcerned, as the SEBI committee had recommended only a 5 per cent cap for majority of minority endorsement.

We were already in March 2019 and the date of enforcement of the SEBI rule was approaching. I proposed the rule be postponed for three months more and the matter be considered fully after the elections. This was agreed to; Nripendra Misra also reluctantly assented. In its board meeting held on 27 March, which both Srinivas and I attended, SEBI postponed the date to the end of June 2019.

Osamu Suzuki Finally Succeeds

Prime Minister Modi was in Japan for the G-20 summit on 28–29 June 2019.

Osamu Suzuki, an octogenarian, is a legend in the Indian automobile industry and greatly respected for the transformational role played by Maruti-Suzuki. I saw him seated very close to the PM during lunch after the foundation stone of the high-speed rail was laid in Ahmedabad in 2017, and also when PM Modi was in Tokyo for his annual summit with the Japanese prime minister in October 2018. I was convinced that Osamu Suzuki would again meet the PM during the G-20 meetings.

After the elections and formation of the new government at the end of May 2019, the proposal had come up for consideration again. The extended deadline was fast approaching and the SEBI Board was scheduled to meet on 27 June 2019. Another meeting with Srinivas and Tyagi led to an agreement that the best course of action was to revert to the 5 per cent limit recommended by the Kotak Committee. After some discussion, the principal secretary also agreed. I did not attend the SEBI board meeting, as I was part of the PM's delegation for the G-20 meeting.

On the afternoon of 27 June, Osamu Suzuki came to the hotel in Tokyo where Prime Minister Modi was staying, to see him in this regard. I had briefed the PM on the developments and the fact that SEBI would raise the limit from 2 per cent to 5 per cent that very day. When Suzuki went to see Modi, I was in the waiting room. I said to him, with a smile, 'Please go in and hear the good news.'

That same day, the SEBI Board amended its decision to make payment of royalty of over 2 per cent of consolidated turnover subject to shareholder approval. Maruti was paying a little over 4 per cent. With the cut-off limit raised to 5 per cent by SEBI, Maruti was not required to take this proposal to its shareholders. The royalty issue was off the back of the venerable Osamu Suzuki.

Data as a Weapon in E-Commerce

Data is the base, lynchpin and pivot of the digital economy. The digital economy cannot exist without data. It grows with data. Data, therefore, has become central to everybody's business, including departments and organizations that are primarily not entrusted with the regulation of data.

During my tenure in DEA, three major initiatives came to the fore that were centred on data. Through a notification issued in April 2018, RBI ordered all payment-related data to be stored only in India. DIPP framed a data regulation policy in the name of an e-commerce policy and released the draft publicly for comments in February 2019. The Ministry of Electronics and Information Technology commissioned the Justice Srikrishna Committee to produce a report and draft of a personal data protection law in July 2018.

Payments, e-commerce and data protection are fundamental to the functioning of the economy and growth. Thus, DEA was vitally interested in all the three initiatives.

RBI's Data Localization Order: Hardly Any Gains

India's IT law did not mandate local storage of any data, including financial and payment data. Therefore, RBI had no jurisdiction to regulate data storage. However, RBI Governor Urjit Patel somehow got convinced that data localization was in the national interest. There was no demand from the public, players or the government for RBI to do so. It was entirely an individual's preference.

RBI found a roundabout way to achieve its objective. On 5 April, it noted in its statement on development and regulatory policy, released along with the statement on monetary policy, that the payment ecosystem had witnessed considerable growth in the country and that such systems were highly technology-dependent and necessitated the adoption of safety and security measures.

As part of these safety and security measures, the next day, on 6 April, RBI decided that it needed unfettered supervisory access to the data stored with payment systems, service providers, intermediaries, third-party vendors and other entities in the payment ecosystem. To get this access, it ordered all payment system providers to ensure that the entire data relating to the payment systems they operated was stored in a system located only in India. To ensure everyone understood that payment data meant all data, it was specifically noted in the notification of April 2018 that payment data included full end-to-end transaction details/ information collected/carried/processed as part of the message/ payment instruction. Data could be stored in a foreign country only for the foreign leg of a transaction.

This created a huge ruckus. This is the age of global financial integration, e-commerce and payments. There are many foreign credit card issuers, payment system operators, money transferers and others who operate in India as they operate all over the world. Financial and payment system data and transactions are under constant threat of hacking, stealing and other abuses. Most of these foreign operators have built strong security systems based on the study and integration of global financial and payment data. If they were to keep Indian payment data only in India, and not as part of global networks, the security and safety of financial and payment transactions and data would be compromised.

In response, foreign payment and financial systems operators got together under the aegis of the US India Business Council (USIBC) and US India Strategic Partnership Forum (USISPF) and made a representation to everyone, including RBI and DEA. After studying their representation and hearing them, I found some basis in their argument. Instead of enhancing the security of transactions, the RBI move was possibly compromising it. I convened a meeting of all concerned, including MEITY and RBI. The RBI executive director tried to unconvincingly defend his boss's decision. There are always some overly nationalistic voices in Indian officialdom, which go more by symptoms than the root cause. After a long meeting, I tried to thrash out a compromise—while all the payment data would be stored in India as RBI wanted, a mirror copy of the data could be kept in foreign data storages.

Nevertheless, RBI refused to budge. It had brought in this regulation to get access to all data for supervisory purposes for building better security in the payment system. By agreeing to keep all the data in local storage, the foreign payment system operators were serving its objective. However, without providing any good reason, RBI kept insisting that Indian payment data would not be kept outside India.

I raised the issue at the finance minister's level as well as the PMO. RBI had given foreign payment system operators six months to comply. In a meeting with the finance minister, the RBI deputy governor informed us that most foreign payment operators had already complied and promised that those who had not done so would be given time; no one's system access would be deactivated.

The US treasury secretary wrote a number of letters to the RBI governor and finance minister. The US undersecretary of commerce came to India and was given an appointment to meet the RBI governor. At the last moment, when the undersecretary was already in Mumbai, the appointment was cancelled. His counterpart Anup Wadhawan, India's commerce secretary, called me desperately to help avoid this diplomatic faux pas. I was able to arrange a meeting only with an executive director of RBI.

RBI continued with its policy even after Urjit Patel demitted office. Later, this resulted in some foreign operators like Mastercard being denied the right to issue new cards.

There is no study available to assess whether India's payment security system improved thanks to the forced data localization. However, India is forced to build its sui-generis security system with loads of OTP-based transactions becoming the prime security system.

Personal Data Protection Bill Hits at Use of Data in Business

Protection of the privacy of critical financial data is very necessary. However, financial transactions have to take place digitally in today's highly digitalized banking, payments and financial services economy. They need to take place efficiently, instantaneously and with the least cost, ensuring the privacy of financial data and its use by only those in a fiduciary relationship with the data principal.

The Personal Data Protection Bill, 2018, later 2019, as drafted by MEITY, based on the architecture proposed by the Justice Srikrishna Committee, was concerned only with the privacy aspect of data, not with its business/financial transactions aspect. The categorization of almost all financial data as critical data, which required an informed consent of the data principal every time it was to be used (and which imposed enormous obligations on the data fiduciaries), appeared to be leading to a situation where the data, on which the digital economy runs, was virtually getting locked up. There were also many provisions relating to data localization.

When the draft cabinet note was received in DEA from MEITY for comments, we held meetings with the secretary and other officers of MEITY. These were people working with good conscience and intent. However, they seemed to be missing the impact on the economy and social lives of people. In their urge to protect people's data, they were probably making people's lives more difficult.

We provided critical comments asking for a balance between business/financial transactions and privacy concerns. There were serious concerns raised by the industry and financial systems as well. There were discussions in the PMO and elsewhere. The PMO also realized that the Bill possibly reflected major overreach. It was not approved by the cabinet before the budget session in February–March 2019. Nor was it approved until late in calendar year 2019.

The Bill was finally introduced in the Lok Sabha in December 2019 and was referred to the Joint Committee of Parliament. The report of the joint parliamentary committee was tabled in the Parliament on 16 December 2021. It recommended wholesale changes, many of which were quite controversial, including extending the protection to non-personal data as well. The government decided not to act on the recommendations of the committee. Instead, a whole new law--Digital Personal Data Protection Bill, 2023--was drafted, which was approved by the cabinet for introduction in the Parliament in July 2023.

DIPP's Data Misadventure in the Name of E-Commerce Policy

DIPP had nothing to do with data protection. E-commerce, which is built on the use of data, is one of several services that use data. It is not the exclusive user of data. There is much greater and more sensitive use of data in the financial services industry, healthcare industry and several other industries. Therefore, there is no reason for DIPP, which is in charge of commerce, physical or e-commerce, to formulate a data policy in the garb of an e-commerce policy.

However, under the administrative leadership of Ramesh Abhishek, this is what DIPP did. It brought out a hurriedly drafted, vaguely worded and poorly articulated Draft National e-Commerce Policy, with the objective of harnessing 'India's Data for India's Development'. This draft was placed on DIPP's website in February 2019. The same draft was sent to the concerned departments, including DEA, for comments.

I was horrified to see the draft. There were only exhortations, no vision or policy proposal. There was no explanation for why DIPP had decided to become the champion and controller of data. It was difficult to separate the proposals in the draft policy from what role data could play in India's growth story, what kind of strategies could be followed for data infrastructure development, what kind of anti-counterfeiting measures and anti-piracy measures could be taken, and more such noise.

We prepared scathing comments, virtually suggesting the initiative be junked. Piyush Goyal, who was holding the additional charge of finance minister, wanted the two departments to harmoniously work out a commonly agreed draft. We tried and held meetings but found no common ground. By the time we finalized our comments, Arun Jaitley had returned. Our comments were approved.

There has not been any progress on the e-commerce/data control policy DIPP had drafted in 2019. The government responded to a question in Parliament in late 2020, saying over 100 people had responded with comments on the policy and these were being studied. There were noises from time to time that a revamped e-commerce policy would be brought about. However, nothing really came out. An e-commerce policy by the Department for Promotion of Industry and Internal Trade (DPIIT), the new avatar of DIPP, is unlikely to see the light of day. It is in the national interest that the policy has been dumped.

9

Apple Starts Manufacturing iPhones in India

India Allows Foreign Investment in Single-Brand Retail

APPLE SELLS IPHONES AND OTHER PRODUCTS LIKE LAPTOPS AND IPADS under its brand name all over the world. When such products are sought to be sold in India to consumers under the company banner, the sales are classified under the single-brand retail trade (SBRT) and regulated by the FDI policy on SBRT.

India allowed FDI in SBRT for the first time in 2006. Such FDI was placed under the government approval route and FDI was permitted only up to 51 per cent, implying that minimum 49 per cent equity had to be brought in by an Indian partner. The single brand was tightly defined—the branding had to be done at the manufacturing stage and the products had to be sold under the same brand internationally.

The 51 per cent FDI in SBRT did not attract any international brand initially, except some food companies like Pizza Hut, which appointed franchisees to make and sell their branded products in the country.

Major companies owning international brands needed 100 per cent equity as they were not interested in diluting their exclusive products.

SBRT FDI Raised to 100 Per Cent, but with Many More Conditions

When the government decided to open up the more controversial multi-brand retail trade (MBRT) in 2011–12, the FDI limit in SBRT was increased to 100 per cent from 51 per cent, albeit under the government approval route, in an effort to address the concerns of brand-owning companies.

However, the government threw in a major googly. In a press note issued in April 2012, it restricted such FDI to only the brand owner. It also imposed a killer condition of sourcing at least 30 per cent of the value of the products sold from 'Indian small industries/village and cottage industries, artisans and craftsmen'. Small industries were enterprises with a total investment in plant and machinery not exceeding $1 million at the time of establishment of the industrial unit.

Imagine Apple or for that matter any major international brand sourcing 30 per cent of the value of its products sold from small industries, village and cottage industries or from sundry artisans and craftsmen! This condition was applicable to only those companies that wanted more than 51 per cent FDI under SBRT. This 'liberalization' in the SBRT FDI regime kept foreign SBRT investors (both under and over 51 per cent) away—first, as it was too risky to give up to a 49 per cent stake to Indian parties, and second because sourcing 30 per cent from domestic small industries was clearly a non-starter.

The government made two modifications in September 2012 to liberalize the FDI regime in SBRT. First, in addition to the owners of the brand making investment directly, other parties having a legally tenable agreement to sell the owner's branded products in India were also allowed to make FDI in SBRT. Second, instead of meeting the 30 per cent sourcing condition every year, the investor was allowed to do it on an average basis in the first five years.

SBRT under the Automatic Route: From 49 Per Cent, Leading Up to 100 Per Cent

In November 2015, the government moved further: FDI in SBRT up to 49 per cent of the total equity investment, was brought under the automatic route; and the government approval route was limited only to those international brand owners who wanted a stake beyond 49 per cent. Further, the condition of local sourcing was limited only to those SBRT FDI investors who wanted an ownership stake over 51 per cent.

This amendment allowed foreign single-brand owners to set up their retail outlets without requiring prior government approval or sourcing 30 per cent from local suppliers provided they sought only up to 49 per cent of investment in the SBRT venture. Despite this supposed liberalization, there were no takers for the SBRT regime as the foreign investors were required to dilute majority stake to Indian partners.

Two more important changes were brought in by this 2015 amendment. First, the mandatory requirement of sourcing 30 per cent from small industries was liberalized by allowing local sourcing of 30 per cent from anyone, though preferably from micro, small and medium enterprises (MSMEs). Another carrot thrown in was the permission to undertake retail trading through e-commerce, though this was conditional on the SBRT entity first setting up brick-and-mortar stores.

Apple Applies for Exemption from Local Sourcing Rule

In 2015, Apple filed an application before FIPB to sell its products in India. It wanted 100 per cent equity as well as exemption from the local sourcing condition. The Government of India was keen to get Apple to India, sell its products (which were anyway getting sold through other trade channels) and, more important, manufacture its products in India. Apple was interested in setting up shop first and later establishing manufacturing facilities as well.

To help Apple cross the line, the Government of India exempted single-brand products that were either 'state-of-the-art' or 'cutting-edge technology' products from the requirement of local sourcing. It appointed a committee of officers to identify the criteria and products that satisfied these conditions. The committee could not come up with any good criteria and no officer in either the committee or FIPB was 'courageous' enough to accept Apple's products as either state-of-the-art or cutting-edge technology.

The application of Apple remained stuck.

Government Starts Diluting Local Sourcing Requirement

The 30 per cent local sourcing requirement had acquired the status of a holy cow. The condition imposed in 2012, probably as an afterthought, could not be deleted. If it could not be deleted, the process to dilute it began to take shape in 2018.

In January 2018, the government decided to bring all FDI in SBRT up to 100 per cent under the automatic route—this would allow officers not to take a call regarding permitting FDI in SBRT. The condition of 30 per cent local sourcing for FDI in excess of 51 per cent remained, with the certification of the local sourcing requirement done on a self-certification basis.

A very significant relaxation regarding the local sourcing requirement was made in the same 2018 press note. Local sourcing, which was earlier meant to be for products sold in India, was expanded to be for 'global operations' of the 'non-resident entities undertaking single-brand retail trading, either directly or through their group companies'.

This meant that if Apple or its manufacturers anywhere in the world bought goods and services equal to at least 30 per cent of the value of Apple products sold in India, it was fine. It would satisfy the local sourcing requirement. The local sourcing norms were also limited to the first five years; for cutting-edge technologies and state-of-the-art products, the requirement was reduced to three years.

DIPP Proposes New Package for Major Single Brands like Apple

There were two conditions holding up Apple marketing its products through SBRT entities in India, owned directly or through its franchisees. The first was the local sourcing condition and the second, the inability to sell iPhones and other Apple products online. A manufacturer of Taiwanese origin had started making preparations to manufacture some Apple products in Bengaluru, but that investment was also moving slowly on account of the inability of Apple to sell its products through its own or franchisee channels in India.

In February 2019, DIPP proposed another package. It had three liberalizations. First, the local sourcing requirement was proposed to be met not only by the company directly or through group companies, but even through a third party under a legally tenable agreement. Second, SBRT entities that proposed FDI in excess of $200 million were to be allowed to begin sales through online channels, subject to the condition that brick-and-mortar stores were opened within two years of the start of online retail. Third, depending on the level of FDI, the condition to meet the local sourcing requirement in five years (on an annual average basis) was proposed to be extended to six years for those who proposed an investment of $100 million, eight years for those that invested $200 million and ten years for those who brought in FDI of $300 million.

Such expanded local sourcing included export of the company's products manufactured in India. Local sourcing of raw materials and intermediates for SBRT products to be sold in India, was literally being converted into sourcing or exporting 30 per cent of value equivalent from India.

The DEA officers were as bureaucratic as DIPP. They agreed with all the proposals of DIPP. In addition, they suggested some tightening of the phraseology used in the draft cabinet note.

'Scrap Requirement for Local Sourcing'

I was away at South Africa for the annual meeting of the New Development Bank (NDB) when I received the proposed comments.

I was aghast that we in DEA were supporting a completely irrational policy. I emailed back terming the requirement of local sourcing for SBRT as impractical and unnecessary. I argued that single-brand products were, by definition, global products manufactured abroad and sold in India, along with other countries. My argument was that as these products were not manufactured in India, imposing the local sourcing requirement was simply irrational.

I recalled my examination of the multi-brand retail proposal in 2011 while I was working as joint secretary, trade, in the Department of Agriculture and Farmers Welfare. Pointing out that the requirement of local sourcing was not there initially when FDI was opened in SBRT in 2006, I argued that DIPP was only trying to neutralize this unimplementable requirement by building in a complex export requirement.

I asked Additional Secretary K. Rajaraman, who was handling DIPP matters, to prepare our comments, clearly recommending scrapping the local sourcing requirement. I further suggested that in case DIPP was completely unwilling to accept this, the SBRT FDI could be linked to a simple 20 per cent export requirement in place of local sourcing.

Rajaraman had a counter argument. In his view, some international brands like Samsung and LG were manufacturing in India to sell their branded products here. He asked me to reconsider my advice. By the time I got his mail and could respond, owing to the urgency shown by the PMO, he got his comments prepared, approved by the finance minister and sent them to the PMO. In my response, I told him that foreign investors who brought in FDI to manufacture their products in India or who entered technology-supply agreements with their branded products sold in India on payment of royalty, was a different class altogether and had nothing to do with FDI in SBRT. In the end, I noted I would deal with the matter when I returned.

Upon my return, I convened a meeting with officers from DIPP, including Ramesh Abhishek, DIPP secretary.

DIPP recognized the rationale of our argument to do away with the local sourcing condition. Ramesh Abhishek viewed the matter from the political prism as well, with the general elections approaching soon. However, DIPP's data suggested that the SBRT policy had failed miserably and was, in fact, a major hindrance in bringing high technology manufacturing to India. In the thirteen years of its existence, a little over a hundred proposals worth about $1 billion of FDI had come in through SBRT. This was minuscule compared to over $500 billion of FDI received by the country during this period.

I placed the matter before the finance minister. He recognized the merit of what I was suggesting and approved the proposal. Finally, we officially conveyed our revised comments to the PMO, which suggested that DEA was of the opinion that there should be no local sourcing requirement for SBRT. We further argued that local sourcing conditions only restricted the original manufacturers of SBRT products from selling their products more reliably and directly.

There were follow-up discussions in the PMO, including a meeting with Prime Minister Modi on FDI proposals. I reiterated our stand and requested the adoption of a FDI policy that was not a hostage of such traps.

The proposals were not taken up for consideration before the general elections.

DIPP Does Away with Local Sourcing Requirement by Stealth

In September 2019, well after I had moved out of the Ministry of Finance, a press note was issued. It did not link any local sourcing compliance periods (five/eight/ten years) to the level of FDI brought in.

The 30 per cent local sourcing requirement was converted into local procurement or export by the SBRT entity, its group companies (resident or non-resident) or indirectly through a third party. This formulation completely unlinked local sourcing to the sale of single-brand products in India. In that sense, it was not local sourcing at all, as local sourcing is commonly understood to mean local value-addition. The SBRT entity was free to procure or export any Indian product directly or through a third party. All Apple needed to do was to either procure, export or ask any of its group companies or associates to buy Indian products to the extent of 30 per cent of value sold. Further, it was all to be self-certified. I don't think any Indian regulator would get into verifying compliance with this condition. It need not, as the requirement in the first place does not make much sense in the context of SBRT.

In addition, the government permitted online sale without first establishing brick-and-mortar stores. Further, it was not necessary for Apple to establish its own stores in India even after the two-year cooling period. It could be done through a franchisee.

As reported in the newspapers, Apple welcomed the September 2019 decision. It has started producing its range of products in India through its original equipment manufacturers (OEMs). It also launched its online store sometime in 2020 and opened its own physical stores in 2023.

The actual local sourcing requirements were almost completely diluted by these changes. These changes negated the formal local sourcing requirements, which still remained formally in the regulations. I think we should have the moral courage to adopt the right policies instead of achieving the same results in a roundabout away.

10

India Junks Bilateral Investment Treaties

INDIA OPENED UP TO FDI IN 1991. ONCE THAT POLICY DIRECTION WAS taken, it was deemed necessary to actively promote inflow of FDI. There was no multilateral investment promotion treaty. Investment promotion was mostly done on a bilateral basis. This led to the formulation of a model bilateral investment promotion agreement (BIPA) in 1993, basically modelled on the investment promotion treaties the US had signed with many other countries. Like others, this model treaty provided protection of investments made by foreigners in India from expropriation, providing fair and equitable treatment to such investments and granting of most favoured nation treatment. The most important remedy offered to investors through these treaties was that the investor could take the Indian government to international arbitration forums for dispute resolution.

India began signing BIPAs in 1994. In all, eighty-three BIPAs were signed by 2015. Out of these, seventy-four were actually brought in force.

After 2010, there was a spurt of investors launching arbitration proceedings against the Government of India. More than thirty such cases were launched. Many of these parties interpreted the BIPA provisions in a highly expansive manner, citing non-protection of rights or unfair and inequitable treatment to their commercial disputes. The Government of India had other domestic problems as well, in relation to these arbitration claims. If a state or even a municipality did something in violation, or was perceived to be in violation, of the rights of investors under BIPA, the Government of India had to defend and pay up if necessary. There was considerable dissatisfaction with the Investor State Dispute Settlement (ISDS) clauses incorporated in such treaties.

In 2015, India decided to overhaul the system. The cabinet approved a new BIPA template that built several safeguards against the potential misuse of the international arbitration process. These safeguards included exhaustion of local remedies before ISDS could be invoked, doing away with most favoured treatment and its replacement by national treatment, making investment protection specific to the enterprise, etc. As most BIPAs had run their life of twenty years, they stood terminated after the notice of termination was given. About five to six BIPAs remained. It was envisaged that these would be modified to bring them in line with the revised 2015 template by signing a 'joint interpretative agreement'. Bangladesh agreed, but others did not.

In 2017, India was negotiating new bilateral investment treaties or BITs with about thirty countries under the new template. Only two to three agreements could be concluded in four years after the adoption of the 2015 template. Brazil had similar concerns as India. A BIT with Brazil was concluded. For petty reasons (their advice tendered earlier was not fully accepted and the role of the foreign ministry in such negotiations was quite limited), the Ministry of External Affairs (MEA) kept sitting on this BIT and it could not be signed until I left the Ministry of Finance. Two other BITs were concluded, one with Belarus and the other with Taiwan. [As per information available on the United Nations Conference on Trade and Development (UNCTAD) website, the BIT with Belarus is the only one signed before 2015 and is currently in force, BIT with Brazil was signed in January 2020, but has still not come into force.]

Everywhere else, including with major investor countries like the US, Canada, UK and the EU countries, DEA faced a complete lack of response. India's bilateral investment promotion regime, as built in the BIPAs and BITs, was as good as dead. However, it did not adversely affect FDI flow as investors all over the world believed that India's legal and business regime was quite trustworthy and something they could live with.

A Sui Generis Law on Investment Promotion

The junking of the BIPA regime in 2015 introduced considerable uncertainty in relation to the protection and promotion of foreign investment. Recourse to international arbitration for breaches of protection to foreign investment that came after the expiry of the respective BIPAs was gone. Efforts to conclude new investment promotion treaties on the 2015 protocol were not leading anywhere.

One possible course of action was to modify the 2015 protocol, bringing in elements such as coverage of a wider class of assets in place of only foreign investment in an enterprise, placing some time limit for the local remedies route, and the like. We prepared specific proposals to redefine the 2015 template. These treaties use international jargon and there was considerable suspicion about what such commitments might lead to. Therefore, there is generally a reluctance in the system to discuss these issues, with most people tending to take minimalistic accommodation positions.

After we prepared the new template and took the approval of the finance minister in principle, the matter was referred to a committee of secretaries headed by Cabinet Secretary P.K. Sinha. Sinha held a couple of meetings. The position taken by DIPP Secretary Ramesh Abhishek, was to not go an inch beyond the 2015 offer. The commerce secretary was a little more supportive but wanted any further concessions to be given only as a trade-off for concessions on the trade side. After P.K. Sinha had finished his meetings, he concluded that DEA might take an appropriate view after approval of the finance minister. The committee did not express any specific view about any of the proposals.

I felt we were not going anywhere. Even if we got some more flexibilities, it would not help much in concluding bilateral investment promotion treaty deals. Moreover, it could introduce so many variations in different treaties that there would be difficulties in managing the contradictions and differentiations. It would be difficult to explain to courts and international tribunals as to why we agreed to certain concessions in one case, but not in the other.

Therefore I proposed a very different solution to my investment division team, first led by Govind Mohan and then Rajaraman. I thought we should come up with our own investment promotion law to specify the protections, concessions, etc., available to all investors, except those countries that were specifically excluded. The same law could also confer authority on the finance minister or a group headed by the secretary, economic affairs, to agree to a differentiated solution from a menu of options for other specified matters.

The team did not understand my proposal. It was not in line with the existing pattern and system. It would have also extinguished the potential of conducting negotiations with half the world to conclude bilateral treaties. The team drafted something that was way off the mark. After a few iterations, the Draft Investment Promotion Law started moving in the direction I wanted.

However, after my transfer from the Ministry of Finance, it appears the whole effort has been abandoned.

Rules on Outward FDI

Indian businesses had also been making FDI abroad. In 2017–18, Indian businesses made outward FDI, also known as overseas direct investment or ODI, of a little over $5 billion, which was somewhat lower than the ODI equity investments of $8 billion and $10 billion in the previous two years. India's ODI was heavily concentrated in some countries, like Mauritius, Singapore, the US, United Arab Emirates (UAE), the Netherlands and the United Kingdom (UK). There was also outward investment in the form of debt and guarantees.

However, there were no structured and well-defined rules and regulations like FDI, relating to ODI. RBI had permitted some specified ODI transactions as part of the Liberalized Remittances Scheme (LRS), essentially meant for current account transactions. In 2015, FEMA had been amended to confer the authority to make rules on non-debt instruments, which included equity investments in the country by non-residents or residents outside India. The government, which had entrusted FDI to DIPP and created an elaborate system in the form of FIPB, had not thought of even recognizing ODI. RBI treated equity, debt and guarantees equally as far as making ODI was concerned.

I decided to bring some order to the situation. Reviews were held with RBI to understand the foreign exchange regulations regime to deal with and promote ODI. RBI put together a note and provided the requisite information. However, it was reluctant to let DEA step into this zone. It wanted us to express what changes we wanted which it promised to consider and incorporate in the existing scheme of things. We cited the 2015 amendment and said it was time the government issued the rules as per authority conferred by the law, like the exercise initiated on the principal non-debt rules to deal with FDI and foreign portfolio investment (FPI).

In his Budget 2018–19 Speech, Finance Minister Arun Jaitley noted that ODI from India had grown to $15 billion per annum and announced that the government would 'review existing guidelines and processes and bring out a coherent and integrated ODI policy.'

The Investment Division team in DEA had not also cared to look at the ODI policy and issues as a material matter of interest. We hired the National Institute of Public Finance and Policy (NIPFP) to prepare an approach paper for ODI policy. After a few months, NIPFP came back with its paper, which was more of a stocktaking and theoretical construct of ODI. It made some broad recommendations, including the government offering fiscal concessions, financial insurances or other incentives to promote ODI in areas where Indian firms could capture a share of manufacturing or other production/distribution goods and services abroad. It also proposed that the role of Indian embassies might be strengthened. However, it did not have much to say on specific foreign exchange-related measures.

After reviewing NIPFP's work, I provided a broad direction and structure of the ODI policy to the team. Sometime in December 2018, the team put together its first draft of the ODI policy. It was pretty much a paraphrased version of the NIPFP paper. It did not even look like a policy document, with the policy content, by and large, completely missing.

The policy was intended to override the existing ODI policy fragmented in various circulars and regulations of RBI. It also had to set the tone for the measures the government would take, including the incentives, to encourage flow of ODI from India in areas where global opportunities existed. After a few iterations, we came closer to presenting the draft ODI policy to the finance minister.

However, this was not to be. After I left the ministry in July 2019, ODI policy work seemed to have slowed down. No activity was seen publicly for at least two years. On 9 August 2021, RBI placed two drafts simultaneously on its website: the Draft Foreign Exchange Management (Non-Debt Instruments-Overseas Investment) Rules, 2021, and the Draft Foreign Exchange Management (Non-Debt Instruments-Overseas Investment) Regulations, 2021. Normally, the rules should be framed first and the Government of India should publish the draft rules. In this case, the draft rules were made in the name of the Government of India but published by RBI. This made it very clear that ODI policy had been fully outsourced by the government to RBI.

The proposed rules treat the International Finance Centre (IFC) in Gujarat International Finance-Tec (GIFT) City, Gandhinagar, as foreign territory and encourage both ODI and OPI (overseas portfolio investments) for entities established in the IFC. Evidently, the ODI policy has become a composite ODI and OPI policy, with greater emphasis on OPI than ODI.

Government notified comprehensive Foreign Exchange Management (Overseas Investment) Rules 2022 on 22 August 2022. RBI notified Foreign Exchange Management (Overseas Investment) Regulations, 2022 on the same day. Finally, India has a comprehensive, integrated and functional outward direct and portfolio investment regime.

Hybrid Instruments Policy

The division of authority between the Central government and RBI, brought about by the 2015 amendment in FEMA—with policy work related to debt instruments being primarily placed with RBI, and policy work related to non-debt instruments assigned to the Government of India—left hybrid instruments with characteristics of both equity and debt somewhat unclear in the middle.

We argued that RBI's role had been specified for only 'debt instruments', whereas all non-debt instruments fell in the jurisdiction of the government. Hybrid instruments like convertible bonds were certainly not debt instruments and therefore should be primarily dealt with by the Government of India in the matter of formulation of policy. In any case, policy matters are primarily in the domain of the Government of India. RBI was only to be consulted before the policy was formulated.

After some discussions, RBI got more or less reconciled to this. Finance Minister Arun Jaitley announced in his 2018–19 Budget Speech that hybrid instruments were suitable for attracting foreign investments in several niche areas, especially for start-ups and venture capital firms, and promised that the 'Government will evolve a separate policy for hybrid instruments'.

Extensive discussions held in the Investment Division and with market participants, especially with start-ups and venture capital funds, led to the formulation of a draft policy framework for hybrid and innovative instruments. The framework noted that besides convertible instruments (initially debt, then equity), instruments that help raise non-dilutive capital or instruments with limited or no voting rights were also hybrid and innovative instruments, which the proposed policy covered. Likewise, many instruments contingent upon certain events or financial performances taking place were also part of the policy framework.

The policy was fairly comprehensively defined and structured, running into over eighty pages. We thought we had developed one of the most innovative and forward-looking policy frameworks to encourage the use of innovative and hybrid instruments in the country. The framework was sent to RBI for comments sometime in December 2018, as was the standard operating procedure. Thereafter, RBI sat on it for over two months without reacting one way or the other. We heard informally that the RBI governor had kept the draft with him for a review.

Elections were announced in March 2019. There was no revert from RBI even during the election period. The whole motivation to bring institutional reforms in DEA was lost after the elections. Nothing has been publicly heard about the hybrid and innovative instruments policy since then. Perhaps policymakers are more comfortable with the status quo.

There is still no well-formulated hybrid instruments policy.

11

'Raiding' RBI's Reserves

Government of India Called a 'Raider' of RBI Reserves

IN A SERIES OF ARTICLES UNDER THE BANNER 'PROTECT RBI'S BALANCE Sheet' in *Business Standard* in October 2018, Rakesh Mohan, former chief economic advisor, secretary, economic affairs, and deputy governor of RBI, called a suggestion in the *Economic Survey* for the year 2016–17 (published about twenty months earlier) to use part of RBI's accumulated reserves for bank recapitalization, a 'raid' on RBI's capital. More immediate provocation was an unofficial report published on 3 August 2018, by market data and financial news provider Cogencis, under a misleading headline, 'Govt pegs RBI excess capital at 3.6 trln rupees, seeks it as surplus'.

Viral Acharya, the incumbent deputy governor of RBI, knowing full well that this was not a fact, sanctified it and gave it wings when he delivered a speech on 26 October titled 'On the Importance of Independent Regulatory Institutions: The Case of the Central Bank'. He legitimized both the news report in Cogencis and Rakesh Mohan's articles in *Business Standard* and lit a fire (more in the media, than in the markets) when he said, 'a thorny ongoing issue on this front has been that of the rules for surplus transfer from the Reserve Bank to the Government', which he said related 'closely to the leading Argentine example' of the dramatic exit of the Argentinian central bank governor in 2010 consequent to the interference of the government in the bank's independence. Viral Acharya then quoted Rakesh Mohan's arguments in favour of retaining the reserves on the balance sheet of RBI: 'Raiding RBI's capital creates no new government revenue on a net basis over time, and only provides an illusion of free money in the short term.'

The expressions 'raiding RBI's capital' and 'raiding RBI's reserves' became part of the public lexicon thereafter. Every business paper in India wrote about it. The BBC spoke about it. *Financial Times* ran a story on the theme. It became an international issue of Indian origin.

Chief Economic Advisor Arvind Subramanian, who authored the suggestion of using RBI's reserves for capitalizing public-sector banks in January 2017, had left the Ministry of Finance in June 2018. In any case, the policy issue of surplus transfers from RBI was looked after by the secretary, economic affairs. I was handling that work in October 2018. We were convinced in 2018 that there was a very strong case for transfer of a part of the accumulated cash surpluses of RBI to the government.

Finance Minister Arun Jaitley and I were convinced that the issue should be settled bilaterally between the government and RBI based on its merit and statutory provisions. We had not spoken to the media about it. Viral Acharya made the entire matter one of great interest to the media.

What is the fact of the matter, why did it come to this pass and where did it finally lead?

My Introduction to the Economic Capital Framework

The table agenda placed in the board meeting of RBI on 10 August 2017, the first meeting I attended as the RBI Board member, proposed the retention of ₹13,400 crore of the RBI surplus of ₹44,200 crore for financial year 2016–17. As it was a table agenda, I had no brief and not much familiarity with the issue.

A quick read of the paper and some other material indicated that in the previous three years, RBI had transferred 100 per cent of the surplus earned to the Government of India. Further, at some point of time, RBI had communicated that approximately ₹30,000 crore would be available for transfer as surplus to the government for the year 2016–17. The table agenda papers indicated that the RBI Board had prepared a staggered surplus distribution policy (SSDP) following the earlier adoption of an economic capital framework (ECF). Retention of ₹13,400 crore of surplus was argued to be in accordance with the ECF and SSDP.

It was difficult to make head or tail of the ECF and SSDP in such a situation. In my papers, there were some copies of correspondence that took place between Rajiv Mehrishi, then finance secretary and economic affairs secretary, and RBI Governor Raghuram Rajan in 2015 that suggested that Rajiv Mehrishi had outright rejected RBI's ECF proposal. There was also some information in my briefs that suggested that the representatives of the Ministry of Finance as board members had not agreed to either the ECF or SSDP. And, here was a board agenda note suggesting that everything regarding the ECF and SSDP was done and dusted and the RBI Board was expected to approve retention of 30 per cent of surplus for the first time after three to four years of 100 per cent surplus transfer in line with the new framework.

The government has two members on the RBI Board: secretary, DEA, and secretary, DFS. Secretary DFS Anjali Duggal had given the board meeting a miss. Rajiv Kumar, the soon-to-be vice-chairman of NITI Aayog, a board member in his individual capacity, was also new. I could not even speak to him. Whatever the background or situation, it appeared to me that I should not agree to the proposal.

I quickly looked at the provision in the RBI Act. Section 47 mandated that all the surplus of RBI shall be transferred to the Government of India after setting aside provisions that the banks would normally make. The critical factor was what provisions the banks (in the context, central banks) normally make. There was no time available in the middle of the meeting to try to comprehend the mechanics of the ECF and SSDP. My instincts suggested that RBI was possibly adopting an improved methodology to determine the provisions required using more market-oriented methodologies, but the result was something that disfavoured the Government of India. It also appeared that the government's case was going by default.

When the item was taken up by the Board, I asked for 100 per cent of surplus to be transferred to the Government of India on the lines of previous years. I also took the stand that the ECF was not agreed to by the government. I suggested that though there seemed to be good technical work behind the ECF, it would need to be understood and suggested that a presentation be made to the government for us to understand the logic, basis and rationale of the framework. I promised to look at the entire thing completely objectively.

My request was not accepted as RBI Governor Urjit Patel insisted and most members of the board were in favour of approving the agenda. Rajiv Kumar suggested that the government's share could be improved somewhat, which was promptly rejected by Urjit Patel.

I had quickly discovered that the earlier 100 per cent surplus was transferred under a formula suggested by noted chartered accountant and former board member Y.H. Malegam. I persisted and asked what amount would have been transferred under the Malegam formula, used in the previous three to four years. The RBI management would not agree to provide this number. Whether it was not being provided deliberately or it could not have been calculated and provided in the meeting, I did not know at that time.

As the board was almost completely behind Governor Urjit Patel and I did not know much about the ECF at that point of time, I finally asked for two points to be recorded in the minutes for the item:

1. Transfer of ₹30,600 crore to be treated as provisional, and if the calculations as per the Malegam formula suggested that transferable surplus was higher than the total surplus of ₹44,200 crore, the retained amount of ₹13,600 crore would be transferred to the Government of India.

2. The ECF be discussed with the government and whatever was agreed upon with mutual consent be adopted as the ECF.

The board agreed to record my observations. However, when I received the minutes, these were not recorded as I stated. I had to ask for amendments in the minutes and wage a battle in the subsequent meetings for the same.

Our calculations later revealed that the entire surplus of ₹44,200 crore was transferable for financial year 2016–17 on the basis of the Malegam formula.

Crystallizing the Government's Position on ECF

I studied the subject after returning to New Delhi from Mumbai. RBI had started work on the ECF sometime in 2014–15, ostensibly under the RBI Act to determine the provisions RBI could make out of the surplus, but in reality to give RBI 'the strongest balance sheet'. The arguments Raghuram Rajan had offered in discussions with the Ministry of Finance were not found convincing. Rajiv Mehrishi wrote a long letter with the approval of the finance minister, rejecting the proposal outright in 2015.

However, RBI continued to work on the framework. The differences between RBI and the Ministry of Finance on quite a few other issues led to Rajiv Mehrishi stepping out of the RBI Board. Ajay Tyagi, additional secretary in DEA, was made a board member in Mehrishi's place. Shaktikanta Das, who replaced Mehrishi as secretary, DEA, and assumed the board seat in RBI, did not take much interest in the matter.

Governor Urjit Patel had the complete support of Prime Minister Modi and believed more fundamentally in the ECF than Raghuram Rajan. Probably realizing this, Shaktikanta Das continued some routine correspondence with RBI though formally maintaining DEA's official stance that the ECF had not been approved by the government.

Sometime in 2016, the RBI Board approved the new ECF, without any participation or opposition from Secretary Shaktikanta Das. The ECF primarily indicated the percentage of total assets that RBI should maintain as provisions and reserves. If the available provisions and reserves fell short of the required percentage, RBI was entitled not to transfer any surplus to the government.

RBI had to hastily evolve the SSDP in June 2017 when it realized the government would not get any part of the surplus for 2016–17 as per the new ECF. The newly minted SSDP permitted part surplus transfer to the government by linking the proportion of the available provisions and reserves to the required provisions and reserves as per the ECF. This designer SSDP formula allowed RBI to transfer 70 per cent and retain 30 per cent of the surplus of ₹44,200 crore for the financial year 2016–17. The SSDP, however, sowed the seeds of retaining a part of the surplus every year.

Earlier, CEA Arvind Subramanian had initiated a public debate about the ECF in 2016.

Arvind included Box 1.6 in the first overview chapter in the *Economic Survey* of 2015–16 released in January 2016, titled 'Addressing the Twin Balance Sheet Challenge'. Here, he highlighted in graphic detail that RBI was holding the second highest level of equity (capital, retained earnings and contingencies) as a percentage of the balance sheet in the world at close to 32 per cent, whereas the median level of equity was only 16 per cent. In this edition of the survey, he said, 'If RBI were to move even to the median of the sample (16 per cent), this would free up a substantial amount of capital to be deployed for recapitalizing the PSBs [public-sector banks].' RBI did not like this analysis.

Arvind revisited the subject in the next year's *Economic Survey* (for 2016–17) published in January 2017. Again, a highlighted box (Box 2: 'Excess Capital of RBI') in Chapter 4 of the survey on the largest financial and fiscal problem of the day—non-performing loans—under the title 'The Festering Twin Balance Sheet Problem' highlighted the equity held by RBI relative to other central banks. Though India had slipped to the fourth highest position by then in terms of equity, it was still holding capital, reserves, provisions and buffers of about 28 per cent of its total assets. In this box, Arvind specifically mentioned that RBI was holding as much as ₹4 lakh crore in excess equity capital and made recommendations on how this amount could be put to better use. The first suggested use was again the recapitalizing of the PSBs.

These conclusions and suggestions were not palatable to RBI. Raghuram Rajan had argued against the conclusions presented in the 2015–16 survey and the use of RBI's excess reserves. There was a public spat between the two. Urjit Patel operated more privately. He bitterly complained to the PMO. The story of Volume 2 of the 2016–17 *Economic Survey*, which I have recounted in an earlier chapter, was influenced to some extent by the specific recommendation in the conclusion of Volume 1 that RBI was holding capital in excess of ₹4 lakh crore.

Secretary Shaktikanta Das maintained complete silence in the matter throughout his time in DEA.

RBI did arrange to make a presentation in North Block following the August 2017 meeting. Its top brass, including deputy governors N.S. Vishwanathan and Viral Acharya also attended the presentation. Arvind Subramanian was also present. The RBI presentation was very comprehensive and quite technical. In sum, it made three points for our understanding. First, the aim of the ECF was to secure the highest possible credit rating for RBI and for that RBI needed to keep the highest possible level of capital. Second, the highest level of capital would require the highest possible valuation reserves and a high degree of cash reserves to be maintained on its balance sheet. Third, for determining the requisite/highest level of valuation reserves, RBI had selected the most stringent formula of valuation: stressed value at risk at the confidence level of 0.999 at an interval of ten days.

It was also apparent in the discussions that RBI was not a borrower and therefore did not present any credit risk to its lenders. No central bank anywhere in the world was rated for credit risk and, thus, the whole objective of making RBI so highly credit-rated was quite unnecessary. The model used by RBI for building the formula for calculation of market risk for valuation reserves (which accounted for about 80–85 per cent of total reserves/provisions required) was also one that none of the central banks had used anywhere in the world. RBI's formula used the tightest version of a formula used for calculating 'credit risk' in case of the banks and other companies for calculating the 'market risk' of a central bank.

We pointed out many areas where there was a lack of clarity, lack of evidence and lack of fairness in the elements chosen to design the formula that hurt the revenue interest of the government badly without really improving the strength of RBI. The additional information and clarification required was included in the minutes issued for the meeting. The deputy governors, including Viral Acharya, stuck to their position, though the RBI officials agreed to provide the information sought. The information was never provided.

I kept raising the subject of the ECF at every meeting of the RBI Board thereafter. While Urjit Patel wanted to bury the subject, I was determined to keep it alive.

Later, when this and some other subjects had gathered more heat and urgency, the finance minister designated Finance Secretary Hasmukh Adhia to try to find an acceptable solution. Again, the RBI deputy governors and officials came to discuss the matter but there was no willingness to review the formula and the issue.

The Matter Gets Raised to the PMO

Urjit Patel, earlier deputy governor, was appointed the RBI governor by Prime Minister Modi in late 2016. After his appointment, Urjit Patel considered Finance Minister Arun Jaitley as his counterpart. He snapped the direct line of communication with the secretary, economic affairs, and established it with P.K. Mishra, the additional principal secretary in the PMO. Nripendra Misra, the principal secretary, though did not like Urjit Patel very much.

Retention of ₹13,800 crore by RBI from the surplus, was causing major concern in view of the precarious fiscal condition. The government had projected a fiscal deficit of 3.2 per cent for the year 2017–18. There was substantial over-projection in non-tax revenues. The lingering impact of demonetization in 2016–17 and introduction of GST from 1 July 2017 had made the fiscal position quite fluid. My most immediate reason for pursuing the ECF agenda was to somehow get this withheld amount of ₹13,800 crore.

About nine months of interactions with him had made Arun Jaitley lose some faith in Urjit Patel. He approved my communications to RBI regarding the need to frame the ECF in consultation with the government, not withholding the ₹13,800 crore, and inclusion of my stand/ask in the minutes of the August 2017 meeting.

Arvind Subramanian had been consistently raising issues where RBI, in his judgement, was in the wrong, such as not reducing the repo rates despite very high levels of real interest rates. RBI had also got its inflation trajectory wrong most of the time during those years. It was holding excess capital which was not being made available for useful purposes like bank recapitalization.

The PMO had also started getting feedback about the lopsided priorities of Urjit Patel and his management of RBI. However, the PM did not like RBI Governor Urjit Patel being publicly attacked by Arvind Subramanian. The PMO seemed inclined not to upset the RBI governor's apple cart. Yet, only the PMO could nudge Urjit Patel into doing something in the matter. Some intervention was definitely necessary on the ECF issue.

In such a situation, I drafted a note bringing out the inherent unsoundness of RBI's ECF, building on the research work Arvind Subramanian had done (his paper was placed in the file) and the unfair retention of ₹13,800 crore by RBI. I requested the PM's orders for the constitution of a committee headed by the finance minister to delve into the ECF issue. I also asked for directions to be issued to RBI to transfer the withheld surplus to the government. Finance Minister Arun Jaitley approved the note and the file went to the PMO.

Some discussions took place with APS P.K. Mishra and Brajendra Navnit, joint secretary in the PMO. While they had some sympathy for my point of view and made some efforts to understand the complexity of the ECF formula, Arvind's paper in the file drew some uncomfortable glances.

No action was taken on the file and it remained unattended in the PMO for months. However, the message was conveyed to the RBI governor that something needed to be considered for transfer of that year's surplus to the government.

First Interim Dividend to Partially Make Up for Loss of Surplus Withheld

I kept up my pressure on the PMO and RBI to give us the ₹13,800 crore that was unfairly retained from the surplus of 2016–17. I wrote a number of letters to the RBI governor with the approval of Arun Jaitley. However, RBI was determined not to cede any ground on the ECF. In one of the meetings, Urjit Patel said that the ECF would be reviewed only over his dead body.

Eventually, RBI came up with an alternative. Internally, it decided to offer an interim dividend from the surplus expected to be generated in financial year 2017–18. It kept this close to the chest (perhaps it kept the PMO informed). Though RBI got an interim assessment made of the surplus generated in the first six months of 2017–18 (July–December) and also thought up every way to keep disposable surplus as low as possible, it shared nothing with us. There was no intimation that the proposal for an interim dividend would be floated in the board meeting held in New Delhi (the post-Budget meeting) on 10 February 2018.

I was in Dubai attending a programme with investors as part of the PM's delegation on that day. I got frantic telephone calls from DFS Secretary Rajiv Kumar in the early hours of 10 February. He informed me about a table agenda item on interim surplus transfer of an amount of ₹10,000 crore and wanted to know what was to be done as he was attending the meeting. I promptly advised him to ask for the transfer of ₹13,800 crore instead of any interim surplus and, if he was not able to get that through, not to accept any interim surplus of an amount less than ₹15,000 crore.

Rajiv batted well but RBI stuck to its number of ₹10,000 crore. Rajiv was told that it was this or nothing. The discussion on the item remained inconclusive. Upon my return, I promptly wrote to Governor Patel, with the concurrence of Finance Minister Arun

Jaitley, requesting him to transfer ₹15,000 crore as interim surplus as well as the withheld amount of ₹13,800 crore.

Quite a few phone calls were exchanged in February and March 2018. Urjit Patel would not agree with any of our requests. The RBI governor literally made it a 'take ₹10,000 crore or forget it' choice for the government. Finally, while not formally agreeing to accept ₹10,000 crore, the government agreed to leave it to the RBI governor to transfer whatever amount it thought appropriate as interim surplus. RBI transferred ₹10,000 crore. This first ever interim surplus to the Government of India arrived on 31 March 2018.

The practice of interim surplus transfer continued the next year as well. In February 2019, RBI proposed the transfer of an amount of ₹28,000 crore. This time, I was able to persuade the board to make a higher transfer of ₹35,000 crore as interim surplus because there was no Urjit Patel. He had resigned in December 2018.

Government Initiates 'Consultations' with RBI under Section 7

The year 2018 witnessed relations between RBI and the government coming under increasing strain. RBI's 12 February circular, a good move for the resolution of non-performing loans in general, created enormous difficulty for banks with regard to the loans given to power-sector companies. The power-sector business and financing model had some peculiar characteristics, which made the insolvency and bankruptcy process unsuitable. Power purchase agreements (PPAs) would become infructuous if the resolution were made through the Insolvency and Bankruptcy Code (IBC) process. There were other material consequences for fuel supply agreements (FSAs) and other matters as well. RBI refused to make any differentiation for any particular sector.

On a petition by power-sector developers, the Allahabad High Court directed the government to invoke Section 7 of the RBI Act, which provided for the government to issue 'directions' to the RBI governor, after consultation with the governor. RBI was bound by law to implement such directions. As such a situation had never arisen (at least from the record available in the ministry) in the past, the step was considered unprecedented and many commentators considered it an attack on the independence of RBI. RBI decided not to work with the government on this. It did not attend the meetings of a committee constituted under the chairmanship of the cabinet secretary to find solutions to the issue.

Some other major issues were building up as well. A number of PSBs were placed by RBI under the prompt corrective framework (PCF), literally depriving them of their business licence. Rising oil prices and the depreciating rupee were running down foreign exchange reserves. It was increasingly dawning on the government that RBI and Governor Urjit Patel had embarked on a path that would hurt India's economy and its financial sector. In these circumstances, the ECF and surplus distribution file also got dusted off. The PMO allowed the finance minister to initiate appropriate action on the matter.

The Ministry of Finance decided to start the process of issuing directions under Section 7 of the RBI Act by initiating consultations with the governor. A total of six communications were sent, four from DEA and two from DFS. Among these communications, a letter sent in July 2018 to RBI Governor Patel asked for his views on the government's proposed direction to bring the matter of ECF for discussion and review in the RBI Board.

Amid this escalating breakdown of trust, a meeting was convened at the level of the PM to discuss matters. RBI's top brass, led by Urjit Patel, was also present. He made a presentation. I also presented certain issues for urgent attention.

Prime Minister Modi had also perhaps had enough of Urjit Patel by that time. He did some serious tough talking. He brought up many subjects where RBI's intransigence was hurting India. He also brought up the subject of the surplus retained. He mentioned that RBI could not be squatting on excess capital like a snake sits on a treasure. He conveyed to Urjit Patel as emphatically as a PM, without issuing directions, to convene a meeting of the board and find solutions for the issues in consultation with Arun Jaitley and the finance team.

Two Tempestuous Meetings Spark the RBI Board Decision to Set Up Expert Committee on ECF

Two meetings of the RBI Board took place in quick succession in October and November and generated enormous attention in the national and international media. There were at least fifty media persons with cameras and mics offering live commentary outside the RBI headquarters in Mumbai on those two days. Experts of every hue were debating on TV channels for days before the meetings and holding forth on what was really going on between RBI and the government. Some speculated on the likely resignation of Governor Urjit Patel. The atmosphere had become quite surcharged on account of leaks relating to references/directions issued under Section 7 as well as the incendiary speech delivered by Deputy Governor Viral Acharya.

The first meeting, on 23 October, lasted for over ten hours. Two government directors—DFS Secretary Rajiv Kumar and I—were to present agenda items for the board's consideration at this meeting. This was probably another first; otherwise, all agenda items are brought in by RBI. Though this is said to be one of the longest meetings ever in the history of RBI (it ended at 9 p.m.), the discussion on the six items initiated by the government directors could not be completed. Only four items initiated by Rajiv were covered, that too not completely. Much emotion was on display. At one stage, a director, Ashok Gulati, vociferously complained that he was being made to agree to something with a gun pointed at his temple. It was also reluctantly agreed by RBI that the minutes of the meeting would be drafted in the meeting itself. However, the minutes draft could not be agreed upon.

In the second meeting, on 19 November, I presented two items: one on the ECF and the other on governance and board reforms in RBI. RBI also made a presentation on the ECF. In my presentation, I had proposed three points for decision, including review of the ECF and transfer of withheld surpluses of the past two years amounting to approximately ₹23,000 crore.

The RBI governor found these two meetings very tough to handle. In one of the meetings, he even suffered some heart spasms and went out for a short rest. We thought we had a very genuine case for referring the matter for review to an expert committee. Whether he was persuaded by our logic, shaken by the plain speak he had received from the PM or whether he found the situation too difficult to sustain, Urjit Patel blinked and agreed to the establishment of an expert committee to examine the question of an appropriate ECF. A communication issued by RBI after the board meeting announced the constitution of an expert committee within two weeks with the terms of reference and composition to be jointly agreed upon by the finance minister and governor.

Expert Committee Gets Set Up

Urjit Patel promptly wrote to the finance minister proposing the terms of reference and the composition of the expert committee. He proposed that Dr Rakesh Mohan head the expert committee, despite Mohan having publicly called the government a raider of RBI reserves and having spoken against any transfer of the accumulated reserves/provisions from RBI to the government. The ToRs proposed were totally loaded to reflect the outcome RBI desired.

Former RBI Governor Bimal Jalan was also commenting in the public domain about the goings on between the government and RBI. He sounded more balanced and his utterances indicated that he understood the issues involved. He also carried the reputation of finding constructive solutions in the past whenever tricky situations had arisen, most particularly relating to the management of foreign exchange reserves, a key issue for many decades.

I redrafted the ToRs to reflect more comprehensively and accurately all the issues involved and suggested making Bimal Jalan the chairman of the expert committee. With the approval of the finance minister, the revised ToRs were sent to RBI along with a recommendation to make Bimal Jalan the chairman.

RBI agreed with the ToRs we proposed except one that related to the committee deliberating on the issue of the use of non-cash accumulated valuation reserves, if these were assessed to be higher than required. As for the chair of the committee, RBI still wanted

Rakesh Mohan. It proposed making Bimal Jalan and Rakesh Mohan co-chairs. With the finance minister's approval, I proposed making Rakesh Mohan vice-chair.

At this stage, quite suddenly, Urjit Patel resigned as the RBI governor on 10 December. Shaktikanta Das, appointed the RBI governor on 11 December, agreed to a slightly tweaked version of the ToR relating to consideration of valuation reserves. With that, the expert committee, its composition and the ToRs were agreed to between the finance minister and the governor. RBI promptly notified the committee.

The Expert Committee Pushes the RBI Viewpoint

RBI did not prepare a discussion paper when the ECF was taken up for board approval in 2016. It made presentations. Even after approval of the ECF, which the government contested, RBI did not issue any document relating to the ECF as its capital framework in the public domain. Nor was any such document shared with the government. Considering the principal impact the ECF had on the extent of the RBI surplus transferred to the government, such black-box regulatory behaviour was simply non-par.

In its presentations, RBI officials presented the ECF in a hugely technocratic manner, banking on abstruse concepts such as value at risk, estimated loss method and confidence levels. Cleaned of legalese and obtuse risk management concepts, our principal concern was to design a fair, simple and robust system of ascertaining whether RBI needed to retain some part of its surplus to strengthen its capital base. It was ironic that RBI had a statutory capital of only ₹5 crore, which was never considered inadequate to be revised upwards in its eighty years of existence, while the RBI system wanted to retain thousands of crores of rupees every year to build a supposedly strong capital base.

To put it simply, the expert committee had the following issues to deliberate:

First, the valuation of RBI's two assets—investment in government bonds and foreign exchange reserves—change depending upon movements in market prices. If government bond yields go up, the value of bond assets goes down, and vice versa. Likewise, if the dollar appreciates vis-à-vis the rupee, the rupee value of foreign exchange goes down, and vice versa. Fluctuations in valuations were taken to a valuation buffer account.

Though the extent of buffers in this account depended entirely on changes in market valuations and was completely automatic in that sense, the ECF had adopted complex formulae to determine that valuation reserves/buffers should be in the order of about 23–24 per cent of RBI's assets. The expert committee was to determine the extent of valuation provisions RBI needed.

Second, RBI was retaining some of the surplus earned over the years as a reserve in an account called the Contingency Fund (CF). This account had accumulated a little over ₹2 lakh crore. The ECF stipulated that the realized profits transferred to the CF should be about 4 per cent of RBI's assets. This was a view not backed by any complex formulae, as was done in the case of valuation reserves. The expert committee was to recommend how much of the reserves and provisions to be built out of cash surplus earned, was needed by RBI.

Third, if the expert committee came to the conclusion that RBI was holding more valuation buffers/reserves, it was to recommend how this excess should be treated. Should such excess valuation be transferred to the Government of India and, if so, what should be the best mode of doing so? On the obverse, if the committee came to the conclusion that RBI was holding less valuation reserves than needed, it was to recommend the means of making up the difference.

Fourth, likewise, if the expert committee came to the conclusion that RBI was holding excess cash reserves/provisions, it was to recommend the extent to which such reserves should be transferred to the Government of India and the best method of doing so.

Finally, the expert committee was to recommend the framework for distribution of surplus year to year.

The committee had two independent members: Chairperson Bimal Jalan and Vice-Chair Rakesh Mohan. There were two RBI Board members on the committee: noted chartered accountant Bharat Joshi and former IAS officer Sudhir Mankad. It also had two officials, Deputy Governor Vishwanathan as the RBI representative and me as the representative of the government.

RBI provided the secretariat of the committee. Its officers prepared all the papers, drafted minutes and provided data and other information sought by the members. I took the assistance of Shashank Saxena, an experienced economic service officer, who was working as an advisor in DEA.

As mentioned earlier, Dr Rakesh Mohan had publicly written and argued against any transfer of accumulated reserves to the government, terming such a move as a 'raid' on RBI. He gave a set of seven loaded questions/tasks to the RBI officials, which convinced me that he had joined the committee with a completely prefixed notion that RBI was not holding any excess reserves/provisions and, therefore, any attempt to make a transfer from the reserves to the government was to be foiled by any means.

Two members of the committee—Sudhir Mankad and Bharat Doshi—were party to the adoption of the ECF formula in 2016, which yielded 28 per cent of RBI's balance sheet/assets as the required level of reserves. It soon became apparent that they believed that any downward revision of the requirement would be an adverse comment on their due diligence and role earlier, whereas the retention of the formula would be a kind of endorsement.

We had banked on Dr Bimal Jalan to play a balancing role. Initially, he displayed considerable enthusiasm to understand the government's viewpoint and appeared keen to find a reasonable solution. However, he found it difficult to understand the complex valuation metric and turned out to be completely clueless about the abstruse formula involved in the assessment of market risk. He conveniently decided to go with the majority.

After two to three meetings of the committee, I was literally ranged against the five.

Credit Rating, the Foundation of ECF-2016 Formula Gets Rejected

The estimated ECF-2016 required valuation buffers at a very high level, something close to 24 per cent of RBI's asset base. Almost the entire valuation buffer requirement was based on the perception of the market risk RBI was exposed to on its two major assets, foreign currency reserves and government securities. RBI's ECF-2016 defined market risk related to assets it held in terms of likelihood of depreciation in their value. In 2019 RBI held a large amount of foreign reserve assets, worth approximately $400 billion dollars (₹28 lakh crore).

The market risk for RBI's foreign currency assets was defined in terms of potential depreciation of their rupee value. The rupee value of dollar assets depreciates when the rupee appreciates. A strong rupee ironically leads to the depreciation of RBI's foreign currency assets! The argument offered was that the stronger the rupee, the greater RBI's reserves and provisions must be, to cover this risk of depreciation. Incidentally, the reserves held by RBI were also invested in foreign currency assets. This meant that its buffers also depreciated in value along with the remaining foreign currency reserves. It was a strange risk matrix but it was the accepted one.

The market risk related to the government securities held was measured in a more conventional manner. Whenever the interest rate of the government securities RBI held goes up compared to the average value of yield on the securities held, the aggregate value of RBI's holding of government securities goes down. The reverse effect takes place when interest rates go down. If you look at it in today's context, by trying to keep the yields low on government securities, RBI is not only enabling the government to borrow at a lower rate of interest, but is also building a valuation buffer for itself.

How do you measure the market risk of RBI's two principal assets? For this purpose, RBI/ECF-2016 used the formula to measure the 'credit risk' that lenders are subject to. RBI's borrowers were sovereigns, which are always considered the least risky. The Government of India's bonds, the US and other sovereign treasuries issuing foreign currency bonds and the central banks, where RBI invested its foreign currency reserves, were the most risk-free investments.

We had argued that market risk was not measured by a formula designed for credit risk. I again took this up in the expert committee meetings right at the beginning. Vishwanathan and the RBI team tried to explain, asserting that the RBI Board wanted to adopt an ECF framework in 2016 that was equal to the highest possible level of credit rating.

The fact that RBI and its board had based the ECF-2016 on a hypothetical highest level of credit rating disturbed even Rakesh Mohan. When the RBI team could not come up with a credible explanation or precedence to adopt credit rating as the means to measure market risk of the central bank's assets in the next meeting, it was agreed to junk credit rating as the foundation for designing the ECF.

In 2016, the RBI Board had decided to measure the required level of valuation buffers by adopting a formula built around three elements.

The first element measured the value of asset at risk, or VaR. Traditionally VaR is assessed through the historical maximum value of assets that had suffered a loss. Two new variants of VaR had come up in the previous few years. One was the stressed value of assets at risk (S-VaR), which assesses the VaR on assets that might suffer under stressed conditions as chosen to be defined by the valuing authority. The newest variant was termed the estimated loss (EL) method to estimate VaR for events outside the normal distribution range, also called tail-end risk.

The second element was the confidence level. The three most prevalent confidence levels chosen by the central banks were 0.99, 0.975 and 0.9.

The third element was the interval at which risk was to be measured.

RBI had decided to adopt S-VaR, a 0.9999 confidence level and ten days interval in 2016. This calculation yielded a value of about 24 per cent of assets as required reserves for financial years 2016–17 and 2017–18.

Our analysis revealed that there was no central bank in the world that had adopted such a conservative framework to assess the required level of valuation buffers. Our assessment further revealed that the modal framework adopted by a few central banks that chose to assess the requisite level of reserves/buffers was VaR with a 0.975

confidence level. A few central banks had adopted S-VaR at a 0.99 confidence level. Only one or two central banks, most prominently the European Central Bank (ECB), had adopted EL under normal conditions at a 0.99 confidence level a few months earlier.

The calculations made by the RBI technical team and the team at the Ministry of Finance confirmed that VaR at a 0.975 confidence level would require only about 12.7 per cent of the assets as required valuation provisions. The required level of provisions for the most conservative formula adopted globally (S-VaR at 0.99) turned out to be only about 13.5 per cent. The required level of provisions went up to at best 14.5 per cent under the EL framework.

When it was asked what formula then led to the requirement of around 24 per cent of valuation reserves and why such an offbeat formula was adopted by RBI in 2016 that had no precedent or parallel, we were told that RBI had adopted the most conservative VaR formula (S-VaR) and the most conservative level of confidence (0.9999). It was also mentioned that a board member, Nichiket Mor, had argued (most likely at the behest of Urjit Patel) to provide an intellectual underpinning for this formula. Sudhir Mankad and Bharat Doshi had gone along without bothering much about the potential consequence on surplus distribution.

The modal formula that resulted in the required level of valuation buffers of 13.5–14.5 per cent was not acceptable to RBI as well as other members of the committee. In search of a formula that would take care of RBI's presumed interests, Sudhir Mankad asked for various other calculations—what if the confidence level were to be kept at 0.995 to 0.998 and other combinations. The EL method with a confidence level of 0.995 under normal to stressed conditions resulted in a calculated range level of 17.4-18.9 per cent of assets. The RBI Four—Vishwanathan, Rakesh Mohan, Joshi and Mankad—decided to settle for this formula even though the 0.995 confidence level was not used anywhere in the world. Chairman Jalan decided to go with the majority.

I was prepared to accept at best the ECB formula, which was the most conservative and yielded a required level of 14.5 per cent. RBI was holding an amount of ₹7.35 lakh crore as revaluation reserves as on 30 June 2018. The difference in reserves/provisions required from the RBI Four and my formula was ₹1,83,000 crore as on 30 June 2018, the last year for which actual data was available at the time.

This became the first major point of difference between the rest of the members of the committee and me.

The RBI Team's Rear-Guard Action to Enhance Required Cash Reserves

RBI had been retaining some part of the surplus as reserves/provisions for meeting contingencies as the revaluation reserves represented value only on paper. For retaining cash surplus, RBI had created the CF, to which retained amounts were transferred from time to time. There were one or two other small accounts like the Asset Development Fund (ADF), which also had some reserves from surplus transfer.

The CF and other small funds had a balance of ₹2.32 lakh crore as on 30 June 2018. RBI had decided in 2016, as part of the ECF package, that a balance equal to 3–4 per cent of the assets should be maintained in the CF. The available CF balance exceeded 7 per cent of the assets as on 30 June 2018. The cash reserves with RBI thus exceeded the levels required by over ₹1 lakh crore. During the course of discussions in the RBI Board before the expert committee was set up, a view had emerged that if some excess reserves had to be transferred to the government, it could be done from the extra cash reserves held in the CF. We were clearly banking on this excess cash reserves held by RBI for a one-time transfer.

That contingency appeared very real for the RBI Four after the available revaluation reserves, even as per their assessment, were higher than their formula. If the required level of realized/cash reserves in the CF stayed at 3–4 per cent, the committee would have to recommend the transfer of excess cash reserves to the government.

This was not acceptable to Rakesh Mohan, Vishwanathan, Sudhir Mankad and Bharat Doshi.

They came up with an audacious proposal as a rear-guard action. They proposed to increase the level of required cash contingency reserves to 5–6 per cent of the assets from the existing norm of 3–4 per cent. Together with two other smaller reserve/provision requirements for credit risk and operations risk, the required cash reserves would have risen to 6–7 per cent to equal the level of free reserves available in the CF and other funds. This would have resulted in either no transfer from the accumulated reserves or at best only a nominal transfer to the government.

As the objective of the RBI Four was clearly to fend off any transfer to the government, I dug my heels in and asked them why RBI needed to hold any cash reserves at all. I was strengthened by our finding that almost no central bank, globally, retained cash reserves. All kinds of complicated jargon was thrown at us—financial stability risk, the lender of last resort function, and so on.

Essentially, the financial stability risk was the risk of the loss RBI might incur in case the banks, most likely PSBs, ran out of their liquid assets (government securities and other high-quality liquid assets held for meeting the statutory liquidity ratio and liquidity coverage ratio, which exceed 25 per cent of the assets held by the PSBs), and they had to borrow from RBI and did not repay what they borrowed.

This possibility was nothing but hogwash. There had never been such a situation in the eighty-four years RBI's existence. It was never required to provide liquidity to PSBs as the lender of last resort without collateral. Whenever PSBs had come under stress, it was the government that had come to their rescue. Since 2017–18 too, the Central government has infused equity of over ₹3.5 lakh crore. If somebody needed money to take care of the PSBs, it was the government and not RBI.

The scenario conjured up by RBI was completely hypothetical. Moreover, if such a contingency were to ever arise, RBI would not have created liquidity by selling off its reserves invested in foreign currency assets or government securities (such an action would suck out liquidity even more). It would meet such an eventuality by simply creating new money, either in the form of new currency issued or by making an accounting entry in the banks' accounts held with RBI. That's why no central bank provided for this kind of risk and held capital in the form of reserves/provisions for this purpose.

I felt that the move of the RBI Four to enhance the CF from 3–4 per cent to 6–7 per cent, was nothing short of extortionary. The evidence I had led me to conclude that RBI did not need a single rupee of cash reserve/provision to meet this hypothetical risk. Despite this, I proposed that only an amount equal to 2 per cent of the assets of RBI could be, at best, maintained in the CF account. While the RBI Four wanted to enhance the CF by 2–3 per cent of the assets, I wanted it to be reduced by 2–4 per cent.

I tried to persuade the committee member to see reason, but it was completely clear that Mohan, Vishwanathan, Mankad and Doshi were acting in concert with the sole objective of ensuring that no reserves got transferred to the government.

This was the second major point of big difference between the RBI Four and me.

There were two issues connected with the transfer of the stock of surpluses/excess provisions held by RBI: transfer of excess stock of revaluation reserves and transfer of excess stock of cash reserves.

In my calculations, RBI was holding excess stock of revaluation reserves of ₹1,83,000 crore as on 30 June 2018. There was some stock of excess revaluation reserves as per the formulation of the RBI Four as well.

To ensure there was no possibility of transferring anything from the excess revaluation reserves, the RBI Four decided to recommend that the revaluation reserves, even if in excess, should not be considered for transfer to the government as these did not represent real cash and were created out of a mark to market (value of security assessed at their current market value in place of their purchase price) movement in value of assets held by RBI. This was a tenuous argument as the same could be monetized by simply selling off the securities anytime in the market, which RBI actually did in 2019–20 and 2021–22.

I proposed that a deposit of ₹1,50,000 crore could be created in RBI favouring the Government of India, as RBI was the banker to the government. This would not have led to any immediate change in the composition of RBI's assets. I further recommended that the deposits made in favour of the government could be used to cancel the government securities held by RBI as per a staggered programme spread over three to five years. This would not have led to any cash outflow as it would only be a balance sheet transaction. It also would not have affected the currency held by the people or reserve money in any manner.

Rakesh Mohan was vehemently opposed to the idea. The other three agreed with him. Chairman Bimal Jalan had ceased to matter, as his constant refrain was that he would go by the majority view.

This was the third major area of difference between the RBI Four and me.

On the issue of transfer of the stock of cash reserves held in excess, there was no disagreement in principle. However, as noted above, the RBI Four sought to frustrate this by proposing an increase in the percentage of the CF required from 3–4 per cent to 5–6 per cent, which would have led to a transfer of only a princely sum of ₹8,000 crore!

According to my calculations based on the requirement to hold 2 per cent for the CF and another 0.9 per cent (0.3 per cent for credit risk and 0.6 per cent for operational risk), or roughly 3 per cent, RBI was holding about ₹1,24,000 crore extra. I accordingly recommended the transfer of ₹1,00,000 crore (again in three annual instalments).

This was the fourth major area of difference between the RBI Four and me.

My Dissent and Exit

The country was in election mode in 2019, from early March to late May. However, the committee met regularly during this period.

Our differences had become quite crystallized and irreconcilable by the fifth meeting held on 24 April 2019. Four major areas of difference described above had emerged. Seeing no possibility of the others accepting what I thought was the reasonable and correct view, I told the chairman and the committee members that I would, in the circumstances, write a comprehensive dissent note. This surprised them a little but they were quite confident that they could write the report in a way that would give my dissent note no traction.

I decided to bring the entire matter to the notice of the finance minister and the PMO after the fifth meeting on 24 April. A note was drafted and delivered to the principal secretary to the PM, explaining the serious implications of what the majority committee members were going to recommend. I explained the entire matter in person to the principal secretary, stating that the issue was serious enough to warrant the personal attention of the PM even though he was in the midst of an election campaign. The principal secretary agreed regarding the seriousness of the matter. Within two days, he reverted to inform me that Prime Minister Modi had desired that the matter be brought to the notice of the finance minister who could take it up with RBI.

Arun Jaitley was quite unwell. I tried for an appointment a number of times but, unfortunately, he could not take up the matter with RBI.

I wrote a comprehensive dissent note, running into about forty pages, with point-by-point arguments and evidence of why the proposed recommendations of the RBI Four on the four major points discussed above were wrong and detailed the right course of action. I used emphatic language to make my points. In our sixth meeting held on 13 May, I formally placed my dissent note before the committee.

The RBI secretariat incorporated my dissent note as an appendix to the main report. The RBI Four decided to respond to my points in their main report at relevant places. The dissent note was also discussed in the next meeting held on 12 June.

The expert committee had attracted huge media attention. At some stage, the media got wind of the fact that there would be a dissent note from the government representative. I was asked this question many times during May–July 2019. I would always take the line that the committee was deliberating the issues. I never confirmed that there was a dissent note.

The draft report of the committee, including my dissent note, made for interesting reading. It also exposed the fallacy and weakness of many arguments of the RBI Four. The RBI Four and RBI got somewhat worried about the possible implications of my dissent when the report became public.

Nirmala Sitharaman Questions My 'Authority'

I mentioned the matter in the first briefing on 1 June 2019, after Nirmala Sitharaman took over as finance minister. On 3 June, I submitted the entire set of documents relating to the ECF matter, along with a copy of the majority report and my dissent note, in a file to her. She promised to look into the matter soon.

I accompanied her to the G-20 Finance Ministers' meeting in Fukuoka, Japan, held from 7–9 June 2019. During this visit, I briefed her extensively about the matter, the issues involved and the reasons for the serious difference of opinion, including the implications of the majority's recommendations for the government. She seemed to appreciate the enormity of the issues involved and promised to take it up with the RBI governor upon her return.

Something transpired in the three days after we came back from Japan. I don't know what actually happened—who briefed her and with what intent. She called me to her room in North Block. Without questioning the contents of the dissent note, she asked me whether I had the government's permission to write a dissent note. I again explained the entire sequence of events, including the fact that the dissent note had been furnished to the PMO and I had sought the intervention of the PM to take the matter up with RBI for protecting the legitimate interest of the government.

However, as the discussion progressed, she got visibly irritated and told me I had no authority or business to file a dissent note. I told her it would not be in the interest of the government if its viewpoint was not reflected in the report. I suggested that she intervene with RBI to develop a consensus. When she appeared uninterested in either taking the matter up with RBI to find a consensus solution, or in permitting me to include the dissent note as a member of the committee, I told her I would need her written instructions on the file, which was already with her office. I received no written instructions for the next ten to twelve days.

The Government Would Have Lost if Realized Reserves Increased to 6–7 Per Cent

Sometime in June, I had realized the massive implications of the RBI Four's proposal to raise the realized reserves to 6–7 per cent of RBI's assets. This proposal would have much bigger and far more damaging implications on the annual transfer to the government from the surpluses earned by RBI year to year as well.

RBI earns a much smaller return on its foreign exchange reserves, which are mostly deployed in highly liquid assets in advanced economies. The purchase of treasury bonds in advanced economies— the US, the European Union (EU) and Japan—by the central banks of emerging market countries like China and India adds to the savings glut in these economies and further depresses effective yields (over $17 trillion of bonds globally were earning negative returns in 2019). Over 80 per cent of RBI's assets were in the form of foreign currency assets. Returns on these assets had varied from 0.6 per cent (or lower) to 2.5 per cent in the recent past. Interest earned on government securities also varied but, effectively, government securities yielded 5–8.5 per cent in recent years.

The RBI Four estimated that RBI would earn approximately 2.2 per cent of the assets in return in the years to come. On that basis, they estimated that given the dynamics of transferring a part of the surplus to the contingency reserves, RBI would require 15–25 per cent of the annual surpluses to be retained and the balance would be available for transfer to the Government of India.

My assessment of the evidence of the past (proportion of assets earned as net surplus) suggested that RBI's net surplus could vary from 0.6–2.5 per cent of its balance sheet assets. If the committee were to recommend that the CF be kept at the rate of 7 per cent per annum, this would require a retention equal to 7 per cent of the increase in the size of the balance sheet. RBI's balance sheet increases by 10–25 per cent per annum.

If we assume that the balance sheet assets grew by 10 per cent in a year, RBI would be required to retain 0.7 per cent of these assets for transfer to the CF from the surplus of that year. If RBI surpluses were to earn 1.4 per cent of the balance sheet size as surplus in that year, part of the surplus equal to 0.7 per cent divided by 1.4 per cent would need to be set aside for transfer to the CF. Thus, 50 per cent of the surplus in that year would have to be transferred to the CF.

In case RBI earned 0.6 per cent of the balance sheet as profit/ surplus, the entire surplus would be insufficient to even meet the CF requirement and the government would get zero rupees as transfer of surplus. This retention of surplus would be unprecedented and totally unjustified. One could plot a simple straight-line fit curve to calculate the proportion of cash profits which would be retained by RBI in different situations.

Government Forms Informal Group of Ministers to Examine the Matter

The eighth meeting of the expert committee was due to be held on 24 June 2019. At 8.45 p.m. on 23 June, while I was returning from the office, I received a call from Nripendra Misra, principal secretary to the PM. He informed me that the finance minister had complained to Prime Minister Modi about my insistence on filing a dissent note. He further said that it was decided that no dissent note needed to be filed. I was shocked, as I had briefed him about the serious implications of the committee's recommendations. I reminded him of these implications. I further stated that I would not file the dissent note only if I was withdrawn as a member of the committee or I was given an order in writing to accept the majority recommendations as they were.

Nripendra Misra called back after about half an hour and asked me to request Chairman Bimal Jalan to cancel the meeting slated for 24 June. I reached out to Bimal Jalan who said he would check with RBI.

It seemed there was a parallel track in operation. Nirmala Sitharaman had informed the RBI governor about her meeting with the PM and told him I was being directed to withdraw my dissent note. After checking with RBI, Bimal Jalan informed me that the meeting would be held as scheduled on 24 June but the report would not be finalized. One more meeting would be held to do so.

When I reported back to Nripendra Misra, he asked me not to attend the meeting on 24 June. I complied. The expert committee met and went over the draft report, including my dissent note. Shashank Saxena (advisor in DEA) attended the meeting. The RBI Four objected to some parts of the language I used in the dissent note, which I decided to modify later.

On 25 June, the PMO constituted an informal Group of Ministers (GoM) under the chairmanship of Home Minister Amit Shah. It included Finance Minister Nirmala Sitharaman and Commerce Minister Piyush Goyal. I was asked to explain the entire issue to the GoM on 25 June itself, which I did in the meeting that took place in the anteroom of the home minister. Brajendra Navnit and Secretary DFS Rajiv Kumar were also present.

Amit Shah and Piyush Goyal understood the entire matter very quickly. Both of them also realized the serious financial implications of the majority's recommendations. After the matter was discussed, Rajiv Kumar and Navnit were asked to leave. I remained. At that stage, Nirmala Sitharaman became openly hostile toward me. She accused me of being totally one-sided and questioned my narrative. While maintaining my cool, I requested the GoM to listen to the RBI governor and representatives before coming to any conclusion.

In its meeting on 24 June, the expert committee had decided to schedule its next meeting on 17 July. The Budget was scheduled to be presented on 5 July. In view of this, the informal GoM decided to meet once more before the next meeting of the expert committee. The home minister asked if the finance minister wanted to discuss the matter with RBI as well.

In the meantime, work continued on finalizing the expert committee's report. With the help of my officers, I kept updating the dissent note, which was, at that stage, an integral part of the report, being continuously updated by RBI. While providing updated versions of the dissent note to the RBI secretariat, I kept the finance minister and PMO apprised of the updated versions and the serious implications of the principal recommendations as they stood at that point of time.

The informal GoM next met on 13 July. Both the home minister and commerce minister were convinced of the strength of my stand. The finance minister remained quiet and did not speak much. There was no open hostility either. At the end of the meeting, the home minister asked the finance minister to reach out to the RBI governor and find an acceptable solution.

The Expert Committee Concludes Deliberations and Its Draft Report

I attended the expert committee meeting on 17 July.

I had received no advice/communication from the finance minister or her office either on the files submitted for her orders or based on the outcome of her discussions with the RBI governor, as she was requested to do by the GoM on 13 July. I checked with the principal secretary to the PM a day before the meeting—I was told Bimal Jalan had been informed that the report of the committee was not to be finalized before 25 July.

I reached the meeting about half an hour late on account of an unavoidable engagement. During this time, the committee had decided to complete its deliberations.

In this meeting, I brought to the notice of the other members the serious implications of their recommendation to raise the normative realized reserves requirement from 3–4 per cent to 5–6 per cent on the annual flow of surplus to the government. I also underlined the inaccuracy of their assumption that the annual surplus would be 2.2 per cent of the balance sheet assets every year. I presented the likely reductions in annual surplus transfers based on different likely levels of surplus earned by RBI.

When I provided these calculations to the committee members, there was a visible current of uneasiness. First, they had to accept that the assumption of earning profits in excess of 2.2 per cent of balance sheet assets was unrealistic and unsustainable. Second, they realized that, very soon, the government would discover the large retention of surpluses by RBI, especially in the years when RBI's earnings were quite low. Still, Rakesh Mohan asserted that they would go by the principle and that their principal recommendation of raising the cash reserves and CF to 6–7 per cent was sound.

Therefore, without giving any credence to the serious implications of their recommendations on the transfer of surplus, the RBI Four decided to stick to their recommendations. My calculations made a key table in the majority recommendations completely untenable. The table was changed.

Chairman Jalan made a feeble plea to the committee members to consider 3–4 per cent as the right level of the CF. He was not given any quarter.

At one stage, Sudhir Mankad took me to the corner of the room and referred to his conversation with the RBI governor and asked if I could agree to accept 4.5 per cent of the assets as an appropriate level of the CF. Pointing to the utterly unsound basis of the recommendation to raise the norm from 3–4 per cent to 6–7 per cent, I said I could agree at best to 3 per cent. When Sudhir Mankad mentioned this to the other members of the committee, they decided to stick to their recommendation.

I had revised the dissent note to highlight the serious implications of the recommendation of the majority group on the transfer of surplus, year to year, to the government.

It was decided that the calculations I had provided regarding the likely profitability scenarios and their implications for the transfer of surplus would also be reflected in the report as one set of assumptions. It was also decided that the RBI secretariat would rewrite the concerned section of the report and it would be sent to me for my final comments after being vetted by Rakesh Mohan. This was to be completed in three days time.

The committee also decided that its job was over and there would be no further requirement to meet on 25 July, as earlier planned. Except for me, all the members, including Chairman Jalan, signed on the cover page of the report under the date '25 July'. I promised to sign it on 25 July, after the draft report was updated.

My Last Meeting

The revised sections of the report dealing with the implications of the recommendations on transfer of surplus to the government did not arrive until 24 July. Consequently, I could not verify the changes agreed to in the last meeting. On 24 July, I was transferred from DEA to the Ministry of Power.

The principal secretary to the PM informed me on 24 July, after my transfer orders were issued, that a meeting had been arranged at the residence of Home Minister Amit Shah the next evening, in which the RBI governor would also participate. The principal secretary reconfirmed on 25 July, the day I handed over charge of the post of finance secretary and secretary, DEA, that the meeting stood as planned.

I reached the residence of Amit Shah at 7.30 p.m. as per the programme. Rajiv Kumar, secretary, DFS was already present. Finance Minister Nirmala Sitharaman arrived at around 7.45 p.m. and the home minister joined us at around 8.10 p.m.; RBI Governor Shaktikanta Das never arrived.

Amit Shah discussed the matter again in critical detail. He seemed to be of the view that the cash/realized reserves should be fixed between 3 per cent and 4 per cent. He noted other implications as well in long hand. He had some sheets of paper with him, which he referred to a couple of times. These sheets seemed to have come from RBI with some indication regarding the landing zone in their opinion. The finance minister did not utter a word. Rajiv Kumar also remained practically silent.

After about fifteen to twenty minutes of conversation, I left. Nirmala Sitharaman and Rajiv Kumar stayed on.

I Get Banished from the Expert Committee

After my departure from the Ministry of Finance, my successor in DEA, Atanu Chakraborty, was not named my replacement in the expert committee. Instead, Rajiv Kumar, DFS secretary, was nominated as the representative of the government.

Rajiv called me a couple of days later. As he requested, I explained the entire matter to him, knowing fully well that it would be quite challenging for him to understand the complexities involved. I particularly emphasized that he should not sacrifice the government's legitimate interests.

From newspaper reports, it appeared that the tenth meeting of the expert committee took place on 4 August. It decided to meet once more to conclude its work.

The RBI Board met on 26 August. In this meeting, it accepted the expert committee's report on the ECF. RBI reported that it earned a surplus of ₹1,23,414 crore in the year 2018–19. The board decided to transfer 100 per cent of this to the government. In addition, the RBI Board also decided to transfer ₹52,637 crore from the CF, which was identified as excess provisions.

I felt good that RBI decided to transfer 100 per cent of the profits and about 50 per cent of the excess cash reserves I had estimated in the CF. It seemed that my struggle had paid off.

However, when I read through the report that RBI placed on its website the same day—26 August—most of my satisfaction withered away. Except in the introductory chapter where it was stated that I was briefly associated with the committee's work, all references to me were removed. The dissent note was cleaned out. The report did not contain the minutes of the nine meetings I had attended and the issues that were debated in those meetings. Nine meetings of the total of ten to eleven meetings that were held were reduced to my being briefly associated with the committee.

The report reflected what the RBI Four wanted on all the major issues I have identified in the preceding paragraphs. Only two changes were made. One, the RBI Board was given discretionary authority to go beyond the committee's recommendations if necessary. Second, the lower limit of both the valuation and cash reserves was somewhat lowered. That said, vesting discretion in the RBI Board virtually nullified the recommendations of the expert committee. These recommendations became only of persuasive value, not directory.

I was convinced that the committee's recommendations would have to be junked sooner or later, as they were based on impractical and analytically weak considerations.

RBI Buries the Jalan Committee Report

The recommendations of the Bimal Jalan-led expert committee have not been used consistently for the surplus transfer of three years—2018–19, 2019–20 and 2020–21. The recommendations were used only for the financial year 2019–20, when RBI reported a surplus of ₹1,30,747 crore. It retained ₹73,615 crore out of the surplus earned, transferring only ₹57,132 crore to the government.

For the years 2018–19 and 2020–21, RBI generated extra surplus by selling its foreign assets to monetize the valuation gains that the ECF committee was against even touching. The accumulated valuation gains and the realized balance in the CF account had to be brought to the lowest permissible limits of the ECF framework recommended by the committee.

If we were to consider all the three years together, RBI effectively transferred 186 per cent of the normal surplus (excluding valuation gains booked as profits) for 2018–19; 57 per cent of normal surplus for 2019–20; and 143 per cent of normal surplus for 2020–21. For the three years from 2018 to 2021 together, RBI earned a normal surplus of ₹2,64,400 crore, whereas it transferred ₹3,32,249 crore to the government. In fact, it ended up transferring 125.66 per cent of the normal surplus earned to the government during the three-year period.

RBI had effectively buried the Jalan committee report by the end of FY2021. Thereafter, RBI transferred surpluses to the government in an ad-hoc manner depending upon growth in its Balance Sheet size and profit or losses it made on the sale of foreign exchange to manage the rupee-dollar exchange rate. In 2021–22, surplus transferred was only ₹30,307 crore out of total income of ₹1,60,112 crore. In 2022–23, RBI earned total income of ₹2,35,457 crore, thanks to higher interest and gains on sale of foreign exchange reserves. Yet, it transferred only ₹87,416 crore as surplus to the government.

12

India Announces Foreign Currency Sovereign Bonds

Paragraph 103 of the Budget 2019–20 Speech delivered by Finance Minister Nirmala Sitharaman on 5 July 2019 announced India's decision to issue sovereign bonds in foreign currencies:

> India's sovereign external debt to GDP is among the lowest globally at less than 5 per cent. The Government would start raising a part of its gross borrowing programme in external markets in external currencies. This will also have a beneficial impact on the demand situation for government securities in the domestic market.

This announcement attracted a lot of attention in the media. The market welcomed it. Yields on government bonds went down by about twelve basis points that day. This was one of the major questions directed to me in the post-Budget media interactions. I provided some more clarity on the move. The government looked to raise about 10 per cent of its gross borrowing programme of ₹7.1 lakh crore, or about $10 billion, in foreign currency sovereign bonds during the year.

While investment bankers, bond market participants and banks, in general, supported it, two groups of people—former RBI top brass, including Raghuram Rajan and Rakesh Mohan, and affiliates of the Rashtriya Swayamsevak Sangh (RSS), including the Swadeshi Jagran Manch—questioned the move. In the days to follow, the debate intensified as opposition from these quarters kept increasing.

The Run-up to Announcement Had an Interesting Backdrop

All the G-20 countries issue foreign currency-denominated sovereign bonds. India was the only country not issuing such bonds to raise resources for government finances. The global stock of sovereign bonds exceeded $50 trillion in 2019 and made up over 60 per cent of the total global bond market.

When raising sovereign bonds in foreign currencies was such a routine matter for the entire world, why was it such an emotive issue in India?

India had toyed with this idea for twenty-five years before it was announced, yet its policymakers were unable to mainstream the issuance of such sovereign bonds when most other areas of capital flows, such as FDI, FPI and external commercial borrowing (ECBs), had been opened up after 1991.

Why?

Indian Sovereign Bonds Opened to Foreigners in the 1990s

India's Central and state governments financed a good part of their fiscal deficit by issuing sovereign bonds in the Indian Rupee (INR). Only resident Indians and Indian institutions were permitted to buy these securities until the 1980s. The debt market, a major constituent of the capital market, was closed to foreigners.

Whenever India was faced with an acute shortage of foreign currency reserves, it resorted to issuing bonds and deposits largely aimed at the non-resident Indian (NRI) community abroad. On four occasions in the past—in 1991 (India Development bonds), 1998

(Resurgent India bonds), 2001 (India Millennium Deposits) and 2013 (special FCNR [Foreign Currency Non-Resident]-B Deposit Scheme)—the country had raised funds from NRIs in foreign currencies. These schemes are commonly known as NRI bonds/deposits. The Government of India/RBI paid higher than prevailing market rates of interest through structured arrangements with SBI and other banks, to raise these bonds/deposits. These bonds/deposits were not listed on any exchange and liquidated upon expiry.

In the 1990s, the government and RBI opened the issuance of Indian domestic sovereign bonds to foreign investors. Foreign institutional investors (FIIs) could buy government securities in both the primary and secondary markets. The government and RBI controlled the overall amount of government securities that FIIs, now called foreign portfolio investors, could buy. In 2019, FPIs owned more than $20 billion of government securities.

The total external debt of the government in 2019 was around $103 billion. Of this, loans (mostly from multilaterals and bilaterals) made up about $70 billion. The external debt in the form of bonds and notes was almost entirely owned by FPIs in the form of government securities issued in the domestic rupee market.

Foreigners did subscribe to, buy and own sovereign bonds in India in 2019. They brought dollars to India and used the rupee proceeds to buy the rupee-denominated sovereign bonds. In their books in their home countries, they always maintained their accounts/investment in foreign currencies. For all practical purposes, their investments in Indian sovereign bonds were in their foreign currencies.

The foreign currency bonds proposed to be issued in the 2019 Budget were different more in form than substance. Foreigners could buy sovereign bonds directly in foreign currencies and these would be listed on foreign stock exchanges. India would get the dollars invested in these bonds and the government in equivalent rupee exactly the same amount as in their participation in bonds issued domestically.

Proposal to Issue Sovereign Bonds Got No Traction in 2018

India had toyed with the idea of issuing foreign currency sovereign bonds in the 1990s. On both these occasions, the proposals were rejected by Montek Singh Ahluwalia, who was finance secretary at the time, offering exactly opposite reasons—first on the ground that it was too risky as India's foreign exchange reserves were too low and second, that India did not need it as foreign exchange reserves had become quite comfortable.

In 2018, India was facing rough weather on the foreign exchange front consequent to oil prices rising from early 2018. By the time oil prices rose to about $80 per barrel in June–July 2018, FPIs started unwinding their investments in government securities. They started selling government securities and Indian corporate debt. They withdrew over $15 billion in 2018–19. The rupee was under pressure on account of rising oil prices. Withdrawal of investments by FPIs added additional pressure. The rupee depreciated below 74 to a dollar. India's foreign exchange reserves declined from the level of $426 billion in April 2018, to less than $400 billion in October 2018.

Piyush Goyal, who was acting finance minister, started building pressure to bring in an NRI deposit scheme on the lines of what India had done in 2013 and on three occasions earlier. The NRI deposit scheme of 2013 had provided 2–3 per cent extra interest over the prevailing FCNR-B dollar deposit rates prevailing at the time. Honestly, it was a bit of a scam! Foreign banks lent to NRIs at 50–75 basis points higher than the prevailing deposit rates. The NRIs invested these borrowed funds in the special FCNR-B account created in 2013 and made a cool 1.5–2 per cent extra interest.

As the rupee had appreciated vis-à-vis the dollar by the time these deposits were liquidated, the Indian government and RBI did not suffer any major loss, but it was not certain that this would be the case this time around. Moreover, there was no justifiable reason to offer this extra interest when India could raise as much as it wanted on the prevailing interest rates.

Therefore, I opposed the proposal of issuing such NRI bonds. Instead, I proposed that India issue sovereign bonds. Piyush Goyal wanted to issue NRI bonds on the grounds that 'the time was not right' for sovereign bonds. He recalled his proposal to issue sovereign bonds in 2016 and kept cursing the Ministry of Finance for rejecting it.

On the directions of the PMO, all the proposals on the table were decided to be placed before a group informally formed for this purpose under the leadership of the ailing Arun Jaitley. The meeting at his residence was attended by Amit Shah, Sushma Swaraj, Suresh Prabhu, Piyush Goyal and RBI Governor Urjit Patel, accompanied by his two deputies. Also present was Nripendra Misra, principal secretary to the PM.

Sushma Swaraj, making her pitch right at the beginning, announced her complete opposition to sovereign bonds. Piyush Goyal pushed for NRI bonds, which Urjit Patel opposed. Another proposal—a rupee-dollar swap with Japan, also came up for consideration. This arrangement provided for India to borrow dollars from Japan under the facility. Nripendra Misra was more inclined towards the swap deal with Japan, provided Japan agreed to allow its use in conditions India considered appropriate. The meeting remained inconclusive and Arun Jaitley ended it by advising us to further explore all the options.

Thankfully, No Costly NRI Deposits

After a few days, Piyush Goyal, showing some desperation, 'directed' me to put up the proposal on file formally for the issuance of NRI bonds. I said that RBI, besides being opposed to the idea in principle, believed the situation was not alarming enough to issue NRI bonds and accordingly was not willing to extend the type of dollar-rupee swap guarantee as was done in 2013. But Piyush Goyal was of the view that the government could bear both foreign exchange risk and additional interest cost in such a case.

This conversation was baffling as no decision had been taken at the meeting held a few days earlier, to issue NRI bonds. Nor had I received any instructions from Arun Jaitley or any advice from the PMO. However, with the involvement of S. Jaishankar, former foreign secretary, and the Japanese ambassador to India, lines of communications had been opened up with the Japanese to negotiate a large rupee-dollar swap deal.

I advised Shashank Saxena, joint secretary, capital markets, to prepare the file with a thorough and complete analysis of the proposal as Piyush Goyal envisaged, and also to record the reasons why NRI bonds should not be issued. Some awkward directions were given by Piyush Goyal to Revenue Secretary Hasmukh Adhia in other matters. We exchanged notes and agreed that the PMO and Prime Minister must be apprised of these matters and the unreasonable expectations/directions of the minister.

We met the PM separately and he listened patiently. I told him that if India were to raise $50 billion via NRI bonds or deposits by paying a 2 per cent extra interest rate, it would cost $100 million extra per annum. And for the five-year bonds/deposits, India would end up paying $500 million or about ₹3,500 crore extra. Raising such costly resources when the country was holding $400 billion of foreign currency reserves could prove to be a little scandalous.

Prime Minister Modi's decision was clear. He asked me not to process the proposal of issuing NRI bonds. He must have passed this on to Piyush Goyal as he did not remind me of the proposal thereafter.

When I suggested that we explore the possibility of issuing sovereign bonds that would raise the amount India wanted at rates even lower than the FCNR-B deposit rates instead of paying a premium over these rates, the PM did not give his go-ahead. Instead, he asked that the proposal be examined further.

We Prepare for Initiating Sovereign Bonds after the Elections in 2019

I saw a lot of merit in India taking up the sovereign bond issuance programme in foreign currency and listing its debt abroad. I also thought this should form part of the bold reforms programme after the 2019 elections.

On my instructions, the Budget Division in DEA, which handles policy relating to government borrowings, examined the proposal formally. The Export-Import (EXIM) Bank of India had been raising bonds in foreign markets for many years. Likewise, the Power Finance Corporation (PFC) and Rural Electrification Corporation (REC) had also been regular issuers of debt in foreign markets. I asked EXIM Bank to work with the Budget Division to guide it about the processes involved and the preparations required to issue sovereign bonds. EXIM Bank CMD David Rasquinha was quite supportive. We also engaged an international investment bank to advise us on the sovereign credit rating and get information on the international sovereign bond markets on a pro-bono basis.

RBI is the debt manager of India, though it had only raised domestic debt. Whenever India went for NRI bonds/deposits, SBI had played a much bigger role in managing the issuance as it had a substantial presence in foreign currency markets and foreign territories. Sovereign bonds would not require any guarantee or other support from RBI unlike the case with the types of bonds/ deposits issued in the 1990s and 2013. Still, it was necessary to discuss the matter with RBI.

The Government of India discusses its borrowing programme formally and comprehensively twice a year. First at the end of March to finalize the borrowing calendar for the first half, and again at the end of September to finalize the borrowing calendar for the second half. Despite the public impression that RBI does everything related to the government's borrowing programme, the key policies, instruments to be issued, composition of borrowings in terms of different tenure and inflation indexing are all finalized in these meetings.

The subject of sovereign bonds was formally taken up in the March 2019 meeting with RBI to finalize the borrowing programme and calendar for the first half of 2019–20. Deputy Governor B.P. Kanungo was present. He indicated that RBI had some reservations but was willing to examine it as a possible option to partly fund the government's borrowing programme.

After the elections, my perception about the lack of interest on the part of the government to frontload any bold reforms programme and my less than collegial relationship with new Finance Minister Nirmala Sitharaman made me realize that the July Budget was not the best time to initiate the sovereign bonds programme. Accordingly, I did not include the proposal to initiate the programme in the first drafts of the Budget speech.

Die for Sovereign Bonds Cast in Most Unlikely Circumstances

Chief Economic Advisor Krishnamurthy Subramanian had joined DEA sometime in December 2018. He was not very involved in the formulation of the interim Budget. Though the *Economic Survey* is not presented at the time of the interim Budget, the task of presenting the full-fledged survey in July 2019 occupied him substantially after he joined.

A Group of Secretaries in the Ministry of Finance, headed by the finance secretary, is always constituted for every Budget. The CEA is a member of this group. They meet among themselves to discuss major macroeconomic and coordination issues. The group also meets with the finance minister regularly to take directions on major issues.

In one of the meetings of the Group of Secretaries with Finance Minister Nirmala Sitharaman, Subramanian proposed that India raise sovereign bonds in external markets to boost investments. He enthusiastically argued that India had a very low foreign debt to GDP ratio, in fact one of the lowest in the world at less than 5 per cent, and could easily raise a lot of cheap foreign money to fund investments.

Obviously, he was not aware of India's chequered history of policymaking related to the issuance of sovereign bonds in foreign currencies in foreign markets, which was more influenced by emotions than the merit of the case. He genuinely believed the country needed to raise its investment to fire its growth story. He argued that sovereign bonds were, in fact, a kind of low-hanging fruit that could be well deployed to boost India's investment-led growth. As he did not discuss this proposal with me before raising it in the meeting, he was also obviously unaware of the fate of the proposal in 2018 when it had been shot down by the concerted opposition of Sushma Swaraj and Piyush Goyal.

After Subramanian had finished his pitch, I thought it was my duty to place the facts and history before the finance minister and the group.

I began by saying that it was indeed a very good idea for India to raise sovereign bonds abroad in reasonable amounts of about 10 per cent of our annual borrowing programme every year. I also enumerated the benefits such a move would bring in terms of reducing the fiscal pre-emption of domestic savings, reduced supply of government paper leading to better transmission of interest rate reductions by RBI, and the private sector being left with higher domestic resources for investment. I also explained how we had opened up investment by foreigners in government securities through the FPI route and how raising external sovereign bonds had less risks in comparison to FPIs investing in government papers.

Thereafter, I apprised the finance minister about the less than enthusiastic support from RBI for such a move and active opposition by certain sections of the RSS and BJP who saw it as the return of the East India Company. I also underlined the need for her to take it up politically within and outside the BJP to enable the proposal to sail through.

While Nirmala Sitharaman viewed me with a little lack of trust, she found CEA Krishnamurthy Subramanian completely reliable. She lapped up the idea and said that issuing sovereign bonds would be a good move. She assured us that she would deal with the political implications.

I could not have been happier at the outcome of this discussion. I drafted a paragraph, more or less on the lines quoted in the beginning of this chapter, and included the same in the next draft of the Budget speech.

The ideas for the Budget were presented before Prime Minister Modi and other senior advisors. The proposed paragraph relating to the issuance of sovereign bonds was read aloud in two subsequent meetings. While several other proposals generated much discussion and some had to be dropped, this proposal invited no objection, including from Piyush Goyal, who was present at some of these meetings. The final draft of the Budget speech was also scrutinized thoroughly in the PMO and by the finance minister. It survived all this scrutiny. Finally, Nirmala Sitharaman made the announcement in her Budget speech in Parliament on 5 July 2019.

The Announcement Triggers a Storm

As mentioned above, the announcement attracted a lot of adverse attention from former central bankers. The most scathing attack was launched by former the RBI Governor Raghuram Rajan.

He termed the argument that borrowing in foreign currencies was cheaper, as bogus. He argued that lower dollar interest rates were offset in the longer run by higher principal repayments (owing to depreciation of the rupee). Making light of the intelligence and the ability of the officials in the Ministry of Finance, he attributed the move to lobbying by foreign bankers. He also reminded the media of previous times of crisis, like the taper tantrum in 2013, when India faced much higher repayment obligations on account of the rupee depreciating sharply, which generated a very bad image for the country. His advice was for India to worry about 'short-term faddish investors buying when India is hot, and dumping us when it is not'.

All the three arguments made by Raghuram Rajan were hollow and showed his lack of understanding. India's foreign exchange markets were reasonably free and exchange rates were largely market-determined. India had also built up a decent stock of foreign exchange reserves. Taking any moving average for a period of ten years, the average rupee depreciation rates had not been more than 3–4 per cent. In the five years from 2014 to 2019, there was hardly any rupee depreciation. In fact, many times, the rupee had appreciated. The 2013 taper tantrum was an isolated event that only lasted for a few months. His raising of the bogey of higher repayment costs in the long run was factually incorrect and reflective of an unnecessarily fearful mindset.

His slur that we were acting under the influence of foreign bankers was also completely baseless. No foreign banker had met officials from the Ministry of Finance in the run-up to the Budget. As I recounted above, the proposal emanated from the CEA only in June 2019, at the Budget group meeting. The ministry officials understood the matter quite well and were convinced on its merits that the sovereign bond proposal was in the national interest.

Finally, his lack of trust in India's ability to manage the sovereign bonds programme prudently was equally misplaced. The apprehension that Indians would load up foreign liabilities once this route was open, betrayed his distrust of India's political and official leadership. India had been quite conservative in building up foreign liabilities and could be trusted to be similarly prudent in building up a foreign sovereign debt portfolio. The 'short-term faddish investors' Raghuram Rajan referred to behaved no differently when they bought and sold Indian debt in domestic currency permissible for more than twenty-five years.

Some other 'knowledgeable' experts also criticized the move. Calling attention to 'the silent fiscal crisis' India was facing, macroeconomist Dr Rathin Roy worried about the 'loss of sovereignty' the country might face if sovereign bonds were issued. He also doubted that sovereign bond liabilities would be relatively cheaper if hedging costs were added. Former RBI Governor C. Rangarajan felt unsure about the benefits of sovereign bonds and suggested that instead of issuing sovereign bonds, FPI limits for investment in government securities could have been raised.

None of these suggestions had any real merit. There was no point in the sovereign hedging its exposure when the foreign exchange rate only reflected the external value of Indian currency. The FPI route was far more troublesome than sovereign bonds.

Instead of buying any hedging cover, it would be much more prudent to provide for likely depreciation by creating a reserve in the Government of India account by transferring an amount equal to the difference between the domestic cost of borrowing and the interest rate of sovereign bonds. This is being done in the case of the gold bonds the Government has been issuing. The difference between the Government's average cost of borrowing and the 2.5 per cent interest it pays on the gold bonds is transferred to a reserve. Such a transfer would also be a prudent financial practice as it would account for a fuller cost of interest in government accounts.

Swadeshi Jagran Manch Troubled by Ghost of East India Company

Ashwini Mahajan, co-convener of the Swadeshi Jagran Manch, termed the proposal 'anti-patriotic'. Mahajan feared sovereign bonds would create long-term risks for the economy, potentially allowing rich foreign nations and their financial institutions to dictate the country's policies. In his view India ought to learn from the experience of countries that took loans from international markets to meet their government deficit. He argued that going overseas might lead to the rupee depreciating at a fast rate, which would allow foreign governments to demand tariff reductions. He further contended that the flow of foreign currency received led to a rise in inflation.

Mahajan's arguments were utter nonsense. They were dismissed by the BJP's national spokesman on economic affairs Gopal Krishna Agarwal, who termed the proposal the 'best alternative' at this point. Agarwal also correctly said that the government should stick to its fiscal deficit target of 3.3 per cent of GDP. India needed to attract a lot of investment and financing from abroad to make the desired investment in the economy to put the country on a higher growth trajectory.

There was hardly any connection between the issuance of sovereign bonds and foreign governments demanding tariff reductions. No one could dictate economic policies to India and there was nothing unpatriotic about it. People like Mahajan were still afflicted by the 'East India Company fear syndrome' and have no idea about the financial and trade integration in the world in the past four centuries.

India is the world's fifth-largest economy. It can grow at a steady rate to become a $10 trillion economy by the mid-2030s only by integrating its economy with global financial, technology, capital and trade markets.

Sovereign Bonds versus the FPI Route

India has permitted foreign investors to buy and sell sovereign bonds issued in domestic currency by bringing foreign currency from abroad. This is now known as the FPI route. The FPIs are allowed to freely invest in Indian government debt, subject to an overall limit and some restrictions relating to investment limits in short-term securities and concentration limits. Another former governor of RBI, Dr Rangarajan, in his comments, suggested enlarging the FPI route. It is instructive to examine the two routes: sovereign bonds issued in domestic currency and sovereign bonds issued in foreign currency.

Foreign investors participate in both routes by investing their foreign currencies. Both the routes result in inflow of foreign exchange to India. In terms of flow of foreign exchange, sovereign bonds do not have any special advantage except that India can choose to raise them in the currency it wants, whereas FPI investment in government securities would come in the currencies that FPIs choose to bring in. India has a large trade deficit with respect to China and Japan. It could raise the sovereign bonds in Chinese or Japanese currencies if it finds it more advantageous.

The first real difference between the two is in terms of interest rate implications.

When FPIs invest in rupee-denominated government securities, they reap the advantage of higher interest rates in India relative to what their debt investments earn in their own countries. Bonds worth $17 trillion in advanced countries were earning negative interest rates in 2019.

German bunds and Japanese bonds issued by these countries required their issuers to pay no interest; in fact, they repay less at the end of the tenure than the amount they got at the time of issuance. Investors pay to hold these bonds instead of earning any interest. If the Government of India issued bonds in these markets in these currencies, it could reap the same advantage of low, if not negative, interest rates.

In 2019 the difference between the interest the Government of India paid to foreigners under the FPI route and under the foreign currency issuance was more than 6 per cent per annum. A $10 billion sovereign bonds programme meant a lower payment of $600 million in interest on this. If India were to build a portfolio of $100 billion over ten years, the annual savings of interest would be $6 billion.

The faddish behaviour of foreigners is also less dangerous for India in case of foreign issuance of sovereign bonds than the FPI route.

The behaviour of FPIs, as can be expected, is determined by their perception of their interest. Many FPIs tend to bring debt investments when India does not need foreign debt flows and take out their debt investments when the rupee is under pressure. This behaviour was on display in 2013 when the taper tantrum took place. The same behaviour was seen in 2018 when the rupee was under pressure during April–October 2018 on account of higher oil prices. Funds worth $15 billion, most of it in debts, were withdrawn by FPIs in 2018–19, putting additional pressure on the rupee.

This behaviour gets fully neutralized when sovereign bonds are raised in foreign currencies in foreign markets. If someone wants to sell, another foreign investor needs to buy it in the stock exchange where the bond is listed. Buying and selling can take place only among themselves, and will have no implication on India's foreign currency reserves. Thus investors do not have recourse to taking their foreign currency investments out of India before the redemption date of the concerned securities. The fear that foreign institutions or speculators could bring the rupee under pressure by dumping the bonds and raising yields is therefore a chimera.

The fearmongering Raghuram Rajan and the Swadeshi Jagran Manch tried to generate, is related more to a situation where there is a concerted speculative attack on the currency of a country. Such an attack can take place only when the central bank of a country tries to keep its currency highly overvalued and has no firepower in the form of reserves to defend such overvalued currency. This situation has nothing to do with the amount of sovereign bonds issued in foreign currency. As India had been maintaining a flexible exchange rate, there was unlikely to be any speculative attack on Indian currency.

There are some other means available to foreign speculators to speculate on India's currency. The Non-Deliverable Forward (NDF) market is one such avenue. That route has to be managed by creating a liquid derivative foreign currency market in India. The issuance of sovereign bonds in foreign currency does not affect the operations of the NDF market either.

On objective considerations, there are more advantages of India issuing sovereign bonds in foreign currency than persisting with the FPI route for foreign investment in India's sovereign debt.

Sovereign Bonds Have Not Seen the Light of Day

I left the Ministry of Finance on 25 July 2019. A part of the media attributed my transfer to the proposal of issuing sovereign bonds. This was not correct. I believed in the merits of the proposal but I was not the real author of the proposal in Budget 2019–20.

Chief Economic Advisor Subramanian boasted about being the father of the sovereign bond proposal in his address at Indian School of Business (ISB), Hyderabad, delivered only a few days after the Budget. He was also quite vocal about it in media interactions for some time thereafter. The finance minister also spoke about implementing the announcement for some weeks after I had left the ministry. Gradually, though, the enthusiasm about sovereign bonds waned, both for the finance minister and CEA. RBI might have also worked with the finance minister to let the proposal die by efflux.

The government has not issued any sovereign bonds in foreign currency since the announcement was made in July 2019. There does not seem to be any interest in the move either.

Instead, the government and RBI agreed to enlarge the FPI's debt investment route by creating a fully accessible route (FAR). The overall caps applicable for investment, including foreign investment, in government securities do not apply to securities under FAR. There is no other difference between FPI's investment in government securities issued under FAR and non-FAR. India continues to suffer excessive interest payments and the risk of faddish behaviour when the chips are down.

The FAR route has not brought in FPI's investment in Indian debt. In fact, there has been a continuous reduction in FPI's overall investment holding in Indian government debt in the last three years.

13

Six Airports Get Monetized

THE AIRPORT AUTHORITY OF INDIA (AAI) CONTROLLED 129 AIRPORTS IN India in 2017–18, including 78 domestic airports and 23 international airports. Delhi and Mumbai, two of the largest airports in the country managed by AAI, were given out on concession in 2006. The AAI, which had managed the airports earlier, then took a 26 per cent share in the joint-venture special purpose vehicles (SPVs)—Delhi International Airport Ltd (DIAL) and Mumbai International Airport Ltd (MIAL)—created for this purpose.

The concession period is thirty years, extendable by another thirty years. The AAI gets about 46 per cent of revenue share for Delhi airport and 39 per cent for Mumbai airport. These two airports have been cash cows for AAI, generating over 25 per cent of its total revenue without any expenditure.

Despite the successful model of concessioning out these two airports in 2006, AAI had not given out any other operating airport on this concession model thereafter. It did take some equity in new greenfield airports developed in the private sector—Kochi, Bengaluru, Hyderabad and so on—but no more 'privatization' was undertaken based on the Delhi and Mumbai model or any other improved model.

In 2015, after the NDA government had settled down and wanted to promote further concessioning of airports, the Ministry of Civil Aviation (MoCA) and AAI came out with a very timid operations and maintenance (O&M) model and got it approved in a review meeting chaired by Prime Minister Modi. This model basically envisaged handing over the non-aeronautical revenues in the terminal building to the concessionaire, with AAI remaining in charge of both airside (all airport operations facilities like runways, ferrying of passengers, etc.) and cityside (development of land and buildings outside the terminal building exits) areas.

This O&M model was actually an excuse to show that some 'privatization' was being done without handing over anything of substance. As it was also technically a public-private partnership (PPP) project, a committee in DEA called the Public Private Partnership Appraisal Committee (PPPAC) had approved the O&M project for the Ahmedabad and Jaipur airports in 2016. It was no surprise that there was no interest in taking over such a function and AAI received only one bid, which was also rejected by MoCA. Some more efforts were made to give out these two airports on this moth-eaten mode, by sweetening the model with the inclusion of airside and cargo facilities in the O&M model.

I started getting invited to these meetings sometime in the middle of 2018. As I found the O&M model a sham, I started raising questions on the desirability of moving in this direction despite the secretary, MoCA, always reminding everyone in the room that the model was approved in a meeting headed by the PM and they were making every conceivable effort to make it work, including hiring professional consultants.

Amitabh Kant, CEO of NITI Aayog, also did not see much sense in the O&M model but had gone along with the same for years to give every chance to MoCA to implement the decision taken in the meeting.

Nripendra Misra, principal secretary to the PM, sick of MoCA's failure to show any success, had started nudging the secretary, MoCA, to change tack and go for bolder 'privatization'. There were quite a few meetings between June and October 2018 when this issue, along with many others in the civil aviation sector, including privatization of Air India, were discussed. With every meeting, Nripendra Misra got more and more exasperated.

Nripendra Misra Loses Patience

At a meeting sometime in the middle of October 2018, where Kant, Secretary (MoCA) R.N. Choubey, AAI Chairman Guruprasad Mohapatra, and I were present along with officials from the PMO, Nripendra Misra finally lost his patience. Cursing Choubey that no real initiative had been taken despite so many meetings and the meetings chaired by him had been utterly useless, Misra announced he was closing the matter of privatization of airports then and there. He said he would not ask for any progress report in the matter from then on and left the room.

This was shocking. Choubey was a hardworking and forward-looking officer. Either on account of his genuine belief that the O&M model had the PM's approval or to avoid any controversy in 'privatizing' an asset (the government had not succeeded in privatizing Air India or for that matter any other public-sector company by then), he had become excessively cautious and unwilling to propose any real privatization from his side.

Though stunned at what had transpired, I quickly gathered my thoughts and took the initiative to speak to Kant, Choubey and Mohapatra, after Nripendra Misra left. I suggested that we discuss the key features of a real PPP concession model and make the privatization of airports a success before the elections, due in May the following year. Somehow, the discussion started and we got going. Possibly shaken by Nripendra Misra's outburst, Secretary Choubey also decided to drop his inhibitions.

In the same room from which Nripendra Misra had just walked out, we thrashed out the key features of real privatization on a PPP concession basis: fifty years of concession against thirty years in the case of DIAL and MIAL, complete freedom for land development on the cityside and increasing the bidder pool by enlarging eligibility to anyone with experience of maintaining a real-estate infrastructure facility (hotel, mall, etc.). We decided to shoot for six airports at one go and not restrict any bidder to a specific number of projects. If the bid was the highest for all six, someone could take all six airports. That said, we believed that such a situation was unlikely to arise with the pool of eligible bidders expanded massively.

I promised that I would get DEA's PPPAC approval in less than two weeks, if MoCA was able to get all the relevant documents— the PPPAC proposal, draft concession agreement, etc.—prepared quickly. R.N. Choubey rose to the occasion and promised to get all the paperwork done in two weeks using his existing consultant for the O&M project. We drafted the minutes of the meeting and decided to deliver what was written off completely a few minutes earlier.

We Set a Scorching Pace

The impromptu meeting of the group held on 20 October 2018 and the ambitious agreement arrived at on the spot, created the momentum for privatizing six non-metro airports. In the next meeting held a day later at NITI Aayog, we decided to set the end of February 2019 as the date by which all the six airports should be awarded and concession agreements signed. This was only four months away. The process involved an enormous amount of procedural work and decision-making.

Both MoCA and AAI would have to prepare the basic documents— request for proposal (RfP) and project reports for the new model and an agreement (operation, management and development agreement or OMDA)—for concessioning away all parts of the airport (airside, terminals and cityside) for fifty years, as well as a proposal for the consideration of PPPAC.

The PPPAC process involved two stages of approval: in principle, and final. As per the prescribed process, both the stages required three weeks of notice to the members of PPPAC. The Infrastructure Division of DEA worked as the secretariat for the PPPAC. The secretariat had to examine all the documents from MoCA and then circulate an appraisal note raising all the issues for the consideration of the PPPAC.

The reserve prices for each of the airports had to be arrived at and agreed to. There were a number of other complications; AAI had commenced infrastructural works in many of these airports and had plans for large capital expenditures. There were a good number of employees involved.

Once the PPPAC approved the structure of the concession agreement and documents, MoCA had to obtain the cabinet's approval. Thereafter, the RfP had to be issued, consultations held with interested bidders, bids received and evaluated, decisions made for finding the best evaluated bidders and the matter placed again for consideration of the cabinet for approval to the winning bids.

There were also intergovernmental issues. Rajasthan had a new government headed by the Congress party, which opposed the privatization of the Jaipur airport. For Thiruvananthapuram, there was fierce opposition from the CPM government in Kerala. It began by opposing the project and later wanted to take over the airport through its own SPV.

When I proposed that we needed to work backwards from the deadline of 28 February 2019, the task to be completed in four months appeared impossible to Guruprasad Mohapatra, otherwise a very sincere and efficient officer (unfortunately, he died from Covid-19 while serving as secretary, DIPP). Considerable discussion followed. We had to cut through the foliage. I promised I would provide PPPAC approval within a week of the documents being received. This process normally takes months.

Eventually, everyone agreed to give the task a sincere and serious try. R.N. Choubey, on whom the bulk of the hard work fell, rendered yeoman support and showed exemplary commitment.

The DEA Joint Secretary Raises Tough Questions in Appraisal Note

The PPPAC is chaired by the secretary, DEA, but the appraisal note for the PPPAC is the property of the joint secretary, Infrastructure

Division. K.V. Pratap, an extremely hardworking officer and an authority on infrastructure contracting issues, was the joint secretary. He was completely uncompromising in his views, which often betrayed an utter lack of pragmatism and innovation. I had taken him in DEA knowing fully well he had fought with his bosses in most places he had served in earlier. I was confident that if his views or approach in any matter were not in the public interest, I would have no hesitation in overruling him on file.

DEA received the documents from MoCA on 6 December 2018 and the draft concession agreement on 7 December 2018. I scheduled the PPPAC meeting for 11 December to consider providing both in principle and final approval by combining the process in one meeting. Kumar Pratap circulated the appraisal note on 10 December. I saw the note only on the morning of 11 December, the day of the meeting. The minutes of this PPPAC meeting are not confidential.

I chaired the meeting and R.N. Choubey attended along with the representatives of NITI Aayog and other concerned organizations. We made several decisions deviating from the standard operating process considering the unique nature of the transaction, overruling at several points the position taken and suggested by Kumar Pratap as well as the economic advisor of the NITI. We offered a rationale for every decision taken which was duly recorded in the minutes. The minutes of this PPPAC meeting are not confidential. These were later taken under the Right to Information (RTI) Act and are available in the public domain on the Internet.

In terms of the structure of the concession agreement, all the features agreed in the two meetings of the group of officers—concession period, widened eligibility, concession for all six airports to one party if that happened to be the outcome and full freedom to make use of cityside land—were adopted.

As for the important technical issues raised in the appraisal note and vigorously presented by Kumar Pratap in the meeting, the PPPAC decided to stick to the qualification of projects undertaken in the harmonized master list of infrastructure issued by DEA, despite it being pointed out that some infrastructure projects in the list (such as the construction of soil-testing laboratories) were too small to be considered. As the PPPAC decided to specify a much higher financial project-capacity threshold of ₹3,500 crore and ₹1,000 crore for the financial capacity threshold, we pointed out that small projects like soil-testing laboratories, which require investments of a few crores, had no likelihood of making anyone eligible. Therefore, instead of picking and choosing particular infrastructure sectors closer to the class of airport projects, out of the master list—which would have complicated the process and restricted the competition—we stuck to the criterion of all projects in the master list for technical and financial eligibility thresholds.

The PPPAC guidelines required the project proponent (the department) to compute a total project cost or TPC. It was impossible for any interested bidder or AAI to work out capital cost investments over a period of fifty years. Further, as we proposed to give complete freedom to the winning bid for cityside development, it was impossible to think ex-ante what kind of development the winner would choose to undertake. The idea of TPC was for projects that were fully conceptualized and costed in the detailed project report (DPR).

In the case before us, there was no DPR. There was only information about the cost already incurred by AAI and the projected cost of the development works proposed by AAI, which it called Phase 1 of the development of these airports. We decided to take only these costs as TPC, consciously deviating from the guidelines despite Kumar Pratap's insistence. I decided to record his views in the minutes and the reasons for overruling him.

There were many other technical issues, such as determining termination payment in the event of default in the concession. Usually, termination payments are set in terms of outstanding debt at the time of termination. We decided to deviate from debt-related determination of the termination payment and fixed it in terms of depreciated value of the assets with no value assigned for the land.

The existing rules capped the land for cityside development at 5 per cent of the total land available for the airport. The available cityside land for the six airports under consideration ranged from 3 per cent to 9 per cent of total land available. It would have been wasteful if the land in excess of 5 per cent was not offered for development, which would have also raised disputes about which 5 per cent was to be given and what to do with the rest.

Again, PPPAC took a pragmatic view and decided to offer all the available cityside land for development, subject only to conforming with applicable municipal laws. The percentage of shareholding in case of conflict of interest was required to be limited to 5 per cent as per the guidelines, but the Companies Act had been amended in the meantime, raising it to 20 per cent. We went by the 20 per cent limit.

Kumar Pratap presented draft minutes of the meeting the next day on the e-filing system—they were comprehensively written, minutely recording the objections/issues he raised. Retaining the pith and substance of each of the issues he raised and recording the rationale we accepted for deviating or overruling the same, I cleared the minutes the same day. The minutes of the PPPAC, duly approving the proposal, were circulated on 13 December 2018, within a week as promised.

AAI Receives Massive Response

The Ministry of Finance had sponsored the National Infrastructure Investment Fund (NIIF) to make investments and bring investments into the infrastructure sector. Sujoy Bose, CEO of NIIF, had done a lot of work to develop the bid structure. The NIIF was keen to bid for the airports. Sujoy and NIIF were, therefore, kept away from the determination of reserve prices and other commercial parts of the bid. Once the bids were out, asking for a response within six weeks or so, he found the bid period quite short. I told him to focus on his bids within the time provided.

The determination of reserve prices was done meticulously taking into account the revenue profile. The bidder was asked to quote a specific amount per passenger. There was no revenue share, as we did not want to go into the contentious issue of what revenues to share and examine the bidder's books of accounts. The airside fee per passenger is determined by the airport's regulator.

The bidder was not permitted to recover the per-passenger fee from the passenger. Therefore, what the bidder offered to pay AAI did not affect the passenger. The formula for increase in the per-passenger fee was specified up front. The bidder had to pay AAI an amount by the per-passenger rate multiplied by the number of passengers who travelled through the airport. Both numbers were objectively determined with no scope for dispute.

Despite the tight schedule, AAI received a tremendous response, much better than anyone expected. In all, thirty-two bids were received for six airports. Jaipur and Ahmedabad received the maximum number of bids (seven each), while Lucknow and Guwahati received six bids each. There were three bids each for Mangalore and Thiruvananthapuram airports, including one from the Kerala government organization. Adani, GMR and NIIF participated for all six airports.

When the financial bids were opened on 25 February, the highest bids for all airports exceeded four to five times their reserve price. Adani's bids were the highest for all six airports. The NIIF had also bid quite aggressively and was only marginally behind Adani in the case of three airports. The incumbent airport operator GMR's bids were very low, only a little higher than reserve prices in most of the cases.

On 28 February, MoCA/AAI, having completed the evaluation process, put the award of the six airports to Adani on file to issue the letter of award. We had pulled off the impossible. All the decisions taken—giving it away for fifty years in one go, allowing development of all the cityside land by the concessionaire freely, a very simple but sound system of revenue share, expanding the pool of bidders, and many others—generated this tremendous response, both in terms of competitiveness of participation and the rate offered.

The PMO Has Second Thoughts

The integrity of the bid process was completely unquestionable. Nothing was done to favour NIIF or Adani. It was only ambitious bids that made Adani a winner in all the six cases. Yet, for some reasons, reservations developed in the PMO. My assessment was that these emanated from A.K. Sharma, additional secretary in the PMO.

The apprehension could have been that the public would find it hard to believe that all six airports were going to Adani without any direct or indirect favour from the government.

The Kerala government raised an objection. Though it lost out in the bidding, it still wanted Thiruvananthapuram airport. It offered to match the price of the highest bidder. The NIIF also wanted two airports by matching Adani's quote.

The PMO decided not to approve the transaction and issue the award letters quickly. The election schedule was announced on 8 March 2019.

After the elections, in July 2019, MoCA moved a proposal for the cabinet to approve the award of three airports—Ahmedabad, Lucknow and Mangalore—to Adani. I was still in DEA when the cabinet considered and approved this proposal on 3 July. It still took time for the government to hand these airports over to Adani; this finally happened on 7 September 2020 after the first wave of Covid-19. The government took much more time for the remaining three. The concession agreements for the remaining three—Jaipur, Guwahati and Thiruvananthapuram—airports were finally signed on 19 January 2021. The whole process was finally complete about two years after the finalization of the bids.

Momentum Is Lost

Privatization of many more airports under this model was to follow.

The government has been talking about privatizing six more airports—Amritsar, Varanasi, Bhubaneswar, Indore, Raipur and Trichy—ever since 2019. The AAI reportedly urged MoCA in November–December 2019 to go ahead with the privatization of these airports, which indicated the right change of mindset in AAI, earlier quite opposed to such concessioning before the successful March 2019 bids. On 16 May 2020, Minister Hardeep Puri publicly spoke of the tender process being initiated for these six airports. Finance Minister Nirmala Sitharaman, in her Budget speech for 2021–22, said that the government would privatize the airports operated by AAI in Tier 2 and Tier 3 cities.

The complete template for privatization had been developed, which had also proved its success after being thoroughly tested. However, there has been no action since the last transaction was concluded in February 2019. It seems there is still some wobbling of the minds with respect to the objectives of privatization. Should the government privatize profitable airports leaving the unprofitable ones with AAI? Should the government allow all or most airports to be taken by one party?

Two significant developments took place in August–September 2021.

On 23 August 2021, the finance minister announced the National Monetization Pipeline (NMP), which included monetization receipts of ₹20,782 crore from twenty-five AAI airports over four years. Besides giving away about twenty-two airports on the OMDA model or another appropriate monetization model, the plan also envisaged the sale of the remainder stake in airports already operated by the private sector—Delhi and Mumbai, where AAI has a 26 per cent equity stake, and Bengaluru, where the government stake is 13 per cent.

On 10 September 2021, the AAI Board approved the privatization of thirteen airports, the six mentioned above and seven other smaller ones, by clubbing these smaller unviable or loss-making airports with six profitable airports. The cabinet had earlier approved a policy decision to bundle loss-making airports to these six airports and invite bids based on this bundle of airports. The AAI press release indicated that it would appoint a consultant to prepare the bid document and determine the concession period and reserve price. It hoped to call the bids by early 2022. The AAI press release indicated that all fundamental parameters, like the concession period and the number of airports a single bidder could bid for, were open for discussion.

This was the a recipe for indecision, if not disaster. These are policy parameters the government should decide on its own rather than waiting for a consultant's advice. It was more troubling in view of the fact that all these issues had been decided earlier and worked to the best advantage of the country and AAI. It looked like the government would not be able to privatize any more airports.

The apprehensions have proved right. After nearly four years of successful bidding out of six airports and two years of NMP and AAI Board decision, nothing has moved. Not a single airport has been privatized. In fact, no process is on at all. It is easy to see that no more airports will be monetized anytime soon.

SECTION III

INSTITUTIONAL ISSUES

14

A Bill to Regulate Cryptocurrencies

Bᴵᵀᶜᴼᴵᴺ, ᴛʜᴇ ᴍᴏsᴛ ᴘᴏᴘᴜʟᴀʀ ᴀɴᴅ ᴋɴᴏᴡɴ ᴄʀʏᴘᴛᴏᴄᴜʀʀᴇɴᴄʏ, ᴡᴀs ᴠᴀʟᴜᴇᴅ at $2 in early 2013. Though quite volatile, its prices continued to rise thereafter and touched $1,000 for the first time in the last quarter of 2016. After trading below $1,000 for the first two months of calendar year 2017, it took off and traded for over $15,000 through most of December 2017. A 1,500 per cent increase in less than one year! No real asset, conceivably, could generate this kind of return. Then it fell with the same ferocity. By the end of calendar year 2018, the price was less than $4,000 per bitcoin. This kind of volatility in any asset price would worry both RBI and the Government of India.

There were other factors of concern. While bitcoin was initially used to make payments, most people drawn to bitcoin in India were 'investors' looking for extraordinary capital gains in no time. Most investors knew nothing about cryptocurrencies, the blockchains that recorded transactions and held bitcoins at any particular time, and the cryptography used in writing codes for this cyber/digital 'currency'. Some cryptocurrency exchanges had come up in India from 2013 onwards that made money by providing a platform to buy and sell bitcoins and other cryptocurrencies. These exchanges ensnared the youth as well as the gullible to buy bitcoins.

Bitcoins and other cryptocurrencies were not 'currencies' and legal tender in India, yet occasionally they were used to make payments, mostly by people operating outside the law, such as smugglers and terrorists, etc. Common and law-abiding people basically bought bitcoins for investment, to make a quick buck. No law defined or regulated cryptocurrencies. This state of no-man's land concerned RBI, but it was unable to do anything about it. It issued press notes, warning of the dangers and pitfalls of investing and dealing in cryptocurrencies.

As these warnings did not make any difference, RBI alerted the government to do something about the matter. The government set up a committee under the chairmanship of Dinesh Sharma, special secretary in DEA, in April 2017. The Sharma Committee, which included members from RBI, the Income Tax Department, MHA, and other connected organizations, consulted stakeholders in the cryptocurrency ecosystem. It felt quite strongly against bitcoin and other cryptocurrencies that were, at the least, complex and suspicious products and appeared akin to fraud.

I joined DEA in July 2017. The Dinesh Sharma Committee submitted its report in August 2017. Its utter discomfort about cryptocurrencies was evident from the conclusions it reached. It was convinced that cryptocurrencies deserve to be banned and recommended a clear warning to be issued to the public to stay away from them. However, instead of recommending an outright ban, it suggested that the subject be studied by another committee to suggest specific action, including legislative changes, to make 'possession, trade and use of cryptocurrencies expressly illegal and punishable'.

I had studied a bit about distributed ledger/blockchain technology. It seemed to be an innovation with a potential to transform how assets/records are stored and transferred directly between the holders/participants, without the need for a government regulator or department. An oft repeated example was that of land records that could be reorganized using distributed ledger technology.

I Chair a Government-Appointed Inter-Ministerial Committee

I discussed the Dinesh Sharma Committee report with others in the know to understand what the fuss was all about and what the government could do. Severe dissentions between the authors of the report and the members of the committee came to light during this review. The National Institute of Public Finance and Policy, the resource organization for the Dinesh Sharma Committee, which was represented at the meeting by a team led by Ashish Agarwal, seemed more inclined towards regulating cryptocurrencies; Dinesh Sharma was completely against it and wanted them to be banned. I was not sure. I wanted to understand cryptocurrencies and blockchain technology in all their dimensions and applications and then examine the policy options.

I recommended to the finance minister that another senior level inter-ministerial committee (IMG) be constituted, to study the issues related to virtual currencies and propose specific action to be taken. As the real stakeholders were DEA, RBI, SEBI and MEITY, to keep the examination and discussions focused, I proposed a smaller IMG of these four organizations represented by the two secretaries as well as the SEBI chairman and the RBI deputy governor. The finance minister approved the committee and it was notified on 2 November 2017. The NIPFP was retained as the resource organization.

The new IMG reached a key understanding in the first meeting held on 27 November. It accepted that cryptocurrencies could not be treated as currency and agreed to explore ways that cryptocurrencies did not use the appellation 'currency' or 'coin'. It was also accepted that the crypto market had developed a fair bit and all gains made in trading were subject to tax, irrespective of legal status.

The IMG recognized that there was a lack of clarity about the true nature of these cryptos—whether these were commodities/financial assets/something else—which was necessary to determine before developing any views/options to regulate them. It also recognized that a ban on cryptocurrencies was very difficult to implement. However, it was concerned that there was a real danger of the public being duped by the cryptocurrency phenomenon and that RBI and the government must issue appropriate advisories to people.

The IMG also noted that some countries had begun experimenting with blockchain technology to issue legal governmental digital currency. It advised RBI to study the matter and present its views at the next meeting.

The Government Spells Out Cryptocurrency Policy in Budget 2018–19

A comprehensive press note was issued by the government in the last week of December 2018, terming cryptocurrencies a 'Ponzi scheme' and warned people of serious losses when the prices of cryptocurrencies collapse.

For its use as currency, the government made a formal announcement of policy in Budget 2018–19. The Budget speech made it abundantly clear that did not 'consider virtual currencies as legal tender or coin' and would take 'all measures to eliminate the use of crypto-assets in financing illegitimate activities or as part of the payment system'.

Differences Emerge

RBI Deputy Governor B.P. Kanungo attended the meeting on 22 February via video-conference. While he was party to the understanding reached at the previous meeting that a ban was very difficult to implement, this time around, he spoke first and argued for a ban on cryptocurrencies. He was strongly supported by Sushil Chandra, chairman, Central Board of Direct Taxes (CBDT), who cited instances of how cryptocurrencies were creating a chain of black money and how even the most uninformed people in the interiors of the country were being lured to buy cryptos. RBI was requested to prepare a paper, including the draft of a law, to ban cryptocurrencies.

Madhabi Buch, the SEBI member, focused on the indeterminate and myriad nature of cryptocurrencies and felt it would be difficult for one regulator to regulate cryptocurrencies. Recognizing the merit of the argument, I stated that even in such a situation the law would have to be one though different aspects would be regulated by different regulators. Madhavi Buch was asked to draft a law recognizing its multifarious nature and the regulatory framework for it.

After arguing that the two primary uses of cryptocurrencies were in the payment system and as investment assets, I stuck to the position that the IMG should continue to develop the option of regulating cryptos as assets. Sawney, secretary, IT, was also in favour of keeping an open mind about the crypto phenomenon.

However, from this point onwards, RBI's drift towards a ban became apparent. While I was also of the same opinion for the use of cryptocurrencies in the payment system as currency, I believed it would be necessary sooner or later to create conducive statutory conditions to regulate cryptos as assets. Accordingly, DEA took it upon itself to draft a regulatory law for cryptocurrencies.

RBI Unilaterally Initiates a Ban

Without further consultations with the committee or even informing it or DEA, RBI issued a notification on 6 April 2018 on 'prohibition of dealing in virtual currencies or VCs'. It used all its statutory powers available under the Banking Regulation Act, 1949, and the Payment and Settlement Systems Act, 2007, to ban cryptocurrencies in India by directing that all 'entities regulated by RBI' desist from dealing in VCs or providing services for 'facilitating any person or entity in dealing with or settling VCs'.

To make it abundantly clear that the services not to be provided were referred to in the widest sense, the notification mentioned services including maintaining accounts, registering, trading, settling, clearing, giving loans against virtual tokens, accepting these as collateral, opening accounts of exchanges dealing with VCs and transfer/receipt of money in accounts relating to purchase/sale of VCs. In short, everyone doing anything with VCs was cut off from the payment and banking system. RBI also directed banks and payment system operators to exit any such relationship, if existing at the time.

The IMG had suggested that RBI propose a draft law to ban cryptocurrencies. After taking this unilateral executive action, RBI did not feel the necessity to propose a draft law, SEBI was also reluctant to propose any draft regulatory law as it did not want to be a regulator for cryptocurrencies. This meant DEA had to do all the work to frame an appropriate legal framework to deal with cryptos working with the resource agency, NIPFP, which also saw the exit of Ashish Agarwal and other senior executives.

Confusion Gets Confounded

The joint secretary, Coins and Currency Division, organized the groundwork for the IMG and for DEA. Anurag Agarwal, who served in this capacity in the first two meetings of the IMG, viewed cryptocurrencies as evil, and took my efforts to bring a balanced debate on the issue as an inclination towards permitting and regulating cryptos. While he could not write the minutes of the meetings as he wanted, he made an anonymous complaint against me after he left DEA in March 2018, prominently highlighting my supposed efforts to legitimize the use of cryptocurrencies in India. Nothing came of this, but it muddied the waters to some extent.

Prashant Goyal, who succeeded Anurag, was more inclined towards regulating cryptocurrencies. From April to June 2018, I waited for CCD and NIPFP to prepare the draft to regulate cryptocurrencies, as decided in the IMG meeting held in February. The idea was to make a consolidated draft later incorporating the 'banning' draft of RBI and the 'definition and classification' draft of SEBI, with the 'regulating' draft of DEA.

I left the work of preparing DEA's draft to Prashant Goyal. He worked closely with the NIPFP team and produced a draft sometime in June 2018. I agreed to convene a meeting of the IMG and approved a date for the meeting without looking at the draft.

Cryptocurrency exchanges hurt by RBI circular of 5 April 2018 filed writ petitions in the Supreme Court. As the apex court was informed by the parties that the IMG was deliberating the issue of banning/regulating cryptocurrencies, it rightly demanded to know what the IMG was doing. Without my specific approval, Prashant Goyal delivered a copy of the draft, tentatively titled 'Crypto-Token Regulation Bill, 2018', to the court.

When I saw the brief along with the draft Crypto-Token Regulation Bill, 2018, a day before the IMG meeting, I was shocked. The bill made only a nominal reference to outlawing private cryptocurrencies but effectively legitimized their ownership and trading in the country by putting in place a regulatory structure. As RBI had spoken publicly by debarring the use of the payment system and banks for transactions in cryptocurrencies, this draft would have been a red herring for them. The draft did not fit in the overall architecture the IMG had in mind either. I postponed the meeting and decided to first hold an internal discussion to clarify our approach.

Setting the Basic Parameters

There was no point in taking the matter to the IMG unless DEA produced, working with NIPFP, a draft bill that it was in full consonance with. I convened a couple of meetings with the officers of DEA and the consultants of NIPFP to get the basic framework and the architecture of dealing with cryptocurrencies right.

In these meetings, we arrived at five fundamental conclusions.

First, cryptocurrencies and distributed ledger/blockchain technology were two different things. Cryptocurrencies, in existence at that time, were meant to be virtual currencies invariably built on the blockchain technology.

Second, distributed ledger/blockchain technology was a digital technology innovation of importance likely to have immense applications in financial markets and products, including to build a system of virtual currencies in place of fiat paper currencies.

Third, cryptocurrencies like bitcoin were intended to substitute official currencies and had serious damaging potential in money laundering and terrorist financing. These were also poor substitutes for official currencies as their value fluctuated violently. Outlawing cryptocurrencies and banning their use as currency was in the larger public interest.

Fourth, most investors in cryptocurrencies and trading and other businesses set up in India around cryptocurrencies were interested in capturing the appreciation in the dollar/rupee price of bitcoins and other cryptos, not using them as currency. Cryptocurrencies, in this sense, were like digital commodities or assets. While the value and appreciation in cryptocurrencies were illusory, it was advisable to regulate cryptos as assets to protect gullible investors from this Ponzi type of asset with violent price fluctuations.

Five, it was time to think of progressing from a physical paper fiat currency to an official digital fiat currency.

I tasked the team of young researchers from NIPFP, which included Nelson Chaudhury, who worked for the US–India Strategic Partnership Forum and, later, Citibank, to make the draft report and bill based on these fundamental features.

IMG Report and Cryptocurrencies Bill Finally Take Shape and Are Adopted

It took the NIPFP team some time to come up with the draft report and bill to meet the expectations I had laid down. It required quite a few meetings and clause-by-clause reading to finally develop a draft report and bill, which I found reasonably satisfactory, sometime in November 2018. The draft bill proposed to ban private cryptocurrencies as currencies, initiate work on the digital rupee as a virtual currency and promote the use of blockchain technology in the financial system. As the primary issue under consideration of the IMG was to ban/regulate the use of private or non-official cryptocurrencies as currencies, the draft bill did not deal with the issue of regulating cryptocurrencies as crypto-assets, but permitted the use of crypto-tokens in a closed loop.

A comprehensive and intensive discussion took place in the next meeting of the IMG held on 9 January 2019. The draft bill, 'Banning and Regulation of Cryptocurrency and Official Digital Currency Bill, 2019', was extensively discussed in this meeting, both in terms of its broader aspects as well as specific clauses.

There was broad support for the draft bill and report. However, Kanungo, deputy governor, RBI, wanted to remove the word 'regulation' from the title of the bill as it could give the impression that some attributes of cryptocurrencies were banned and some regulated. He also wanted to remove the provision relating to the use of cryptocurrencies in a closed loop, which RBI thought could be used to create cryptocurrency-based payment systems by large companies like Amazon for its operations. The SEBI chairman wanted specific clauses on the prohibition of investment and fund-raising through initial coin/currency offerings (ICOs). Both RBI and SEBI wanted the punitive provisions to be strengthened and enforced by the police, not by them. The IT secretary wanted the removal of provisions relating to the regulation and development of blockchain technology, which he felt was the job of the IT ministry.

Over the next few weeks, much to and fro took place with RBI and SEBI. Drafts were improved and modified to accommodate their concerns. The word 'regulation' was shifted in the title to make it applicable only to the regulation of official digital currency. The use of cryptocurrencies in a closed loop was removed at the insistence of RBI, but the draft retained the use of cryptocurrencies for research and development (R&D) purposes.

The report, including the draft bill, was signed by everyone in early February. RBI still held out till the use of cryptocurrencies for R&D purposes was also removed from the bill. Finally, everyone signed the IMG report on 28 February 2019.

My Departure from the Finance Ministry Gets a Crypto Flavour

The IMG report, along with the draft bill, was immediately placed for the consideration of Finance Minister Arun Jaitley. We also proposed to permit its release on the website of the ministry to generate public discussion. Arun Jaitley wanted to see a presentation on the report. We tried to schedule a meeting with him several times even after the elections were announced on 8 March. Despite this meeting being formally scheduled a couple of times, it did not materialize.

After the elections, the new finance minister, Nirmala Sitharaman, scheduled a presentation. After her approval, the IMG report and bill were placed on the website of the Ministry of Finance on 22 July 2019. I tweeted that day: 'Committee is very receptive and supportive of distributed ledger technologies and recommends its widespread use in delivering financial services. It also opens up door for a possible official digital rupee. Private crypto currencies are of no real value. Rightly banned.' [9]

The crypto community took the proposed ban on private cryptocurrencies as currencies as a complete ban on cryptos. The tweet generated a lot of response—165 retweets over the next week. While there were many likes, there was a large hate commentary in 810 comments on the tweet.

Three days later, I handed over the charge of secretary, DEA, and finance secretary. I also announced my decision to take voluntary retirement from the IAS. I tweeted while travelling home from North Block: 'Handed over charge of Economic Affairs today. Learnt so much in the Finance Ministry and Economic Affairs Dept. Will take charge in Power Ministry tomorrow. Have also applied for Voluntary Retirement from the IAS with effect from 31st October. Last tweet from this handle.' [10]

This tweet was liked by over 1,000 people and retweeted 264 times. The comments were fewer, at 289. There was appreciation for my services and good wishes for the future, but the bulk of the commentary still characterized me as an enemy of the crypto community and relished my departure.

The Bill Is Still to Make Any Headway

RBI had separately decided to debar crypto-exchanges from the payment system. In April 2018, it issued a circular that mandated the entities regulated by it not to deal with virtual currencies or provide services to facilitate any person or entity dealing with such virtual or cryptocurrencies. This was challenged in the courts.

In a major judgement on crypto currencies delivered by the Supreme Court on 4 March 2020, the court, relying on, among others, the submission of the preliminary and half-baked first

---

9   https://twitter.com/Subhashgarg1960/status/1153302518815
     834119?s=20
10 https://twitter.com/Subhashgarg1960/status/115435568469
     2992002?s=20

draft of the Crypto-Token Regulation Bill, 2018, held RBI circular unconstitutional. With some reluctance, finally in May 2021, RBI instructed all its regulated entities not to cite its April 2018 circular while providing/or not providing services to crypto-exchanges and other entities dealing with cryptocurrencies.

The government kept mulling over the draft Cryptocurrencies Bill 2019 for many more months after I left the ministry. For the Budget session for 2021–22, the government included a bill named 'The Cryptocurrency and Regulation of Official Digital Currency Bill, 2021' in the list of the twenty bills it intended to move in that session. The text of the bill was not released by the Government.

Fearing that the government might bring in the 2019 bill, which proposed banning private cryptocurrencies, only by changing its title, there was considerable activity in the cryptocurrency and crypto-assets world. The government did not present the bill despite the Budget session transacting record business. The bill was not moved in the following monsoon session in August 2021. The government again intimated its intention to bring up the bill in the winter session of the Parliament in 2021. The bill was not presented in that session as well.

In December 2022, in response to a specific question (unstarred no. 2039 dated 19.12.2022, Lok Sabha) about 'the current state of the crypto-currency bill, which was due for being tabled during the winter session, 2021 of the Parliament' and 'the timeline within which the cryptocurrency bill would be tabled and subsequently be open for public inputs', the government informed: 'Crypto assets are by definition borderless and require international collaboration to prevent regulatory arbitrage. Therefore, any legislation on the subject can be effective only with significant international collaboration on evaluation of the risks and benefits and evolution of common taxonomy and standards.'

While the reply was more cryptic than crypto-currencies are, it was abundantly clear that the government had abandoned the efforts to bring a bill to legislate on and regulate cryptocurrencies and assets.

15

Privatization Policy Falters

THE GOVERNMENT OF INDIA MADE MASSIVE INVESTMENTS IN PUBLIC-sector enterprises and through other state instrumentalities in the production of goods and construction of infrastructure. Most public-sector enterprises were created in the heydays of policy obsession on building a socialist society and nation from the 1950s to the 1970s. Many private enterprises were also nationalized.

The policy changed in the 1990s and the Government of India scaled down new investment in existing enterprises and virtually stopped setting up new public-sector enterprises. From the first decade of the twenty-first century, it started divesting its stake in public enterprises and also privatized a few during 2002–04. The privatization process remained stalled until 2015. Willingness to recommence privatization was indicated in the policy revamp creating the Department of Investment and Public Asset Management in place of the more appropriately named, but non-delivering Department of Disinvestment. The privatization policy was again announced in the 2020–21 Budget.

The Government of India started the monetization of public-sector assets when the shut-down mills of the National Textiles Corporation (NTC) started getting sold in the 1990s. The government has carried out monetization transactions in power distribution, airports and roads since 2005–06. In August 2021, it announced a comprehensive plan for the monetization of public-sector assets, the National Monetization Pipeline.

However, the government still makes considerable investments in existing public-sector enterprises, mostly in sick enterprises or those operating in the infrastructure space. It announced an investment of ₹70,000 crore in two telecom undertakings, Bharat Sanchar Nigam Ltd (BSNL) and Mahanagar Telephone Nigam Ltd (MTNL), in 2019, followed up by a still bigger package in 2022. It also established the National Infrastructure Investment Fund to encourage investment in infrastructure assets with NIIF having skin in the game.

In this chapter, I discuss my policy engagement with the privatization of central public-sector undertakings, monetization of public assets of the government and the organizations it controls, and investment still being made in the public sector and private sector though NIIF.

Abortive Privatization of Air India in 2017–19

The government had announced the privatization of Air India in 2017. A committee chaired by Finance and Expenditure Secretary Ashok Lavasa, of which I was a member as secretary, economic affairs, met a few weeks after I joined to deliberate two major issues on which the Air India privatization transaction essentially hinged. The first concerned dealing with the debt of Air India and how to wriggle out of/structure the guarantees the government (through DEA) had given for certain loans to buy aircraft and facilitate short-term borrowings.

Air India's debt ran in excess of ₹65,000 crore. Its balance sheet for 2016–17 recognized long-term borrowings of ₹33,500 crore, short-term borrowings of ₹12,500 crore, trade payables of ₹9,000 crore and other current liabilities of ₹8,500 crore. Air India was carrying accumulated losses of over ₹47,000 crore, which were funded by these excessive borrowings. Its annual financing cost exceeded ₹4,200 crore, which was eight times its earnings before interest and taxes (EBIT).

Air India had gone through a reform and restructuring programme over the previous five years, with the Government of India infusing about ₹18,000 crore of equity in those years, raising its equity to over ₹27,000 crore, which was 125 per cent of its operating revenue in 2016–17.

There was no way anyone would buy such an equity and cash-haemorrhaging organization. I proposed that we retain only the sustainable debt on Air India's balance sheet and take the rest out to an SPV to be managed and serviced by the Government of India. A debt of over ₹28,000 crore was later transferred to Air India Asset Holdings Ltd. We also agreed to continue the guarantees to the buyer until it refinanced the debt on better terms.

These terms were broadly recommended by the committee and accepted by the Alternative Mechanism (a committee on strategic disinvestment) under the chairmanship of Finance Minister Arun Jaitley. DEA also participated through the joint secretary/additional secretary handling the Investment Division, in an evaluation committee headed by the financial advisor of the Ministry of Finance. The minimum net worth criterion agreed to was ₹5,000 crore and bidders were allowed to form consortiums.

A major issue arose while the evaluation committee was at work. Most Indian scheduled airline operators were making losses and had negative or very small net worth. The civil aviation ministry proposed that the consortium's net worth be so calculated that all Indian airline companies became eligible to participate. This appeared quite unfair and unviable. We objected to the development of such an eligibility criterion. However, to increase potential bidders for Air India, we eventually agreed to an exception in this respect. Indian scheduled airlines could be the lead consortium partner and hold 51 per cent stake in the consortium despite having zero or negative net worth, with the total requisite net worth being made up by the consortium partners. For obvious reasons, foreign airlines were not granted this liberty.

The preliminary information memorandum (PIM) was finally issued on 28 March 2018. Despite waiting with bated breath and making many further concessions, not a single bid came in. The result was the same even after an extension. The effort was finally abandoned. There were no credible ways to find out why no one bid. Informal feedback suggested that the remainder debt was still considered very high and that potential bidders were not interested in the government holding a 24 per cent share, which might lead to government engaging in backseat driving.

Airlines Scene Gets Murkier

The government decided to restructure Air India on the lines it had proposed in the PIM.

To clear and transfer Air India's unsustainable long-term loan liabilities, Air India Asset Holding Ltd was registered and made operational in 2018-19. We placed the joint secretary, budget, on the board of this SPV. I also worked with the debt providers to refinance these borrowings by issuing fully serviced government debt of the SPV. This helped reduce the cost of servicing by over 2 per cent. Despite these efforts, Air India's total debt ballooned to over ₹80,000 crore by the end of 2018–19.

Air India was also required, as per the privatization plan, to transfer most of its non-core assets to the Air India Asset Holding Company. It transferred many of these assets. We wanted these assets to be managed by professional real-estate agencies and wanted to set up an appropriate real-estate investment trust (REIT) for these assets. However, the government permitted Air India management to continue finding buyers for these assets. They were unable to sell any major property, including the iconic Air India headquarters on Mumbai's Marine Drive. Air India Express and two other subsidiaries were agreed to be sold separately, but this was also not done.

By the time I left the Ministry of Finance in July 2019, the PIM for the second bid of Air India was not ready. Considering the state of Air India, at one stage I had proposed that instead of selling it as a company and an active concern, it might be advisable to sell Air India's operating assets, its brand name and bilateral rights. However, this did not gain any traction.

Meanwhile Jet Airways, considered a potential bidder for Air India in 2017–18, also collapsed in 2019. As the lead lender to Jet Airways, SBI tried to find some takers and offered to restructure the debt. When these efforts did not seem to yield any result, I requested the principal secretary to the PM to get SBI to refer it to the National Company Law Tribunal (NCLT). It was taken to NCLT under the Insolvency and Bankruptcy Code. The matter was resolved and new owners found. However, it was taking a lot of time for the new owners to pump in the money. Many new issues also cropped up, which the new owners did not find acceptable. Finally, the lenders decided to call it off; they have moved the court to declare the NCLT award infructous.

The Government Finally Gets Air India Off Its Back

The government came out with another PIM on Air India in January 2020 offering to limit the debt to about ₹23,000 crore and to sell 100 per cent equity. It also issued eleven corrigenda during calendar year 2020 to clarify the bid conditions. Finally, in the month of October 2021, the government sold Air India to the Tata Group at the enterprise value of ₹18,000 crore, which included taking over Air India's ₹15,300 crore debt. The government retained the rest of the debt and some of Air India's assets. For the remainder of Air India, the Tata Group made a payment of ₹2,700 crore. Air India became the first real privatization effected by the government in seven years.

Selling the Public Sector to the Public Sector

The first genuine strategic sale/privatization transaction took place during the first NDA government (1999–2004) when major central public-sector enterprises (CPSEs) like Bharat Aluminium (BALCO), CMC Ltd, Hindustan Zinc, Indian Petrochemicals Corporation Ltd (IPCL), Maruti Suzuki and Videsh Sanchar Nigam Ltd (VSNL) were privatized. This policy was abandoned by the UPA (United Progressive Alliance) government. No privatization transaction took place in the ten years of the UPA government (2004–14).

The NDA Government officially adopted the policy of strategic sale in 2015. The privatization of Air India was part of this policy. However, it was not able to carry out any genuine privatization/ strategic disinvestment until 2017.

During the first flush of privatization during 1999–2004, besides undertaking quite a few genuine privatizations, the government had sold a public oil sector company, IBP Ltd., to another public-sector company, Indian Oil Corporation, in 2002, when the latter came out as the highest bidder in an open bidding process.

HPCL Sold to ONGC without Losing Real Control

Just about the time I joined DEA, the Cabinet Committee on Economic Affairs granted in-principle approval for the strategic sale of the government's 51 per cent stake in Hindustan Petroleum Corporation Ltd (HPCL) to the Oil and Natural Gas Corporation (ONGC) along with transfer of management control to make HPCL a subsidiary of ONGC. This was done to combine the strengths of the two companies that operated in two different streams of the oil and gas business: ONGC upstream, and HPCL downstream. The government was not ready to sell HPCL to private players.

As this strategic sale and purchase was between two CPSEs, it was not a complicated process. The DIPAM, the evaluation committee, a committee of secretaries under the cabinet secretary, Alternate Mechanism, and CCEA went through the motions. The government's stake sale in HPCL was finally approved on 31 January 2018 for a consideration of ₹36,915 crore. Oil and Natural Gas Corporation borrowed to pay the government for its stake in HPCL. However, HPCL refused to acknowledge ONGC as its promoter/owner for many years.

In October 2019 Petroleum Minister Dharmendra Pradhan said ONGC was free to offload its HPCL stake in the market. However, ONGC has not dared to enter the market to sell its stake in HPCL, which would result in the true privatization of HPCL. Meanwhile, it (ONGC) continues to get much less dividend, than the interest it paid out, on the funds it borrowed to buy out the government's stake in HPCL.

REC Sale to PFC: Not Even a Fiscally Beneficial Bargain

Before the close of financial year 2018–19, the government concluded another ONGC–HPCL type of strategic divestment when one of the two power-sector finance NBFCs, PFC, acquired the Government of India's 52.63 per cent stake in the Rural Electrification Corporation for a consideration of ₹14,500 crore. Even in terms of the proceeds it generated for the government, this transaction was much smaller than the other pseudo-strategic divestment of HPCL being sold to ONGC.

Power Finance Corporation had paid a total dividend of ₹2,059 crore in 2017–18, of which the government got a little over ₹1,050 crore. Rural Electrification Corporation had separately paid a dividend of over ₹1,250 crore to the government for that year. Both these organizations are heavily leveraged. With a net worth of around ₹40,000 crore, PFC had lent out more than ₹3.5 lakh crore in 2018–19. With all the net worth fully deployed, PFC had to borrow to pay the purchase consideration to the government.

Both these companies paid over 80 per cent of their dividends in the form of interim dividends. During the year 2018–19, PFC pleaded that it would not be able to pay any dividend to the government, which meant that the government would not get an amount of over ₹1,000 crore. Once the government interest in REC got transferred to PFC, the government would not get the REC dividend—a loss of over ₹1,250 crore per annum.

In the years before this PFC–REC transaction, the companies had faced a tough situation that had resulted in a reduction of their dividend payout. In 2015–16 REC, paid a total of ₹17 per share as dividend, in 2016–17 and 2017–18, it paid only ₹9.65 and ₹9.15 per share as dividend, respectively. At ₹17, the REC dividend would be in excess of ₹2,000 crore to the Government of India per year. This was a fair estimate. In 2020–21, REC paid ₹22 per share as dividend. Similarly, PFC had paid about ₹14 per share as dividend in 2015–16, which came down to only ₹11 per share in 2016–17. For 2017–18, it paid only ₹1.8 per share.

I was concerned. If REC's annual dividend of ₹2,000 crore was getting jeopardized by this transaction, with PFC also probably missing the payment of dividend for some time to come, was a one-time receipt of ₹14,000 crore worth this sacrifice? I raised my doubts before Arun Jaitley, who said I could find any other way to secure the government interest but should not risk the transaction. I told him the dividends from PFC should not be sacrificed.

Atanu Chakraborty had obtained orders from the finance minister that PFC would not pay interim dividend for 2018–19. This was hurting our revenue projections. Atanu was not concerned with either the dividend receipts or the government's overall revenue situation. He was totally focused on meeting his disinvestment target by any means. In another matter, he had started counting the sale of 'enemy' property and shares (these were shares mainly of WIPRO that were seized by the government from people who had gone to Pakistan after Partition) as disinvestment receipts!

Upon my suggestion, the finance minister agreed that PFC would pay interim dividend as per the usual practice. I conveyed this to Atanu Chakraborty and PFC. Atanu went to Arun Jaitley and again obtained an order that PFC need not pay any dividend, which he communicated to PFC. The government did not get an interim dividend from PFC in 2018–19.

My fears were not unjustified. After PFC paying no dividend for 2018–19, the combined entity of PFC–REC paid the government only ₹9.5 per share for 2019–20 as against a combined dividend of over ₹30 per share in 2016–17.

The Ministry of Power refused to concede any control to PFC over REC, and continued to appoint REC's chairman and managing director. As REC was never merged with PFC, PFC did not exercise any real management control over REC. All decisions relating to REC continued to be made by the ministry even after the transfer of the government's entire stake in REC to PFC. The government continues to appoint its nominee director as well as all independent directors on the REC Board.

Not only was the transaction a sham strategic divestment, it also did not make much sense for the government financially.

Disinvestment Proceeds Come in Handy to Cover Some Fiscal Gap in 2017–18

The disinvestment target for 2017–18 was ₹72,500 crore. The government's projection for non-tax revenues was higher by about ₹1 lakh crore for the year. The economy faced headwinds thanks to transitional issues connected with GST replacing myriad central and state indirect taxes in 2017–19. There was also demand for fiscal stimulus.

In this situation, the resources raised by DIPAM, irrespective of their nature, provided some welcome relief. Secretary, DIPAM, Neeraj Gupta was able to carry out market transactions (through offer for sale or OFS and exchange traded funds or ETFs) in a number of companies. The HPCL–ONGC transaction was also a shot in the arm, at least from the resource viewpoint.

A record thirty-five transactions were carried out by DIPAM during the year. These included about five IPOs, over ten buy-backs, a few OFS, including OFS only for employees and by means of ETFs. Neeraj Gupta reluctantly agreed to raise the disinvestment target to ₹90,000 crore in the revised budget estimates. We included a statement in the budget speech that the finance minister expected final disinvestment receipts to exceed ₹1 lakh crore. It happened. When the final receipts were counted by DIPAM, they totalled ₹1,00,057 crore. The year 2017–18 has been the year with the largest disinvestment receipts under the BJP government. After another reasonably satisfactory year in 2018–19, when ₹94,727 crore was received in disinvestment receipts, unfortunately, the government's disinvestment programme floundered with the three subsequent years (2019–20, 2020–21 and 2021–22) receiving only ₹50,299 crore, ₹32,815 crore and ₹13,627 crore, respectively.

DIPAM Got Distracted in Arranging Borrowings for CPSEs

Department of Investment and Public Asset Management's primary mandate is to sell the government's equity in CPSEs. However, Neeraj Gupta wanted to raise debt for them. Buoyed by the success of the

ETFs created by building a pool of shares from a number of CPSEs, he wanted DIPAM to create a debt ETF to raise debt resources for CPSEs. He drafted a proposal and handed it over to me to include in the Budget speech for 2018–19.

The proposal made no sense to me. First of all, why should DIPAM get into raising and managing the debt of CPSEs? Depending on their needs and experience, CPSEs had a well-developed system of raising debt, either as loans from banks and financial institutions or by issuing bonds in the market. There was no value DIPAM could have added to raising debt. On a more fundamental level, the idea of creating an ETF of debt raised by CPSEs with different credit profiles and ratings was bad and unworkable. Why would higher credit-rated institutions agree to borrow at the same rates as the lower-rated CPSEs?

I did not include it in the draft Budget speech. Two days later, when Neeraj enquired about it, I told him I did not find the proposal worthwhile. He was upset and we had an argument. He went to Finance Minister Arun Jaitley, who told me to include it. Reluctantly, I made his debt announcement a part of the ETF programme. The announcement in the Budget speech read: 'The Government introduced Exchange Traded Fund Bharat-22 to raise ₹14,500 crore, which was over-subscribed in all segments. DIPAM will come up with more ETF offers, including debt ETF.'

After the Budget was done, Neeraj created a committee to implement the idea. I placed joint secretary, Budget, in this committee. It conducted deliberations for the next few months, including under the leadership of Neeraj Gupta's successor, Atanu Chakraborty. Despite our opposition, which was based entirely on merit and with the intention to keep DIPAM focused on disinvestment, DIPAM diversified into raising debt ETFs for CPSEs. But, the product that DIPAM blessed, the Bharat Bond Fund, was not the right avenue to raise debt for CPSEs. It became another corporate debt fund, which the mutual fund industry runs in the hundreds. Investors invest in the Bharat Bond ETF, which in turn buys public-sector bonds, already issued, from the market.

The first Bharat Bond Fund ETF was raised in December 2019. It garnered ₹12,000 crore. The second was raised in July 2020, which collected a little under ₹11,000 crore. None of the CPSEs like Power Finance Corporation and Powergrid Corporation, or public authorities like the National Highways Authority of India (NHAI), whose bonds these two ETFs bought, got any fresh borrowings. The bonds the ETF bought were already in the market. The DIPAM contributed nothing to the management of assets of CPSEs. It did not come up with Bharat Bond Fund ETF issues in 2021. In fact, it announced the suspension of equity ETFs as well. An unnecessary diversion into managing borrowings came to a halt only thereafter.

The Government Announces a Big Policy Tweak in Budget 2019–20

The government had been following the policy of divesting small stakes in listed CPSEs by way of selling them directly under the OFS route or building small stakes of a number of CPSEs as part of an ETF. In some CPSEs, the government's stake had already fallen to less than 55 per cent, severely diminishing the ability of DIPAM to offer more stakes, even as small stakes. In Powergrid Corporation, which had the second largest market capitalization amongst listed CPSEs in 2018–19, government shareholding was only 51.34 per cent.

At that time sales of minor stakes were also not yielding any good disinvestment proceeds. Generally speaking, the announcement of minority stake sales was followed by a fall in share prices. The policy was not getting anywhere. Despite the difficulty I faced in putting together the draft Budget speech for 2019–20, I was able to include a paragraph that signalled a material shift in the disinvestment policy. The government signalled willingness to go below 50 per cent in CPSEs.

The government announced in Budget 2019–20 that it would be 'open' to let its shareholding fall 'below 51 per cent to an appropriate level on a case-to-case basis' where deemed necessary, subject to retention of management control. Further, to meet the situation of CPSEs where it was felt that public-sector shareholding should not fall below 51 per cent, the Budget announcement said that the government had 'decided to modify the present policy of retaining 51 per cent government stake to retaining 51 per cent stake inclusive of the stake of government-controlled institutions'.

This announcement marked a threefold deviation from the earlier policy of selling only a minority stake.

First, the government was open to make a strategic sale or privatize by going below a 51 per cent stake, which included selling the complete stake as well.

Second, wherever it was necessary to retain management control, it could go below 51 per cent but retain management control.

Third, it was also agreeable to apply the 51 per cent threshold, taking the composite stake of the government and government-controlled institutions into consideration.

I thought this was a big policy shift. Unfortunately, DIPAM did not follow it up well. The policy announcement died a slow death and was later replaced by the new public-sector disinvestment policy announcement in May 2020 (as part of the Atmanirbhar agenda) that the government would privatize or close every public-sector undertaking except a maximum of four companies in the strategic sector. This new announcement was certainly bolder than the announcement made in Budget 2019–20.

No BPCL Strategic Divestment and LIC Listing Announcement in Budget 2019–20

Sometime in March 2019, Nripendra Misra started a discussion to prepare a meaningful disinvestment agenda for the consideration of the government after the elections. In the first meeting he convened on this matter, Atanu Chakraborty, secretary, DIPAM, was also present. I proposed that the government sell at least one major oil company, the combined general insurance entity and at least 10 per cent stake in Life Insurance Corporation of India (LIC). This, I said, would not only bring in excellent disinvestment proceeds but also establish that the government meant business.

The discussions rolled on. When the time for the Budget came in June/July 2019, I included an announcement relating to these three specific companies in the draft speech. This paragraph was also read out in the Budget meeting chaired by Prime Minister Modi. Some eyebrows were raised about including specific companies—BPCL and LIC—in the announcement, but there was no serious objection from anybody. I took this as confirmation that the government was willing to bite the bullet and make this big announcement on the floor of the House.

The paragraph remained in the draft Budget speech for long. However, a day before the Budget, I was told by Nripendra Misra to remove it from the speech. He assured me, though, that the strategic disinvestment of BPCL was still very much on the cards.

In November 2019, after I had taken voluntary retirement, the government made the big announcement. The cabinet approved a total stake sale in BPCL, excluding the Numaligarh Refinery, which was to be sold to another public-sector undertaking. In addition, the government also announced a stake sale of 30.8 per cent out of its total stake of 54 per cent in the Container Corporation (CONCOR) and its entire stake of 63.75 per cent in the Shipping Corporation of India (SCI).

Many steps were taken out to carry out these transactions. Transaction advisors and legal advisors were appointed, PIMs issued, and RFPs invited. After some postponements, ostensibly on account of Covid-19, some bids for BPCL were received.

The government was reluctant to sort out all the basic policy issues involved. In the case of BPCL, foreign investment rules were tweaked to allow 100 per cent foreign ownership but the regime relating to non-interference in determining prices of diesel and petrol was not reformed and the sale of BPCL stake in Indraprastha Gas Ltd (IGL) and Petronet was not decided.

BPCL privatization was cancelled in 2022–23.

Privatization Policy Receives a Shot in the Arm in 2020

In May 2020, Finance Minister Nirmala Sitharaman spoke about a new PSU privatization policy as part of her announcements under the Atmanirbhar stimulus package of ₹21 lakh crore. She stated that the government would privatize public-sector enterprises in 'non-strategic sectors'. She further announced that a list of strategic sectors would be announced soon and that even in these sectors, only one to four public-sector enterprises (PSEs) would remain.

The government did not follow up on the announcement for quite some time. The distinction between strategic and non-strategic sectors of the economy, in my judgement, is phoney. Indian policy has been fascinated by the notion of 'strategic sectors and enterprises' without ever explaining why any sector or enterprise was or is strategic.

In the heydays of the policy of the socialistic pattern of society from the 1950s to 1980s in India, industrial policy resolutions had identified several sectors as strategic. Investment and operational performance in these large sectors of the economy suffered massively as only the public sector was permitted to establish new enterprises in these sectors. These policies and laws, which produced the so-called low Hindu rate of growth, were gradually done away with after liberalization in 1991. From the vast list of several sectors identified as strategic in 1951, only two sectors currently remain classified as strategic under the industrial policies and laws of the country.

The Department of Public Enterprises conducts an annual survey of CPSEs, classifying them into four sectors and twenty cognate groups. It did not classify any CPSE as strategic in the 2018–19 survey. The phoney nature of the strategic and non-strategic sector debate becomes apparent when one asks a fundamental question: is a sector strategic from the perspective of the economy or from the universe of CPSEs? The classification of any economic sector as strategic was abandoned thirty years ago. Is it that some sectors out of the twenty groups recorded in the CPSE surveys are strategic or is there some other criterion?

Which CPSE can be termed strategic and on what basis? No CPSE wants to be privatized. If you ask the management of CPSEs and the administrative ministries that control them, every CPSE and department would like the CPSE and the sector to be classified as strategic, simply to ward off the possibility of sale. The Ministry of Power would argue that power generation, power transmission and even power distribution are all strategic. The Ministry of Petroleum would argue that all the companies in its sector are strategic. The PSBs would want to be classified as strategic, though none of them were strategic before they were nationalized in 1969. Is telecom strategic enough to retain MTNL and BSNL in the public sector, when they serve less than 10 per cent of subscribers?

There is no sector in which the CPSEs are operating that is really strategic; no CPSE that is strategic; and no objective criteria that can be evolved to define any sector or CPSE as strategic. It leads nowhere. Of course, if you do not want to privatize a particular CPSE, you can always call it strategic. If you don't want to privatize, don't do it, but do not take shelter under the excuse of calling any sector or CPSE strategic.

The finance minister listed certain sectors as strategic in the 2021–22 Budget, without listing the criteria. There was also an apparent contradiction between what the policy said and the companies picked up for privatization. The oil and gas sector is strategic, but BPCL has been put on the block. The insurance sector is strategic, though the government announced it would privatize one general insurance company in 2021–22. Banks are strategic, though the same Budget speech announced the privatization of two banks.

The Privatization Bullet in Budget 2021–22 Did Not Fire

The government finally announced the CPSE privatization policy in Budget 2021–22. There were three planks of the policy. First, strategic sectors were said to include only four groups of sectors: a. atomic energy, space and defence; b. transport and telecommunications; c. power, petroleum, coal and other minerals; and, d. banking, insurance and financial services. This, however, takes out 90 per cent of CPSEs by valuation. There is nothing of value that is non-strategic. Second, in strategic sectors, a bare minimum presence of CPSEs (which was stated to be four earlier) would be retained with the rest privatized, merged, subsidiarized with other CPSEs or closed. Third, in non-strategic sectors, CPSEs would be privatized or closed.

The hollowness of this privatization policy, however, was totally overshadowed by the big bold announcement of privatization of two

PSBs and one general insurance company in budget 2021–22. To signal the serious resolve of the government, the finance minister mentioned that a bill to bring about the necessary legislative amendments to enable privatization of banks would be introduced in the Budget session itself.

I welcomed these announcements and sincerely believed the government could be turning a new leaf. However, there were serious doubts about government actually delivering on these announcements. My fears turned out to be true very soon. The government failed to introduce any bill to amend the Banking Regulations Act and other banking laws in the Budget session of Parliament. For that matter, the amendment bill has not been brought in until the time this book goes to print. All indications appear to confirm that the government will not do it in the current term of the Lok Sabha.

For the insurance company, in place of privatization, the government ended up shoring their capital to make sure that they did not fall foul of the solvency ratio requirement.

In March 2023, the finance minister declared that the government was in no terrible rush to privatize. Forget being in a terrible rush, the government speed on privatization can put a sloth to shame.

16

Getting on the Monetization Bandwagon

NIIF Has a Major Monetization Mandate

INDIA'S FIRST SOVEREIGN INVESTMENT FUND—THE NATIONAL INFRASTRUCTURE Investment Fund—had been launched and its first CEO, Sujoy Bose, appointed in 2016–17 when I was still in World Bank. Bose had worked in the International Finance Corporation (IFC) and had excellent credentials and the requisite experience to make the structuring and roll out of NIIF, a smooth affair. He met me in Washington, D.C. before and after I was appointed secretary, economic affairs. We discussed how to make NIIF functional quickly and get it to sort out and shape up India's infrastructure, both by making investments and developing the right policy framework. It is a hell of a process to create these structures. The kind of documentation needed is mind-boggling. It confirmed my long-held view about the constraints upon the private sector in India in setting up and pursuing businesses.

The NIIF is mandated to invest in greenfield infrastructure projects. It can also bid up and take controlling or minority stake in brownfield projects. The most significant role it played, in my judgement, was to help the government monetize public assets by working with concerned departments and organizations under the broader guidance of the Ministry of Finance to develop the right policy framework, structuring transactions and then participating on a fully competitive basis. This model, I found, was highly suitable and effective for the Indian situation.

Under Sujoy Bose, the NIIF played this role admirably. It helped NHAI and the Ministry of Road Transport and Highways (MoRTH) to structure the toll, operate and transfer (TOT) model to monetize fully constructed road assets. It also participated in the bids after roping in foreign and domestic partners in the joint venture it led. In the first bid, the NIIF did not win despite bidding quite aggressively, as Australian company Macquarie had bid even more aggressively. That was quite fine as the real value addition was to settle the TOT model, not the NIIF getting the concession.

The NIIF worked with the Ministry of Finance, MoCA and AAI to help me translate our vision of airport concessions, as articulated and described in the airport privatization chapter. When we set an overambitious timetable to complete the transaction in four months, even Sujoy felt for a while that we were probably being impractical. However, he and his team pooled in all their abilities and experience to bid for all the six airports offered on concession. The NIIF again bid aggressively. Yet again, the Adanis proved more ambitious. Eventually, the NIIF was second in almost all the six bids; quite close in at least three of these. It offered to take two airports by matching the Adani bid. However, that would have been a violation of tender conditions. Again, I felt the NIIF did its job well. Getting the concessions was not the real objective.

NHAI Brings TOT Proposal to the Board

The economic affairs secretary was on the NHAI Board when I joined the Ministry of Finance. However, for some reason, the outgoing

DEA secretary had decided that this was not advisable. This was possibly as some NHAI cases would come to the PPPAC, headed by him, which could be perceived as some sort of conflict of interest. To me, however, this appeared to be a flimsy reason. The proposal to let the secretary, DEA, leave the NHAI Board had been built-in as part of the Bharatmala Project Cabinet Note, which took about four months' time after I joined to be finally approved and implemented. So I attended the three meetings of the NHAI Board only.

The first TOT proposal came up in these meetings. There was some discussion about whether to structure a big bundle of road assets or go in for smaller bundles. My feedback from the NIIF as well as foreign pension and sovereign funds, indicated that a ticket size of under $1 billion would not interest people much. Ashok Lavasa, who actually chaired the board meeting in place of the NHAI chairman, who is formally chairman of the NHAI Board, felt that NHAI should consider smaller bundles as well to get domestic funds interested.

We decided to go with a larger bundle as policy and also advised NHAI to do a pilot for a smaller bundle.

India Pitches for Brownfield Monetization in G-20

The Argentinian presidency of G-20 had brought up the development of infrastructure as an asset class, as its premier agenda for the meeting of finance ministers and central bank governors. It wanted this to be remembered as its signal contribution to G-20.

As India was building up a brownfield infrastructure asset monetization programme, I proposed very early that the presidency should include the development of brownfield infrastructure asset monetization as a distinct subclass of the broader agenda of development of infrastructure as an asset class. We did a lot of work on the matter. K.V. Pratap, joint secretary, infrastructure, DEA, who represented India on the G-20 working group on infrastructure, pushed this agenda seriously.

Most members were focused mostly on the greenfield infrastructure agenda, on account of lack of standardization of infrastructure contracts and bidding documents, which was considered a difficult asset for financing. While we sympathized with this concern, we were convinced that the enormous variety and risks involved in greenfield infrastructure would make it difficult to develop greenfield infrastructure assets as a standard asset class. There would be too much work required to develop standardization even for sectoral infrastructural asset classes, whether in energy, real estate, pipelines or others.

The Argentinian presidency realized the futility of developing an agenda on greenfield infrastructure as an asset class. It finally settled for framing principles for development of infrastructure as asset class. Though this was adopted by G-20 and we also acquiesced to it after repeatedly pointing out the hollowness of what was sought to be achieved, the principles finally adopted remained buried in the G-20 minutes and papers. Nothing has come out of it.

The monetization of brownfield assets did not get any major traction but it was recognized as a promising area to work on.

The Government Adopts a Monetization Policy in 2019

Finance Minister Nirmala Sitharaman, while announcing the National Monetization Policy (NMP) on 23 August 2021, traced its formulation to her announcement in Budget 2021–22. Recognizing that monetization of 'operating public infrastructure assets is a very important financing option for new infrastructure construction', she had announced in paragraph 47 of her Budget speech that a 'national monetization pipeline' would be launched and an 'asset monetization dashboard' would be created for tracking visibility for investors.

However, the idea of or the policy of infrastructure asset monetization was not hers. Three years earlier, Finance Minister Arun Jaitley had announced in Budget 2018–19 that the 'Government would initiate monetizing select CPSE assets using Infrastructure Investment Trusts (InvITs) from next year'. To operationalize this announcement, DEA had prepared a detailed list of monetizable assets of over ₹3 lakh crore and proposed a policy framework to nudge the line ministries and concerned CPSEs to undertake monetization of their operational assets.

The release of the National Monetization Policy, along with guidelines and the listing of assets (pipeline), is actually the culmination of the process started in 2017—in terms of articulating policy and formally listing monetizable assets in Budget announcements and actual steps/transactions undertaken in monetization of roads, airport and transmission assets.

DIPAM Gets Monetization Policy Mandate

After the announcement of monetization in Budget 2018–19, K.V. Pratap did a lot of work in putting together the Indian and global experience in monetization of brownfield assets, identification of potential infrastructure assets that could be monetized and the likely resources the government could raise through monetization.

After I had finalized and approved the concept paper and the presentation over a few meetings with the Infrastructure Division of DEA, I discussed the matter with Nripendra Misra, who promptly scheduled a meeting to consider the way forward in June 2018. We finalized the list of approximately ₹3 lakh crore of assets that were good for monetization. A major meeting was held at the PMO, attended by representatives of all infrastructure departments and major organizations, including the railways, telecom and GAIL.

The concept of monetization was new to most people in the government in 2018. Except for MoRTH, no one had undertaken a monetization transaction. Almost no ministry or CPSE was enthusiastic about the idea. The railways had always had a fundamental objection to even the idea of corporatization of basic railway services, such as tracks and stations. Yet, the idea of taking the monetization agenda forward was agreed upon. I offered to lead the drive as DEA was the most clued-in organization in this regard. It had been instrumental in developing REITs and InvITs, including the regulatory regime for the same in India. It had carried out all the PPP transactions in the country and also operated the viability gap funding scheme, which enabled many PPP transactions.

Nripendra Misra thought otherwise. Instead of DEA, DIPAM was entrusted with the task of driving the monetization agenda, presumably on the grounds that monetization of public and CPSE assets amounted to management of public assets. I sensed that the decision would probably sound the death knell of the monetization agenda in the country.

DIPAM Got into a Rut of Mimicking the Disinvestment Processes

The monetization agenda got into a slow grind thereafter. The DIPAM viewed monetization as a kind of disinvestment or sale of land and buildings. It proposed a process to carry out monetization transactions that mirrored the process in vogue for disinvestment or privatization transactions. Our comments were requested on the cabinet note prepared to lay down the process for implementing the monetization agenda. I informed the principal secretary and DEA, commenting that the proposed process would take India nowhere.

The process proposed by DIPAM was approved in the rush to clear the pending agenda before the general elections. It was notified on 8 March 2019, a few days before the general elections were announced. The office memorandum prescribed procedure and mechanism of 'asset monetization of central public-sector enterprises (CPSEs), public-sector undertakings (PSUs)/other government organizations and immovable enemy properties'.

This order implemented the decision of the cabinet taken on 28 February 2019 to delegate power in favour of an Alternate Mechanism for granting approval for disposal of assets and to lay down the detailed process for asset monetization. A key prescription in the cabinet decision and the order issued was that the Alternate Mechanism would set a threshold based on the value of asset(s) and/or any other criteria to determine the assets that would be monetized by the government through this mechanism. Assets below this threshold would be disposed of by the concerned administrative ministry/CPSE, etc. Later, in April 2019, a monetization threshold of ₹100 crore was prescribed.

The government prescribed an overly bureaucratic process for asset monetization. Besides the Alternate Mechanism, a Core Group of Secretaries on Asset Monetization (CGAM) was constituted under the chairpersonship of the cabinet secretary to recommend to the Alternate Mechanism the process for asset monetization, threshold value of assets, selection of CPSEs and assets for monetization and the like. An inter-ministerial group was created to carry out exactly the same tasks to make recommendations to the CGAM.

Direct contractual approaches (PPPs of various types) and structured finance approaches (REITs, InvITs, etc.) for asset monetization were listed, along with various means of land monetization, including sale of land and various models that the Department of Public Enterprises had laid out for disposal of assets of closed and sick CPSEs, including disposal of land and other models/approaches like transferable drawing rights (TDRs).

I was still in the Ministry of Finance when these orders were issued. We had initiated the monetization agenda a year earlier. When DIPAM was put in charge, half the life in the monetization agenda got sucked out. When the monetization process was established in March–April 2019 and the thresholds set, it became clear to me that the monetization policy was dead and nothing worthwhile would happen.

Putting Powergrid on the Path of Monetization through the InvIT Route

Amitabh Kant established a process in NITI Aayog to identify and finalize the assets for monetization during the election recess. Young professionals of NITI Aayog worked on all the potential assets earlier identified by DEA. The list of potential monetizable assets also included stadiums like New Delhi's Jawaharlal Nehru Stadium, ONGC's golf courses and a few other sports assets.

The discussions in the meetings Amitabh Kant convened, which I attended, reflected much the same attitude that was seen in the meeting Principal Secretary Nripendra Misra had convened ten months earlier. The sports secretary completely opposed the monetization of sports assets. In the two meetings held between April and June, nothing concrete emerged.

I also told Nripendra Misra that monetization was not moving in DIPAM. Agreeing that DEA had to be brought in the forefront of pushing the agenda, the PMO created a small group under the chairmanship of Amitabh Kant, which included secretary, DEA, as the other key member. By the time this group was to hold its first meeting, I got transferred from DEA.

The first meeting was held in the first week of August. I participated as secretary, power, to speak on behalf of Powergrid and other power companies. Before going to the meeting, I asked K. Sreekanth, director of finance, Powergrid, to let me know how the company could do an InvIT of ₹10,000 crore. The Powergrid team came over and presented a case why the company should not be asked to undertake any monetization by InvIT, or even otherwise.

It took me over forty-five minutes to answer every point raised by Powergrid and clear all the cobwebs. After the discussion, while Powergrid was still not convinced about the InvIT, the team had no argument or reason to justify their lack of willingness. I told Sreekanth, who was also holding the charge of CMD, that I would commit to a ₹10,000 crore InvIT and provide him the government's direction to do it.

The meeting chaired by Amitabh Kant that evening had a very different complexion. Atanu Chakraborty, erstwhile DIPAM secretary, was present as secretary, DEA. I was on the other side, representing a ministry and organization generally reluctant to undertake such transactions. As soon as the meeting opened, I said I had discussed the matter thoroughly with Sreekanth and that the Ministry of Power would commit to an InvIT for ₹10,000 crore to monetize the transmission assets of Powergrid. That was the only monetization transaction committed before the group in that meeting.

I managed to provide Powergrid due approval from Power Minister R.K. Singh. This was in August–September 2019. It took Powergrid more than one-and-a-half years to carry out its first transaction. That was also for half the amount committed in 2019. Powergrid raised

₹5,000 crore in its first InvIT, which was successfully completed in May 2021. Interestingly, it announced thereafter that it would not be doing any more InvITs in 2021–22, though the National Monetization Policy, released on 23 August, set a much larger target for the year from Powergrid. Powergrid did not carry out any monetization in 2022–23 as well.

PPPAC Could Not Resolve the Hyderabad Metro Stalemate

The PPPAC, under the secretary, DEA, decides the modalities and key parameters of PPP transactions besides approving the offer of request for calling bids and the final PPP contract. The Hyderabad Metro project, sponsored by the Andhra Pradesh government and awarded to L&T, was a PPP project for which the PPPAC had approved viability gap funding (VGF) of about ₹1,450 crore in 2013. Such funding goes as a grant and is disbursed linked to the disbursement of debt sanctioned for the project. All the instalments of the VGF, except the last three instalments totalling a little over ₹250 crore had been disbursed by early 2018.

The VGF was determined on revenue calculated on the basis of the tariff determined in accordance with the applicable Andhra Pradesh Tramways Law. In November 2017, the Telangana government (Hyderabad had become part of Telangana) changed the applicable law and allowed the fare to be determined in accordance with the Metro Railways (Operation and Maintenance) Act, 2002. Incidentally, there was no provision in the Central Metro Act to determine the fare for PPP projects. When this material change was made, Joint Secretary Kumar Pratap proposed that the remaining VGF for the project be cancelled and action taken for recovery of the VGF disbursed. I did not agree with this proposal as I wanted to hear the concessionaire and the Telangana government. I only ordered suspension of disbursement of the remaining VGF grant pending consideration of the case.

Metro projects fall in the administrative jurisdiction of the Ministry of Housing and Urban Affairs (MoHUA). Secretary D.P. Mishra took offence to the suspension of VGF instalments. He tried to persuade me to change the decision and disburse the remaining VGF as the project was prestigious, it was the first real PPP in the metros, and that it had faced cost overruns. I said I would be able to do so only if we determined that the change of the applicable law for determination of tariff/fare was legal and the revised viability gap was calculated after taking into account the new fare proceeds.

This did not satisfy him. He took the matter to Nripendra Misra, who felt I was being obstructionist. I stood my ground. The Telangana government also took up the matter aggressively. On the other side, Gajendra Haldia, the conscience-keeper of the nation on infrastructure projects who also claimed to be the author of the Hyderabad Metro concession, wrote letter after letter alleging gross irregularity on the part of the Telangana government and concessionaire Hyderabad Metro Project. His ask was to scrap the VGF and recover the amount released, which was echoed by his one-time director Kumar Pratap.

I convened two meetings over the next three to four months on the matter. However, MoHUA could not convince us that the tariff could be determined legally for the PPP project under the Central Act (though secretary, MoHUA did obtain a legal opinion to that effect through the Ministry of Law). Nor did the concessionaire come clean on the financials. They did not provide financial numbers and computations to convince that the viability gap had gone up in the meantime than the one originally determined, which would justify a higher viability gap funding.

Hyderabad Metro is indeed a flagship PPP project of India. It is also the only private-sector metro project. I was convinced that if the same metro project were undertaken by a company of the Andhra Pradesh/Telangana government on the pattern of other projects in the country, the equity and grant support from the Government of India would have been much higher. Thus, I was in favour of disbursing the entire ₹1,450 crore VGF grant approved for the project. But a case had to be made, at least on the point that the viability gap had not decreased after the change in determination of tariff.

The discussions were still ongoing till the time I left the Ministry of Finance. From the newspaper report, it appears that the Government of India has not agreed to release the remaining ₹254 crore even until now.

The Government's Monetization Track Record

The government has carried out monetization of three kinds of assets in the past three years: NHAI road assets, AAI airports and the transmission line of Powergrid.

Monetization of NHAI road assets using the TOT model started back in 2018. The contract for the first TOT transaction was signed in April 2018 when NHAI concessioned a road bundle of nine select stretches of national highways, approximately 700 km, for ₹9,681 crore to the Australian company, Macquarie Group. Another nine road stretches totalling 566 km were given to Singapore-based Cube Highways for a total capital payment of ₹5,011 crore in November 2019. The NHAI's fifth TOT bundle was a smaller transaction involving a twenty-year lease of two road stretches of 160 km. This was won by two companies, Adani and DP Jain & Co, for an aggregate sum of about ₹2,250 crore. Two TOT transactions— bundles two and four—were cancelled. The NHAI carried out a total of three transactions in the past four years aggregating a total of about ₹17,000 crore until 2021.

In all, the government had been able to monetize a little over ₹25,000 crore in the past four years and about ₹7,250 crore in 2021–22. A target of ₹6 lakh crore or ₹1.5 lakh crore envisaged in the National Monetization Pipeline every year therefore appeared audacious, perhaps impossible.

Structuring Monetization Transaction Is the Real Challenge

Monetization of CPSE assets is more complex than privatization of CPSEs. It involves transfer of an operating asset or a company with operating assets to a private partner. The NHAI keeps most of its road stretches in a single pool of roads. When some road stretches are to be monetized, they need to be transferred to one or more SPVs before they can be bid out. Important decisions need to be taken about the period of concession, kind of rights transferred, regulation of the tariffs, standards of service to be maintained and so on. Moreover, as these are operating assets and their cash flows are known with a reasonable degree of certainty (there would be some scope for improvement but only within a narrow range), the estimation of upside in revenues already being collected from monetization and then a fair sharing thereof are tricky matters. There are also conflicting public policy issues and preferences.

One of the principal reasons why the government has not been able to carry out a second airport monetization transaction since 2019 is the conflict in policy preference—can a single party be given all six airports or should it be limited to a maximum of two or three airports? The first monetization transaction had solved this policy cobweb by leaving it open to a single party to take all the six airports if it bid the highest for each of the six. But this decision is said to be haunting the government since then.

There is another policy confusion. What would happen to the loss-making airports of AAI? While there is no change in the fortunes of AAI if loss-making airports continue to remain with AAI, the government has recently fallen in the trap of bundling loss-making airports with profit-making ones. The monetization of these bundles is going to be extremely difficult. The second TOT bundle of NHAI roads could not find takers as it included some roads in West Bengal where there were problems in collecting toll revenues.

Monetization transactions are for a long period of time. Six airports were given away for fifty years. The shorter the timeframe, the less remunerative the asset becomes for the recipient to make large investments to develop its full potential. Whenever governments have given away assets on long leases, such as the Taj Man Singh Hotel or the Delhi Golf Club, both in the capital— it becomes very difficult for the concessionaire to leave and the government to give it to anyone else. There is no need for the government to be overly defensive while monetizing these assets to assure that the land would come back to it after the period of concession.

There are many questions about the appropriate choice of instruments. Privatization and divestments are simple transactions as these are standard transactions carried out only by selling equity. Monetization requires very comprehensive contracts to be structured and negotiated. The government has been talking about developing standard bid and contract documents for years. There are some basic standard documents for one or two sectors like roads but not for most. Assets differ so much. It is difficult to standardize monetization transactions. It will be extremely difficult to structure these monetization transactions across twenty different asset classes.

Monetization of warehouses, sports stadiums, power plants and ports would present another set of issues. Monetization of FCI warehouses would mean FCI handing them over to private operators to run. It would get a one-time payment but would pay for the services private contractors would render. The risk of mismatch in capital receipts and payment of services has the potential to create enormous problems. Powerplants, if handed over to private concessionaires for operation, would have similar problems. The uncertainties created by the PPAs with state agencies and payment delays would also complicate matters. If the NTPC, which is a reasonably efficient plant operator, were to see its manpower rendered jobless, it might create serious issues.

Implementation Mechanism is Quite Weak

Most of the assets listed in the National Monetization Policy are those of CPSEs. Powergrid has built up transmission lines. GAIL has built gas pipelines. Railways has built railway tracks. And NHAI has built road assets. For their construction and financing, these CPSEs and government organizations have been delegated adequate powers to take decisions in most investments and borrowing. In the National Monetization Policy mechanism, the government is attempting a reverse delegation of powers. All monetization transactions involving ₹100 crore or more are to be structured, processed and approved by the government; ₹100 crore is a pittance. It means almost every monetization transaction would be undertaken by the government while the CPSEs and government organizations would be only bystanders supplying information.

The complex multi-layered institutional mechanism created by the government for overall implementation and monitoring of asset monetization is likely to become a millstone around the neck of the programme. The IMG, the CGAM, the Alternate Mechanism and Oversight Committee, with their non-commercial DNA, are likely to ensure that no transaction is structured commercially and undertaken swiftly. The entire programme is likely to become a victim of process overload and excessive government interference.

The government has said that it is committed to making the asset monetization programme a value-accretive proposition for both the public sector and private investors/developers. However, its inability to structure commercial contracts will lead to all transactions being questioned by the officers involved, auditors and investigative agencies.

The government has said that asset monetization will ensure improved infrastructure quality, operations and maintenance. It is claimed the programme will also help achieve the broader and longer-term vision of inclusiveness and empowerment of common citizens through best-in-class infrastructure and increased investments in infrastructure creation using the proceeds of monetization. This is getting way ahead of the facts. Most monetization proceeds would accrue to the respective organizations/CPSEs. For some organizations, the cost of raising investible funds through traditional modes and monetization would also become an issue as they structure and carry out transactions. The effective cost per ₹1 crore raised by Powergrid through the recent InvIT is likely to be much higher than resources raised through bonds or other borrowings. The monetization proceeds through InvITs for NHAI might turn out to be lower than TOT. As transactions get carried out and these variations come out in the open, there will be a clamour for enquiries and action.

The procedural mechanism created by the government is poorly equipped to handle these issues. When these matters come up for decision, chances are that there would be a lot of passing the buck and upward delegation, with decision-making suffering.

Is the ₹6 Lakh Crore Monetization Plan Getting Delivered?

The ₹6,00,000 crore National Monetization Policy unveiled to the nation on 23 August follows another pipeline, the ₹1,02,50,704 crore

National Infrastructure Pipeline (NIP), launched on 31 December 2019. The NIP was projected to be implemented over a six-year period (2019–25). The National Monetization Policy was prepared for a four-year period (2022–25), to coincide with the NIP timeframe. At ₹6 lakh crore, the estimated value of the National Monetization Policy unveiled was stated to correspond to ~14 per cent of the proposed outlay for the Centre under NIP (₹43 lakh crore).

The NIP indicates estimated capital expenditure on new infrastructure projects (greenfield projects), whereas the National Monetization Policy indicates the capital value the government can recover from infrastructure projects already implemented (brownfield projects) and the capital expenditure the concessionaire (the party to whom the government will transfer specified rights in the brownfield infrastructure project under a contract) would also incur for exploiting the rights transferred. The National Monetization Policy is thus a resource-raising pipeline, whereas the NIP is a resource-spending pipeline of projects.

The National Monetization Policy is quite ambitious in scope in terms of the type of assets proposed to be monetized. As the PIB note and the two volumes of the National Monetization Policy released by NITI Aayog indicated, the policy included more than twelve line ministries and more than twenty asset classes. The sectoral width of assets identified for monetization was impressive: roads, ports, airports, railways, warehousing, gas and product pipeline, power generation and transmission, mining, telecom, stadiums, hospitality and housing.

The National Monetization Policy eyed government assets (such as stadiums), non-commercial organizations and authorities under the government (such as roads of NHAI, warehouses of FCI) and commercial CPSEs (such as gas and product pipelines of GAIL, power transmission lines of Powergrid). Some of these assets have been taken up for monetization in the past (transmission lines, airports and roads). However, some of the assets offered for monetization (railway lines, power-generation plants) were new asset classes.

The top five sectors—roads (27 per cent), railways (25 per cent), power (15 per cent), oil and gas pipelines (8 per cent) and telecom (6 per cent)—captured approximately 83 per cent of the aggregate estimated pipeline value. The National Monetization Policy envisaged a 15 per cent monetization target to be achieved in financial year 2021–22, which implied that the government should be able to monetize assets worth about ₹88,000 crore in that year. The target for 2022–23 was ₹1,62,422 crore, for 2023–24 it was ₹1,79,544 crore, and for 2024–25 it was ₹1,67,345 crore.

A serious analysis done immediately after the NMP was unveiled indicated that the government would find it extremely hard to undertake monetization of railways, gas and oil pipelines and telecom assets. Achievements in roads and the power sector would also be much smaller given the state of play in the sectors. I estimated and wrote that the government was unlikely to achieve more than 20 per cent of the target.

The experience of 2021–22 and 2022–23 has proved the same. The government could not undertake even a single transaction in railways, gas and oil pipelines and the telecom sector. Even in the power sector, no second transaction after the one by Powergrid was undertaken. The road programme has also been underwhelming.

The government has not brought out NMP progress reports. Occasionally, there have been some informal briefings claiming 50 to 70 per cent achievement of NMP targets. However, no sectoral data is provided. The government has reportedly included grant of coal concessions as monetization. The grant of mining concessions by auctions is not monetization.

Privatization, Monetization, or Both?

In her press conference, Finance Minister Nirmala Sitharaman was at pains to emphasize that asset monetization was not privatization and that the government was not selling these assets. The opposition leaders slammed the government and the monetization pipeline as selling the family silver and handing over valuable assets created in seventy years to friends and relatives of the ruling party.

The government had announced the policy of strategic disinvestment in Budget 2021–22. Strategic disinvestment is nothing but privatization. It had also boldly announced in the Budget that it would undertake privatization of two PSBs and one general insurance company in 2021–22. In addition, the government was quite confident that the strategic disinvestment of BPCL, Air India, SCI, CONCOR, IDBI Bank, BEML, Pawan Hans and Neelachal Ispat Nigam would be completed in 2021. The strategic disinvestment policy of the government had declared that in all sectors classified as strategic, a bare minimum presence of public-sector enterprises would be retained and the remaining CPSEs would be privatized, merged or subsidiarized with other CPSEs or closed; CPSEs of non-strategic sectors would be either privatized or closed.

In the face of the announced policy of strategic disinvestment and privatization of at least ten major financial and non-financial CPSEs, why was Finance Minister Nirmala Sitharaman at pains to stress that the government was not undertaking any privatization of CPSEs and other assets?

Following policies based on the socialist pattern of society and placing the 'commanding heights of the economy' in the public sector, the Government of India built many CPSEs that finished off or stymied the growth of the private sector in most sectors, which was further constrained by the policies of the licence and permit raj. After liberalization was adopted from 1991, the private sector made deeper inroads in most sectors where CPSEs operate, reducing the latter to insignificant and inefficient players.

In telecom, the earlier monopoly DOT/BSNL is down in the dumps (the government had to sink in ₹70,000 crore to keep it afloat though it still keeps turning out massive losses every year). The CPSEs are fast losing market share in banking, insurance, power generation, power transmission and so on. There is no economic or public policy rationale not to privatize or close these CPSEs. There are some profitable and comparatively well-managed CPSEs as well—NTPC, Powergrid, BPCL—but there is no economic or public policy rationale for these companies also to continue operating with government ownership.

Most infrastructure, like roads, sports stadiums and railways, was a public good until it was figured out that these assets could operate better under concession arrangements with the private sector. Some of these infrastructure assets could be profitably run and others could see government expenditure reduced with the better operating efficiency of the private sector. This gave rise to PPP, or public-private partnership, structures. Infrastructure assets have been entrusted to the private sector all over the world under various forms of PPP.

In India too, numerous infrastructure assets have been constructed by and handed over to the private sector under PPP arrangements. Roads have been constructed under build-own-operate-transfer (BOT) arrangements where the private sector has invested in constructing the roads and operating them, collecting government-approved tolls to recover its capital investment and make profits. The government has also handed over roads constructed by NHAI under the TOT scheme to the private sector. In fact, NHAI was able to monetize roads worth about ₹15,000 crore in three TOT transactions undertaken in the past three years. Greenfield airports have been constructed by private operators (Cochin, Bengaluru, Hyderabad) under PPP arrangements. The government has also handed over AAI airports to the private sector under the OMDA model of PPP, beginning with Delhi and Mumbai in 2006 and six airports (Ahmedabad, Mangalore, Thiruvananthapuram, Jaipur, Lucknow and Guwahati) in 2019.

There is no reason for the government to continue in business. Its responsibility is to deliver public goods, formulate policies for businesses and redistribute income from the rich to the poor. Operating businesses is none of its business. It is a waste of fiscal resources and governance. Privatization is the most appropriate model and the need of the hour for the government to get out of most CPSEs producing goods and services; PPP (both greenfield and monetization) is the most appropriate model for creation and operation of infrastructure assets. The government need not be defensive about either privatization or monetization. It has to adopt both means to serve the country.

What Can Be Done to Better Design and Execute the Monetization Programme?

First and foremost, a clear distinction must be made between government assets and CPSE assets, or non-commercial and commercial assets. Stadiums and FCI godowns are non-commercial assets whereas transmission lines, airports, railway tracks and stations are commercial assets. Except for a promotional and monitoring role, the government should have nothing to do with the monetization of commercial assets. It is the job of the CPSEs and the organizations concerned. It should be left to them.

Second, the government should dismantle the decision-making structure created copying the disinvestment process. Disinvestment relates to equity owned by the government. It is entitled to create an appropriate mechanism to carry out the divestment of equity, including strategic divestment. Operating commercial assets are the assets of the organization concerned. The government should manage its assets, not those of CPSEs. Therefore, the Alternate Mechanism–CGAM–IMG mechanism should be dismantled for CPSEs. Even for government assets, monetization is akin to the creation of PPP. There is a much better evolved process under the rubric of PPPAC in DEA. The monetization of government assets should be brought under the purview of PPPAC. The Alternate Mechanism created for the monetization programme should be completely abolished.

Third, DEA has been instrumental in evolving most monetization mechanisms, like REITs, InvITs and the OMDA model. It is also the administrative department for SEBI, the capital markets and operation of the financial system. Further, it deals with FDI and FPI. The DIPAM has the limited task of selling government equity in the CPSEs. Monitoring of the asset monetization programme should be handed over to DEA.

Fourth, the government should clearly lay down that the proceeds of monetization belong to the organization that owns the assets and that the government has no intention of taking over even a single rupee for its purposes, directly or indirectly. The CPSEs/organizations concerned should have full liberty to assess the relative financial advantage of asset monetization vis-à-vis traditional ways of funding further infrastructure creation. These organizations should also have complete freedom to choose the model of monetization that suits them best. The government should only focus on selling off/privatizing CPSEs that cannot operate competitively and profitably.

17

Government Still Invests More Than It Disinvests

Getting NIIF Off the Ground

IN JULY 2015, THE GOVERNMENT DECIDED TO SET UP THE NATIONAL Infrastructure Investment Fund, an alternative investment fund (AIF), as India's sovereign wealth fund (SWF) to principally provide equity support for infrastructure projects. The government committed to provide ₹20,000 crore (about $3 billion) initially to take a 49 per cent stake in NIIF to build a corpus of about $6 billion. The NIIF was to be set up as a Category II AIF with a trust structure. Its assets were to be managed by NIIF Ltd, registered under the Companies Act, 2013, and SEBI approved the establishment of NIIF in December 2015.

The NIIF was still to get its first investor when I took over as secretary, DEA, and chairperson, NIIF. Working with CEO Sujay Bose and a team from IDBI Capital, all the requisite documents and policies were finalized. To get 51 per cent investment in NIIF, the government had earlier approached LIC to take a 10 per cent stake and the Abu Dhabi Investment Authority (Adhia) to be a major investor.

We decided to first finalize the fund structure. It was agreed there would be three funds: a Master Fund, a Strategic Opportunities Fund and a Fund of Funds. Most infrastructure investments with a time span of five to seven years would be made from the Master Fund. Long-term, somewhat riskier investments where the policy structure was still evolving would be made from the Strategic Opportunities Fund. The Fund of Funds would take a stake in other funds set up to serve the investment objectives of NIIF. The NIIF Trust, therefore, would be a combined entity of three separate trusts for each fund. The government had initially registered the Master Fund as NIIF. This was corrected and three trusts registered in due course.

We decided to split the ₹20,000 crore government investment between the three funds. The size of the Master Fund was kept at $2.1 billion with the government contributing $1 billion equivalent. It was also decided that the government would retain a 49 per cent stake in NIIF Ltd and the position of investment manager and give other investors in the Master Fund the opportunity to hold a majority stake. We aimed to get foreign sovereign funds and pension funds in a major way in the Master Fund. It was agreed that such foreign investors should hold a 49 per cent stake as well. The remaining 2 per cent was to be offered to Indian financial institutions.

With the broad structure of financial contribution decided, we decided to reach out to investors. LIC had never made an investment in AIFs. It was not sure what this new animal was. LIC Chairman V.K. Sharma was evasive and diversionary whenever the topic was discussed. We decided to leave out LIC. I wrote to the heads of Indian financial institutions. ICICI Bank, HDFC, Kotak Mahindra Bank and Axis Bank enthusiastically responded. The 2 per cent stake was split between these four institutions.

The Abu Dhabi Investment Authority (ADIA) was the first foreign domiciled SWF to commit to investing in the Master Fund. In October 2017, we made the first close of NIIF with Mubadala, an associate of ADIA SWF, with an investment of $300 million.

We wanted Singapore SWFs GIC and Temasek to come on board as well. It took some time. With Temasek committing $100 million, the second close of the Master Fund was completed in September 2018.

We worked with pension funds in Australia and Canada to pitch in the remaining funds. With Australian Super and Ontario Teachers' Pension Fund each committing $250 million each, the third close was completed in August 2019 (the transaction was fully structured but was formalized after I left DEA in July 2019). With this, about $900 million of the targeted $1.1 billion was in the kitty. Finally, with two more closes in December 2019 and December 2020, NIIF closed the Master Fund at $2.34 billion.

We targeted multilateral institutions like the NDB, Asian Development Bank (ADB) and Asian Infrastructure Investment Bank (AIIB) to invest in the Strategic Opportunities Fund. The AIIB was the first to respond with a proposal to invest $200 million. Its chief, Jin Liqun wanted to use this strategic investment to get India to agree to some governance misadventure he wanted to effect in AIIB. I have recounted the story of AIIB wanting to concentrate all project approval authority in the hands of its president in a subsequent chapter on India's economic engagement with the rest of the world. As we did not play ball, the investment in the Strategic Opportunities Fund was reduced to $100 million. This was fine with us.

The Strategic Opportunities Fund made its first strategic acquisition in July 2019 when it bought IDFC Infrastructure Finance Ltd, an infrastructure debt NBFC, to create an infrastructure debt financing platform. Both ADB and NDB also made investments in the Strategic Opportunities Fund after AIIB. I could facilitate NIIF's Fund of Funds' investment in a renewable energy fund, the Green Growth Fund, jointly established by NIIF and the UK Treasury.

It is quite a laborious process to structure and launch an AIF incubated by the Government of India, more so, if the ask is to get foreign SWF and pension funds to invest in such a fund with the government's presence being a massive 49 per cent stake. The expectation from the government was that NIIF would start dispensing loads of money within a few months of it being announced. That was an entirely impractical ask. In the first meeting of NIIF's Governing

Council, DFS Secretary Anjali Duggal said she wanted NIIF to pump in money in stalled real-estate projects in NOIDA and elsewhere.

The NIIF made its first investment in January 2018, when it partnered with DP World to create an investment platform for ports, terminals, transportation and logistics in India named Hindustan Infralog Ltd. The pace of investment disappointed the PMO. Nripendra Misra discussed this with me a couple of times. Twice, I organized a presentation from Sujoy Bose for the PMO. The concept and rollout of an AIF was perhaps too complicated for the team.

Once, sometime in July 2018, Nripendra Misra told me the government was contemplating appointing Haseeb Drabu, former J&K finance minister, as chairman of NIIF. I told him the PMO could go ahead if it thought he could push faster execution of NIIF, but again explained what it requires to set up an SWF like NIIF and how important it was that the team be allowed to make all investment decisions as they had to earn enough returns to satisfy the foreign investors. The NIIF was not a public-sector bank.

The PMO did not proceed with the replacement. I continued to be chairman of NIIF until I left DEA in July 2019. Over time, other renowned professionals joined the board of NIIF Ltd. By September 2021, NIIF had completed five years of its existence and developed a good portfolio of assets under management, exceeding $4.5 billion.

Equity investment is a far more serious business than debt and more susceptible to wrong decision-making. So far, no investment made by NIIF has been questioned for its soundness.

Corporatize NHAI for Investment Efficiency

Infrastructure assets are almost always organized in SPVs to specifically house investments made therein, debt taken and revenue receipts. The SPVs help in better valuation of infrastructure assets, their financing, servicing and, if required, divestment.

Road assets are such infrastructure assets. Most private-sector entities that have taken road projects on BOT or any other basis have also housed them in SPVs. Many private investors in road assets have been able to raise equity for their projects and monetized the same by transferring these assets/companies to InvITs and other monetizing structures. Even those who mismanaged their road assets, like IL&FS, could get the right valuation of the SPVs holding these assets.

Unfortunately, the NHAI, following the model of the state public works departments (PWDs), treated road projects as a common expenditure proposition. It would raise bulk finance from the government by issuing corporate bonds or taking corporate loans from LIC and other financial institutions. It was impossible to identify specific investment on a road project, its revenue stream and profitability or loss being made thereon.

When the proposals for Budget 2018–19 were being discussed in the PMO, I proposed that both NHAI and AAI be corporatized. There was enthusiastic support from Tarun Bajaj, who was joint secretary in the PMO. However, immediately after this discussion, MoRTH went into overdrive to oppose the proposal. A few weeks earlier, Road Minister Nitin Gadkari had publicly spoken about corporatizing NHAI. He was also persuaded to backtrack. With this strong opposition, the PMO gave up. Nripendra Misra told me to drop the proposal. Instead, monetization of infrastructure assets was to be addressed in the Budget.

The NHAI's finances were in a deep hole. In 2018–19, I presented the true state of NHAI's finances to the government. This led to the PMO restraining the unabated expansion of national highways in the garb of 'in-principle' approval. The NHAI was also asked to set its finances in order. I attempted to persuade the NHAI chairman and officers to change the structure and management of their road assets by creating an appropriate number of SPVs and placing all the road assets in one or the other SPVs. They promised, but did not do anything.

The NIIF worked with NHAI to create a separate SPV for the new Delhi–Mumbai Expressway with a completely new alignment and offered to part-fund the same. When I presented my 100 points of reform to Prime Minister Modi in early August 2019, I again proposed to turn NHAI into a road asset management company. Noting that it was completely 'logjammed', I proposed NHAI be asked to place all its road projects in an appropriate number of SPVs and the completed road assets auctioned on TOT basis. I contended that NHAI should undertake projects mostly on BOT basis so that under-recoveries in road construction are known right at the beginning.

My proposals (without identifying me) were sent by Principal Secretary Nripendra Misra to the roads secretary with his covering letter to take action or comment upon. These suggestions found their way to the media. The ministry asked NHAI to streamline its road asset management system but nothing came of it.

In fact, instead of being corporatized and made a commercial entity, NHAI has become 100 per cent dependent on budgetary support now. Its access from market was literally withdrawn in 2021–22, when government decided to meet its 100 per cent requirement of funds from the Budget. NHAI is a 100 per cent government dependent organization now.

Don't Waste Money on BSNL and MTNL

Secretary, DEA, is a member of the Telecom Commission (later renamed the Digital Communications Commission or DCC). Sometime in December–January 2018–19, the Department of Telecommunications (DoT) which services DCC, brought a proposal of a revival package for BSNL and MTNL for the consideration of the DCC for recommendation to the government. I severely questioned the proposal and essentially ticked them off by noting that there was no rationale for the government to revive BSNL. Aruna Sundararajan, secretary, DoT, tried to plead their case. Other members were sympathetic to BSNL but did not strongly support it. At the end, it was officially noted that BSNL would rework its proposals.

A few days later, Aruna Sundararajan told me that the proposals were discussed in the PMO and she had been asked to move a cabinet note on the matter. She wanted the proposal to be approved by DCC first. I reiterated that there was no rationale in these proposals and if the Ministry of Finance had to record its views, it would be better if it did so by commenting on the draft cabinet note. I refused to agree to the proposals in the DCC. She dropped the idea of taking the proposal to the DCC and instead circulated the draft cabinet note.

In one of my discussions with Nripendra Misra, I brought up the subject of the revival package of BSNL and MTNL. I said it amounted to throwing good money after bad. It made no sense for BSNL to establish networks for 4G after other companies had already done so. As BSNL was fast losing consumers, it was unlikely it would get consumers to shift from other operators. I also said that it was unfair and a market distortion if BSNL and MTNL were given a 4G licence and spectrum free when others were expected to pay a good amount for the same.

For some reason, Nripendra Misra was completely convinced that there was a strategic need for BSNL and MTNL to continue to exist. Apparently, no cost was too large for this. When I tried to argue, he told me no arguments would work. He quoted some old cases, especially the award of a fertilizer plant to Italian firm Snamprogetti despite the opposition of the secretary at the time. I said I should at least have the freedom to record my views in the matter on file, as perhaps the fertilizer secretary of that time had done. He said I was free to do so, however, whether I liked it or not, the government would approve the revival package of BSNL and MTNL.

When the draft cabinet note was received, I recorded a comprehensive note highlighting the sheer waste of fiscal resources the proposal would lead to. I also noted that BSNL and MTNL had not been successful even in acquiring technologies and equipment in the past and they probably would not be able to do so this time and, therefore, there might not even be any technical revival. I recommended that the proposal not be approved by the cabinet.

The finance minister approved my note. This possibly led to the proposal not being discussed by the cabinet before the declaration of the general elections. After the elections, the comments of DEA were again requested with the approval of Nirmala Sitharaman, the new finance minister. She also approved DEA's comments. The proposals were not approved until I was in the Ministry of Finance.

Eventually, the revival package of ₹69,000 crore was approved in October 2019. Much fiscal expenditure has taken place with the

BSNL and MTNL staff getting a bonanza in the form of the voluntary retirement scheme (VRS). The package had proposed a merger of BSNL and MTNL, which has since been dropped. The cost of the package was to be part-funded by selling the land and buildings of the two companies. The DoT and DIPAM kept sparring and passing the blame for not being able to sell any asset. Both BSNL and MTNL could not award contracts for 4G technology and equipment.

In July 2022, the government came out with another package of ₹1.64 lakh crore for reviving BSNL/MTNL. The government took out these companies from market and started meeting all their equity and debt needs from the Budget. Thousands of crores of tax-payers' money has been pumped in BSNL, yet there is no turning around. BSNL continues to be the largest loss-making public-sector company. Its market share is down to less than 10 per cent. Even in the fixed line business, it has slipped to third place.

Government Investment in Indradhanush Gas Grid

Five public-sector enterprises, Indian Oil Corporation (IOC), GAIL, Oil India, ONGC and Numaligarh Refinery, contributing a 20 per cent share each, formed the Indradhanush Gas Grid Ltd (IGGL) to lay down a 'gas grid' in the Northeast. The project was estimated to cost ₹9,265 crore and the government was to provide viability gap funding of 60 per cent of the cost or ₹5,559 crore. The company was registered sometime in August 2018 and Prime Minister Modi had laid the foundation stone of the project in Guwahati on 9 February 2019.

Sometime in late February, Brajendra Navnit, joint secretary in the PMO, called me to check whether I had seen the proposal for the project. I checked and found it had not come to DEA and had been cleared by the expenditure department. I also collected the basic details of the project. After a short while, I informed him of the facts and my first impression that the government was being ripped off.

An official letter came from the PMO the next day asking me to examine the facts of the project and give my report. A meeting with Petroleum Secretary M.M. Kutty and the heads of IOC and GAIL brought out all the facts. The pipeline project was basically intended to provide natural gas to the Numaligarh Refinery to be used in place of fuel. There were some populist eye-catching proposals, like providing piped gas to state capitals like Kohima in place of LPG cylinders. Considering the fact that the population was so small and LPG was an equally good fuel and more convenient to deliver in hilly terrain, it did not make sense from this perspective as well.

I sent my report with the finding that the project was utterly unjustified and designed to make the government cough up fiscal funds for providing gas as fuel to the Numaligarh Refinery. I suggested that the government not provide any subsidy to this project and if the project proponents wanted to go ahead with it, they should do so at their cost. This led to the project being placed in cold storage.

It was later revived and approved on 8 January 2020, in its original form.

BPCL Investment in Mozambique Gas Field Difficult to Digest

When the country was in the midst of general elections, the Ministry of Petroleum and Natural Gas (MoPNG) brought a proposal before the Committee of Secretaries (CoS) headed by NITI Aayog Member Secretary Amitabh Kant in April 2019. The proposal asked for its recommendation for an investment by a BPCL subsidiary, Bharat Petro Resources Ltd (BPRL), over and above its originally approved limit towards its share of cost in an offshore block in a gas field in Mozambique. The note mentioned that BPCL/BPRL was also negotiating with the operator of the field to buy the natural landed cost of about $9 per MMBtu.[11] No approval was sought for this.

The proposal raised my eyebrows. Petroleum and natural gas assets had fallen in value all over the world after the heydays of 2007–09. The investment of BPCL/BPRL must have devalued materially. Was it wiser to make further investments? Buying gas at $9 per MMBtu when the landed cost of gas prices had fallen to around $4–5 per

---

11 MMBtu = Metric Million British Thermal Unit

MMBtu seemed outrageous. I also did not have all the facts relating to the investments made by Indian companies. Further, there were reports that the main investor Anadarko had sold its stake in the field to another company sometime back.

Most members thought that MoPNG and BPCL were the best to judge the advisability of the investment and they were not asking for any financial support from the government. However, I felt I needed to know the full facts. I raised all these questions in the meeting. The BPCL/BPRL officials tried to say that there was volatility in oil and gas prices and the $9 price was cost-based. If there was any surplus profit at any stage, it would come back to them as a share of profit being the owner of the block. We were also informed that Indian companies (Oil India Ltd [OIL], ONGC and BPCL) together owned a 30 per cent stake in the company. If BPCL/BPRL did not agree to provide the additional cost, the contract provided that their original investment would stand forfeited. Finally, we were informed that ONGC, which was also to make additional payments, had agreed to do so as the amount required was covered under its original approval.

While I agreed to recommend the case to the cabinet, I made the CoS record categorically the facts/position as stated by the MoPNG/BPCL in the cabinet note with a request to the cabinet to take a decision after considering these. When the note, with these observations, reached the PMO, their antennae were raised. I was asked to explain the matter to them, which I did.

This led to the formation of a Group of Ministers (GoM) headed by Home Minister Amit Shah, with the finance and petroleum ministers represented. In the first meeting of the GoM, after the petroleum secretary had made a formal presentation, I was asked to provide my assessment. I said it was a case of Hobson's choice. There was already considerable loss in the investment. Investing more would most likely increase the losses. However, if it was decided not to make any further investment, the initial investment would stand completely lost. The decision should be based on what led to fewer losses.

The home minister asked whether the petroleum secretary had seen all the records relating to when BPCL had made the initial investment of a 10 per cent stake. M.M. Kutty was not fully sure.

He promised to look into it. The home minister then asked whether it was true that BPCL was initially offered a 20 per cent stake and took only 10 per cent. This was extremely significant in view of the fact that BPCL had got the initial 10 per cent stake for only about $75 million whereas Videocon, which purchased the 10 per cent stake not taken by BPCL at about the same price, later sold it to ONGC for close to $2.5 billion.

M.M. Kutty checked the record. He did not find anything there. Another meeting of the GoM was held. The whole issue had acquired an entirely different hue. Again, no decision was taken.

Later, sometime in September 2020, approval seemed to have been granted as per a news report, with the condition that CBI would investigate the matter. In April 2021, French energy company Total SE, which was the lead operator of the field, suspended the project citing force majeure on account of violence in the area, and literally abandoned the project.

Global disruption in gas markets and shortage post the Russia–Ukraine war seems to have re-energized interest in the Mozambique gas-field. Indian public-sector investors have also become active. However, nothing seems to have really fructified.

18

Taming the IL&FS Bull

THE REFORMS OF THE 1990S OPENED INFRASTRUCTURE—ROADS, POWER, urban development, industrial parks—to private enterprise. Infrastructure development, however, required land, water and other concessions from the government. Further, the nature of infrastructure investment was very long-term—investments were upfront whereas returns came over many decades; in many cases. returns were not adequate to pay back investments. Viability support from the government appeared essential for investment to be made in infrastructure. The infrastructure sector was also highly controlled and regulated.

Considering the very nature of infrastructure investment—long-term and risky—the private sector did not come forward to invest. The government developed a PPP model for most infrastructure sectors, provided regulated and guaranteed returns or provided support with viability gap funding. The peculiar nature of infrastructure development led to the formation of the Infrastructure Leasing and Financial Services Corporation (later IL&FS).

The government supported the creation of IL&FS in the late 1990s and the first decade of the twenty-first century and structured it as a private-sector company with its equity being subscribed to primarily by PSBs, IFC, LIC, etc. The Banking Division of DEA incubated IL&FS. After this division was spun off as a full-fledged Department of Financial Services, matters concerning IL&FS were allocated to DFS.

The government provided all kinds of support to IL&FS. It got loans from multilateral institutions such as the World Bank, ADB and IFC, for IL&FS's infrastructure projects. As infrastructure development involved intricate issues of land management, concessions and interface with the government in different forms, many IAS and other officers went to IL&FS on lucrative deputation terms. Entry 13 in the Allocation of Business Rules, mentioning 'matters relating to Infrastructure Development Finance Corporation (IDFC) and Infrastructure Leasing and Financial Services (IL&FS)'— still described this work as allocated to DFS in 2018.

IL&FS was nurtured by some intrepid professionals, Ravi Parthasarathy and Hari Sankaran in particular. They brought enormous innovation to structuring infrastructure projects and got financing for them. IL&FS permeated many departments/ministries of the Government of India (principally sourcing equity and policy support for projects like textile parks, food parks, road development and so on), and in the state governments (roads, power, GIFT city and many others). Over the years, it evolved into a behemoth with 169 Indian companies undertaking numerous infrastructure projects. Somewhere down the line, hubris and overconfidence got the better of these IL&FS pioneers and they not only made highly risky bets but, in some cases, leveraged frauds, not innovations.

Hari Sankaran met me for the first time in 2002 when IL&FS wanted to cancel the unused funding of a World Bank-financed project in the urban sector. I found him highly motivated and persuasive. Cancellation of the line of credit from the World Bank, though unusual, was fine as it saved commitment fees. Later, we crossed paths in connection with a road sector company, RIDCOR, in which the Rajasthan government had an equity stake and had also committed to provide a loan. We also had very intense interactions for the Bhamashah Project of Rajasthan—a multidimensional identity, a direct benefit delivery project, a precursor of the Aadhaar project of the Government of India.

The two IL&FS leaders—Ravi Parthasarathy and Hari Sankaran— had developed the reputation of selling dreams to state governments and taking land, equity and financial support from them at terms highly favourable to IL&FS. I had not allowed their designs to succeed in the Bhamashah project.

Hari Sankaran Came Calling with an SOS

One Friday in the middle of September 2018, Hari Sankaran called to say he wanted to see me urgently. He came alone with only a few sheets of paper. In sum, he told me IL&FS was facing an enormous liquidity problem and needed the government's support to nudge LIC or SBI to lend it ₹10,000 crore for some time against its assets. He wanted this to be arranged in a day or two; otherwise, he said, IL&FS might default.

A few days earlier, market perception about the difficulty in terms of liquidity faced by a major housing finance company (DHFL) and a fund had led to the yields on their papers spiking sharply. Rising crude oil prices and the tight monetary policy RBI had been following had not only created a liquidity squeeze in the financial markets but had also raised the yields on government borrowing to over 8 per cent. A default by IL&FS, a massive NBFC and AAA-rated infrastructure powerhouse, would surely upend the financial markets.

Hari Sankaran insisted IL&FS was perfectly solvent. It had assets exceeding ₹1.2 lakh crore whereas its total debt was less than ₹80,000 crore. He also said the government had over ₹10,000 crore to pay IL&FS. He said he was close to concluding a deal for selling some of IL&FS's assets to raise this much money, but something cropped up that scuppered the deal. He also said they had plans to raise equity on a rights basis, which would be considered by the IL&FS Board early next month.

I was not prepared to accept what Hari Sankaran said at face value. At the same time, I did not want a situation where IL&FS defaulted purely on account of liquidity problems. I wanted more details. I also wanted to hear from the CFO of IL&FS. We agreed that Hari and the IL&FS CFO would visit me the next Monday to go over the numbers and assess the liquidity situation based on IL&FS's documents and financial details.

India Faced a Lehman Moment?

The next day in the forenoon, Nripendra Misra, principal secretary to the prime minister, called me to say he had received an alarming report about the state of affairs in IL&FS. I thought Hari Sankaran might have met him as well the previous evening. I told Nripendra Misra that I had also been informed about the precarious state of finances in IL&FS and the matter appeared to be serious. He said he was sending me a presentation titled 'India's Lehman Moment'. He wanted me to study it and meet him in the afternoon.

The presentation had no authorship. It was certainly not from IL&FS. It appeared to be made either by an IL&FS insider or a market analyst or academic think-tank. The presentation argued that IL&FS's assets were heavily overvalued and its debts grossly underrepresented. There were large sums of money that government departments—in particular, NHAI and other organizations under MoRTH—owed IL&FS.

The presentation urged the government to do something urgently, including taking IL&FS over if necessary, and warned that if immediate action was not taken, India would witness its Lehman moment. Several NBFCs and other companies would default, the banking crisis would worsen and the financial system would collapse.

The presentation appeared to be grossly exaggerating the situation. The possibility of IL&FS choreographing this could also not be completely ruled out. Hari Sankaran meeting me and Nripendra Misra receiving such a scary presentation on the same day was too much of a coincidence.

We met in the afternoon and agreed that the situation was serious and the government would have to do something soon. I promised to come back to him two days later after having studied the matter in greater detail. Secretary, DFS, was also present. The DFS controls LIC, SBI and other PSBs that were principal lenders and equity investors in IL&FS. He related how LIC Managing Director Hemant Bhargava was tricked into becoming chairman of the IL&FS Board after Ravi Parthasarathy suddenly decided to bolt. Secretary, DFS, talked about taking serious action against IL&FS and the public-sector officials. Bhargava stepped down from the chairmanship of IL&FS the same day.

Meeting with the IL&FS Brass Convinced Us It Was a Sinkhole

I went over IL&FS's last balance sheet and other documents brought by Hari Sankaran and the IL&FS CFO. Additional Secretary K. Rajaraman was also present at this meeting.

Nominally, the assets exceeded the liabilities by over ₹20,000 crore. However, there was a substantial amount of assets claimed to be 'work in progress'. The completed assets and work in progress assets had entries that were 'invisibles', possibly representing hugely exaggerated arbitration and other claims filed by IL&FS. There were inter-corporate loans within the IL&FS group, for which no provisions for doubtful or loss assets were made. In all, the real value of assets, including financial assets, seemed to be much lower than the debt on the consolidated balance sheet, which by no means contained any exaggeration.

Desperation for resources had made the IL&FS entities borrow against all possible means. Almost all the equity was pledged. All the assets, including the corporate headquarters in Mumbai, had been mortgaged. There was virtually no asset that could be sold freely. It had taken up several projects, in many cases where the cost of land had gone up sharply after the 2013 land acquisition law, and which were going to make big losses.

While IL&FS had approximately ₹16,000 crore of payment obligations for the remaining year, it had no cash flow after incurring operational expenditure. The equity rights issue that Hari Sankaran said would bring about ₹6,000 crore looked unlikely to go through or have any subscribers.

Hari Sankaran was still at his confident best—get me ₹10,000 crore for three months and everything will be great, he repeated. I don't think he genuinely believed that IL&FS had only a temporary liquidity problem. Though many details were still not available, it appeared fairly clear that if the government provided any budgetary support or asked any PSB or LIC to put in money, it was bound to be lost.

I told Hari Sankaran I would discuss the matter with the finance minister and the PMO. I was convinced that the time to send Sankaran and his partners in crime out of IL&FS had arrived.

The Government Debated Options

Two days later, Nripendra Misra convened a meeting in the PMO to decide what the government could do. Injeti Srinivas, secretary, corporate affairs, who had been tasked to study the matter keeping the precedent of Satyam in mind, was also present besides secretary, DFS, and I. Brajendra Navnit from the PMO was part of all the discussions. Vineet Nayyar, who had been instrumental in resolving the Satyam case, was also invited.

Everybody agreed something had to be done. Allowing the matter to dither would be disastrous for the banks, financial markets, infrastructure development and growth momentum of the country.

There were two issues. First, should the government provide financial support in some manner as had happened in the US in the 2008 financial crisis? And second, if not, what was the most appropriate option in the situation—sending IL&FS to the bankruptcy process, make a Satyam type of intervention by replacing the IL&FS Board or something else?

I had earlier explained to Nripendra Misra that any kind of budgetary support or guarantees from the government to provide financial support to IL&FS would set a very bad precedent—we did not know how much support would be adequate; chances of the money coming back were very slim, as the underlying assets of IL&FS were also hollow; and it would send a very bad signal that would make every fraudster and loser come to the government. I again explained the reasons for the government not providing any financial support. This seemed to be the common assessment.

There was a long discussion on what non-financial action the government could take. We were informed that IL&FS had already gone to the National Company Law Tribunal under Section 230 of the Companies Act asking for directions to lenders to enter into a compromise for restructuring/waiving debt. The IBC (insolvency and bankruptcy) process was not available for IL&FS and one of its principal subsidiaries, IL&FS Financial Services Ltd (IFIN), as financial companies were not covered by the IBC Code at the time. Further, with over 300 companies in the IL&FS group, the IBC process would prove to be completely unmanageable. One option was to act under sections 241 and 242 of the Companies Act and replace the IL&FS Board with NCLT orders, as was done with Satyam.

I favoured superseding the IL&FS Board and replacing it with a set of competent people to resolve the problem on the basis of IBC principles but under the orders of NCLT. There was good support for this viewpoint.

Srinivas had more in-depth information about other NBFCs that were facing tough times and were, in his view, likely to go belly up soon like IL&FS. Section 241-242 Companies Act process required intense involvement of the Ministry of Company Affairs (MCA), which he headed. Either because he did not feel very confident about the matter going through successfully in case of a complex company like IL&FS, or because he wanted to avoid getting entangled in more such cases, Srinivas argued against taking action under the Companies Act to supersede the IL&FS Board. He suggested that whatever action was required should be taken under IBC.

Nripendra Misra wanted still wider consultation. A meeting was organized on Saturday, 22 September, in NITI Aayog to be chaired by the vice chairman. The SEBI chairman, former SEBI chairmen G.N. Bajpai and Sinha, Vineet Nayyar and some others were also invited. In this meeting too, Srinivas took pains to explain why the government should not invoke sections 241-242 of the Companies Act. However, the overwhelming opinion was in favour of superseding the IL&FS Board with NCLT orders under Section 241-242. Realizing the futility of his resistance, Srinivas also came on board.

The PM Blessed the Action

With complete clarity on the course of action, we moved to the next necessary steps to execute the plan: identifying a new chairman and board of directors for IL&FS, initiating the paperwork, drafting a justification, and so on. Srinivas marshalled his resources very well thereafter, to do all the hard work. Uday Kotak was identified as the man of the moment for chairing the IL&FS Board. He agreed to take on the responsibility.

Within a couple of days, a meeting was organized at the level of Prime Minister Modi. He gave his go-ahead. With that, the die was cast. It was decided that the NCLT order would be obtained on 1 October, the following Monday.

Srinivas ordered a Serious Fraud Investigating Office (SFIO) investigation, collected as many details as he could through his Mumbai office and compiled a mammoth petition. He also spoke to the NCLT judge and briefed him on the gravity of the situation. We all worked on identifying directors for the board. Again, Srinivas did most of the work.

The government could move an application before NCLT under Section 241(2) if it was of the opinion that the affairs of the company were being conducted in a manner prejudicial to public interest. A case needed to be made to show how the affairs of the company were conducted in this manner. Srinivas wanted DEA to make this case while he took care of all the procedural aspects.

I gave Shashank Saxena, economic advisor and an ace drafter of economic memos, forty-eight hours to do the job. He delivered. I found his memo well drafted. With minimal changes to strengthen the public interest aspect involved in the infrastructure aspects of IL&FS, and also how its mismanagement was affecting the financial system, I sent the final version to Srinivas on Sunday, 30 September.

Discredited IL&FS Board Booted Out

The MCA's lawyers filed the petition before the Mumbai branch of NCLT on the morning of 1 October 2018 and NCLT heard the matter the same day in view of its urgent nature. The petition pleaded for immediate suspension of the entire IL&FS Board and its replacement by directors proposed by the government. The IL&FS lawyers did not support or oppose the petition, which amounted to their having no issue with the request made by the government.

The NCLT ordered the immediate suspension of the IL&FS Board, which included fallen professionals like Hari Sankaran, Arun Saha and others, representatives of equity holders including LIC and SBI, and independent directors like R.C. Bhargava, Jerry Rao and others. Upon the recommendation of the government, NCLT appointed Uday Kotak, Vineet Nayyar, G.N. Bajpai, G.C. Chaturvedi, Malini Shankar and Nand Kishore as directors. A few days later, the appointment of former Rajasthan chief secretary, C.S. Rajan, was also confirmed by NCLT. Bajpai left within a month's time as he had some conflict of interest.

The same day (1 October), DEA issued a comprehensive press note highlighting how the supersession of the discredited IL&FS Board by the one appointed by NCLT, could bring the financial system of the country back from the brink.

The new board assumed its responsibility on 4 October. IL&FS was considered by many as a government organization and its equity and loans were predominantly contributed by government-owned banks and other financial institutions. After being run by Ravi Parthasarathy, Hari Sankaran and company as their personal fiefdom, IL&FS had finally come into the hands of government-appointed directors.

Government Expected the New Board to Resolve IL&FS in a Year

Throwing out the cabal was necessary to resolve the IL&FS matter. The PMO appointed a committee under my chairmanship, with MCA Secretary Srinivas, DFS Secretary Rajeev Kumar and PMO Joint Secretary Navnit as members to set the policy for resolution of the issues that troubled IL&FS and its hundreds of subsidiaries and associate companies. Considering the sensitivity of the situation and the formal authority of the IL&FS Board and NCLT in the matter, the committee was asked to operate informally. The idea was that it would regularly sit with Uday Kotak and Vineet Nayyar to set policy goals, review progress and sort out issues and glitches.

There were considerable discussions on the issues involved and options available. In the first two meetings, there was broad agreement on key policy and strategic issues. It was agreed that the board would follow asset-by-asset resolution (with each SPV accounted as one asset) instead of group resolution, which in any case was not permissible even under IBC. In addition, it was recognized that group resolution would be impossible to achieve as the rights of lenders, investors and other stakeholders were more clearly aligned with the SPVs.

There was also clear agreement that the IL&FS Board would basically adopt the strategy of selling whichever SPVs could be sold; those that could not be sold would be liquidated. The IBC waterfall structure would be followed for distribution of sales proceeds at the SPV level. The board would follow a transparent auction process to sell the SPVs.

The IL&FS Board quickly assessed the solvency and liquidity position of the major group-level companies. There were companies that were profitable and those that were losing cash heavily and carried debt that was completely unserviceable. Uday Kotak proposed a two-way classification of the companies: green and red. I suggested another category—orange. This classification basically recognized debt-servicing ability at the SPV level. The SPVs that could service both secured and unsecured debt (after meeting operational expenses) were green companies, those that could service only secured debt were orange, and those that could not service even secured debt were categorized as red companies.

The secretary, DFS, lost interest in the committee's proceedings fairly soon. He stopped attending after two or three meetings. Srinivas attended quite regularly for the first two months. The committee meetings became irregular thereafter. Once the policy issues and broad strategy for carrying out the resolution mandate were agreed upon, I also felt there was no great necessity for the informal committee to meet. After two months or so, the interface with the NCLT became the principal matter. Every month, MCA filed a report based on the progress furnished by the IL&FS Board. In between, a number of interlocutory applications were also required for obtaining the NCLT's orders. The NCLT granted moratorium on debt service in the middle of October and approved the basic scheme of resolution, including the classification of companies as green, red and orange, a few weeks later.

Meanwhile, IL&FS defaulted on servicing two loans taken from ADB, guaranteed by the Government of India. While the division handling these loans wanted IL&FS to service these loans from whatever repayments it was receiving or to obtain relief from ADB by directly approaching the bank, I ruled that the Government of India should assume these loan liabilities. IL&FS's defaulting not only affected the two loans concerned, but could have led to India becoming a defaulter of ADB, which was a much larger cost than servicing these two small loans. I also processed and explained all the tax-related concessions that were available in case of an IBC resolution being granted to IL&FS, which were finally granted through the Finance Act presented along with Budget 2019–20.

The format of interaction with the IL&FS Board shifted to meeting Uday Kotak on a one-on-one basis. This went on until February 2019. Thereafter, it became episodic. If Srinivas wanted to get any issue sorted out, he would call up. After I shifted from the Ministry of Finance in July 2019, I stopped interacting with anyone, except once in the Ministry of Power, when C.S. Rajan wanted me to persuade NTPC to take over one of the IL&FS power companies in Tamil Nadu.

Good Housekeeping but Little to Show after a Year

The IL&FS Board undertook serious efforts to sell assets. The fourth progress report that IL&FS filed with the government and NCLT in August 2019, informed that the asset divestment process for IL&FS

Security Services Ltd (ISSL), ISSL Settlement and Transaction Services Ltd (ISTSL) and the renewable energy business assets was proceeding well, with eleven expressions of interest (EoIs) received for ISSL and ISTSL and twenty for the renewable energy business. Further, IL&FS had issued advertisements for twenty-two road assets and over thirty EoIs had been received. The sale process was also launched for the education vertical and the alternative investment fund business.

On 1 October 2019 the IL&FS Board released a media presentation upon completion of one year of the new board. It recognized the key objective of the new board as achieving an orderly resolution of the IL&FS Group through a fair and transparent process. In one year, the board had taken stock and recognized that there were 302 entities in the group: 133 foreign and 169 domestic. The group also had twelve specific verticals comprising all but six companies. The transport vertical (IL&FS Transportation Networks Ltd or ITNL) was the largest with 160 entities, followed by energy (IL&FS Energy Development Company Ltd or IEDCL) with thirty-five entities and financial services (IFIN, and IL&FS Investment Managers Limited or IIML) with thirty entities.

The IL&FS Board further informed that it had completed the solvency test for all the 169 domestic companies and had classified them into green, orange and red categories. These domestic companies carried 95 per cent of the total debt. The external (other than intra-group) borrowings of the group were in excess of ₹94,000 crore. The board announced that resolution plans had been readied for all 302 entities. Of the 169 domestic entities, 'entity monetization' was being undertaken for fifty-five entities and real-estate monetization for eight; of the external entities, only sixteen out of 133 entities were found worthy of being monetized.

An actual sale purchase agreement (SPA) had been signed for only one vertical with seven renewable SPV companies. This deal was made with ORIX, which was already a 49 per cent investor in these seven SPVs and was also a leading shareholder of IL&FS. Other than this one deal, nothing else had crystallized.

The government had expected the IL&FS group's issues to be fully resolved in one year's time. The media presentation talked a lot about what the board had been doing in preparation and addressing debt-related issues, but in terms of real resolution, there was only one sale to show.

The IL&FS Board Got Overwhelmed by Debt

Lenders' debt was placed under moratorium and they stopped accruing interest the day IL&FS was admitted to NCLT in October 2019. The NCLT process for IL&FS was intended to get the maximum of their debts, like any other insolvency process. It was quite understandable that the government-appointed IL&FS Board was focused on the external debt of IL&FS as soon as it took over.

In the first year, no lender got any money back. Banks and financial institutions were not the only lenders to IL&FS. Besides them, a large number of pension funds, provident funds and public-sector companies had invested, particularly in the deposits and bonds of the holding companies of IL&FS. These groups, including a fund of army soldiers, being unsecured creditors, were at the lowest rung of the creditor recipients. They panicked and reached out to the government and NCLT.

As of the end of September 2022, IL&FS claimed (in the report to NCLT filed in December 2022) to have achieved debt resolution of ₹56,943 crore out of estimated external debt of ₹99,355 crore (a little over 57 percent).

Of this, the debt resolved through monetization/termination was claimed to be of ₹16,452 crore, and the debt actually discharged by payment to be ₹4,725 crore. In all, debt of ₹21,177 crore only was effectively discharged (about 21 per cent). The lenders had lost interest for three years during this period, which perhaps was higher than the total pay-out/effective discharges.

Available cash balance of ₹19,699 crore and InvIT units of ₹2,213 crore were also counted as debt resolution. In addition, the IL&FS Board also claimed that the debt of ₹7,254 crore, which was indicated to have been approved by courts but was pending closure, and debt of ₹5,269 crore, for which applications had been filed with courts pending approvals, amounted to debt resolution. In addition, debt to be serviced by green entities of ₹1,331 crore was rightly taken as resolved.

As is quite evident, a very small amount of debt has actually been paid out in cash after three years. Most proceeds of sales were still with IL&FS. There is definitely a major inadequacy of cash-funds for the creditors in the system. The NCLT ordered IL&FS to make provision of a fair distribution, which included part payment to pension funds and other public investors. The IL&FS management is neck deep in the debt quagmire.

By the third anniversary of the IL&FS takeover (1 October 2022) by appointment of the government-appointed board, the character of the IL&FS resolution had changed drastically from what was initially envisaged. The IL&FS Board is primarily engaged in 'addressing debt' in place of selling out businesses and closing IL&FS.

One-Year Mandate Has Become an Open-Ended Mandate

After two years went by, IL&FS released another media briefing in October 2020. In this briefing, it gave no specific information about the sale of any particular entity.

The moth started turning thereafter. In December 2020, it announced that it had received approval from Supreme Court Judge D.K. Jain, who was appointed to supervise the process, for the sale of its two Chinese road assets. In April 2021, it announced that it had sold the environmental business with its five subsidiaries to Eversource. In its April 2021 presentation, IL&FS also informed that it was adopting the InvIT model for its road assets and expected the resolution of six road SPVs via InvITs with a value of ₹9,300 crore to be completed in Phase 1, with the rest to follow in subsequent phases.

In its report to NCLT in December 2022, IL&FS has submitted a very detailed account of the sale/monetization/other action taken with respect to the resolution of the 302 entities it began with in

2018. It claimed that as on 30 September 2022, only 101 entities remained to be resolved—eighty-eight domestic (from 169) and thirteen off-shore (from 133).

Fifty-four of the 169 domestic entities were identified for monetization. Of these thirty-one had been resolved and twenty-three under the process. In addition, IL&FS changed the mode of resolution for twelve road assets from sale to the InvIT model. It created an InvIT-Roadstar Infra Investment Trust (InvIT). In December 2022, IL&FS claimed to have resolved ten road assets, though only four road assets/SPVs were actually transferred to Roadstar InvIT by the end of December 2022. There are six key holding companies, which in any case would be the last ones to be resolved. Larger resolution took place by closer/insolvency/residual entities, where out of eighty-six such identified entities, thirty-seven were claimed to have been resolved and the rest of the forty-nine under different stages of process. The last mode of resolution was 'termination of concession'. Three of such ten concessions had been terminated and the rest under process. Most of the off-shore entities were subsidiaries of a road company registered abroad. Most of these were de-rostered by merging or closing.

After four years of its existence, much of the IL&FS task is unfinished. It has now become a sponsor of Roadstar InvIT and holds ownership units. This model supposes that IL&FS will remain in existence as a sponsor for quite some time to come. IL&FS has become an asset management company, rather than closing shop, as envisaged.

The mandate to resolve IL&FS's assets and close the group in a year's time has become less of a 'resolution'. It has acquired a certain form of permanence without any expiry date for undertaking 'asset monetization' and 'liquidity management', as IL&FS indicated in its December 2022 report to the NCLT.

IL&FS survives and carries on. Its mandate has become an open-ended mandate.

19

Wrath of the Markets

NO SPECIAL MEETING WAS CONVENED BUT THE EFFECT OF THE consultations initiated under Section 7 of the RBI Act and the dressing down Urjit Patel received at the hands of the PM at the meeting on 14 September 2018, as referred in the chapter 'Raiding RBI's Reserves' and described in the chapter 'Governor Urjit Patel Resigns' (see later), led to contentious issues being discussed at the Central Board meeting held on 23 October and in the meeting that followed. Deputy Governor Viral Acharya had very strong views about the banking sector in India and the independence of the central bank. As we would discover later, much of the policy framework adopted in handling non-performing loans and the Prompt Corrective Action (PCA) framework also reflected the ideas of Viral Acharya, which Urjit Patel fully shared.

Viral Acharya had a strong dislike for Indian PSBs. Several times during his tenure in RBI, he spoke about the need to privatize them. As early as April 2017, in one of his speeches, Acharya said: 'Perhaps re-privatizing some of the nationalized banks is an idea whose time has come ... this would reduce the overall money government needs to inject as bank capital.'

Since 2015 the PSBs had been undergoing the worst phase in their existence, on account of their excesses and imprudent loans made in the gung-ho phase of 2005–13. Non-performing loans kept rising until they peaked in 2018–19. Several measures had to be taken. The government provided additional capital infusion exceeding ₹2.5 lakh crore until 2018, more than 50 per cent of the capital provided in the entire history of the PSBs. RBI placed several PSBs under the PCA framework, which placed several restrictions on these banks, including on their lending operations.

The extent of capital to be provided to PSBs had become a major headache for the government. It also did not like the situation where PSBs had been stripped of their authority to lend as this was affecting credit growth to industries, including MSMEs. The government wanted its recapitalization burden to be reduced and PSBs to be brought out of the PCA framework for them to resume lending.

The DFS worked hard on the matter. It went into the Basel norms (a global effort to coordinate banking regulations) for different types of capital required: Tier 1, Tier 2 and Contingency Buffer. It also looked at the international practice of placing banks under PCA or a similar framework. Three issues where RBI had adopted practices at variance with global practice were identified: a. Capital adequacy, basically on account of higher Tier-1 capital norms in India, was higher by 1 per cent compared to the Basel norms; b. RBI was asking the banks to make a provision for a capital contingency buffer (CCB) in 'bad' times, whereas the norms required the provision of CCB only in 'good' times; and c. the criteria adopted by RBI for bringing the banks under the PCA framework was excessively severe in comparison to global norms.

A long and passionate debate took place at the Central Board meeting on 23 October 2018 on these issues. Dr Viral Acharya took an extreme position. In his opinion, the PSBs were pathologically incompetent. He argued that they could not be trusted to manage anything—from the interest rate risks of their investments to extending credit. Referring to the American example, he said, 'Elsewhere in the world, a "to sell" notice is hung on the door of a bank on Friday and, by Monday, the bank has new owners.' He wanted the Government of India to sell off these banks, instead of asking for any dilution in the norms for PCA framework. Alternatively, he argued that the Government of India must provide whatever capital these banks needed for meeting capital adequacy and other norms. His view was that Indian banks actually held a very low level of capital.

In the long debate that took place in the board on the issue, Urjit Patel fully backed Viral Acharya. It was quite apparent that they held similar views.

The 'Saviour' of Central Bank Independence Delivers a Fiery Speech

Three days later, Viral Acharya delivered the famous 'Wrath of the markets' speech.

On 26 October 2018, only three days after the RBI Board meeting on 23 October, which was perhaps one of the most contentious and dramatic meetings of the board where pitched battles were fought between RBI and government teams, there had been rampant talk of Governor Urjit Patel resigning. The media and politicians were debating the rumoured raid of the central bank's reserves by the government and the threat to RBI's independence owing to the communications issued under Section 7. The setting could not have been more undesirable for a partisan public debate on central bank independence.

Viral Acharya, the incumbent deputy governor of RBI, delivered the A.D. Shroff Memorial Lecture in Mumbai on that day. He left no one in doubt that this speech was delivered at the instance of RBI Governor Urjit Patel. The first footnote of the speech noted that Viral Acharya was 'grateful to Governor Dr Urjit R. Patel, Reserve Bank of India (RBI), for his suggestion to explore this theme for a speech, for referring me to the work of the late Deena Khatkhate (2005) and for his constant encouragement, feedback and guidance.'

Viral Acharya's theme of the day was the trampling of central banking institutions by governments and its consequences, which led the governors of central banks to resign from their positions to protect the independence of the central banks. To conjure up a parallel with the Indian situation, right at the beginning of his speech, Viral Acharya quoted Martin Redrado, Argentina's former central bank chief, who had called a news conference on 29 January 2010 and had said: 'My time at the central bank is up and that is why I have decided to leave my post definitively, with the satisfaction of my duty fulfilled.' The audience was rapt as Acharya quoted the next sentence from Redrado's speech: 'We have arrived at this situation because of the national government's permanent trampling of institutions.' He went on to quote Redrado, saying, 'Basically, I am defending two main concepts: the independence of the central bank in our decision-making process and that the reserves should be used for monetary and financial stability.'

While the quotes used by Viral Acharya were crystal clear to drive home the point that India was facing an exactly similar situation as Argentina in 2018, to leave no one in any doubt at all, he specifically outlined the 'attempts' of the Government of India to raid the reserves of RBI: 'A thorny ongoing issue on this front has been that of the rules for surplus transfer from the Reserve Bank to the government (Cogencis, 2018, 'Govt pegs RBI excess capital at 3.6 trln rupees, seeks it as surplus'), an issue that relates closely to the leading Argentine example in my introductory remarks.'

Viral Acharya drew heavily from the articles of Dr Rakesh Mohan, describing his conclusions as 'deft'. While quoting him, Dr Acharya highlighted the line: 'Raiding RBI's capital creates no new government revenue on a net basis over time, and only provides an illusion of free money in the short term.' Viral Acharya knew that there was no such move by the government, which he acknowledged in the later part of the speech by stating that better sense prevailed on the government and it did not raid RBI's balance sheet.

Viral Acharya is an eloquent speaker. He chose words, analogies and quotes to make his points very strongly. His speech left no one in doubt that he did not expect anything fair and reasonable from the government, which made him bring in the markets as the referee where the consequences of such unfortunate events get fully reflected and make nations suffer.

Before invoking the virtues of markets and how they punish governments that undermine the independence of central banks, he first warned that such actions severely affect the macroeconomic stability of the country. Equating macroeconomic stability to central bank autonomy in decision-making and delivery of its core functions, Viral Acharya warned, 'When such a measured perspective of an independent central bank as a key element of durable economic prosperity is missing and/or government myopia so rife as to lead to regular inroads into central banking apparatus and decisions, unfortunate accidents can arise.'

Paying tribute to the correcting power of markets, he went on, 'As this dynamic plays out, markets watch keenly and if uncertainty grows and confidence in central bank independence and credibility erodes, markets rap bond yields and exchange rate on the knuckles!'

Reposing his faith in the ability of the markets to discipline governments, Viral Acharya continued, 'The presence of this third player—the market—in the back and forth between a government and the central bank (more generally, regulatory institutions) is an important feedback mechanism. The market can discipline the government not to erode central bank independence, and it can also make the government pay for its transgressions.'

Concluding his speech with fire and brimstone, Viral Acharya issued a direct warning to the Government of India:

> Governments that do not respect central bank independence will sooner or later incur the wrath of financial markets, ignite economic fire, and come to rue the day they undermined an important regulatory institution; their wiser counterparts who invest in central bank independence will enjoy lower costs of borrowing, the love of international investors and longer lifespans.

The public speeches of governors and deputy governors of RBI rarely occupy the top headlines and become 'viral'. On the evening of 26 October 2018, the provocative parts of this speech were making headlines in the media and trending as 'breaking news'.

The Government Takes Note of the Speech

Viral Acharya had delivered many speeches before. He always spoke with eloquence. But the government always took note of official communications from RBI and not his speeches. This time, it was different.

The secretaries gathered in the room of Finance Minister Arun Jaitley. There was general unhappiness about the content, tenor and accusatory tone of Viral Acharya's speech. It was felt that it would only worsen the climate. However, the government was determined not to weaken its efforts to continuously engage with RBI to find solutions for the problems of the day. There was no doubt in the mind of anyone present in the meeting that the government truly respected the independence of RBI and did not want to encourage the impression that this provocative speech would force the government to shun restraint.

Finance Minister Arun Jaitley issued a public statement, which I had drafted, on 31 October 2018, on the subject of the central bank's independence, without directly referring to Viral Acharya's speech. It emphasized the need for continuous dialogue between the government and RBI to resolve issues of public interest.

It read:

Autonomy for the Central Bank, within the framework of the RBI Act, is an essential and accepted governance requirement. Governments in India have nurtured and respected this. Both the Government and the Central Bank, in their functioning, have to be guided by public interest and the requirements of the Indian economy. For the purpose, extensive consultations on several issues take place between the Government and RBI from time to time. This is equally true of all other regulators. The Government of India has never made public the subject matter of those consultations. Only the final decisions taken are communicated. The Government, through these consultations, places its assessment on issues and suggests possible solutions. The Government will continue to do so.

Argentinian Data Quoted by Viral Acharya Was Suspect

Argentina is far away from India. It has not been an exemplar for either following virtuous monetary and fiscal policy or establishing good governance standards. At that point, it had constantly defaulted in its sovereign bond obligations. The fact that Viral Acharya chose examples from Argentina appeared a desperate attempt to find something from somewhere in the world to take potshots at the Government of India.

Not much is known in India about Argentina and most people who heard or read Viral Acharya's speech perhaps thought the country was a paragon of virtue and had to suffer catastrophic consequences when its government interfered with the independence of the central bank, leading the governor of the bank to resign in protest.

Viral Acharya used data from the sovereign bond markets of Argentina to make the point that bonds were sold off and yields and credit default swap rates rose massively when the governor of the central bank resigned in the wake of the government's interference. No one in the country cared to look at this data. We, however, decided to examine the facts.

To make the point that markets revolt by re-pricing sovereign bonds when governments do not respect central bank independence, Viral Acharya chose this quote:

> Within a month of Mr Redrado's resignation, Argentine sovereign bond yields and the annual premium cost for buying insurance against loss from default on Argentina government bonds (measured as sovereign credit default swap spread) shot up by about 2.5 per cent or 250 basis points, *by more than a fourth of their prior levels.*
> [Emphasis added, as Viral Acharya implied that credit default swap spreads effectively rose by as high as 25 per cent.]

Shashank Saxena and two other technical experts in the Economic Division investigated. They looked at the actual data of the monthly average of the Argentinian sovereign bond spread over US bonds in 2009 and 2010 to learn what had happened.

Credit default swap rates of five-year bonds in Argentina did go up from 919.72 basis points to 1012.50 basis points in February 2010. This was an increase of less than 10 per cent, not one-fourth or 25 per cent. Moreover, in March 2010, the very next month, they came down to 907.08 basis points, lower than the rates in January 2010. The credit default swap rates fell further to 817.57 basis points in April 2010, which were over 10 per cent lower than the rates in January 2010.

A similar trend was observed in credit default swap rates of ten-year bonds. From 989.86 basis points in January 2010, they went up temporarily to 1092.60 basis points in February 2010 but came down to 975.47 basis points in March 2010 and 851.91 basis points in April.

The conclusions drawn by Viral Acharya about credit default swap rates going up by 25 per cent were patently false. We collected the monthly series of credit default swap rates for both five and ten-year bonds and placed them in our records.

The question was, did Viral Acharya use wrong data knowingly or unknowingly? Further, if he knew the data to be false, did he deliberately use it to create a major storm?

Markets Start Turning Benign after 'Wrath of Markets' Speech

In a bad turn of events for Viral Acharya, most markets started turning for the better within days of his speech. Oil prices started declining, leading to the prospects of improvement in the current account as well. Stock, fixed securities and currency markets all started indicating a turnaround for the better.

India also concluded a highly favourable dollar-rupee swap agreement with Japan for $75 billion. I had negotiated this agreement with Japan, which was finalized at the summit meeting of Prime Ministers Narendra Modi and Shinzo Abe in Tokyo. This swap agreement was unique in the sense that it provided for accessing a good portion of the amount practically on demand, which India wanted.

I tweeted on 2 November 2018[12]: 'Rupee trading at less than 73 to a dollar. Brent crude below $73 a barrel. Markets up by over 4 per cent during the week and bond yields below 7.8 per cent. Wrath of the markets?'

Viral Acharya's speech had led to much being written in the media about the government's alleged attempts to raid RBI's reserves. Figures of ₹3.6 lakh crore and ₹1 lakh crore were bandied about by many commentators, including knowledgeable people like former Finance Minister Chidambaram.

I issued a long tweet[13] to make the position clear on this front as well:

Lot of misinformed speculation is going around in media. Government's fiscal math is completely on track. There is no proposal to ask RBI to transfer 3.6 or 1 lakh crore, as speculated. Government's FD in FY 2013-14 was 5.1%. From 2014-15 onwards, Government has succeeded in bringing it down substantially. We will end FY 2018-19 with FD of 3.3%. Government has actually foregone 70,000 crore of budgeted borrowing this year. Only proposal under consideration is to fix appropriate economic capital framework of RBI.

These tweets led to front-page stories in the pink papers and media. We could effectively make the point that Viral Acharya had made a false case about RBI's independence being under threat. Further, the

---

12 https://twitter.com/subhashgarg1960/status/105822812598787686 5?s=51&t=4W55xdXV8yNP3LctT66QEA

13 https://twitter.com/subhashgarg1960/status/10608022114402222 08?s=51&t=4W55xdXV8yNP3LctT66QEA, https://twitter.com/ subhashgarg1960/status/1060803807297368065?s=51&t=4W55 xdXV8yNP3LctT66QEA and https://twitter.com/subhashgarg1960/ status/1060803856395833346?s=51&t=4W55xdXV8yNP3LctT 66QEA

connection between the markets and the perceived independence, or lack of it, for central banks was not as direct as he wanted everyone to believe.

There was no wrath of the markets in India.

Proposal Drafted Calling for Explanation from Viral Acharya

Dr Viral Acharya had used false data to make his point about the so-called parallels between Argentina and India. This was not expected from a researcher of his stature. He had also delivered an incendiary speech, probably with no parallel in the annals of central banking, knowing well that the speech could further spoil the relationship between the government and RBI. Finance Minister Arun Jaitley was also shocked when he was apprised of the data. With his consent, it was decided to call for an explanation from Viral Acharya.

A letter was drafted that basically contained four allegations.

First, Viral Acharya delivered a public speech on theme 'On the Importance of Independent Regulatory Institutions: The Case of the Central Bank' on 26 October 2018, which created a strong impression in India in the media and the minds of economic and financial analysts, participants and commentators that the independence of RBI was under threat, as a result of the Government of India allegedly taking measures to stifle its independence and taking measures to raid the reserves/buffers built in the balance sheet of RBI.

Second, the language used in the lecture was unusually incendiary/fiery, which was very unusual for a central banker, and accused the government of having a short-term perspective and mindset, brandishing it as unfit to take policy decisions of a long-term nature. Further, all these accusations were made in public without even first bringing them to the notice of the government and discussing the same.

Third, Viral Acharya used false data to make his points.

Fourth, making a false accusation that the Government of India was trying to raid RBI's reserves despite knowing fully well that the government had made no such move and no such proposal was made or direction issued to this effect to RBI.

It was proposed in the draft letter that Viral Acharya provide the proof of his research and the actual source of the data he relied upon to reach the conclusion that Argentine sovereign bond yields spiked by as much as a fourth after Redrado's resignation.

Further, it was proposed that Viral Acharya be asked to explain why he used a media/agency report, which was nothing more than a false rumour as the reason to use intemperate, incendiary, half-baked, emotive and harsh language in his speech.

However, this letter was never issued. The file remained in the custody of Arun Jaitley for some time before the matter died in due course. Viral Acharya put in his papers six months in advance of the completion of his three-year tenure in July 2019 for 'personal reasons'.

20

Governor Urjit Patel Resigns

B Y JULY 2018, THE GOVERNMENT WAS FRUSTRATED WITH RBI UNDER Dr Urjit Patel. A big build-up had led the situation to rise to this unfortunate level, a level that had upset even a person like Arun Jaitley.

Its seeds started germinating on 12 February 2018, when RBI Governor Urjit Patel had come out with an extremely straitjacketed formulation for dealing with the non-performing loans of the banking sector and taking these defaulters for resolution under the IBC. This had created major problems for bank loans to power-generation companies. RBI also refused to participate in the High-Level Empowered Committee, constituted under the chairmanship of the cabinet secretary, to resolve stress in the power sector consequent to the Allahabad High Court order that called for examination of issuance of a direction under Section 7 of the RBI Act.

On 14 March 2018, Urjit Patel had delivered a scathing speech at the Centre for Law & Economics at Gujarat National Law University in Gandhinagar. In this speech, he questioned the government's inability to shed regulatory authority over nationalized banks, leaving RBI with inadequate regulatory authority over the PSBs compared to private-sector banks. By elevating himself to the status of the mythical 'Neelkantha', Urjit Patel indicated that he was willing to drink all the poison. This speech and characterization painted the government in a poor light.

Through March and April 2018, Urjit Patel had tried to scuttle the government's electoral bonds scheme by insisting, as an afterthought (after first agreeing to the proposal of designing and issuing these bonds through the banking system), that the electoral bonds should be issued only by RBI, that too in the digital mode. This would have made the electoral bonds a non-starter on account of complete traceability of the donors.

While the real interest rates were still quite high in India, RBI, under Urjit Patel, had raised the repo rate to 6.25 per cent in June 2018, attributing a potential rise in inflationary pressures to the government's decision to hike minimum support prices. He followed it up with another rise of 25 per cent in August 2018. RBI was maintaining a very tight liquidity situation, with banks being forced to continuously borrow from it under the liquidity window. Liquidity had also become tighter on account of RBI selling foreign exchange reserves to manage the rupee-dollar exchange rate.

RBI had also put as many as eight PSBs under the PCA framework, rendering them unable to lend. The DFS secretary was always emphasizing that RBI had made the PCA framework the tightest in the world. Pressure was building on the government to put additional capital in banks to the tune of lakhs of crores.

The government was immensely concerned about all these issues and wanted the liquidity situation to be eased, measures to be taken to shore up foreign exchange reserves, a pragmatic approach to be adopted to resolve the non-performing loans crisis and a more supportive framework to deal with the PCA framework.

Growing Distrust Leads to Lines of Communication Snapping

The more the government wanted to discuss these matters with RBI, the more intransigent and non-communicative Urjit Patel became.

Piyush Goyal, officiating as finance minister from the middle of May to August 2018, had become quite miffed with Urjit Patel and communications between the two got strained. To discuss monetary policy in June 2018, Urjit Patel chose to see Arun Jaitley instead of Piyush Goyal.

Arun Jaitley resumed work formally as finance minister only on 22 August 2018, though he had continued to be involved in all major policy decisions during the period April–August 2018, when he was undergoing medical treatment. But by August 2018, Urjit Patel had apparently decided to bid goodbye to the age-old practice of holding consultations with the finance minister, and did not see Arun Jaitley or Piyush Goyal for the monetary policy review that month.

An unusually tolerant and accommodative man, Finance Minister Arun Jaitley felt bad about the way RBI, in particular Urjit Patel, was conducting himself. He expected minimum courtesies from the governor, with whom he was always extracourteous. He genuinely wanted RBI to be reasonable and do only the minimum necessary in the public interest to keep the economy going. However, Urjit Patel seemed to behave as though he did not want to do anything at the behest of the government. The perception was widely gaining ground, which Arun Jaitley also shared, that Urjit Patel wanted to go down in history as the most independent governor of RBI.

Unusual Situations Call for an Unusual Response

In this extraordinary situation, the government felt it was left with no choice but to invoke Section 7 of the RBI Act, 1934, to issue directions to RBI to do what the government felt was absolutely necessary in the interest of the public and the economy. Section 7 (1) of the RBI Act provides that the 'Central government may from time to time give such directions to the Bank as it may, after consultation with the Governor of the Bank, consider necessary in the public interest.'

The government decided to initiate consultations on the matters it felt were not being conducted in the right public interest by RBI.

In all, six letters were issued—three each from DEA and DFS—requesting the views of RBI Governor Urjit Patel.

The letters from DEA covered the following subjects: establishing a special window for providing liquidity support to non-banks and businesses; issuing NRI bonds for an amount of $50 billion; and discussing the issue of the Economic Capital Framework in a meeting of RBI Central Board.

The letters from DFS sought views on the subjects of implementing the circular dated 12 February, in light of the Allahabad High Court judgement for the affected, including SMEs; appropriate regulatory provisions for the Tier 1 capital and contingency capital reserve; and a more balanced PCA framework.

In addition, the government initiated some key changes in the RBI Board, through the DFS. Nachiket Mor, who was considered to be the intellectual force backing Urjit Patel in the Central Board, was made to resign and S. Gurumurthy, an ideologue considered close to the party in government, was brought in. Some other changes were made in the board by including more directors. This brought some balance to the complexion and composition of the board.

At a meeting of the Central Board on 8 August 2018, it agreed to a much higher dividend to the government than RBI had earlier proposed.

The letters did initiate a process of consultation on the issues identified. Though kept confidential, they also led to considerable comment in the media.

The PM Reviews the State of the Economy

It was against this backdrop that Prime Minister Modi decided to convene a meeting to review the state of the economy and what RBI could be asked to do. This meeting took place on 14 September 2018. The meeting was attended by Urjit Patel with his two deputy governors, Viral Acharya and N.S. Vishwanathan. From the government, Finance Minister Arun Jaitley, Railways Minister Piyush Goyal, Principal Secretary to the Prime Minister Nripendra

Misra, Additional Principal Secretary P.K. Mishra, DFS Secretary Rajiv Kumar, and I, were present.

The meeting took place in the wake of a difficult economic situation, especially on account of rising crude oil prices, a deteriorating current account position and slowing GDP growth. Crude oil prices had just touched the high of $80 per barrel. The rupee had fallen to 72–73 to a dollar. The FPIs were selling off Indian bonds; they had pulled out $1.3 billion in the first fortnight of September 2018. The current account deficit (CAD) was widening, threatening to go beyond 3 per cent of GDP on an annualized basis. There was enormous pressure to reduce excise duties on petrol and diesel to bring down prices. Foreign exchange reserves had started falling and there was a fear that they could run down by over $50 billion in the year. The economic situation was indeed tough.

Governor Urjit Patel made a presentation, where his diagnosis was even more alarmist than the prevailing economic situation, and painted a horrible picture. Indian currency, he pointed out, was the worst performer globally. The oil situation, in his judgement, was unlikely to improve. The situation would become wholly disastrous by November 2018, when US sanctions against Iran came into play.

He believed oil prices would shoot up beyond $100 per barrel. He said RBI had already used $30 billion of reserves in spot and forward markets and feared its firepower was simply inadequate in the developing situation, with the CAD likely to go beyond 3.5 per cent of GDP. He underlined that India was running one of the highest fiscal deficits in the world. He also pointed out that India was one of the fragile-five countries in 2013 and concluded that, taking into account the fiscal deficit, current account situation and performance of the rupee, India had become one of the five worst-performing and vulnerable economies in 2018.

He offered some recommendations—all for the government to take and nothing for RBI to do, besides what it had been doing already. He proposed four major solutions. He asked that the long-term capital gains (LTCG) tax, imposed in Budget 2018–19 in February 2018, be scrapped. He emphasized the urgent need to bring down the fiscal deficit drastically for a macroeconomy reset. For this, he proposed the government scale-up disinvestment targets massively. His other suggestion was to go to the new multilateral institutions like the Asian Infrastructure and Investment Bank and New Development Bank to persuade them to invest in Government of India bonds. Last, he proposed that the government pay up the pending bills of several companies, including MSMEs, which, in his judgement, amounted to thousands of crores.

Finance Minister Arun Jaitley rarely showed frustration publicly. Nor did he normally contradict and question senior functionaries. That day, he could not contain himself. He intervened to say that the solutions presented by Governor Urjit Patel were no solutions at all; they were totally impractical and generally undesirable.

Rajiv Kumar apprised the PM of how difficult the situation had become with respect to non-performing loans, especially of the power sector and MSMEs, because of the stand RBI had taken. He also complained against RBI for not even consulting DFS or him, when RBI decided to issue the 12 February circular. He recited how embarrassing it was for him to learn about the circular from the newspapers and how he had to still publicly defend the circular only to ensure there were no wrong perceptions about the relationship between the government and RBI.

In my comments on the presentation, I questioned the very premise of the RBI governor's diagnosis and the impossibility of bringing down the fiscal deficit further or raising disinvestment targets dramatically. I pointed out that suggestions like approaching AIIB and NDB would be quite slow-moving and at best yield not more than $2–3 billion in inflows over a period of one to two years. I brought up the subject of the ECF and the excess reserves RBI was carrying, which could possibly be used for bank recapitalization.

Earlier in the day, the principal secretary had asked me to prepare a note on specific measures RBI could be asked to take. I provided this list of six specific measures at the meeting, ranging from liberalizing ECBs to placing some restrictions on current account payments.

The governor agreed to two of these, agreed to examine two and disagreed with the other two. Finance Minister Arun Jaitley held a hurriedly convened press conference at about 9.45 p.m., to announce the decisions taken in consultation with RBI aimed at improving the flow of foreign exchange in the country.

Governor Patel Receives Some Plain-speak from the PM

Besides the worsening economic situation, the considerable strain that had developed between the government and RBI also weighed on the mind of Prime Minister Modi. He had selected Dr Urjit Patel as governor and had been defending him all along. Any proposal that was seen as causing any discomfort to RBI or Urjit Patel would be nipped in the bid by the PMO.

Urjit Patel was a poor communicator. He had virtually stopped communicating with me by July 2018. His communication lines with officiating Finance Minister Piyush Goyal and Finance Minister Arun Jaitley had also broken down. The only communication took place through P.K. Mishra in the PMO. There was some breakdown in communication with P.K. Mishra as well, after Urjit Patel made a 180-degree turn with respect to electoral bonds. The PM was not happy with the situation that had developed in the past few months when the government had to resort to Section 7 of the RBI Act, 1934. His patience had possibly been fully tested and he was sick of the situation.

Prime Minister Modi had listened to Governor Urjit Patel very carefully and patiently. After about two hours of presentations and discussions, he saw no solution emerging. His assessment appeared to be that RBI was not on top of the situation and was unwilling to do anything meaningful to address the economic situation and resolve its differences with the government.

At that stage, the PM lost his cool and took on Urjit Patel. I saw him in such an angry mood for the first time. He was scathing in his attack on RBI's stance on the resolution of non-performing assets (NPAs) and its intransigent, impractical and inflexible attitude to finding solutions. He criticized Governor Patel for proposing the withdrawal of the LTCG tax, which had since stabilized with hardly anyone objecting to it, and asking for fiscal deficits to be cut down further in the middle of the financial year. He compared Urjit Patel to the snake who sits over a hoard of money, for being unreceptive to putting RBI's accumulated reserves to any use.

Prime Minister Modi had also been briefed about the reluctance of Governor Urjit Patel to convene a special meeting of the Central Board despite agreeing to do so in the last meeting of the board held on 8 August 2018. The governor had agreed to convene this special meeting on 30 or 31 August subject to 'all directors attending it'. RBI had also sought the convenience of the directors by writing letters the following week. However, Governor Patel had developed second thoughts and had not convened the meeting. The PM was critical of the governor for not calling this special meeting to discuss burning issues and take decisions.

When we were leaving after the meeting I asked Urjit Patel, tongue-in-cheek, whether he would convene the special meeting of the Central Board. Sticking to his intransigent stance, he responded without batting an eyelid: 'I will not.'

Should, or Would, the Governor Resign?

The invocation of Section 7 of the RBI Act 1934 by initiation of consultation for the issues mentioned above, and the change brought about in the Central Board, unnerved Governor Urjit Patel. The change in the attitude of Arun Jaitley and the deterioration in his relationship with the PMO also affected his confidence.

He had some health issues as well. At the Central Board meeting on 8 August, I noted (as I would sit next to him) that he was physically uncomfortable at one stage. When a similar episode occurred at the next meeting and lasted for a much longer period, I asked him about his well-being. He told me that he had a tendency of getting spasms in his body if he had to sit for long. I suspected that the stress of these meetings also had something to do with it.

In a couple of meetings that took place in Finance Minister Arun Jaitley's chamber, we discussed the subject of differences between the government and RBI on policy issues. As such cases in the past could provide valuable precedents, the history books were searched, including the volumes of RBI's official history. There were indeed quite a few instances of governors resigning on account of either them losing the confidence of the government or serious differences developing on policy issues.

The most celebrated case that was germane to the evolving situation in August–October 2018 was that of former RBI Governor Benegal Rama Rau. The circumstances surrounding his resignation had some similarities to the current situation. The government had upwardly revised the stamp duty payable on the bills of the exchange that had an impact on the monetary policy transmission RBI was making through the discount rate on bills of exchange.

While no directive was issued to Rama Rau under Section 7 of the RBI Act, he strongly felt that the policy decision of the government had affected the independence of the RBI governor. There was a breakdown in communication between him and Finance Minister T.T. Krishnamachari. Protracted correspondence between Governor Rama Rau and Prime Minister Jawaharlal Nehru is available in the public domain, published by RBI.

Prime Minister Nehru had told Rama Rau unambiguously about the government's right to take policy decisions in the interest of the planned development of the country and conveyed clearly that it was RBI's duty to work in accordance with such policy decisions. Rama Rau offered to resign in his correspondence with Nehru, who categorically told him that he was free to do so but that the policy decision of the government would stay unchanged. When Rama Rau tendered his resignation, it was promptly accepted.

Arun Jaitley did not want Urjit Patel to resign. He seemed sincere in his expectation that better sense would prevail and Urjit Patel would facilitate appropriate decisions to ease the liquidity situation and deal with non-performing loans. He genuinely felt Urjit Patel need not and should not resign and expected the situation to be resolved.

The opinion among officers was not unanimous. The secretaries were not sure how Governor Urjit Patel would react and what he would do in the circumstances. Some felt he would resign. Some felt that he should resign, but would not. I was of the view that he should not and would not resign. I believed there were solutions that could provide a middle ground. Urjit Patel was honest, technically very sound and was doing, in his judgement, what was in the interest of the country and the banking and financial sectors. His judgement betrayed a lack of balance, which I felt could be sorted out.

I sincerely believed that the objective of issuing the letters invoking Section 7 was not to seek or force the resignation of Urjit Patel as the RBI governor but to nudge him towards a workable solution to the problems at hand.

Governance in RBI Gets a Look-in during This Tussle

The meeting held with Prime Minister Modi and the issuance of several letters invoking Section 7 of the RBI Act made no difference in the attitude and working of RBI and Governor Urjit Patel. Deputy Governor Vishwanathan responded to all the three letters issued from DEA, virtually dismissing all the suggested measures as either unnecessary or irrelevant for RBI. On the issue of the ECF, he informed us that the subject would be placed for discussion in the next board meeting.

To evolve the government's response, it became necessary to look at the governance structure of RBI more closely, especially the power and authority of the Central Board and the government as per the RBI Act and policy decisions taken over the years. When the government examined the governance of RBI in more depth, several matters came to light.

Section 7(2) of the RBI Act vests the general superintendence and direction of the affairs and business of RBI in the Central Board of Directors. These powers are quite broad and the board is authorized to exercise all powers and undertake any acts that may be exercised and done by RBI under the RBI Act.

However, in the 1950s, the Central Board entrusted all its powers to be exercised by a Committee of the Central Board and the governor. Over the years, the governor exercised all executive powers directly or through the CCB. The Central Board became more of a decorative body that met six times a year, for a talk followed by lunch. It ceased to make any executive decisions. The 12 February circular was not only issued without any reference to the government, but also without any discussion in or approval of RBI Central Board.

All general powers were exercised by the CCB which met every week, with the meeting attended by directors who happened to be in Mumbai that day. This ensured that government directors never participated in CCB meetings. At best, one or two non-RBI directors attended. Otherwise, it became an internal RBI committee comprising the governor and the deputy governors. The CCB took all the decisions, which came to the board for information as part of thousands of pages of the board agenda after a considerable amount of time, and the decisions having been implemented.

RBI created some specialized committees as well, without the participation of government directors. All powers relating to banking supervision were concentrated in the Board of Financial Supervision (BFS) headed by the governor with no representative of the government. All of RBI's decisions relating to the implementation of the PCA framework were rubber-stamped in the BFS, though these vitally affected the PSBs owned by the Government of India.

RBI is the regulator of the banking and financial system. But it seemed to be functioning without following the modern practices and standards other regulators followed. Very rarely were concept papers issued and discussions held with stakeholders. Most regulations were made in the form of circulars, internally drafted and issued unilaterally.

The government decided it was time to revisit the governance of RBI.

We examined the governance structure thoroughly and proposed some fundamental reforms. We wanted the primacy of the Central Board restored, the CCB's mandate and composition changed, and other specialized committees made more broad-based and functional. A comprehensive governance reforms note was drafted and proposed for the consideration of the Central Board meeting on 23 October. Finance Minister Arun Jaitley approved this agenda along with the agenda related to the ECF.

We sent the two agenda notes well in time. In the run up to the board meeting on 23 October, RBI did not react to the items I had proposed. On the issue of governance, RBI circulated an agenda item from its side. This item wanted the board to acknowledge that there was no issue with RBI's governance and the existing structure of delegation of powers, the CCB and other committees. In addition, RBI note proposed a new code of conduct for the directors aimed at restricting them from speaking to the media.

Urjit Patel Fights Hard

The meeting on 23 October was unprecedented in several respects. There was a virtual live coverage of the meeting throughout the day, although no one in the media had any access to the actual proceedings. Over fifty correspondents with their cameras were sitting at the main gate of RBI building. Directors were brought to RBI through a side road. The meeting began at 10 a.m. and lasted until 6 p.m., without finishing the agenda.

Four items relating to banking were agreed to be taken up first. Agenda items brought up by the government-nominated directors were taken up for consideration and presentations were made by them. Counter presentations were made by RBI officials. The discussions generated a fair amount of heat and argument.

The government directors insisted that the decisions/sense of the board be recorded then and there at the meeting. Two sets of drafts were prepared, with a gulf between them. Voices were raised and tempers flew. The governor fought every proposal or change that was different from the existing state of regulation. He was supported by his entire team: four deputy governors, executive directors and other officers brought in specifically for the item concerned. At times, he choked. He also had spasms, longer than usual, at this meeting. He took a break to rest in the attached anteroom. He skipped lunch.

Gurumurthy tried to play the role of umpire to bring about some rapprochement. At around 5 p.m., he began separate parleys with the governor and DFS Secretary Rajiv Kumar, whose agenda items had mainly taken up the day. At one stage, he announced there was agreement on the minutes/package relating to four items. When these were read out to everyone at about 5.30 p.m., there seemed to be little clarity. In my view, Gurumurthy seemed to have given up more ground than required. I told Rajiv and Gurumurthy that I had difficulty relating to two items. The minutes were not finalized.

It was decided that the next meeting to approve the minutes and discuss the remaining items would be convened within fifteen days.

The governor seemed to be under a lot of pressure. While his worldview remained alarmist and excessively negative, he stood his ground. His team fought well. They had also prepared well. It appeared to me that he had decided to dig in his heels and carry on with the battle.

Agreement on Decisions of 23 October Meeting Become Contentious

Gurumurthy was assertive and proactive. He flashed his draft of agreement on the four issues to the PMO and Finance Minister Arun Jaitley. He indicated to them that while the RBI governor and Rajiv Kumar were in agreement with his formulation, I had a disagreement. To be fair, he added that I did have a point.

I had also conveyed my takeaways of the meeting to Arun Jaitley, who noted that there were significant differences between Gurumurthy's version and mine. Two days later, Gurumurthy was asked to come to Delhi from Chennai. A meeting was held at Finance Minister Arun Jaitley's residence. Party President Amit Shah, Railway Minister Piyush Goyal and the principal secretary and additional principal secretary to the prime minister were present, besides Rajiv Kumar and me. Soon, different interpretations of what Gurumurthy thought he had presented and what the RBI governor had thought he had agreed to appeared. There was also an acknowledgement of the imprecise nature of Gurumurthy's draft. Amit Shah had more inside and accurate information about what had transpired at the meeting and he seemed to agree with my version of the event.

It was agreed that Rajiv Kumar would prepare the first draft in precise language of what we considered was confirmed by the

RBI governor. As this would form the record of minutes of the meeting, we also decided we would agree on every word of the draft. After that, the draft would be sent to Governor Urjit Patel for confirmation so there was no ambiguity.

The draft prepared by Rajiv and somewhat refined by me was quite different than what Gurumurthy had attempted sketchily. This draft was sent to Governor Patel for confirmation. He refused to acknowledge it, let alone accept it. However, we decided to stick to our draft. This was taken up at the next board meeting on 20 November 2018. The RBI team objected to the method of drawing up the minutes of the board meeting in this manner. We had also discussed that the consensus decisions should be conveyed as the directions of the board. RBI team objected to this idea as well.

After many points of order and other objections to the content, Rajiv Kumar and Viral Acharya were asked to agree on an acceptable draft of the agreed decisions. Again, there was an hour-long discussion, with some attempts to go back on decisions made. Finally, everyone agreed to the draft minutes of the meeting. At the end of the board meeting on 20 November, a press release was issued by RBI announcing these and other decisions on the ECF and governance framework of RBI.

An Unlikely Resignation

The fierceness with which Governor Urjit Patel fought to protect the turf of RBI in the meeting of 23 October had convinced me that the likelihood of him resigning was almost non-existent.

Then came the onslaught in which he made his 'war' with the government public, by asking Deputy Governor Viral Acharya to deliver his incendiary speech on 26 October. These were clear indications that Urjit Patel had decided to fight it out.

I had negotiated a swap agreement with the Japanese in late October, which involved an exchange of messages with Governor Urjit Patel. The oil prices situation had also eased substantially sometime in November, after the worst did not happen in the enforcement of sanctions against Iran. The FPI inflows started coming back as well. The worst seemed to be over for the current account. The swap deal with Japan gave RBI another option to bring in dollars if temporarily needed. Although the IL&FS blowout had taken place in September–October 2018, the macroeconomic and foreign exchange situation as well as the rupee appeared to be much more stable and the emergency seemed to be abating.

At the board meeting on 20 November, another marathon meeting, Urjit Patel was in much better shape. He stayed put during the meeting that lasted over nine hours. We agreed to the formation of an expert committee to go into the issue of the ECF as well. There was some active progress.

By the end of November, there was general consensus in the government that the situation had eased materially, though large concerns remained on liquidity conditions and governance and the ECF agenda was still only at the beginning. Banking issues seemed to have been resolved. The idea of Urjit Patel resigning had virtually disappeared from the minds of the finance minister and government secretaries.

The unexpected happened on 10 December.

I was chairing a meeting in the committee room close to my chamber in North Block from 5 p.m. onwards. Around 6 p.m. as I entered my room, I saw the news flashing on the television channels: RBI Governor Urjit Patel had resigned.

Urjit Patel resigned in a most unusual manner. He put his resignation letter on RBI website. He did not send in his resignation to the government as required under the rules and established procedure. After posting his resignation letter on RBI website, he simply went home. He referred to 'personal reasons' for his decision to step down. He recalled his association with RBI in various capacities over the years and attributed the considerable accomplishments of the bank to its staff, officers and management. He also expressed his gratitude to his colleagues and directors of RBI.

There was something very conspicuous by its absence—there was no reference to the government, PM and finance minister in the resignation letter.

I called Arun Jaitley who confirmed that he had no prior knowledge of the resignation. However, he said he intended to accept his resignation forthwith and not ask for any reconsideration. Within an hour or so, the finance minister issued a statement noting his deep appreciation for the services rendered by Dr Urjit Patel to India, in his capacity as the governor and the deputy governor of RBI. He further noted it was a pleasure to deal with him and benefit from his scholarship. Arun Jaitley wished Dr Patel all the very best and 'many more years of public service'.

Urjit Patel's elevation as governor was solely the decision of Narendra Modi and the PMO. However, he did not express any gratitude towards the PM. I thought he did not meet the PM before deciding to resign; later, I discovered that he had.

An important public figure, who happened to be seated next to Dr Urjit Patel on a flight on 7 December from Mumbai to Delhi, told me about ten days later that Patel appeared to be edgy as the flight had got somewhat delayed. He had an appointment with Prime Minister Modi at 4 p.m. that day. Prime Minister Modi also publicly acknowledged in January 2019 that Urjit Patel had discussed his intention to resign with him, some months earlier.

The PM offered a laudatory tribute to Dr Urjit Patel on 10 December. He tweeted: 'Dr Urjit Patel is an economist of a very high calibre with a deep and insightful understanding of macroeconomic issues. He steered the banking system from chaos to order and ensured discipline. Under his leadership, RBI brought financial stability.'

I tried to call Urjit Patel that day. He did not pick up the phone. It was not unexpected. Our paths had crossed for about eighteen months and, professionally, it was quite a satisfying journey together.

Selection of a New Governor: A Sideshow in Which I Featured

The Central government appoints the governor of RBI. For all kinds of casual vacancies arising in the office of the governor, except in circumstances not involving vacation of appointment by a governor under Section 11(1) of the RBI Act, the Central government has to appoint an officer to officiate as governor on the recommendation of the Central Board. This provision was not applicable in this case. As Dr Urjit Patel had 'vacated' his office, there could not have been any temporary or officiating appointment.

The government needed to select the next governor without any loss of time as the office could not have been left unattended.

I was holding the charge of secretary, DFS, which is the administrative department for RBI, as Rajiv Kumar was on leave with his daughter's marriage approaching. It is the job of DFS to convene the meeting of the selection committee chaired by the cabinet secretary to recommend a panel for the governor. I immediately checked the relevant provisions. From the records of DFS, it appeared that the role of DFS was largely secretarial.

I received a call from the cabinet secretariat to come at 8 p.m. the same evening to participate in the meeting of the search-cum-selection committee. I reached with whatever sketchy records were available in DFS and a copy of the RBI Act as the Section 11 (1) provision was significant in the context.

When I got there, I found Rajiv Kumar also present. It intrigued me and I wondered why I was also called for the meeting if he was there as secretary, DFS. Rajiv had also served as establishment officer of the government for long and was much more informed and knowledgeable about personnel matters.

I asked him why he was there. He responded cryptically, in half jest, that both of us were possibly under consideration for the post. For my part, I thought that both of us were called to be on surer ground about the rules and regulations applicable, as I was only temporarily holding the charge while he knew much more about the matter. However, I started thinking about the possibility in case I was offered the job.

I had about two years of service left in the IAS. I was enjoying my job in the Ministry of Finance. I felt it was not in my best interest to go to RBI at this stage. At the same time, the job of the RBI governor is among the most prestigious in the country. It also offered enormous potential to contribute to the development of India's economic and financial system. It would indeed have been an honour and a privilege.

In terms of professional abilities and competence, I thought I was qualified to be the RBI governor. However, I also realized that I had been virtually at the forefront of the tussles between RBI and the government in the past six months. As I was the face of the government, I was quite likely to be persona non grata for RBI management and staff.

On the whole, I felt it was premature for me to move to RBI. I preferred to continue as secretary, DEA, which would soon morph into the job of finance secretary. I decided to say very frankly that I would not like to be considered for the job. However, if the government decided to send me as governor, I would abide by its decision.

I joined the meeting as officiating secretary, DFS. As mentioned, Rajiv Kumar was also present. As the meeting progressed, macroeconomist Dr Rathin Roy, who was at the meeting as an expert member, proposed that I should also be considered for the job as he felt I fit the bill the best. Whether it was a part of the choreography or a spontaneous suggestion, I have never asked Dr Roy about the matter. The cabinet secretary immediately asked me to go to his chamber and wait for him. As soon as I got up and neared the exit to the committee room, he asked me to stop. He mentioned that he thought I had a lot of service left and might not be interested in the job at this stage. He wanted me to indicate my preference before I left.

Fortunately, I had thought the matter through earlier. Standing at the end of the table in the cabinet secretariat's committee room, just near the exit gate, I told him that as I had about two years of service left, I did not think it was an appropriate time for me to go to RBI from a personal point of view. However, as RBI was in a very difficult situation at that point of time, I would be willing to go only if the government needed my services.

The meeting ended after about forty-five minutes. The committee decided to shortlist a panel of three IAS officers for the job. I was part of the panel with Shaktikanta Das, former secretary, DEA, and Ajay Tyagi, chairman, SEBI. I was told that Shaktikanta Das and I were the two serious contenders.

The next day, on 11 December, the selection process played out in which I had no role. I was told later that Prime Minister Modi was not in favour of letting me leave the government at that juncture. Shaktikanta Das was appointed governor of RBI.

I was quite happy with the outcome. DEA had to complete a small formality—Shaktikanta Das had to resign from membership of the XV Finance Commission. I processed his resignation quickly and got the President's formal orders.

India had a new the RBI governor on 12 December 2018.

21

There Were Issues with SEBI as Well

IN THE DOMESTIC FINANCE SPHERE, BESIDES CURRENCY AND COINAGE, THE most important function assigned to DEA relates to the capital markets. The allocation of business rules assigns the work relating to 'policy measures for the regulation and development of the securities market and investor protection' and 'new investments and securities for mobilizing resources from the capital markets, investment policy, including investment policy of Life Insurance Corporation of India and General Insurance Corporation of India' to DEA. Further, all matters relating to forward contracts and the Forward Markets Commission (FMC) have also been transferred to DEA.

Equity is raised only through issuance of securities. Forward markets have also become increasingly security-based. Credit markets still have a substantial presence of non-securitized loans from the banking and non-banking space, though bonds markets have also developed enormously in India. There is also an increasing preference to securitize loans, both performing and non-performing. Currently, the capital markets are predominantly a securities market. Therefore, DEA has an extremely important role to play in the development and growth of capital markets in India.

Over the years, DEA has undertaken substantial legislative development work for the orderly development of capital markets in the country. The principal law for development of regulation of capital markets is the Securities Contract (Regulation) Act, 1956, or SCRA 1956.

An independent regulatory system for the securities market—the Securities and Exchange Board of India—was established in the country by the Securities and Exchange Board of India Act, 1992. To establish the dematerialized securities system, the Depositories Act, 1996, was enacted. Futures trade in commodities was regulated under the Forward Contracts (Regulation) Act, 1952, which has also been majorly converted into securities; for this reason, the administration of this Act was transferred from the Ministry of Consumer Affairs (MCA) to DEA in 2013.

Over the years, SEBI has developed into a formidable organization and has increasingly led the securities regulation and development work. However, DEA retains considerable authority under the SCRA Act, including recognition of stock exchanges, and has the authority to issue policy directions to SEBI. DEA is also represented in the SEBI Board. Usually, secretary, DEA, or the joint secretary in charge of capital markets in DEA sits on the SEBI board.

Depository Receipts Scheme 2014, a Long Wait to Operationalization

Indian companies got foreign investments both through the FDI and FPI routes, but they could not raise capital by listing their equities abroad. In 1993, the government had opened a route to indirectly issue/list equity shares of Indian companies abroad by bringing in the Foreign Currency Convertible Bonds and Ordinary Shares (through depository receipt mechanism) Scheme, 1993. This scheme enabled issuance of over $20 billion of global depository receipts (GDRs) and American depository receipts (ADRs) by over 350 companies. However, it had certain serious shortcomings: only listed companies issuing DRs; the permission of the government/SEBI; weaknesses in jurisdictions where DRs could be issued; lack of transparency on the subscribers of DRs; and concerns about it being used as an instrument for money-laundering.

The government formulated a new set of rules to facilitate issue of DRs outside India and notified a new scheme, the Depository Receipts Scheme, 2014, which was to come into effect from 15 December 2014. This scheme permitted 'permissible securities' (securities issued under SCRA, which could be acquired by non-residents under FEMA), to be turned into DRs (foreign currency-denominated instruments, whether listed on an international exchange or not) issued by a foreign depository (a person not prohibited from acquiring permissible securities) and regulated in a permissible jurisdiction (of a member country of the Financial Action Task Force, or FATF, with the securities regulator of that country being a member of the International Organization of Securities Commission, or IOSCO).

The scheme was comprehensively defined and laid out all aspects of the DR regime in clear terms. With this scheme, the 1993 Scheme was repealed. While SEBI was required to issue guidelines under the 2014 scheme to implement it, it did not do so. Consequently, DR issues came to a crashing halt. When I reviewed the implementation status of the scheme in late 2017, the DR scheme seemed to have literally been dismissed as something inherently unimplementable.

Interested in getting to the root of the issue, I convened meetings of all concerned, including SEBI, RBI and foreign investment banks that had earlier acted as sponsors of DRs. The examination led to the crystallization of one issue that had become insurmountable. As SEBI had mandated for domestic holders of securities, it wanted the details of all the holders, including final beneficiaries of the DRs; whereas international stock exchanges permitted what is called 'omnibus holding' of securities, where foreign depositories did not need to hold details of individual subscribers and holders of securities.

Having found several cases of misuse, where Indian residents and non-residents had used the GDR/ADR route to launder money, SEBI had its reasons to demand these details. However, this demand could simply not be met as most foreign jurisdictions where DRs were to be issued did not require and collect the details of individual beneficiary owners.

It took a few months to bring SEBI around to accept the reality that it could not get this information. We gave instances of bond subscribers in masala bonds and Euro-bond issuances, where RBI did not insist on getting these details. Once SEBI accepted the fact of the situation, it clutched onto another excuse. It discovered that the Department of Revenue under the Prevention of Money-Laundering (Maintenance of Records) Rules, 2005, had made regulators like SEBI responsible for framing guidelines/regulations to collect requisite details to ensure there was no money-laundering. Now SEBI asked these rules be amended such that there was no obligation to collect details of the final beneficial holders under the omnibus securities holding schemes of the permissible jurisdiction.

It took another six months to persuade the Department of Revenue to agree to amend the rules. Finally, sometime in March 2019, we had agreed to a draft of the amendment that the Department of Revenue would make and, thereafter, SEBI would notify the guidelines to bring the 2014 DR scheme into effect.

The wheels of rule-making move quite slowly in the Government of India in the normal course. The notification incorporating the gist of the agreed language arrived in March 2019 and after all kinds of vetting was finally issued in September 2019. It incorporated two explicit provisions that provided the necessary comfort to SEBI.

First, it stated that where a client subscribing to or dealing in DRs or equity share (this was to provide for the additional situation when direct listing would be permitted) issues or lists DRs, determination, identification and verification of the ultimate beneficial owner would be done as per the norms of such jurisdiction. Second, even when an Indian listed or resident entity is the client or owner with controlling interest in such a DR entity, it would not be necessary to identify and verify the identity of any shareholder or beneficial owner of such an entity.

Once the Department of Revenue issued this unambiguous notification in September 2019, SEBI issued the Framework for Issue of Depository Receipts on 10 October 2019, five years after the Depository Scheme, 2014, was notified in October 2014. While it based the framework on relaxations notified by the Department of Revenue, it enjoined upon the Indian depositories to develop a good system to monitor foreign holdings by DR sponsors in terms of observing various limits and constraints; for instance, if there was a sectoral limit on foreign holding, foreign holdings, including through DRs, had to be within that limit.

In February 2020, expecting Indian companies to issue DRs, the Government of India notified that the proceeds of foreign contribution to DRs could be brought and retained at the International Finance Centre, GIFT City, Gandhinagar.

Indian depositories took some time to develop this monitoring framework. Again, after another year had gone by, in October 2020 SEBI notified 'broad operational guidelines' for the purpose of monitoring the foreign holdings, including those held by way of DRs. Through this circular, SEBI authorized Indian depositories to 'prescribe the formats and other details' as might be necessary to operationalize the framework in consultation with each other and market participants.

We are still to see the DR route being used by Indian companies to raise foreign equity capital. In the meantime, a new instrument— special purpose, acquisition companies (SPAC)—also called blank cheque companies, has come into existence globally that bypasses all the Indian regulations incorporated in the DR Scheme, 2014. Renew Power, the first SPAC company, was listed in August 2021 on the New York Stock Exchange with a market cap of $4.5 billion. A few other India focussed SPACs raised funds in the US, but no other company actually listed. At one stage, SEBI also toyed with the idea of coming up with regulations for Indian SPACs. However, this was not followed through. Lately the fascination for SPACs has been evaporating globally.

The UAE Insists on Categorization as Sovereign Wealth Fund

The Abu Dhabi Investment Authority is the sovereign wealth fund established by the Abu Dhabi Emirate of the UAE. There are other

SWFs in Abu Dhabi like Mubadala. There are seven emirates in the UAE; Abu Dhabi is the richest. All the emirates have set up one or more investment funds, which are operationally independent from each other. To some extent, these funds compete with each other and don't share information with each other.

As per the limit placed by SEBI, a single foreign portfolio investor could not own more than 10 per cent of the issued equity of a company. If more than one FPI was part of a group, the 10 per cent limit applied to the entire group. As SWFs like ADIA and Mubadala are ultimately owned by the Abu Dhabi government or the sheikh ruling the emirate, SEBI treated Abu Dhabi entities as part of one FPI group. This made the 10 per cent total investment limit applicable to ADIA, Mubadala and other SWFs/government entities as a group.

In 2015, during the visit of Prime Minister Modi to the UAE, a joint statement was issued that mentioned the establishment of a UAE–India Infrastructure Investment Fund with the aim of reaching a target of $75 billion to support investment in India's infrastructure, especially in railways, ports, roads, airports, industrial corridors and industrial parks. The Abu Dhabi government and its investment vehicles like ADIA, expected exceptional treatment from India as this was one of the largest ever investment commitments made by any foreign government entity to India.

The SEBI regulation on clubbing the investment limit by various Abu Dhabi investment vehicles irritated them, and rightly, to a great extent. The clubbing regime of SEBI assumed that different investment entities, ostensibly owned by the same beneficial owner, operated like a single entity. This was far off the mark. Once the funds were released by the Abu Dhabi government or its ruling family from their personal estates to ADIA or Mubadala, the government or its officers played no role in the matter of the investment made. Even among the investing vehicles, there was no exchange of information or coordination in making specific investments. As a senior authority of ADIA told me once, all or any Abu Dhabi authorities might apply for allotment of a share in the same company in its IPO without knowing whether the other was applying.

Their petitions to SEBI to treat these entities as separate and not part of a group did not yield any response. To make their irritation worse, they did not know how much any of the others owned in a particular company and, therefore, had no way to even know whether they had breached the 10 per cent limit and when. The SEBI's regulations were tough. If any group entity breached the 10 per cent limit, the excess had to be divested within five working days; else, there were penalties.

The Abu Dhabi entities were quite scared of falling on the wrong side of the regulations and being penalized. They flagged this issue with me at every meeting chaired by the PM or the finance minister. This constant refrain had a dampening impact on the otherwise enthusiastic and growing investment relationship between India and Abu Dhabi.

Some other parties were also upset. Investment and pension funds of different Canadian provinces had also set up investment vehicles in India. They did not want to be treated as part of a single group as they were structurally different governments—not only different from the federal Government of Canada, but also different from each other.

I took the matter up with SEBI Chairman Ajay Tyagi. He appreciated our concerns but did not agree to frame or interpret the regulations to treat the Abu Dhabi entities as separate. He cited the case of Singapore entities GIC and Temasek, which were exempted from being treated as part of one group as per a bilateral treaty between India and Singapore. He lobbed the ball back by saying that if the government wanted to treat Abu Dhabi entities as separate, it could be done by entering into a treaty to that effect.

Continuous follow-up with Tyagi and SEBI resulted in some movement. After agreement with DEA, SEBI issued a circular making certain clarifications regarding the clubbing of investment limits of foreign governments/foreign government-related entities. By this, it clarified that investment by foreign governments/related entities from provinces/states of countries with a federal structure, were excluded from being clubbed. Further, SEBI worked with the National Securities Depository Ltd (NSDL) to create a system of aggregate holdings of FPIs/investor groups in any particular scrip. It claimed that by referring to the NSDL, ADIA and other investment entities of Abu Dhabi could ascertain their combined holding in any particular group.

This did not satisfy ADIA and the Abu Dhabi authorities. I drafted a rule distinguishing the investor entities of one single beneficial owner, if the entities operated under separate management and did not share information or coordinated with each other. However, SEBI found that too difficult to enforce operationally and objectively.

Finally, I decided that the government had to assume the power to declare, by way of a notification, which countries' entities it would treat as separate entities and not part of a group. I incorporated this in the draft Foreign Exchange Management (Non-Debt) Rules, which DEA drafted to implement the separation of authority between the government and RBI under FEMA. The FEMA amendment in 2015 had given the government authority over non-debt regulation, and RBI over debt regulation.

These rules were finally notified in October 2019. They provide that investment by foreign government agencies shall be clubbed with the investment by the foreign government or its related agencies for the purpose of the calculation of a 10 per cent limit for FPI in a single company. However, 'certain foreign government agencies and their related entities may be exempted from such clubbing requirements and other investment conditions either by way of an agreement or treaty with other sovereign government or by an order of the Central Government'.

Abu Dhabi investment vehicles, including ADIA, have finally been exempted from the clubbing requirement.

Reporting Loan Defaults to Stock Exchanges Faces Hostile Opposition

The SEBI's listing rules require listed entities to disclose all material events of default to the stock exchanges. For all listed equities, debentures and other securities, the issuing listed corporates have been obligated to disclose delay or default in payment of interest, principal, dividend, etc., to the stock exchanges since 2015.

As per this, if a company defaulted even one rupee of interest payment on any listed debenture, it was required to report the event to the stock exchanges within one working day of such default. This reporting regime came to be known as the 'one rupee one day' default regime. However, it was not applicable to loans and other credit facilities taken by the listed companies from banks, non-banks and other lenders.

Based on approval from its board before I joined DEA in July 2017, SEBI issued a circular on 4 August 2017 additionally mandating listed corporates to report to the stock exchanges within one working day of not paying interest or principal repayment on the due date. For cash credit facilities, the day of default was defined as thirty days from the account becoming overdrawn.

Secretary, DFS, Rajiv Kumar immediately raised a storm. Ajay Tyagi, SEBI chairman, was his batchmate from the IAS. He spoke to him but did not get much of a response. Rajiv took it up with the finance minister. Beleaguered as Rajiv was after the asset quality review in the banks, which had saddled PSBs with huge non-performing debt, he did not want another trigger to worsen his woes.

However, the SEBI circular was intended to promote transparency and good corporate behaviour. By bringing information relating to delay and default in servicing loans taken to the notice of the stock exchanges, investors could take more informed decisions about the true state of the financial strength of the listed corporates. Moreover, there was no good reason to follow a different regime for delays and defaults on bonds and loans.

The finance minister convened a discussion. Rajiv Kumar was emphatic that the SEBI circular must be withdrawn. He stated that the non-performing loans of PSBs would go up by over ₹50,000 crore if the circular was implemented. The government was in the midst of considering a capitalization package for PSBs, which was turning out to be quite hefty even without the additional implications on account of this new problem. I argued against asking SEBI to withdraw the circular. I felt sunlight was a better cure. I also suspected that the real reason for Rajiv's insistence was that this move would bring all the mess in the PSB loans system into the public domain, leaving no scope for the banks to manage widespread loan defaults. I was on the SEBI Board; Rajiv Kumar wasn't. The finance minister saw the merit of my viewpoint but was not prepared to overrule Rajiv. He asked me to find a way out.

Rajiv took the matter to the PMO. Nripendra Misra called the two of us for a meeting. He was clear that the banks could not be asked to take another hit on account of this new regulatory overreach. I argued that the banks were governed by RBI regulations on recognition of non-performing loans. The mandatory disclosure of default by the listed corporates (not banks) did not alter RBI regime. The banks classified such delays/defaults in three categories of special mention accounts (SMAs) depending on the period of delay: thirty days (SMA 1), thirty-one to sixty days (SMA 2), and sixty-one to ninety days (SMA 3). Only after the default persisted beyond ninety days (i.e., after SMA 3) did the banks classify such defaulted loans as NPAs.

Rajiv countered by saying that most corporates clear the due payment with a few days of delay and, therefore, if the delay was publicly reported on Day 1, such delayed payments that were not actually defaults would create an adverse public impact. Nripendra Misra asked me to take up the matter with SEBI to find a solution.

The 4 August circular was to come into effect from 1 October 2017. I discussed the matter with Ajay Tyagi who took an uncompromising stand on the DFS request to withdraw the circular. The circular had generated public interest. I was asked questions by the media. I took the official line that the government was studying the matter and would take a view before 1 October 2017. The matter came up in a board meeting in RBI as well. Deputy Governor Viral Acharya and board member Manish Sabharwal were scathing in their comments about the government trying to stop the right thing from happening.

The SEBI Board meeting was scheduled in the last week of September 2017. I informed the finance minister that I would not ask for either withdrawal or postponement of the 'one day one rupee' default circular in the meeting. However, I favoured a slight modification. To ensure that owing to frictional delays by a few days, which could happen for many reasons, the listed corporates were not made to rush to report to the stock exchanges, I believed they should be mandated to report delays/defaults only if these extended beyond thirty days of the due date, i.e., only if the loan were in SMA 1 should the reporting requirement be mandatorily imposed.

The finance minister convened another meeting. I proposed my solution. Rajiv did not find it agreeable. He still wanted the circular to be withdrawn. I told the finance minister that I would try to persuade Ajay Tyagi to postpone the date of the circular coming into force, to redefine the reporting obligations to only SMA 1 accounts. But Rajiv did not budge. I said that what Rajiv was asking for could only be done if the DFS were to ask SEBI officially for withdrawal/ postponement.

On 29 September 2017, DFS wrote to SEBI, also citing RBI's assessment, that the SEBI circular would warrant additional capital infusion of ₹26,000 crore in the banks. A request was made that as the matter needed to be further studied, implementation of the circular might be deferred. Ajay Tyagi deferred it to 1 January 2018.

In this postponement period, Nripendra Misra took it upon himself to resolve the matter in view of the fiscal and financial implications. He also established direct contact with Ajay Tyagi. Ajay started wavering under the PMO's direct fire. However, I persuaded Nripendra Misra to agree (with some reluctance) to the thirty-day default regime that I was championing. However, Ajay Tyagi developed second thoughts about the wisdom of moving ahead with the circular.

Before the board meeting held in the last week of December 2017, I told Ajay Tyagi to modify the requirement from one working day to thirty working days and bring in a much-needed and transparent regime to bring loan defaults to the notice of investors. By that time, he had got quite weary about the circular and told me he was withdrawing it from the board agenda. The circular agenda was indeed withdrawn by SEBI. Ajay Tyagi informed the media after the board meeting.

A good move died but it could not remain dead forever as this disclosure requirement was absolutely necessary in the interest of investors and for cleaning up the mess in public-sector loans.

According to media reports, SEBI, still under Ajay Tyagi, revived the proposal in late 2019 and proposed (the SEBI Board's note is available on the Internet) to bring in the August 2017 circular as is, with only one change: the listed entities were to make default disclosures within thirty days from the date of default. This circular was notified on 21 November 2019 and did not create any flutter. The PSBs also took it in their stride. What SEBI could have done in December 2017 it finally did in November 2019, and on the lines that I had argued.

Taking Over SEBI's Excessive Reserves

The SEBI is the state, commonly equated with government as 'all local or other authorities within the territory of India or under the control of Government of India' are the 'state' within the meaning of Article 12 of the Constitution of India. Securities and stock exchanges were earlier regulated directly by the Government of India under the SCRA 1956, before SEBI was formed in 1992. Many functions and authorities of the Government of India under SCRA 1956 have been transferred to SEBI. What SEBI does is a pure and simple state and government function.

It collects three kinds of revenues: fees and income for registering and servicing market intermediaries; income by way of fines and penalties imposed for offences and infractions under the SEBI Act and collection of proceeds of disgorgement and other receipts levied for insider trading and other stock-market malpractices.

The SEBI Act created a Securities and Exchange Board of India General Fund (SEBI General Fund) and provided for crediting all grants, fees and charges received by the board under the Section 14(a) of the SEBI Act: all sums realized by way of penalties under the SEBI Act Section 14 (aa) and all sums received by SEBI from other sources as may be decided upon by the Central government (Section 14(b). Section 14 (aa) was omitted in 2002 to pave the way for the penalties to go directly to the Consolidated Fund of India in place of the SEBI General Fund.

The SEBI General Fund was to be applied to meet salaries, allowances and other remuneration of members, officers and other employees of the board, the expenses of the board in discharge of its functions described in Section 11 of the Act, and the expenses on objects and for purposes authorized by the Act.

Levying fees and charges for its services at rates that were far higher than its expenditure requirement, SEBI was quite liberal in incurring capital expenditure and establishing investor education institutions. Still, SEBI could not utilize its annual revenues fully. Consequently, it had a balance of over ₹4,000 crore in the corpus fund at the end of financial year 2018–19, held bank deposits and other short-term investments of over ₹2,000 crore and had an annual surplus of over ₹400 crore in the year. In our assessment, SEBI had no plans to utilize the accumulated income.

There was a deficiency in the SEBI law—nowhere was it defined how it would treat its surplus income. Therefore, I felt that the government should establish a reserve fund in SEBI, in addition to the general fund. While SEBI should be allowed to retain 25 per cent of its annual surplus, subject to an overall level of two years' expenditure in the reserve fund, the remainder of the surplus should flow to the government like the income flow from penalties and fines. Section 13 of the SEBI Act provides for the government to give grants to SEBI. In the unlikely event of SEBI's reserve fund running out, the government could always provide grants, as it did to many other regulators.

These proposals were prepared and presented to Finance Minister Nirmala Sitharaman for consideration and approval for inclusion in the Finance Bill 2019 to be presented along with Budget 2019. I also informed Ajay Tyagi of the government's intent. He was not amused and took the matter up with the finance minister. For a change, Nirmala Sitharaman agreed with me and approved the proposal.

Part IX of the Finance Act in July 2019 amended the SEBI Act to provide for taking 'capital expenditure' specifically on board as legitimate SEBI expenditure. However, to ensure that capital expenditure was reasonable, it provided for capital expenditure as per the plan approved by the SEBI Board and the Central government.

The Finance Act also created a reserve fund and mandated transfer of 25 per cent of the annual surplus in the general fund to the reserve fund.

After the budget was presented, the media, which was already excited by what was going on with RBI with respect to its capital framework, latched onto this news and labelled the government's move as an intent to take over SEBI's reserves as well. Tyagi wrote a letter to the finance minister terming the move as one that weakened the independence of SEBI and asked for its rollback. His request was not heeded and the Finance Bill, July 2019, was approved. With this, the SEBI Act stood amended.

The question of transfer of surplus, however, has still not been finally settled.

We also proposed a revised format for the annual report of SEBI, which, after a lot of to-and-fro, was finally notified by the government in 2020–21. The SEBI Annual Report 2020–21 was in this new format.

SEBI Seeks to Regulate Chartered Accountants and Other Professionals

A consultative paper was prepared by SEBI, which made a case for it to register and regulate professionals like chartered accountants, company secretaries and others. The argument made in the consultative paper was that professionals like chartered accountants, company secretaries, cost accountants, valuers and others are engaged by listed companies. These professionals perform functions like auditing accounts, providing various certifications and giving valuation certificates that market participants and investors rely on to make investment decisions. In this manner, these professionals perform the functions of market intermediaries.

As SEBI had an obligation to register and regulate market intermediaries, it believed it should register and regulate these professionals as well.

All these professionals have their own association bodies, most created by acts of Parliament, which also have comprehensive rules of conduct. In their scheme of things, if any chartered accountant or company secretary, for example, were to commit any misconduct in relation to auditing accounts or providing certification, as the case might be, action could be taken against the defaulting professional. All these professionals are registered and regulated by their own professional bodies.

This consultative paper came up for consideration and approval in one of the meetings of the SEBI Board. I found SEBI's intent and approach excessively over-reaching. In my understanding, SEBI had every right to act against any of these professionals if their actions led to the commission of any offence, insider trading or market manipulation specified in the SEBI Act. Further, in my judgement, SEBI had enough powers to act against such offences. In fact, at that point of time, SEBI had initiated many investigations against chartered accountants and other professionals, exercising its power under the SEBI Act. The more famous cases included those against the partnership firm PWC and its auditors for alleged misdeeds in the Satyam case and many other chartered accountant firms in the National Spot Exchange case.

Therefore, I argued that there was neither any justification nor any authority with SEBI to register and regulate chartered accountants and other professionals. Instead, I said SEBI might specify specific rules and regulations that define the obligations of market intermediaries and the fiduciary obligations of chartered accountants and other professionals for better clarity.

After a debate, the SEBI team saw the logic of what I was saying and SEBI agreed to incorporate specific obligations in specific fiduciary obligations. It was agreed that chartered accountants and other professionals would not be registered and regulated. This also avoided a potential clash between SEBI and the statutory bodies regulating these professionals.

Nominating a Joint Secretary to the SEBI Board

DEA had been mostly represented on the SEBI Board by the joint secretary handling capital markets. In the recent past,

Arvind Mayaram was the first secretary, economic affairs, to join the board in 2012. When Rajiv Mehrishi replaced Arvind Mayaram in DEA in late 2014, he nominated Joint Secretary Manoj Joshi to the SEBI Board. The clock turned again in 2015 when Shaktikanta Das took charge as secretary, economic affairs, and decided to be on the board. When I joined DEA in 2017, the file was placed before me to ask for the finance minister's recommendation for my nomination to the SEBI Board.

I thought over the matter. Secretary, DEA, was on the board of three major institutions at that time—the Central Board of RBI, the SEBI Board and the LIC Board. I decided to continue with the current arrangement as I believed there was a need to treat both RBI and SEBI on a par. Moreover, the joint secretary, capital markets, at the time was not a very assertive and reform-minded officer. I thought I would review the status after a year or so.

The arrangement worked well. A number of issues were sorted out with the arrangement of broader policy issues discussed and solutions found in meetings chaired by me as secretary, with Ajay Tyagi joining in and SEBI-related specific capital market issues debated and decided in the SEBI Board. I attended almost all the SEBI board meetings.

There was an unfair practice in vogue in DEA about handling the SEBI agenda. DEA would examine the SEBI agenda in the Capital Markets Division and then propose specific comments on each item. Shaktikanta Das was not able to attend many meetings. The comments prepared by the Capital Markets Division, approved by the secretary, economic affairs, were communicated to SEBI which was expected to take every comment on record and act as per the advice tendered. If there was any comment that SEBI did not like or want to incorporate, it was expected to revert for resolution of the issue.

Ajay Tyagi rightly complained to me about this bad corporate governance practice. I agreed that a DEA representative must attend SEBI board meetings to present DEA's point of view. There were good chances that members would agree if the proposal or amendment sought, was in order. I discontinued the practice of sending written comments. In the several meetings that I attended, there were occasions when I saw the merit in what SEBI officials or other board members were saying. Whatever decisions the board took were incorporated in the meetings. There were very few occasions when I had to ask for the minutes to be modified.

Anand Mohan Bajaj, an officer of the Indian Audit Service, had earlier served as director in the Capital Markets Division. He knew the subject quite well. I inducted him as joint secretary, capital markets. He worked hard and with considerable application of mind. Sometime in January 2019, I thought he had accumulated adequate experience as joint secretary and could be trusted to represent DEA on the SEBI Board. I recommended his name to the finance minister.

Over the next few months, he ably represented DEA on the SEBI Board. He and the Capital Markets Division would prepare thoroughly for every board meeting and bring the entire agenda and possible views he should articulate before me. After a thorough discussion, we would decide on DEA's views on the matter, which were then formally approved on file.

The arrangement continued for some time. Recently, however, secretary, economic affairs has again assumed his place on the SEBI Board.

22

Recapitalizing Banks

Stressed Assets Pile Up in PSBs

BANK LOANS THAT ARE NOT SERVICED—PAYMENT OF INTEREST AND principal—on due dates, are termed stressed assets. RBI's regulations require banks to classify such stressed loans under one of three SMA categories, serviced within thirty/sixty/ninety days of the due date respectively. When a loan was not serviced even after a lapse of ninety days, it was classified as an NPA. Banks, particularly PSBs, would 'restructure' a loan that had either become an NPA or was about to turn into one.

Restructured loans were accounted as 'performing' as they would have revised repayment and interest payment schedules, but would actually be 'stressed'. Thus, stressed bank loan assets included SMA and restructured loans. In addition, if the banks had 'written off' some loans in their books (to claim deduction in income tax without foregoing the right to recover, treating such loans as unlikely to yield much in recovery), those were also added to the total quantum of stressed loans.

The banking system, especially PSBs, had opened the floodgates of loans, in particular to the industry and infrastructure sectors, from 2004–05 onwards when the animal spirits of the Indian industry were at their peak. Loans to this segment grew by more than 25 per cent every year between 2004–05 and 2007–08, and more than 20 per cent annually until 2011–12. Many of these loans became stressed. Banks liberally restructured loans with the proportion of restructured loans in total stressed loans rising from about 35 per cent in 2011 to over 50 per cent in 2014.

When RBI ordered an asset quality review in 2015, the skeletons in the cupboard started tumbling out. Total stressed assets of PSBs were found to be about 15 per cent of their gross loans and advances at the end of financial year 2015–16. In 2015–16, the highest ratio of gross NPAs (12 per cent) and stressed assets (about 20 per cent) in the banking industry, was from the industry sector.

In July 2017, the government was worried about the state of affairs in the PSBs. The fact that there was low economic growth on account of demonetization and GST implementation, as well as low growth in credit offtake, did not help matters. The government's 'Indradhanush' package, which had provided for infusion of ₹10,000 crore of equity in the PSBs during 2017–18, seemed to be peanuts.

Government Announces ₹2.11 Lakh Crore Capital Infusion Package

The government was in a very tough spot with respect to the PSBs. While the Basel norms that required banks' capital to be shored up, including building contingency capital buffers, were kicking in, the resolution of non-performing loans was virtually grounded. Privatizing banks was still not on the agenda. The only option left was to infuse capital in the banks.

The DFS, based on the advice of RBI, demanded ₹1 lakh crore of capital infusion. After a few days, it raised the requirement to over ₹2 lakh crore. The fiscal deficit situation did not allow the equity infusion to come from the Budget. Some people suggested to the PMO that the capital infusion should be off-Budget. An earlier infusion done in this manner a few years ago had invited scathing comments from the Comptroller and Auditor General (CAG).

I favoured transparent accounting of banks' capitalization as the government's capital expenditure. However, it was decided that the capital infusion would be 'below the line', making it fiscal deficit neutral. The PSBs would subscribe to special government securities issued for this purpose, with the proceeds used to invest in the same PSBs as equity.

To ward off the IMF, which treated such capital infusion as Budget expenditure if done in a non-market manner, the equity infusion was priced at SEBI's pricing formula. The special securities were priced the same as Government of India securities of similar tenor, plus 0.5 per cent for the non-tradable nature of the bonds.

Of the total package of ₹2.11 lakh crore, the government was to infuse ₹1.35 lakh crore and the rest was to be raised by issuing equity in the market and selling 'non-core' assets. The government shelled out, but very little was raised by the PSBs in the market. Only Punjab National Bank (PNB) raised money, but this came into question later on account of the Nirav Modi affair and other scams. No non-core assets could be sold. The government had to make up the balance capital infusion later.

I had favoured raising equity by the PSBs from the market. There were many people in the government, most prominently Piyush Goyal, who felt the PSBs' market share price was very low compared to their real worth and that the government should sell its shares only after recapitalization.

The capital infusion was announced with a big show. All the secretaries accompanied Finance Minister Arun Jaitley to the PIB Media Conference Hall on 24 October 2017. I made a presentation on the macroeconomic situation and answered questions on the features of recapitalization bonds, as the bonds were to be issued with the terms and conditions decided by the Budget Division in DEA.

Rajiv Kumar presented a new Enhanced Access and Service Excellence (EASE) framework to be used to assess the performance of recapitalized banks. The recapitalization package was well received by the market. The NSE PSU Bank index soared by 24 per cent that day; PNB rallied highest at 36 per cent, followed by SBI and Bank of Baroda.

The rally did not last the remaining five months of the financial year. With fresh frauds discovered, the PSB stocks cracked and PNB fell to nearly half its pre-October 2017 levels. The whole exercise ended up with the government infusing equity of ₹80,000 crore in that year (the rest was for the next year). Its equity investment got halved by the end of the financing year, but interest liability went up by over ₹7,000 crore a year.

Making IDBI Bank a Private Bank

IDBI Bank was the worst performing PSB. In 2018, its non-performing loans exceeded 27 per cent of the loan book. It was making large losses continuously. The government owned more than 94 per cent of the bank. IDBI Bank did not become a PSB on account of being nationalized. It was promoted by IDBI, a development finance institution created by an Act of Parliament, which promoted IDBI Bank when banking licences were granted to public and private institutions in 1993. Later, IDBI merged into IDBI Bank, bringing along loads of non-performing loans.

Unlike other PSBs, there was no legislative restriction of retaining a minimum 51 per cent stake with the government. The government was free to sell IDBI Bank like Air India or any other PSU. When I was in Washington, D.C., I was asked to explore the possibility of the International Finance Corporation taking over a majority stake in IDBI Bank, on its own or with other associates. I had done some good groundwork on the matter. Jin-Yong Cai, the IFC CEO, was keen to acquire the stake and was willing to offer about ₹100 a share to acquire a controlling interest along with other associates (IFC on its own was allowed to take a maximum 20 per cent stake). However, the officials in DFS could not structure the deal despite considerable support from the PMO, and it fell through.

In April/May 2018, the government offered IDBI Bank to LIC. Rajiv Kumar expected LIC Chairman V.K. Sharma to take over the bank upon the government's informal advice, but V.K. Sharma found the deal appalling for various reasons. RBI did not allow any single stakeholder to have more than 10 per cent voting rights in a bank. IDBI Bank was sitting over a big pile of non-performing loans. It had very little on the retail book and was feared to be making losses continuously.

Rightly, Sharma felt LIC did not know how to run a bank and could not be expected to turn it around. Sharma also pointed out that LIC's regulator, the Insurance Regulatory and Development Authority (IRDA), would not permit LIC to have more than a 15 per cent stake in IDBI Bank as a higher stake was not permissible under the investment rules framed under the Insurance Act and IRDA Act. The transaction was stuck.

Nripendra Misra called me and asked me to work the government–LIC deal to sell IDBI Bank. He further informed me that new IRDA Chairman Subhash Khuntia was not feeling secure enough to provide approval to LIC to take over a majority stake in IDBI Bank, which LIC Chairman V.K. Sharma required, to agree to do the transaction.

This sensitive matter could not have been discussed with the IRDA chairman, secretary, DFS, and LIC chairman in North Block. We met at a hotel over dinner. The IRDA chairman had genuine concerns. Giving such permission to LIC would have meant making a massive exception. Earlier, LIC was allowed to acquire 28 per cent of equity in Corporation Bank, which was also asked to be diluted over a five-year period. He was also concerned about the impact of this transaction on the LIC shareholders' fund, the protection of which was IRDA's biggest obligation in his judgement. V.K. Sharma sounded much more positive that day and was prepared to take 51 per cent stake from the government. I was on the LIC Board as well.

Rajiv explained the actual state of affairs of IDBI Bank to him and how it was slowly coming out of the woods. I argued with Subhash Khuntia to accept the proposed transaction as inevitable, if the privatization of IDBI Bank were to be carried out. V.K. Sharma talked about how synergetic the relationship between LIC and IDBI Bank was, as LIC needed a bank to distribute its products and manage its treasury operations. We gave assurances to IRDA and LIC that LIC would be able to sell the bank after some time if the latter found it advisable/necessary. We also assured them that RBI would provide a very long timeframe for LIC to dilute its stake if it wanted to retain the bank.

An issue also arose about how LIC would acquire a majority stake. There were two options: one was to sell an adequate number of shares out of the government's existing stock; the other was to make a preferential issue of fresh shares to give 51 per cent stake to LIC. My inclination was to sell the government's existing stock. This would have brought some disinvestment receipts to the government. However, Rajiv argued that IDBI Bank needed much larger capital to meet capital adequacy norms. I agreed with him.

Subhash Khuntia finally agreed with a lot of conditions. We fleshed out the major conditions and IRDA gave its approval to LIC's purchase of the 51 per cent government stake in IDBI Bank on 30 June 2018.

Some more time was taken to get RBI and cabinet approval. SEBI refused to exempt LIC from making a public offer. I advised the LIC Board not to insist on it in the interest of minority shareholders. In any case, LIC held about 8 per cent stake in IDBI Bank, which was classified as a public holding. Excluding that, only about 6 per cent of shares were really with the public. The LIC Board approved acquisition of up to 26 per cent of shares at a price of ₹61.73 per share; LIC got about 3 per cent of shares in the public offer.

The government was required to sell about 40 per cent of IDBI-issued capital to LIC to enable the 51 per cent equity stake. LIC completed the acquisition of the 51 per cent stake in IDBI Bank in January 2019.

The government announced its intent to privatize IDBI Bank in a real sense, i.e. selling majority shares (which required LIC to also off-load its shares) to a private party in 2020. The finance minister specifically referred to IDBI's privatization in the Budget speech 2021–22, while announcing a major policy decision to privatize two public-sector banks. She said: 'Other than IDBI Bank, we propose to take up the privatization of two public-sector banks and one general insurance company in the year 2021–22.'

Progress has, however, been quite slow. After lots of delay, a Preliminary Information Memorandum was finally issued on 7 October 2022 for selling the Government of India stake representing 30.48 per cent of IDBI equity and LIC stake representing 30.24 per cent of the IDBI equity (together a 60.72 per cent stake).

Several Pre-EOI queries were reportedly received from interested parties (specific details not disclosed by the government), which were responded to on behalf of the government on 25 November 2022. The government, on 14 December, extended the last date and time for submission of EoIs to 7 January 2023. The government reportedly received five responses/expressions of interest (names not officially disclosed until the writing of this book).

The next stage is to invite financial bids. There is no word about that bid. While there are still a lot of grey areas in strategic divestment of IDBI bank, there is some likelihood that the government might be able to complete this transaction in 2023–24.

Recapitalization to Free PSBs from PCA Framework

RBI had placed more than half the public-sector banks under a prompt corrective action (PCA) framework. In December 2018–19, as many as eleven out of twenty-one PSBs were under the PCA framework. A bank under the PCA framework is a 'narrow' bank. It can accept deposits but is barred from extending loans by and large. It can invest its resources in buying government securities.

Sometime in January 2019, a few weeks before the presentation of the Budget, Nripendra Misra called me over. He said a few PSBs would have to be brought out of the PCA framework and an amount of over ₹1.5 lakh crore would be needed for that. It was a shocker. We were separately fighting/working with RBI to lower the capital adequacy requirements for banks in line with global standards, postpone the contingency reserve capital requirement and use RBI's excess capital for bank recapitalization.

Rajiv Kumar sent in a file demanding over ₹1 lakh crore to bring six banks out of the PCA framework and also to prevent four others from getting covered under PCA (in addition to the eleven already in). His requirement included capital both for meeting the minimum capital adequacy and 'growth capital' (needed to expand the loan book).

RBI's PCA framework essentially revolved around two asks. First, risk-adjusted capital (capital to risk [weighted] assets ratio [CRAR]) should be 9 per cent and the net non-performing loans should be less than 6 per cent of the total risk-weighted loans. In fact, to meet both, DFS was relying only on capital infusion. The minimum capital requirement under these conditions literally meant that the banks needed capital of 9 per cent plus the amount by which the net NPAs were greater than 6 per cent. In addition, DFS asked for growth capital of about ₹50,000 crore (over and above the minimum regulatory capital for allowing banks to expand lending).

I went to the finance minister and also discussed the matter with Nripendra Misra. The DFS projections were based on the estimated situation at the end of financial year 2018–19. These were extra conservative. The PSBs to be brought out of the PCA framework were also reduced to three or four. The growth capital requirement was also brought down a notch. All this reduced the demand to about ₹90,000 crore. I proposed that the PSBs raise these amounts by issuing equity from the market and argued that their shares were unlikely to recover anytime soon (I pointed to the expectations raised the year before by Piyush Goyal and others). I also felt that the government was unnecessarily rushing in and we should wait for the results of 31 March to determine the actual amount required.

Perhaps the urgency of bringing some PSBs out of the PCA framework was owing to the imminent declaration of the 2019 general elections. I recorded a comprehensive note on the file, basically arguing that the capitalization of the identified PSBs was premature and that whatever amount was required to boost capital should be raised by the banks by issuing public equity if RBI could not be persuaded to part with the excess capital held.

I was overruled. Arun Jaitley wrote the longest note I had seen in my twenty months working with him. He rebutted every point I wrote, not convincingly but at least formally, and approved the proposal of DFS for capital infusion in PCA banks. My note also led Nripendra Misra to comment that I was not in tune with the thinking of the government.

RBI issued a press release on 31 January 2019, a day before the presentation of the 2019–20 interim Budget, removing restrictions under the PCA framework for three PSBs: Bank of India, Bank of Maharashtra and Oriental Bank of Commerce.

Over the years, all public-sector banks have been brought out of the PCA framework. Central Bank of India was the last one to get its honour back in September 2022.

23

Economic Policy Business with the Rest of the World

THE ECONOMIC POLICY BUSINESS WITH THE REST OF THE WORLD IS primarily conducted between three departments/ministries of the Government of India: DEA in the Ministry of Finance, the Department of Commerce (DoC) in the Ministry of Commerce and Industry, and the Ministry of External Affairs (MEA). DEA has the broadest assignment covering economic functions and India's interaction with the rest of the world, while DoC handles all international functions relating to trade and commerce. The MEA has the smallest number of economic functions allocated to it.

It is DEA that has been allocated the functions of foreign exchange management, which includes administration of the Foreign Exchange Management Act, policy relating to the exchange value of the rupee, management of foreign exchange resources, foreign and non-resident Indian investment, Indian direct overseas investment, matters concerning commercial borrowing from abroad, matters concerning gold and silver and management of external debt.

Another big chunk of work is the broad rubric of foreign aid for economic development, which includes matters relating to loan, credits and grants from foreign countries, special agencies, non-governmental foundation agencies, loans, credits and grants from multilateral agencies, borrowings from the International Monetary Fund and policy for private-sector financing from the International Finance Corporation.

DEA has been allocated all matters relating to credit extended by the Government of India to any country other than Nepal, Bhutan and Bangladesh, which is with MEA. DEA is also responsible for dealing with the United Nations Development Programme (UNDP), which is the economic and developmental wing of the UN system. Likewise, contribution to the specialized agencies of the UN and other UN bodies lies with DEA. Further, DEA deals with matters relating to any type of funding from UN agencies. The administration of legislation relating to the IMF and World Bank, ADB, African Development Bank and IFC is also with DEA.

The MEA does not have a single specific entry relating to work allocation for economic policy interface with the rest of the world, except with respect to matters relating to the Law of the Sea and questions of international law arising on the high seas, including fishery rights and piracies and crimes committed on the high seas or in the air. Economic and technical assistance given by India and received under the Colombo Plan is the only specific entry in the work allocated to MEA, other than the grant of loans and credits to Nepal, Bhutan and Bangladesh.

Despite this clear and unambiguous allocation of work under the Government of India (Allocation of Business) Rules, 1961, there is always a concerted attempt on the part of MEA to assume as much external economic policy interaction it can and exclude DEA from it.

BRICS

A Taste of MEA Dominance during the 2017 BRICS Summit

The acronym 'BRIC' for Brazil, Russia, India and China was coined and popularized by American investment banking and financial services company Goldman Sachs in 2001 when its economist Jim O'Neill invented the term and postulated that these four countries would dominate the global economy by 2050. When South Africa was added in 2010, it became BRICS. Goldman Sachs built a lot of hype around this and launched investment funds to capitalize on the economic growth bonanza these countries would generate.

The idea of BRICS was essentially an economic one. The BRIC leaders held their first summit in Yekaterinburg, Russia, in June 2009. They issued a short and concise joint statement. Of the sixteen paragraphs in the statement, the first ten deal exclusively with economic issues: cooperating in G-20, cooperating to deal with the global financial crisis, advancing the reforms of international financial institutions, building a reformed financial and economic architecture, taking action to achieve the UN's millennium development goals (MDGs), and so on. All these matters are handled by DEA in India.

However, the interface with BRICS in India got housed in MEA and MEA became the primary organizer of both, the BRICS summit in India and the country's participation in BRICS. The economic and financial agenda was dealt with by the BRICS finance ministers and central bank governors. As BRICS created many more forums, in agriculture, trade, energy and the like, the finance ministers' meeting became one of many meetings. While DEA led the work relating to the meeting of the finance ministers and central bank governors, its feeding into the leaders' summit was heavily controlled by MEA.

The BRICS leaders met in Xiamen, China, in September 2017. I had joined DEA in July 2017 and was included in Prime Minister Modi's delegation. The BRICS finance ministers had met three months earlier; BRICS had also floated a development bank, the New Development Bank. In their meeting, the finance ministers had also recommended some important institutional development measures, including floating an Asian Bond Fund and a BRICS rating agency. In fact, the proposal for the BRICS rating agency was India's idea and presented vigorously in the leaders' summit held in 2016 in Goa under India's chairmanship.

The most visible output of the leaders' summit is the joint communique. DEA was interested in getting certain references to the expansion of the NDB and progressing towards setting up the rating agency in the communique and DEA officers were negotiating hard on these issues. With great difficulty, I sent a DEA officer to participate in the negotiation of the joint communique, which was otherwise entirely in the hands of MEA officers.

The MEA communique team was headed by a joint secretary whose specialization was terrorism. For quite some time, India's primary theme in the leaders' statement was focused on terrorism. While that was fine, there was a deliberate attempt to exclude India's proposal for the BRICS rating agency. The leaders issued a long communique containing over seventy paragraphs. But the rating agency did not find mention in it.

DEA Blanked Out of 2018 BRICS Leaders Summit

The next BRICS Summit was held in Johannesburg, South Africa, from 25 July to 27 July 2018. Working closely with the South African presidency, we had got a paragraph included on the BRICS rating agency in the leaders' communique at a meeting of the G-20 finance ministers a few days earlier.

The MEA did not include the secretary, economic affairs, in the leaders' delegation for the Johannesburg summit. It was a massive departure but no reason was given. There was not even a courtesy call. The MEA officers who accompanied the PM to this meeting saw to it that there was no reference to the BRICS rating agency in that year's communique as well, despite business leaders submitting their report and substantial progress having been made on that front.

G-20

The G-20 was born at the finance ministers' level from the global financial challenges after the Russian and Asian financial crises in the late 1990s. The global financial crisis (GFC) in 2008 made G-20 the premier economic and financial policy coordination forum when the US realized that the emerging market economies had become systemically important for the global economy. The US also hosted the first G-20 leaders' summit at the heads-of-state level.

As the G-20 was an economic and financial forum led by finance ministers, it was righty housed in DEA—the economic and financial policy seat of the Government of India. India's participation in G-20 continued to be led and coordinated by DEA for some time after 2008. However, as MEA monopolizes the PM's external interaction, the G-20 leaders' summit gradually came to be coordinated by MEA. As MEA is not primarily concerned with economic and financial policy, the PM's participation in G-20 was channelized by MEA to bilateral meetings with the G-20 prime ministers and presidents, as the forum provided an ideal opportunity to organize these bilateral discussions. The economic and financial agenda gradually became, at best, a sideshow or formality.

Until the leaders were brought into the G-20 in 2008, the finance minister led all the interactions with G-20 as it had been dominated by economic and financial issues (finance track) of global concern. To give leaders a wider landscape to work with, and to enable finance ministers to assist them on financial and economic issues, a development track was built into the G-20 after 2008. This development track was entrusted to a 'Sherpa'. As the Planning Commission and subsequently NITI Aayog coordinated development policy in India, Montek Ahluwalia and Arvind Panagariya acted as India's Sherpas on G-20 for most years until 2017.

India Made No Strategic Use of G-20

Secretary, DEA, has always acted as deputy to the finance minister (finance deputy), and the Sherpa as deputy to the PM. These two tracks worked in tandem and were coordinated by DEA with a G-20 advisory council headed by the finance minister providing all the requisite coordination. DEA, the pivot for G-20, provided all the inputs and content for the participation of the PM in the G-20 leaders' meet. However over the years, as PMs increasingly went to attend G-20 meetings more for bilateral dialogue and only to read out one or two interventions in the real G-20 meetings, DEA could not create much value out of India's participation in G-20.

The lack of deep interest on the part of the PM in the economic and financial agenda gradually rubbed off on the finance minister as well. India had been building financial integration with the rest of the world since 1991. Increasing FDI, opening up the equity and debt markets for portfolio investors, rising trade with the rest of the world and calibrated opening up of the capital account had made the country a significant player in the global economic and financial system. Meanwhile G-20 had emerged as a material economic grouping. All this should have normally made India's finance minister as well as the RBI governor a deeply interested participant in G-20. The G-20 held three to four meetings of finance ministers and central bank governors every year, two of them coinciding with the annual and spring meetings of the IMF and World Bank.

Arun Jaitley visited Washington, D.C. and Lima for the five IMF and World Bank meetings that took place during my tenure with the World Bank as India's ED from 2015 to 2017. India was always billed as a lead speaker in the first of the three/four sessions that the G-20 finance ministers and central bank governors usually held over two days alongside the IMF–World Bank meetings. Almost invariably, Arun Jaitley would attend the first session and read out his written intervention text. In the evening dinner session, he would go into the meeting for a short time, sample the staid food that G-20 meetings served, and leave. With him, the secretary, DEA, would also leave. India's seat at the meeting for the G-20 finance ministers and central bank governors, for the most time, would be occupied by either ED, IMF, or joint secretary, DEA, who would only have a listening brief.

India had become a proforma participant in the meetings of the G-20 finance ministers and central bank governors.

Raising India's Profile and Participation in G-20

I was determined to raise India's profile and participation in G-20 when I joined as secretary, economic affairs, in July 2017, which made me assume the responsibility of finance deputy for G-20.

DEA was India's economic and financial policy face for the rest of the world. Unfortunately, on account of the closed economic policies pursued in the first forty years after Independence, DEA's external economic and financial interactions were predominantly built around multilateral institutions like the World Bank and ADB. Weaker trade and controlled capital investment regimes made DEA literally organize itself, as far as the interaction with the rest of the world was concerned, with only aid and finance flowing from multilateral and bilateral institutions.

There was not much interaction on real economic issues, such as trade and investment financing, capital flows, tax and economic policy coordination. In my earlier days in DEA, the Fund-Bank Division, which dealt with the IMF and World Bank, was literally the showstopper in the department with the ADB and Bilateral Cooperation Division playing a supporting role. Bilateral economic dialogues with the US and Japan were in their infancy after the G-20 finance ministers' forum was created in 1999.

One of the first institutional development tasks I took up after joining DEA was to create an International Economic Relations (IER) Division with the mandate to consolidate and organize all the economic and financial interaction (other than institution-specific interactions with multilaterals and bilaterals for loans, grant and technical assistance financing). The IER Division was staffed with a very good team of economists and other experienced officers. When Govind Mohan joined as joint secretary in DEA, I entrusted the IER Division to him to leverage his enormous international experience. The IER Division started looking at the agenda of G-20 meetings very closely. The practice of going through each agenda item very carefully, including understanding the entire background, significance and value for India and what leadership role we could play, brought a lot of heft to these issues.

The meeting of finance deputies in Argentina at the end of November 2017 provided me the first opportunity to participate in the G-20 process. Govind Mohan and I attended the meeting. We participated meaningfully in the entire process and contributed to the press statement.

After Arvind Panagariya left NITI Aayog, the government made a departure in the appointment of Sherpa. Instead of new NITI Aayog Vice Chairman Rajiv Kumar, it appointed Shaktikanta Das (the former DEA secretary who had joined the Fifteenth Finance Commission as a member), as India's Sherpa. DEA was to service the new Sherpa; we welcomed this as it would ensure that all the G-20 preparations (both the Sherpa and finance track) would get coordinated at DEA.

The first meeting of the finance ministers and central bank governors of the Argentinian presidency took place in Buenos Aires on 19–20 March 2018. Finance Minister Arun Jaitley decided to skip the meeting owing to health considerations. Along with Govind Mohan, I prepared hard for the meeting, assuming that I would represent the finance minister being the finance deputy. Two days before the meeting (the formal approval for the delegation would usually come a day or sometimes even a few hours before departure), the PMO decided that Minister of State for Finance Ponny Radhakrishnan (who was not handling DEA matters) would represent India and Govind Mohan would go as finance deputy. My name was struck off the delegation.

This was amazing not for the fact that I was excluded, but for the fact that Radhakrishnan had no clue about the economic and financial issues G-20 discussed. Govind Mohan would have done the job but he would have no opportunity to speak or participate as Radhakrishnan would occupy the only chair at the head of the table available to the finance minister or his deputy. In my opinion, Radhakrishnan's participation turned out to be a disaster. He was either a mute spectator in most of the sessions or read the given text with a lot of difficulty. Govind Mohan had another responsibility. He had to negotiate the communique. We had a number of points but on the critical ones where he needed the support of the head of the delegation—the Minister of State for Finance Radhakrishnan—he received none. India's interventions were excluded by default. Govind Mohan filed a report later that essentially said that India was wasting itself in G-20 and unless it took G-20 seriously it was no good for the country.

I took the matter up with the finance minister and Nripendra Misra. The IER Division made a comprehensive presentation detailing India's contribution to G-20, what it had missed out on and the major financial and economic areas where the country could and should make contributions going forward. I made this presentation to Nripendra Misra with Shaktikanta Das and the foreign secretary present in the room. This interaction changed the mood and approach of the PMO.

With Arun Jaitley not keeping good health and his stand-in Piyush Goyal more concerned about the domestic economy, I attended all the G-20 finance ministers' meetings, representing India's finance minister. I would remain present through all the sessions. One of the G-20 meetings, which took place alongside the IMF/World Bank meeting in Washington, D.C., which Arun Jaitley did not attend despite being in Washington, D.C., I attended. In all these meetings, I would not only make remarks as a lead speaker but also speak in most of the other sessions. I never read from a written text. As these remarks usually commented on the flow of discussions and suggested a course of action, my interventions started getting noticed and responded to.

When Shaktikanta Das moved as the RBI governor, the government appointed me India's Sherpa. I attended one of the meetings in the Japan presidency as India's Sherpa. India's entire economic, financial and development policy interaction in G-20 received well-coordinated attention. At least, for some time.

India Gets to Host 2022[14] G-20 Presidency

The G-20 has a system of rotating its annual presidency, which also serves as the secretariat for the year, as G-20 has no permanent secretariat. For choosing the presidency, G-20 informally divides the nineteen member countries in five buckets (the EU is the twentieth member). India was placed in Bucket 2 along with Russia, South Africa and Turkey. Of the Bucket 2 countries, Russia hosted the G-20 presidency in 2013 and Turkey in 2015. Japan is part of Bucket 5

---

14 Later changed to 2023.

with China, Indonesia and South Korea. China had hosted G-20 in 2016 and South Korea in 2010.

Bucket 2 was slated to schedule the G-20 presidency for the year 2019. India was the obvious choice; South Africa was not even ready. This also happened to be the year of the general elections. India worked with Japan to 'swap' presidencies. Japan agreed. In 2018, during the Argentinian presidency, a formal announcement for the 2021 presidency was to be made.

Going by the informal agreement in 2016 for the swap with Japan, we began preparing for a formal announcement in the leaders' summit scheduled to be held in Buenos Aires from 30 November to 2 December. The PMO, however, had different ideas. To coincide with seventy-five years of India's independence, the PMO informally communicated Prime Minister Modi's preference for hosting the G-20 presidency in 2022.

This complicated matters a little bit more. The year 2022 was 'reserved' for the Bucket 4 countries, which comprised Italy, France, Germany and the UK. All the countries, other than Italy, had hosted it. For India to host in 2022, Italy had to be persuaded to do it a year earlier, in 2021. As 2021 was the postponed year for Bucket 2 (in lieu of its original slot of 2019), the other country in Bucket 2, South Africa, had to agree not to press a claim for 2021 or 2022. Further, as Indonesia was in Bucket 5 (Japan's group), it also had a claim for 2021. If 2021 were to go to Italy, Indonesia also had to be persuaded not to press its claim for 2022, which India wanted.

I worked with South Africa, Indonesia and Italy on the matter. Shaktikanta Das also worked with the Sherpas of these countries. I was able to persuade South Africa and Italy relatively easily. For Indonesia, I banked on Finance Minister Sri Indrawati Mulyani, with whom I had worked closely in the World Bank (she was MD and CEO of the Bank). Her finance deputy Rionald Silaban was also Indonesia's ED in the World Bank and our terms had coincided. Silaban had assured me he would get Mulyani on board.

A few days before the leaders' summit in Buenos Aires, Shaktikanta Das received a mail from his counterpart Sherpa in Indonesia indicating the country's interest in hosting the presidency in 2021. We worked on Indonesia not to press its case for 2021 or 2022 and do it only in 2024. Finance Minister Mulyani said that it was the Sherpa track in Indonesia that had persuaded Indonesian President Joko Widodo to go for 2021 or 2022. She spoke to the President at my request again. After some persuasion, he agreed during the summit meeting that Indonesia would not press its claim for 2021 or 2022. I conveyed the same to the PM and the Argentinians.

In the last session, Prime Minister Modi made a statement indicating India's interest in hosting the presidency in 2022 when the country would also be celebrating seventy-five years of Independence. Everyone was supportive. The order of the next presidencies was announced in the last session of the leaders' meeting: Japan in 2019, Saudi Arabia in 2020, Italy in 2021 and India in 2022.

Prime Minister Modi tweeted and invited the world to attend the G-20 meeting in India in 2022: 'In 2022, India completes 75 years since Independence. In that special year, India looks forward to welcoming the world to the G-20 Summit! Come to India, the world's fastest growing large economy! Know India's rich history and diversity, and experience the warm Indian hospitality.'

The G-20 formally announced the next two presidencies in the leaders' communique. Because of the swap of presidencies involved, the leaders' summit communique at the June 2019 summit in Osaka, Japan, stated: 'We thank Japan for its Presidency and for hosting a successful Osaka Summit and its contribution to the G-20 process, and we look forward to meeting again in Saudi Arabia in 2020, in Italy in 2021 and in India in 2022.'

I took to Twitter on 1 December[15]: 'G-20 Leaders' Meet in Buenos Aires just concluded. It was also announced with unanimous approval that India will host G-20 Presidency in 2022 and Italy will do so in 2021.'

India had three years' time between the determination of its G-20 presidency in 2018 and hosting it in 2022. This was sufficient to

---

15 https://twitter.com/Subhashgarg1960/status/10689189115534
70464?s=20

conceptualize, prepare and present a first-rate G-20 presidency to herald the country's leadership in the economic and financial field. However, for reasons that were not publicly explained, the newspapers carried a statement from MEA (not DEA) on 23 November 2020 that India would host the G-20 summit in 2023.

The formal communique issued at the G-20 leaders' meet (virtually held) under the Saudi Arabian presidency in 2020 said: 'We thank Saudi Arabia for hosting a successful Riyadh Summit and its contribution to the G-20 process. We look forward to our next meetings in Italy in 2021, Indonesia in 2022, India in 2023 and Brazil in 2024.' This confirmed that India had got its presidency shifted to 2023.

MEA Rushes in to Get Suresh Prabhu Appointed G-20 Sherpa

India had no designated Sherpa after Shaktikanta Das had moved as the RBI governor in December 2018. As the Japanese had begun G-20 preparations earnestly as soon as their presidency commenced in 2019, including scheduling the first Sherpa meeting during 19–20 January 2019, we needed a new Sherpa soon.

We proposed certain names with the approval of Finance Minister Arun Jaitley before the elections. The PMO appeared not to like any of the proposals. In the meantime, the first meeting was held. Preparations for the interim Budget were in full swing. With Arun Jaitley indisposed and in the US for medical treatment, there was no question of me being in a position to represent India. We sent Aparna Bhatia, advisor in the Multilateral Relations Division of DEA, as a stand-in Sherpa.

The PMO could not decide on a name before the elections. They designated me as interim Sherpa till they made up their mind. We proposed a new set of names that were also discussed during the elections but no decision was made. Japan's Sherpa came to India in March 2019 to canvass for the issues the Japanese were most serious about. The second Sherpa meeting was convened on 30 April–1 May 2019. I led the delegation as India's Sherpa. India's Sherpa is accompanied by one joint secretary-level officer from DEA and another from MEA as what is called the 'Sous Sherpa' or 'under Sherpa'. For some inexplicable reason, the PMO struck out the name of the MEA joint secretary from the delegation. Familiar with all the issues, I was able to participate very well in the meeting and India registered its weighty presence.

After the elections, I had briefed new Finance Minister Nirmala Sitharaman on the necessity to appoint a full-fledged G-20 Sherpa immediately after she took over at the end of May 2019. Some discussions were held with the PMO, but it seemed to be in no hurry. The meeting of the G-20 finance ministers and central bank governors was held in early June. The G-20 leaders' meeting was scheduled for 27–29 June 2019. We were making preparations to help the participation of the PM on all G-20 issues.

The PM would be accompanied by India's G-20 Sherpa and finance deputy (secretary, DEA) at the leaders' meeting. As a convention, the finance minister and foreign minister did not travel with the PM for G-20 meetings. The Sherpa leads in briefing the PM on development issues and the secretary, DEA, on economic and financial issues. As I was handling both positions, I was fully prepared to brief the PM on all G-20 issues.

To our surprise, the PMO decided to appoint Suresh Prabhu as India's Sherpa on 24 June three days before the leaders' meeting was to be held. It was a shocker, not because Suresh Prabhu did not fit the bill but as it was done just before the meeting. How on earth could Suresh Prabhu familiarize himself with all the G-20 issues and assist the PM? It became apparent to us that we would have to prepare Suresh Prabhu as well, especially because the Sherpa steps in to occupy the PM's chair when the PM steps out for other meetings or engagements.

I checked with Nripendra Misra and P.K. Mishra as to why Suresh Prabhu's appointment was made just a few days before the leaders' meeting. Apparently, MEA had moved a separate note sometime around 20 June, without consulting the Ministry of Finance, of course, and received the PM's order directly appointing Suresh Prabhu as the new Sherpa. Further, MEA also secured orders that Suresh Prabhu would be serviced by MEA. This was against the long-standing convention and arrangement that the Planning Commission/ NITI Aayog and DEA serviced the Sherpa. This move was clearly intended to prise the Sherpa away from DEA.

The MEA had earlier converted the PM's participation in G-20 to predominantly bilateral engagements. With the move to take away the Sherpa from NITI Aayog and DEA, it was poaching the core G-20 agenda as well. This move also effectively excluded the secretary, DEA, from the G-20 leaders' meeting hall. The G-20 hosts provide three seats behind the leader in the leaders' meet. In India's case, unusual as it may sound, the national security advisor (NSA) accompanies the PM to the leaders' meet, ostensibly to assist the Prime Minister in bilateral engagements. This time around, as always, the NSA took one seat and Suresh Prabhu as the Sherpa took another. However, breaking another convention, the new Foreign Minister S. Jaishankar decided to accompany Prime Minister Modi. He took the third seat. With all three seats gone, I had to settle in an overflow room in Osaka to watch the proceedings of the G-20 leaders' summit.

Suresh Prabhu was replaced as G-10 Sherpa in September 2021 by Piyush Goyal, indicating a lack of faith in his ability to spearhead India's hosting of G-20.

Should the PM Participate in the 'Data Free Flow with Trust' Event?

Japanese Prime Minister Shinzo Abe planned two additional side events in addition to the leaders' summit. One was on women's empowerment and the other was what the Japanese termed the Data Free Flow with Trust (DFFT) event. Abe was not only a major global leader but a personal friend of Prime Minister Modi. Japan expected Narendra Modi to participate in both events and consent to the two declarations. India had no issue with the declaration on women's empowerment but the Osaka Declaration on DFFT was hugely controversial. Since the draft of this proposed declaration was received sometime in the middle of June 2019, there was considerable discussion on whether Prime Minister Modi should be part of this event.

Japanese Prime Minister Abe had taken a global leadership role in persuading all countries to move into a new global data governance framework, to create what he called Society 5.0. He had pitched his preposition in Davos in January 2019, where he proposed two fundamental elements of his vision of data governance. Dividing data into two principal blocks, he had proposed that all personal data, data embodying intellectual property, national security intelligence and the like be placed under careful protection, whereas all medical, traffic and other useful, non-personal, anonymous data should flow freely across borders. He termed this data governance regime DFFT.

Separately, on the sidelines of the World Trade Organization (WTO), over seventy countries had launched an Initiative on Electronic Commerce in 2017. This initiative intended to discuss and negotiate the trade-related aspects of e-commerce. India did not join this initiative. In fact, we opposed the opening of any negotiations on e-commerce in WTO. Japan was an enthusiastic participant in the joint statement that seventy-eight countries issued in Davos in 2019, confirming their intention to commence WTO negotiations on e-commerce. India remained opposed to this initiative.

India had drafted the Personal Data Privacy Bill, 2019, to place substantial control over collection, storage and flow of data. The bill was primarily concerned with control and regulation of personal data, which was widely defined, and contained no governance regime for non-personal data. Indian regulators, especially RBI, had mandated data localization. The 2019 Bill also had a number of provisions to restrict the flow of data, including retaining data in India.

Against this backdrop, there was no way Prime Minister Modi would have participated in the leaders' side-event on DFFT. However, Prime Minister Modi was not keen to decline the invitation of Prime Minister Abe.

I was not in complete agreement with India's approach towards controlling and localizing data. I thought we were missing the biggest growth driver in the digital economy as we had missed the mechanization and automation that ushered in the industrial revolution. However, the official view, widely shared by MEITY,

DIPP, DFS and others, was not in favour of a liberal policy for data flows.

In a meeting convened at the PM's residence to discuss India's strategy, I made a presentation and articulated the official view. But I also squeezed in my opinion that we should have a more open view about data use and flow to capture the opportunities generated by the digital economy. I also proposed that we work with the Japanese to either drop the event or rework the language of the proposed declaration to make it acceptable to countries like India.

After listening to a spirited debate in which four ministers also participated, Prime Minister Modi signalled that India needed to understand the digital economy better. He pointed out that none of the people—ministers and secretaries—present in the meeting understood the digital economy well. He directed that the matter—that MEITY should assemble quickly to formulate India's approach and policy towards data and the digital economy—be studied by a group of technical leaders. For the G-20 Event, he asked the foreign secretary and me to convey to the Japanese, without causing any offence, India's disinterest in participating in the event with the draft as proposed, and simultaneously work with our Japanese counterparts to rework the language.

It took some effort to get India's version of the Osaka Declaration finalized with the approval of the finance minister and foreign minister. Some more work, including by MEA, led the Japanese to shift the objective of working for DFFT to the leaders' statement, with the adequate caveats countries like India wanted, and the launch of the Osaka Track basically on the WTO e-commerce matter. India did not participate in the Osaka Declaration on Digital Economy (not on DFFT), which conveyed the resolve of the eighty-odd members who were signatories to the e-commerce initiative 'to make further efforts to achieve substantial progress in the negotiations by the 12th WTO Ministerial Conference in June 2020'.

The leaders' declaration was more of a compromise statement, which India was comfortable with. It noted that cross-border flow of data, information, ideas and knowledge generated higher productivity, greater innovation and improved sustainable development. It also recognized that such cross-border flows raised challenges related to privacy, data protection, intellectual property rights and security. The leaders agreed that they should continue to address these challenges that could further facilitate free flow of data and strengthen consumer and business trust. They also recognized the necessity to respect legal frameworks, both domestic and international. The leaders acknowledged that the DTFF, so governed, would harness the opportunities of the digital economy.

Prime Minister Modi's direction to consult technical experts to formulate India's approach and policy regarding data and the digital economy led to the formation of the K. Gopalakrishnan Committee on a non-personal data governance framework. The committee has completed its work while the joint parliamentary committee (JPC) was still working on the personal data protection bill. While India has not gone down the path of excessive data control and localization, barring a few actions, there is still much hesitation to accept that data and the digital economy are drivers of growth and prosperity and, therefore, more sagacious policies are needed to harness their potential for India.

OECD

The Organization of Economic Cooperation and Development (OECD) is a policy, standards and deliberative think-tank of thirty-six industrialized and emerging market countries. Industrialized countries are economically and financially strong and collaboration on all major economic, financial, taxation and other global issues, under the aegis of OECD, empowers these thirty-six countries and pools their resources to set the global economic agenda.

India has maintained a minimalistic relationship with OECD. Whatever little relationship has developed has been largely at the initiative of OECD. India has never sought to take advantage of the research and policy development that OECD has painstakingly built over the years. The OECD has wanted to enhance its engagement with India and other major emerging market economies: China, Indonesia, Brazil and South Africa. In 2007, OECD offered to designate India as a 'key partner country' and open its agencies and instruments to India (and the four other countries). It also invited India to enter into an enhanced partnership and develop a work programme to define India's relationship with OECD for mutual benefit.

MEA Always Blocked India's Enhanced Engagement with OECD

Interaction with OECD is not specifically allocated to either MEA or DEA. However, as most global agencies for economic cooperation and collaboration are allocated to DEA and none to MEA, the work relating to developing economic partnership should rightfully be handled in DEA. Extending its exclusive instrument of granting 'political clearance' to every minister and government official to travel outside the country, MEA usurped control over India's engagement with OECD without any formal and real authority. From 2007 to 2018, MEA evolved a concept of 'limited sectoral engagement' with OECD.

The OECD's highest governing body is its council, which makes all policy decisions and sets the agenda for work that takes place in myriad committees, working groups and expert groups—in 2018, these numbered about 250. The executive committee (EC) of OECD is its executive arm. Only members are represented in the council and EC. The OECD formalized its outcome of work in five different forms of instruments: decisions, recommendations, declaration, international agreement and 'arrangement, understanding and others'. It also maintains an enormous database on every attribute of economic, financial and fiscal functioning of the world, besides conducting numerous surveys and bringing out publications that influence global economic thinking.

The OECD's non-members engage with it primarily in three forms: as associates (right to full participation in a specific committee or group's work; also bound by its decisions); as participants (invited to the meeting of the committee, with a right to participate and share data but not bound by its decision); and as invitees (part of non-confidential meetings and can speak with permission but carry no obligation).

India's 'limited sectoral engagement' in 2018 amounted to India participating in three of 250 OECD working bodies as an associate, six bodies as a participant and twenty-nine bodies as an invitee. Over the years, however, India had agreed to participate in about 160 databases of approximately 300 databases maintained by OECD. India had agreed to OECD publishing an economic survey (once in two years); OECD had also brought out a number of other thematic publications.

Convinced that it was absolutely necessary for India to engage with OECD (most intellectual work for G-20 was also done by OECD) to get into the development of global principles, standards, agreements and treaties in the economic and financial field, I, with the approval of the finance minister, created a specialized OECD wing in DEA and put a director-level officer in charge.

Our internal examination in DEA convinced us that India should accept the OECD's offer to develop a joint work programme (JWP) to define the contours of India's enhanced engagement. In DEA, we had identified the areas we wanted to expand our work with OECD. We had also tentatively screened and preliminarily identified potential areas of interest for other ministries and departments.

I wrote to the foreign secretary about the desirability of enhancing India's engagement with OECD and offered to discuss the subject. Vijay Gokhale had taken over as foreign secretary and was more sympathetic and open to the idea. But, the team under him, including T.S. Tirumurti, secretary, economic affairs, in MEA, were not prepared. Some formal and informal discussion took place, including a meeting I chaired with Tirumurti. The way MEA drafted the minutes of the meeting was an indication about its intent. Much valuable time was lost in the process.

I had to take the matter to the PMO.

Nripendra Misra chaired a meeting and we made a strong case. The PMO authorized me to develop the content of the enhanced engagement. By the time I began this exercise, however, my time in DEA was over. MEA continued to put roadblocks in the way. At the end of my tenure, we were exactly where I began in 2017. India continues to avoid engaging with OECD.

Negotiating a Rupee-Dollar Swap with the Japanese

The year 2018 was a difficult year for India on the foreign exchange management front. As oil prices rose during the year and current account deficit threatened to cross about 2.5 to 3 per cent of GDP, the rupee depreciated by more than 14 per cent and foreign exchange reserves declined by more than $40 billion. As I have recounted in the chapter on issuance of sovereign bonds, it was decided not to go for another NRI bond or deposit scheme. The PMO preferred the currency swap deal with Japan.

I made a visit to Tokyo, accompanied by RBI Deputy Governor B.P. Kanungo and Executive Director Michael Patra, to discuss the broad contours of the rupee-dollar swap with my counterpart in the Japanese finance ministry, Masatsugu Asakawa. In Japan, foreign currency reserves primarily belong to the government and their Ministry of Finance negotiates bilateral and multilateral swap arrangements, besides deciding on the use of exchange reserves.

India had entered into a $50 billion bilateral currency swap arrangement with Japan earlier, which had expired in 2016. Japan held the second largest dollar reserves and being a current account surplus country, its reserves were always growing. India wanted to access these dollar reserves in situations when the rupee was under pressure. The critical elements in any such bilateral swap arrangement is the swap currency, the size of swap, freely accessible portion (swaps generally have two portions; one can be drawn when the country has no programme with IMF, and the other only along with withdrawals made from IMF), the rate of interest payable in case of funds drawn and the frequency at which you can roll it over.

India wanted a $100 billion swap, 50 per cent unlinked portion (it was 20 per cent in the previous arrangement), an interest rate of only 1 per cent and rollovers in six months. Asakawa (who is currently president of ADB) started by offering the 2016 swap arrangement. The rate of interest offered was six months LIBOR (London Inter-Bank Offered Rate) plus 150 basis points. Though our discussions were held in quite a cordial atmosphere, the Japanese did not budge an inch. They explained their constraints candidly, such as other swap deals, approval of the Diet and many other considerations. The Japanese wanted some concessions on ECBs. India was insisting on compulsory hedging of infrastructure ECB financing of five to ten years. This was an unnecessary condition. I was prepared to give a concession on this front but decided to use it as a bargaining chip. We kept up the negotiations.

In Delhi, the negotiations were taking place on two tracks. The perception in the PMO (with Nripendra Misra leading the track) was that Japanese PM Shinzo Abe would facilitate the deal on India's terms. Nripendra Misra roped in former Foreign Secretary S. Jaishankar and carried out the discussion through him and the Japanese ambassador to India. Japan's Finance Minister Taro Aso, perceived to be in a rival camp, who was opposed to giving any terms more favourable than the previous arrangement, was expected to fall in line but only with active nudging from PM Abe. I was to carry on the negotiations on the official track and bring around the hardliner Asakawa.

The discussions went on. The next big step in the process was a long bilateral meeting I had with Asakawa on the sidelines of the annual meetings of IMF and World Bank in October 2018 in Bali. Asakawa was all charm but showed little flexibility. After the meeting in Bali, we shifted to an email conversation. Coordinating with Nripendra Misra, I offered Asakawa India's final offer: $75 billion swap amount, 30 per cent unlinked portion, interest rate 1.25 per cent over LIBOR and a six-month rollover.

Prime Minister Modi took up the swap negotiations to break the ice when he met PM Abe in Tokyo at the end of October 2018. India got a $75 billion swap deal. The Japanese PM also agreed to the 25 per cent unlinked portion, a fraction less than the 30 per cent that we had given as our final offer. The rate of interest and rollover were also agreed to. In return, Modi agreed to remove hedging restrictions on infrastructure ECBs. The bilateral swap agreement was signed in Tokyo on 29 October. For some reason, the MoU was signed by Indian Ambassador Sujan Chinoy, even though I was present in Tokyo and had led all the negotiations.

Urjit Patel had reluctantly given RBI's consent to do away with the ECB hedging condition. When it came to implementing the understanding, RBI threw another googly. Infrastructure ECBs were defined to be ECBs of five years or more for financing infrastructure projects. There was no mandatory hedging condition for infrastructure ECBs of ten years or more. There was no class of infrastructure ECBs for less than five years and, accordingly, there were no hedging restrictions on these. Therefore, the condition operated only for infrastructure ECBs of five to ten years.

RBI decided to redefine infrastructure ECBs as ECBs for infrastructure financing for three years or more and imposed a condition that infrastructure ECBs of three to five years would require 70 per cent hedging. The Japanese were miffed, and rightly so. Asakawa held up the formal draft of the swap agreement to get clarity on ECBs of three to five years. After some persuasion, RBI relented and redefined infrastructure ECBs as ECBs of five years or more, which closed the matter. Swap agreements are administered by RBI. We authorized RBI to sign the swap agreement on behalf of the Government of India. Finally, the India–Japan bilateral swap agreement of $75 billion with 25 per cent unlinked portion was signed and became effective.

24
New Multilateral Banks Off the Block

NDB

NEW DEVELOPMENT BANK WAS PROMOTED AND ESTABLISHED BY THE FIVE BRICS countries for the purpose, to use the language of the declaration in 2014, 'of mobilizing resources for infrastructure and sustainable development projects in BRICS and other emerging and developing economies'.

A Mutual-Benefit Society of Five Members

While NDB was equally owned by the five members of BRICS and the equity provided by these members was to be leveraged for financing development projects in their countries, the real idea was for BRICS to assume leadership in financing development and infrastructure in developing and emerging market countries. Two multilateral development finance institutions established by developing/borrowing countries—NDB and AIIB—were their answer to the

World Bank, ADB and other 'donor' established organizations. Expansion of membership of NDB beyond BRICS was, therefore, fundamental to the raison d'etre of NDB.

India had pitched for the first presidentship of NDB and ace banker K.V. Kamath was our choice for the position. Predominantly owned and led by China, AIIB was expanding fast. It had fifty-seven founding members by 2016, when it became operational. India was expected to lead the expansion of NDB working closely with Kamath.

The articles of agreement (AoA) of NDB provided for the membership to be open to all members of the UN in accordance with the terms and conditions determined by the special majority of the board of governors. The basic final capital structure was also agreed upon in the AoA. The voting powers of the five founding members would not be reduced below 55 per cent (with 11 per cent each), non-borrowing members would not collectively have voting rights exceeding 20 per cent, and no single non-founding member would have voting power in excess of 7 per cent. The credit rating of NDB, crucial to keep its borrowing costs low, was also dependent upon the strength of non-borrowing members joining and the concentration risk of its lending reducing substantially. Expanding NDB's membership was a no-brainer.

DEA was quite supportive of the membership expansion. Unfortunately, MEA had different ideas. For reasons it best understood, MEA saw merit in keeping the membership limited to the five BRICS members. Nonetheless, Kamath did some documentation and preparatory work. He got the terms, conditions and procedures for the admission of new members prepared, which were approved in the annual meeting of NDB's governors held in India in April 2017. The NDB management prepared a list of over forty countries as potential candidates for expansion and proposed it be allowed to commence discussions with them, which was what happened in other multilateral institutions. However, MEA took a myopic stand and started putting pressure on DEA's representatives on the NDB Board to go slow on the membership issue. Constrained by MEA's advice, DEA's representatives sought more clarifications and slower movement, and signalled to Kamath to not consider the membership expansion a priority.

This was the status when I joined DEA in July 2017. I found the whole thing bizarre. The economic and developmental rationale for NDB's membership expansion was sound. India could earn the goodwill of the new members if it pushed for membership expansion and was seen as opening the doors of the bank to them. India had the presidentship of the institution (which was to last only up to 2020) to implement this mission. Yet, we were playing spoiler.

I took it up with the foreign secretary. It helped, but only a little. I started signalling India's preference for membership expansion in NDB meetings and expressed India's keenness on the same on informal networks. However, an open endorsement and pushing Kamath to lead the expansion aggressively required MEA to stop regressing the agenda. In fact, MEA had begun to adopt subtle ways of sabotaging the agenda. As noted in the previous chapter, I was not included in the delegation for the leaders' summit in Johannesburg in 2018. The resolution passed by the BRICS finance ministers in 2018 (prior to the leaders' meeting) to gradually open the membership to new members was scuttled by the MEA team from inclusion in the leaders' statement.

After this meeting, there was no option left for us except to take the matter to the PMO. A few meetings took place at the level of Principal Secretary Nripendra Misra, in which the foreign secretary and Economic Relations Secretary Tirumurti participated. After these discussions, Nripendra Misra gave clear directions that India must support membership expansion. Despite this, Tirumurti wrote a letter questioning India's support for membership expansion. I wrote back. Finally, the PMO issued instructions in writing to the effect that India should lead the membership expansion work.

That became the policy of DEA and its representatives on the board of governors and board of directors of NDB. Kamath got some strength to pursue this agenda. However, MEA continued to work against it, though subtly. Though there was some progress, nothing really changed. Kamath left NDB in 2020. India's governors and directors continue to express support for membership expansion and

NDB kept recording this in its minutes. Admission of new members has taken place only after India vacated the seat of president, NDB. Bangladesh, the UAE, Uruguay and Egypt have joined as members of NDB by now.

AIIB

Asian Infrastructure Investment Bank, headquartered in Beijing, is almost totally a China-controlled multilateral bank. The country had the largest shareholding, literally giving it veto power. Its president was a Chinese national and is likely to remain one. The AIIB did not have a resident board and, therefore, even member countries with a board seat carried out very little oversight. The board was always pressed for time, as it was overwhelmed by inadequacy of time and skills to examine papers closely. The Chinese and the President literally had a free run over the affairs of AIIB. India was the second largest shareholder and had the right to appoint a vice-president. Former Gujarat Chief Secretary D.J. Pandian occupied this position in AIIB and was entrusted with the functions of chief investment officer.

India Acquiesces to Over-Delegation of Authority in AIIB

In this setting, AIIB President Jin Liqun came up with an unprecedented proposal. A board agenda was brought up at a meeting in December 2017, proposing the delegation of sanctioning powers for all projects—other than a small exception of proposals of setting new policy and sovereign loan projects exceeding $300 million—to the President. No other multilateral had delegated such powers to its President. Our fact-check suggested that 80 per cent of the projects sanctioned by AIIB until then would have fallen in the jurisdiction of the President if this power was granted.

Dinesh Sharma, India's director in AIIB, had just retired and his successor was not in place. I sent Bandana Preyashi, a director-level officer, to attend the board meeting with the clear brief that this agenda item was to be strongly opposed. When she raised India's official objection to the agenda, Pandian had a problem and tried to overpower Bandana by alluding to his seniority and connections with the PMO (he was chief secretary when Prime Minister Modi was Gujarat chief minister). She called me. When I told her to stay firm, she remained resolute. It appeared that Pandian had assured Jin Liqun of India's support for that agenda. Pandian has since been succeeded by former RBI governor Urjit Patel.

Pandian texted me a little later, saying it was unfair for India to object to the proposal. Then he threw some weight and said that he had spoken to the finance minister and P.K. Mishra, additional secretary to the PM. I discussed the matter with Nripendra Misra. He was horrified by the proposal. I also spoke to the finance minister, who saw reason in our objection. I told Pandian in response that I had consulted the finance minister and the PMO and that our position, and objection, remained very clear. When he texted back to say that this was not what the finance minister told him in the morning, I reiterated that this was unambiguously the official position of the Government of India.

While the board meeting postponed discussion on the item, Jin Liqun continued to press for the move. He was completely determined to hold complete sway over AIIB. Pandian, for reasons best known to him, continued to support him. Foreign Secretary Vijay Gokhale, who had served as India's ambassador to China, understood the dangers of virtually handing over AIIB to the Chinese via the proposed delegation to the President. Nripendra Misra authorized the foreign secretary and I, to work with member countries on the matter. I drafted letters that Gokhale sent out to Indian missions in the countries represented on the board of AIIB. The ambassadors took the matter up. Feedback went back to Jin Liqun. He wrote to Prime Minister Modi in March, though he had no business to do so.

The AIIB's annual meeting was scheduled for June 2018 in Mumbai. Both the bank and its President were very keen to ensure delegation of powers to the President was approved before this meeting. With India's encouragement, some more members started questioning the move. Liqun sent Pandian to India to persuade Prime Minister Modi. We continued to oppose the move vehemently with the PMO. Pandian threatened to resign from AIIB and possibly asked the PM to save his honour. Prime Minister Modi finally came up with a compromise: giving the President power to sanction projects up to $150 million.

Once a decision was made by the PM, we had to go along. We expanded the list of exceptions to the $150 million rule a little more by including a few more types of projects. Still, as per our understanding, the decision meant that about 50 per cent of the projects funded by AIIB would not come to the board for consideration and approval thereafter. It also opened the door for the possibility that the Chinese or Liqun would not bring a proposal to further increase the threshold for lending operations to go to the board. The AIIB was clearly on the way to becoming a multilateral where the board will become an unnecessary appendage.

World Bank

India Punctures the Badly Constructed Human Capital Index

Impressed with the impact of credit ratings on political leaders, World Bank President Jim Yong Kim had ordered the development of a human capital index (HCI) as a means to accelerate investment in human capital. The first HCI was constructed and released on 9 October 2018, just a week before the annual meetings of the IMF and the World Bank in Bali, Indonesia. India was assigned a score of only 0.44 on a scale of 1 and ranked 115 out of 157 countries. India's score in the UNDP's human development index (HDI) was 0.64 in a report released a month earlier in September 2018.

India had been opposing the construction of HCI, as it appeared to be a deformed version of the HDI. The HCI had three changes when compared to the HDI. First, it eliminated per-capita income, which was one of three key measures of HDI. Second, it added rate of stunting among children below the age of five (a pet theme for Jim Yong Kim) to the life expectancy rate. Third, it brought in a hugely suspect quality dimension to years of schooling by assigning quality scores based on relative performance of students in a country to the best scores earned in international test programmes like the Programme for International Student Assessment (PISA) and Trends in International Maths and Science Study (TIMSS).

While it was running very large programmes to address malnutrition in children and mothers, India hated the excessive emphasis on child stunting. India and most countries had not participated in international testing programmes regularly (there were issues regarding their testing methodologies and standards as well). World Bank did not have the latest quality scores for more than a handful of countries, except the advanced economies. For India, the score available was for the year 2009 when PISA tests were conducted in two cities.

In existence for decades, HDI had not excited the world leaders enough to focus on human capital. There was nothing in the HCI to suggest there would be any additional reason to do so. Moreover, HCI rankings were based on incomplete and dated data. India's rank suffered (compared to HDI) on account of the faulty methodology for assessing the quality of school education. India's average for years of schooling was 10.2 (maximum 12) but the quality of school education was a paltry 355 out of a maximum of 625. This made India's score on 'learning-adjusted years of school'—one of the three key measures—only 5.8 out of a maximum 12, contributing substantially to its miserly score of 0.44.

We had tried to persuade the World Bank not to enter the misadventure of constructing this faulty and meaningless index. Jim Yong Kim's persistence, however, won the day. (For inexplicable reasons, he left World Bank five months later.)

We could not have allowed the new index a place under the sun without bringing out its deficiencies. On 11 October 2018, after getting the finance minister's and the PMO's clearance, after running through the Ministry of Education as well, an official statement was released through PIB. It was also communicated to the World Bank. We questioned the advisability and utility of the exercise of constructing HCI, pointing out major methodological weaknesses and data and quality gaps. We termed its metric too simplistic at one level and too ignorant of development realities on another. We expressed our fears that HCI, with its emphasis on country scores and rankings, could trivialize the importance of World Bank's Human Capital Project. Finally, we conveyed the Government of India's decision—it would ignore HCI and continue to focus on its development programmes to transform the quality and ease of life for all our children.

No country criticizes the World Bank or one of its initiatives so categorically. However, we called a spade a spade. This attracted a lot of attention at the annual meeting in Bali. Jim Yong Kim organized an exclusive event for finance ministers on HCI. As I was representing India's finance minister, I attended the event. In the three minutes each minister gets to speak, I precisely and clearly conveyed India's objections to HCI. While summing up, Jim Yong Kim assured us all that the data and other deficiencies in HCI would be addressed.

World Bank released the next edition of HCI in September 2020. At the press conference organized for the release, people asked what World Bank was doing to address the issues raised by India.

World Bank's HCI does not attract much attention. It has been mostly forgotten by now.

Green Climate Fund

A Self-Goal

The Green Climate Fund (GCF) was created as a financial instrumentality to implement the commitment made by developed countries to contribute $100 billion a year to support developing countries to move towards adopting less carbon-emitting and climate-friendly technical choices. It began modestly after it was formally established and started operating in 2012 with its headquarters in South Korea. Until 2017–18, contributions of only about $10 billion, in all, were committed. All the same, GCF started approving projects for financial assistance, generally grants, for developing countries.

India had played a major role in the evolution of climate policies under the United Nations Framework Convention on Climate Change (UNFCCC). India was also a permanent member of the Global Environment Facility (GEF). The Ministry of Environment and Forests (MoEF) had played a pioneering role in presenting India's case in climate negotiations and had been able to secure a kind of leadership role. DEA had handled the finance aspect of

India's participation in the climate negotiations, including for GCF. A Climate Finance Unit (CFU) was created in the economic wing of DEA. Dipak Dasgupta, who headed CFU in DEA, was nominated India's representative to the GCF.

The GCF has a twenty-four-member board, divided equally between developed and developing countries. Twelve developing country members come from six regions: Asia-Pacific; Africa; Latin America and the Caribbean; small island developing states; least developed countries; and developing countries outside regional groups and constituencies. The first three groups, including the Asia-Pacific group, select three board members each and the remaining three select one each.

India became a board member from the Asia-Pacific group and Dipak Dasgupta occupied India's chair in the first three-year cycle of the GCF Board. In the second cycle (2016–18), India decided to nominate Additional Secretary Dinesh Sharma to the board. Malaysia was India's alternate. Saudi Arabia and China were the two other board members from the Asia-Pacific group.

For GCF, the concerned administrative department in the Government of India is the MoEF. The process of selecting India's nominee for the GCF Board involves DEA making the selection with the approval of the finance minister and the MoEF securing the approval of the Appointments Committee of the Cabinet (ACC) and thereafter undertaking the necessary processes within GCF for the nominee to be formally selected and elected. The first forum to make the rollout selection process in any new cycle is the regional grouping. In the Asia-Pacific grouping, joint/additional secretary of MoEF represented India.

Dinesh Sharma retired at the end of November 2017. Rajasree Ray, a senior officer from the Indian Economic Service (IES), was heading CFU and doing stellar work. I sent her to attend the GCF board meetings and, after the finance minister's approval, I sent her name to MoEF to formally nominate her to the GCF Board. I had expected that this would be a routine affair as earlier, too, Dipak Dasgupta, who had headed the CFU, had been India's representative.

Possibly, Rajasree Ray was considered as a competitor by the MoEF officers at the joint and additional secretary levels in climate matters. Or perhaps the ministry wanted to keep the post for one of its own officers. Whatever the reason, the MoEF took time to move the file. I asked C.K. Mishra, my batchmate and secretary, MoEF, why it was taking so long. He assured me that it was being processed and would be done.

The GCF set in motion the process for selection of board members for the 2019–21 cycle. In DEA, GCF work, other than climate finance work, was handled in the Other Multilaterals Division, headed by Joint Secretary Prashant Goyal. While our correspondence with MoEF was going on to nominate Rajasree for the position, quite unknown to us, a meeting of the Asia-Pacific group took place in Bangkok sometime in September 2018, which was attended by a joint secretary of MoEF. DEA was not consulted about the strategy to be adopted to get India's representative selected for the 2019–21 cycle.

After about two months we came to know that at the Bangkok meeting, while China and Saudi Arabia secured renominations for one board seat each, India's seat was lost to South Korea. India was not even selected for the alternate position, which went to Iran, who at that time was coordinating the Asia-Pacific group. Pakistan retained its alternate position with Saudi Arabia. This was an amazing development. However, MoEF not only did not ensure India's selection but also kept totally silent about it. It was difficult to believe that MoEF was prepared to let India lose its board seat in GCF rather than nominate Rajasree Ray. After we came to know about it, we tried to take some action but it was too late. India had edged itself out of the GCF Board by a self-goal.

There have been some other instances of India not doing enough to get her candidates selected for major global positions. A few years back, the country did not vote for Indian scientist Ajay Mathur for the post of vice-president and CEO of Global Environment Facility; instead, our vote went to his Japanese rival because the finance minister had committed to the Japanese that India would support their candidate.

SECTION IV

GOVERNMENT OF INDIA BUDGETS

25
Budget 2018–19

Run-Up to the Budget

BUDGET 2017–18 WAS UNPRECEDENTED IN TERMS OF FISCAL ARCHITECTURE, reforms and management of the Central government's finances. The distinction between Five-Year Plan and non-Plan expenditure, which had defined India's expenditures since the 1950s, had been done away with. The institutional arrangement of a separate railways budget, prevailing since 1924, had been discontinued and the 2017–18 Budget was a single integrated budget of the Centre's finances. The budget had been presented on 1 February 2017 and all parliamentary approvals obtained, with the demands for grants, appropriation bills and Finance Act passed before the beginning of financial year 2017–18. This enabled all fiscal expenditures to be taken up from the very commencement of the financial year. These three reforms had transformed the Budget implementation system much more drastically than any budgetary reforms undertaken in the past.

There was another big fiscal reform implemented twelve days before I joined DEA. The nation's indirect taxation system had been transformed by integrating most of the Central and state indirect taxation laws in the Goods and Services Tax system. While this makeover posed enormous systemic change in the administration of indirect taxes, it also had profound implications for the Budget. Budget 2017–18 had not factored in the implication of the introduction of GST for taxation receipts. The 2017–18 tax receipt estimates were all based on expected receipts from the old system of taxation—customs, excise and service tax receipts. There was no estimate of receipts from GST in Budget 2017–18.

The changeover from 1 July 2017 had made the estimates of excise and service tax estimates for the year irrelevant. Further, as the GST system required tax for a month to be deposited by the twentieth of the following month, GST revenues were to come for only eight months. The introduction of the GST system had profound consequences on production and distribution of goods and services. Producers were expected to clear their old inventory soon after the introduction of GST and, therefore, there was a sharp reduction in production and sales of goods, leading to a sharp drop in GDP growth in the April–June quarter (Q2) 2017–18 to 5.7 per cent (7.9 per cent in Q1 2016–17).

The government had totally committed to the path of fiscal consolidation in 2017–18. Despite these big changes in the fiscal architecture of the country, Finance Minister Arun Jaitley had committed to bring down the fiscal deficit to 3.2 per cent in 2017–18,with the goal of 3 per cent in the following year.

When I joined DEA in July 2017, implementing Budget 2017–18 became my responsibility. There is no year without a major challenge in the fiscal management of a vast country like India; 2017–18 was a year where uncertainty about the fiscal outcome was perhaps most intense.

Budget Edifice Starts Unravelling by September

In July 2017, GST revenues were nominal and continued to be quite muted in the next two months. The contraction of economic activities hurt corporate performance as well. Tax performance was faltering compared to budgetary estimates. Fall in GDP growth rates led to all-round calls for fiscal stimulus. The government was quite sensitive and wanted to undertake additional measures to protect employment, assist MSMEs and promote exports. This meant an increase in budgeted expenditures. Falling tax revenues and increasing expenditures had bad portents for fiscal consolidation.

Non-tax revenues delivered the nastiest surprise. By the end of September 2017, non-tax revenues were about ₹89,000 crore, which was only 28 per cent of the Budget target of ₹2.88 lakh crore. In the previous year, the government had collected 37 per cent of a much higher Budget estimate.

The largest shrinkage was in the dividends and profits head that accounted for dividends from non-financial and financial public-sector companies as well as surplus transfer from RBI. Whereas 64 per cent of the budgeted estimates in this head had been collected by September end in the previous year, in 2017–18, it was down to merely 28 per cent of the Budget estimate of ₹1.42 lakh crore. RBI surplus transfer usually came in the month of September. As against transfer of ₹65,876 crore in financial year 2016–17, RBI had transferred only ₹30,659 crore in 2017–18. A quick assessment of realistic likelihood of non-tax revenue collections for the full year 2017–18 suggested a shortfall of about ₹1 lakh crore against the budget estimate of ₹2.88 lakh crore.

The government and RBI sit together every six months to plan for its borrowing strategy, instruments and calendar for the next six months. This meeting, chaired by secretary, economic affairs, is attended by the deputy governor in charge of debt management in RBI. I reviewed the fiscal position with B.P. Kanungo with both the Budget Division and RBI team present. There was complete agreement that the situation was quite fluid. While it looked reasonably likely that government borrowing would have to be increased from budgeted levels to make up for the revenue shortfall, it was not possible to quantify the same.

As an unusual measure, we decided to announce the borrowing calendar for only the next three months—until December 2017—and meet again in the last week of December to finalize the quantum and calendar of the borrowing programme for the last quarter of financial year 2017–18.

Let Us Raise the Fiscal Deficit to 3.7 Per Cent

The continued after-effects of demonetization of ₹500 and ₹1,000 notes carried out in November 2016, the disruption (hoped to be short-term) caused by the switchover to the GST system of taxation and falling GDP growth rates, put the government in a bother. There were incessant calls to provide stimulus in the media and by the Opposition. The government accepted internally that something had to be done.

Various exercises were set afoot. I was also tasked to come up with some ideas. I thought it would be inadvisable to let the fiscal purse loosen on account of factors that appeared short-term in nature. I was convinced that the April–June 2017 quarter represented the lowest point and that the positive effects of GST and demonetization would start kicking in soon. I was also worried about the deteriorating fiscal math. The commitment of the government to stick to the path of fiscal consolidation had been stated very seriously quite often, including by Prime Minister Modi, at some meetings I attended.

I decided to shed light on the true state of the fiscal situation while presenting some options for developmental and ameliorative measures. Re-estimation carried out for the fiscal math revealed that there would be a shortfall of about ₹1 lakh crore on the receipt side (primarily on account of GST revenues of one less month and sharp overestimation of non-tax revenues).

Building a few scenarios assuming the government succeeding in persuading RBI to release more funds, the disinvestment revenue target raised upwards from the estimated ₹72,500 crore to ₹1 lakh crore, additional expenditures being limited to ₹50,000 crore and the like, the estimates worked out indicated that the fiscal deficit would increase by ₹75,000 crore (minimum) to ₹1,50,000 crore, which was about 0.4 per cent to 1 per cent of the projected GDP of about ₹155 lakh crore.

These numbers, presented along with the proposals for a stimulus package, provided a sobering context. In the PMO, Nripendra Misra and Additional Secretary T.V. Somanathan were clearly for expansion of expenditures, while Additional Principal Secretary P.K. Mishra was strictly in favour of maintaining fiscal discipline. The finance minister and the team of secretaries in the Ministry of Finance were also, by and large, in favour of fiscal discipline and consolidation. Chief Economic Advisor Arvind Subramanian had been vociferously in favour of loosening the purse strings, but after seeing the sobering fiscal numbers he had changed his stance to either not expanding expenditures or doing so by letting go of the fiscal deficit constraint.

I proposed that we relax the fiscal deficit constraint by at least 0.5 per cent to account for the shortfall in revenues without expanding expenditures; if some expenditures needed to be undertaken, this could be done by eliminating some other budgeted expenditures.

Several rounds of discussions took place in the Ministry of Finance and the PMO. The final decision-makers were not prepared to see any departure from the budgeted fiscal deficit of 3.2 per cent, though this was increasingly looking indefensible. The fiscal consolidation glide path was sacrosanct. Finally, the idea of any large-scale fiscal stimulus was abandoned. Only some small measures were announced. This approach, however, did not provide any solution for the developing unsustainable situation of sticking to the fiscal deficit in the face of falling revenues.

Flip-flop on Additional Market Borrowings

The MoF–RBI teams met on 27 December to take stock of the fiscal situation and finalize the borrowing plan for the last quarter. Various fiscal scenarios were also doing the rounds in parallel with the finance minister and PMO. There was a realization that there was no escape from increasing the fiscal space by at least 0.5 per cent of GDP. At one stage, the Ministry of Finance team was given a signal that the Budget could go for 3.7 per cent fiscal deficit. There was much reluctance and unwillingness though.

There was considerable discussion in the borrowings calendar group. The Budget Division and I were very clear in our assessment that there was no escape from making additional borrowings of about ₹50,000 crore though the deficit was much wider. Seeing the writing on the wall and no escape, RBI team and Deputy Governor Kanungo agreed. The group decided to raise this additional borrowing and fixed the calendar accordingly. It was released the same day. I also tweeted[16]: 'government's final borrowing program issued today. Additional market borrowing of only ₹50,000 crore would be taken during the current year. No more than that.'

As expected, the yields on government paper moved up by ten basis points or so. We were prepared for that. the RBI governor, however, was not. The next morning, he called P.K. Mishra, who in turn spoke to me. I explained the entire matter, including the participation of Kanungo in the unanimous decision taken. He understood.

A whisper campaign began against me, principally encouraged by DFS. Increase in yields affected the quarter-end valuation of the securities portfolios of the PSBs, which were in any case in very poor health after the quality review. Separately, Finance Secretary Hasmukh Adhia wanted a very clear decision on the size of the fiscal deficit for the year to be included in the Budget to be presented very soon. While the finance minister had accepted the inevitability of fiscal deficit slippage, Nripendra Misra, possibly echoing the PM's mind, conveyed one day that the fiscal deficit would have to be kept at very close to 3.2 per cent.

When I realized that there was no likelihood of the fiscal deficit being allowed to be raised to 3.7 per cent, there was no point in borrowing the additional ₹50,000 crore. After informing the finance minister, I announced the government's decision on 17 January by tweeting[17]: 'Government has reassessed the additional borrowing requirements taking note of revenue receipts and expenditure pattern. Requirement of additional borrowing being reduced from ₹50,000 crore as notified earlier to ₹20,000 crore.'

This brought a lot of cheer to the bond market. Yields came down by about fifteen basis points, within an hour of my tweet—much more than the increase recorded in the bond markets after the 27 December announcement.

---

16 h t t p s : / / t w i t t e r . c o m / S u b h a s h g a r g 1 9 6 0 / status/946052313205972992?s=20

17 h t t p s : / / t w i t t e r . c o m / S u b h a s h g a r g 1 9 6 0 / status/953477683110817792?s=20

Budget Division Wanted to Alter States' Tax Share Transfer and Salary Payment Arrangements

Prashant Goyal, joint secretary, Budget, proposed modifications in a few long-standing fiscal transfer and payment arrangements. States get their share in central taxes in fourteen instalments; eleven instalments of the budgeted amount of states' share in taxes were released on the first of every month from April to February. The difference between the revised estimates and the amounts released in the first eleven instalments was released in three instalments in the month of March.

The new GST system had come into operation from 1 July 2017, which envisaged payment of the tax due (after adjusting for input credits) in the following month by the twentieth in place of by the end of operating month as earlier for value added tax (VAT) and quarterly filing of returns. Advance income tax was paid quarterly even earlier. Arguing that the current collection of taxes and the arrangement of transfer of the share of states led to a mismatch in the Central government's cash management, Prashant Goyal proposed that the Government of India transfer the states' share of taxes only on a quarterly basis and on the twentieth of the month of transfer.

The proposal reflected a superficial understanding of the way taxes were collected and how important it was to provide states a steady transfer of resources instead of lumpy and fewer transfers. The Government of India collected a good chunk of its income and corporate taxes by way of tax deducted at source (TDS).

Likewise, most GST taxes came by way of input taxes. I saw no merit in the proposal of disturbing the fourteen-instalment arrangement. However, to bring the states' perspective on board, I permitted him to seek their views, though I recorded my own assessment that it did not make much sense. The only part I had some sympathy with, was transferring the payment of monthly instalment to the middle of the month.

All the states opposed the proposal, as expected. In the pre-Budget meeting for Budget 2018–19 with the state finance ministers, some raised the matter a bit agitatedly. After the meeting, I took the orders of the finance minister to continue with the fourteen-instalment arrangement and shift the payment of the monthly instalment to the fifteenth of the month. Most states accepted this. One or two states—particularly Madhya Pradesh—raised the issue of liquidity difficulty on account of transfer of their tax share to the middle of the month. These apprehensions were addressed by explaining the correct implications, but the new system of transferring on 15th stayed.

Another proposal Prashant Goyal made was to shift the payment of salary to the first of every month in place of the last working day of the preceding month. It was an article of faith between the government and its employees that they should receive their salary before the month closed. Sometimes, when the last two or three days were holidays, employees received their salaries a couple of days before the month closed.

There were practical difficulties in the proposal to pay salaries precisely on the first of the following month. Banks did not make deposit entries on Sundays or other gazetted holidays even if the government had transferred the funds to them for payment of salaries. This might lead to actual credit of salaries in the employees' accounts later, by one, two or even more days.

I rejected the proposal outright and closed the matter. It is not good to be so penny-wise.

The Budget

The Cabinet Discusses and Approves the Budget

I had worked as additional secretary in the cabinet secretariat in 2013 and attended a number of cabinet and cabinet committee meetings. The PM was flanked by the cabinet secretary and the principal secretary to the PM on the head table. The cabinet secretary would present a summary of the Cabinet Note and Proposal which, after discussion, would be adopted with or without changes. It was quite usual to call secretaries to explain the intricate matters and participate in the discussion.

After I joined as secretary economic affairs in July 2017, I was invited to a number of cabinet meetings. However, never was I called inside for discussion on any agenda item. Nor did I see any other secretary being so called. All of the invited secretaries stayed in the adjoining room and left after additional/joint secretary from the cabinet secretariat announced that the meeting was over.

The cabinet meeting to discuss and approve the Budget 2018––19 was the first meeting I had opportunity to go inside the cabinet room. On my entrance, I noted the big change in the cabinet meeting set-up for the first time. The cabinet secretary and the principal and additional principal secretaries to the PM had moved to the other side of the room after the ministers. The PM was the only one at the head table, so to say.

My directors and deputy secretaries had brought adequate physical copies of the Cabinet Note for circulation among ministers. We were signalled to do so only when the cabinet meeting actually started. Finance Minister Arun Jaitley made some introductory remarks. The PM requested him not to go into 'details' lest he and the finance team be delayed for the presentation in the Lok Sabha. The cabinet meeting was over in less than ten minutes.

We collected the Cabinet Notes, which were barely distributed, and I reached the Officers' Gallery for the FM's Budget presentation by 10.30 a.m. I was well before time, the Budget reading was to begin at 11 a.m.

Government Goes for 3.5 Per Cent Fiscal Deficit

The fiscal math had gone awry. Considerable GST revenues (over ₹2 lakh crore) came in the form of integrated GST (IGST), which was to be assigned to be shared between the Centre and states equally after ten months. The IGST was to be kept in the public account until shared. Non-tax revenues had shortfall across all segments—financial sector company dividends, including RBI; non-financial sector company dividends; and receipts from departments like telecom on account of no spectrum sale taking place.

The government decided to allocate some IGST (₹35,000 crore) between the states and Centre but keep over ₹1.6 lakh crore in the Consolidated Fund of India and give out a 42 per cent share thereof

to the states as devolution. Had it been shared, the Government of
India would have retained only 58 per cent of 50 per cent, or 29 per
cent of ₹1.6 lakh crore. By using this method, it effectively retained
58 per cent (100-42 per cent) or about ₹46,000 crore more. This
treatment allowed the Government of India to report higher tax
revenues in the revised estimates of 2017–18. By keeping the hope of
getting ₹15,000 crore as further transfer from RBI, non-tax revenues
were estimated down only by about ₹53,000 crore. Disinvestment
was expected to pull in additional capital receipts of ₹27,500 crore
(₹1 lakh crore against ₹72,500 crore).

With all these adjustments on the revenue side, the government
decided to present somewhat higher revised estimates by about
₹17,000 crore (including disinvestment) than what was budgeted.
Expenditure estimates also came in higher than Budget estimates.
Despite some expenditures being taken off-Budget (food subsidy,
PM Awas Yojana, etc.) and some restraint on capital expenditures
(₹2.73 lakh crore against budgeted estimates of ₹3.10 lakh crore),
expenditure estimates had to be revised upwards by ₹71,000 crore, as
revenue expenditures had expanded by more than ₹1.07 lakh crore.

The government, perhaps, had no choice but to deviate from
the budgeted fiscal deficit of 3.2 per cent. Tracing the credible
fiscal consolidation record of his government, the finance minister
declared in his Budget speech 2018–19, after noting that fiscal
deficit was running at a very high level of 4.4 per cent of GDP
when the government assumed office in May 2014, that 'the Prime
Minister and the Government have always attached utmost priority
to prudent fiscal management and controlling fiscal deficit'. He
recounted that the government 'embarked on the path of consistent
fiscal reduction and consolidation in 2014' and 'fiscal deficit was
brought down to 4.1 per cent in 2014-15, to 3.9 per cent in 2015-
16, and to 3.5 per cent in 2016-17'.

To maintain there was no reversal of the fiscal glide path, the
finance minister decided to keep the fiscal deficit for 2017–18 at 3.5
per cent of GDP. Further, to assure that the journey on the glide path
would continue, he told the House that he was projecting a fiscal
deficit of 3.3 per cent of GDP for the year 2018–19.

The finance minister reaffirmed the government's commitment to fiscal consolidation when he announced the acceptance of the key recommendations of the Fiscal Reform and Budget Management Committee 'to impart unquestionable credibility to the Government's commitment for the revised fiscal glide path'. The government decided to adopt the debt rule recommended by the committee and to bring down the Central government's debt-to-GDP ratio to 40 per cent and use the fiscal deficit target as the key operational parameter.

A Big Package for the Agriculture Sector

Besides raising minimum support prices for all the field crops to provide minimum 50 per cent profit over the cost of cultivation, which I discussed in a previous chapter, the 2018–19 Budget had a big package for the agriculture sector and farmers aimed at realizing the government's goal of doubling farmers' income by 2022.

To replicate the success of Operation Flood in the dairy sector, the government announced the initiation of 'Operation Greens' for the horticulture sector. The finance minister announced, 'Operation Greens' shall promote farmer producers organizations (FPOs), agri-logistics, processing facilities and professional management.' He allocated a sum of ₹500 crore for this purpose by building it as a component of a much larger food processing promotion scheme, Prime Minister Krishi Sampada Yojana.

Rural infrastructure development had been assisted by the Central government since early 2000 by channelizing the bank shortfalls in priority-sector lending to the Rural Infrastructure Development Fund (RIDF) created in the National Bank for Agriculture and Rural Development (NABARD). The RIDF also funded irrigation and other agriculture infrastructure projects. The government also provided budgetary funds for identified major irrigation projects through the Accelerated Irrigation Benefit Programme (AIBP). After the grant component was done away with from the centrally sponsored schemes in 2005, the Government of India provided its share through AIBP and states raised loans from market or financial institutions, including NABARD, for funding their part of the project cost.

The Government of India had decided to off-Budget the Central loan component in 2016–17 and set up a Long Term Irrigation Fund (LTIF) in NABARD to meet the funding requirement of irrigation works. In turn, NABARD issued fully serviced bonds and handed over the funds to an SPV—Water Development Corporation, under the Water Resources Department—which in turn provided these funds to states as the Central government's share of AIBP. In the 2017–18 Budget, the government had announced the establishment of a Micro Irrigation Fund (MIF) to facilitate expansion of coverage under micro irrigation and a Dairy Processing Infrastructure Development Fund (DPIDF) to help finance investment in dairy infrastructure.

In the 2018–19 Budget, the finance minister announced further expansion of such focused investment funds and announced a Fisheries and Aquaculture Infrastructure Development Fund (FAIDF) for the fisheries sector and an Animal Husbandry Infrastructure Development Fund (AHIDF) to finance the infrastructure requirements of the animal husbandry sector with the total corpus of both funds at ₹10,000 crore.

Setting up so many funds, funded mostly by off-Budget borrowing, was not a good practice at all. Overlapping funding objectives, a small corpus, fuzzy governance structure and funding mechanisms made these funds quite a weak fiscal mechanism. The government also continued with the practice of announcing the target for crop loans from banks to the agriculture sector, with the loan target being raised from ₹10 lakh crore to ₹11 lakh crore, which was neither the government's fiscal operation nor good banking practice.

Ayushman Bharat Makes Its Debut

The Government of India had made a beginning to provide health insurance coverage to the poor in 2007, by initiating the Rashtriya Swasthya Bima Yojana (RSBY), which provided annual coverage of ₹30,000 to poor families. Several state governments had also implemented their own version of health insurance schemes, providing varying coverage. Using smart card technology and a deduplicated database, RSBY and the state initiatives had introduced good health insurance coverage but it was fragmented and patchy.

The government decided to take health protection to a more aspirational level. The finance minister announced the launch of a new flagship national health protection scheme, called Ayushman Bharat, to cover over ten crore poor and vulnerable families, with up to ₹5 lakh of health expenditure per family per year for secondary and tertiary care hospitalization. The scheme was expected to provide health services to approximately fifty crore beneficiaries and help in expanding health facilities to smaller cities and towns. Thus it would provide a decent cover to all the poor and lower middle-income families in the country, saving them from the financial ruination that visited them whenever health emergencies struck.

There had been considerable pre-Budget debate about the scale at which Ayushman Bharat should be included. Some wanted universal coverage; others wanted it to be limited to those identified to be living below the poverty line or those who could be identified as vulnerable based on the socioeconomic caste census carried out in 2011. The final decision to limit it to ten crore 'poor and vulnerable' people was taken very close to Budget day. As expenditure Budget documents get printed a few days before the day of the Budget speech, no specific provision could be made specifically in the Budget demand (RSBY allocation was to serve it initially).

The media and analysts also had serious doubts about the likely financial implication of this initiative. While we estimated that it would not exceed ₹10,000 crore a year, their numbers were much higher. I tried to explain but doubts persisted.

Infrastructure Package Turns a New Leaf

The bulk of the infrastructure package was designed on traditional lines. Progress on the Smart Cities Mission, which aims to build 100 smart cities with the selection of ninety-nine cities with an outlay of ₹2.04 lakh crore, was intimated with various projects like smart command-and-control centres, smart roads, etc., worth ₹2,350 crore having been completed and works worth ₹20,852 crore under progress.

Likewise, the achievements of the government in scaling new heights in the development of road infrastructure, completion of National Highways projects exceeding 9,000 km during 2017–18 and approval of the ambitious Bharatmala Pariyojana to develop about 35,000 km in Phase 1 at an estimated cost of ₹5,35,000 crore were addressed. It was reaffirmed that strengthening the railway network and enhancing the railways' carrying capacity was a major focus of the government. Railways' capex for 2018–19 was pegged at ₹1,48,528 crore with a large part going towards capacity creation.

In the run-up to the Budget, I had proposed a number of initiatives to put infrastructure financing on a fast track. Corporatization of NHAI or, as an alternative, corporatization of road assets by organizing these assets in a suitable number of SPVs was proposed. Corporatization of AAI and converting it into an airports asset-management company was suggested. A policy paper for monetization of the infrastructure assets of the railways, power companies and gas networks was also suggested.

These were discussed extensively and paragraphs relating to these remained in the draft Budget speech for quite some time. There was, however, fierce resistance from the line ministries. The final infrastructure package, as announced in the Budget, was quite a toned-down version but still had a few new and innovative ideas.

To get NHAI to raise equity from the market by monetizing its mature road assets, it was announced that it would organize its road assets into SPVs and use innovative monetizing structures like toll, operate and transfer, and infrastructure investment trust funds. The NHAI's road asset-management function was in a mess, with all the roads being treated as one lump of capital expenditure. The NHAI had initiated TOT by identifying some road stretches and bundling them for franchising on TOT basis, but this was not expected to move much unless NHAI could organize all its road assets into specific SPVs.

With policy and regulatory work on development of monetizing vehicles like InvITs and real-estate investment trusts in India having been largely completed, the government announced that it would initiate monetizing select CPSE assets using InvITs from 2018–19 onwards.

Streamlining Policy on Capital Account Non-Debt Transactions

Foreign direct investment, which is inward flow of equity capital from the rest of the world, had received considerable policy attention but not outward direct investment from India, which had grown to $15 billion per annum in 2017–18. Likewise, investment flows through hybrid instruments, such as convertible bonds and differential voting rights, had not received enough policy attention in India.

In 2015, FEMA had been amended to provide for a neat division of policy work relating to capital account instruments. For debt instruments, the initiative was left with RBI whereas for non-debt instruments that comprised equity and hybrid instruments, the policy initiative was left with the Government of India. Earlier, for almost all these instruments, the primary mover was RBI. The new regime envisaged the Government of India framing policy, law and regulations on equity and hybrid instruments, consulting RBI and then notifying the same.

I had initiated considerable work in these areas. The finance minister announced in the Budget that the government would review existing guidelines and processes and bring out a coherent and integrated ODI policy. Likewise, noting that hybrid instruments were suitable for attracting foreign investments in several niche areas, especially for start-ups and venture capital firms, the finance minister announced that the government would evolve a separate policy for hybrid instruments.

After the Budget, work on implementing these initiatives was taken up with all seriousness along with consolidation and renotification of work on FDI and FPI under FEMA, by the Government of India. While the Foreign Exchange Management (Non-Debt Instruments) Rules were finally notified in 2020, the work on ODI policy and rules as well as the hybrid instruments policy and rules were relegated to much lower priority. ODI Rules have been finally notified in 2022. Hybrid instruments policy is still to see the light of the day.

Long-Term Capital Gains Tax

While the Budget, including the taxation proposals that are typically taken up in Part B of the Budget speech, is the responsibility of the secretary, DEA, a very strict convention has developed that taxation proposals are handled only by the secretary, revenue. Secretary, DEA, is not associated with taxation proposals. It is only the night prior to the Budget Day that the secretary, DEA, gets to glance over the taxation part.

Capital markets policy, however, comes under the secretary, DEA. We had made several proposals relating to strengthening various aspects of capital market taxation. I was also consulting Hasmukh Adhia on the proposals relating to the rest of the Budget speech as he was also the finance secretary and enjoyed the confidence of Prime Minister Modi. In one of our meetings on Budget matters, the subject of long-term capital gains taxation came up.

The proposal, as it stood at that stage, envisaged all capital gains earned on sale of securities one year after purchase (long-term capital gains) in excess of ₹10 lakh to be taxed at a 10 per cent rate, with the indexation benefits to be given in addition. I found the proposal horrible and a public relations disaster. Giving exemption of ₹10 lakh to a person on capital gains and taxing salaries over ₹2.5 lakh was atrocious. The regime of exempting long-term capital gains fully, provided that the transaction was carried out in the stock exchange and the securities transaction tax (which was minuscule) had been paid, rewarded profits on capital unfairly compared to income earned by wage earners. I suggested that the regime be altered drastically.

Adhia saw the point. I was invited to a rare taxation-related meeting chaired by the PM. The proposal relating to exemption up to ₹10 lakh had the blessings of Nripendra Misra. However, the moment I explained its implications for the public, the PM immediately agreed and asked for the proposal to be modified.

The modified proposal was announced in the Budget. Informing that long-term capital gains arising from transfer of listed equity shares, units of equity-oriented funds and units of a business trust that amounted to ₹3,67,000 crore as per returns filed for assessment year (AY) 2017–18 were exempt from tax, the finance minister proposed that long-term capital gains exceeding ₹1 lakh be taxed at the rate of 10 per cent without allowing the benefit of any indexation with all gains up to 31 January 2018 to be grandfathered.

Long-term capital gains tax was a red rag for the capital markets, but the equity and reasonable nature of the proposal made by the finance minister ensured that there were no convulsions in the market. The tax has stayed until now.

26
Interim Budget 2019–20

Run-Up to the Interim Budget

Double-Headed Stewardship of the Finance Ministry

LIFE IS NEVER DULL IN THE MINISTRY OF FINANCE. EVERY YEAR IS SPECIAL and unusual for some reason or the other. The year 2018–19 was unusual and special for the reason that the Ministry of Finance had two bosses, working simultaneously sometimes or alternately, through the year.

Finance Minister Arun Jaitley announced in the first week of April 2018 that he would be taking some time off owing to health considerations. However, there was no formal change in his responsibility and he started operating from home. He trusted his secretaries and left much of the operational and implementation work to them. A system was designed where important matters could be discussed with him on the phone and important files could be sent to his office, which would obtain his orders by printing the note sheet in a fully sanitized manner. As the period of April–May is usually somewhat slack, the arrangement worked quite satisfactorily.

Later in May, he needed some deeper treatment. He was also likely to travel to the US for this. On 14 May 2018, Arun Jaitley was designated a minister without portfolio and the charge of the Ministry of Finance was assigned to Piyush Goyal. The orders issued by Prime Minister Modi made it clear that Piyush Goyal would work under the guidance of Arun Jaitley and all important files would be disposed of and decisions taken only after consulting Arun Jaitley.

This arrangement went on for more than three months. Piyush Goyal, a very active minister, took his responsibility quite seriously and wanted many changes to be made, especially in matters of transfers of grants to the states, credit flow from banks and their capitalization, and the like. On account of tight liquidity management by RBI, there were issues concerning interaction with the central bank. Rising oil prices also queered the pitch.

Arun Jaitley returned formally as finance minister in August 2018, but continued to operate from home for considerations of medical safety. He started coming to office sometime in late September. He also travelled to the US for annual meetings of the IMF–World Bank in October 2018, but could not go to Washington, D.C. from New York as some complications developed. He returned to India after some time and the Ministry of Finance continued to work under his guidance from October to January.

The preparations for the Interim Budget 2019–20 were in full swing under his leadership, when his doctors suddenly advised him to go back to the US for treatment. The notification issued by the President of India on 24 January 2019 (just seven days before the scheduled presentation of the Budget) directed that during the period of Arun Jaitley's indisposition, the portfolio of Minister of Finance would be held temporarily by Piyush Goyal again.

Piyush Goyal presented the Interim Budget 2019–20 on 1 February 2019.

Taking Loans from Public Sector Banks

In the second week of June 2018, while I was chairing a meeting in North Block at around 6.30 p.m., an aide to Piyush Goyal, officiating finance minister, came to inform me that the minister wanted me to come to the committee room on the ground floor. When I reached there, I saw that Piyush Goyal was chairing a meeting with the PSB chiefs and heads of treasuries.

As soon as I took a seat, Piyush Goyal briefly mentioned that they were discussing his proposal for the government to borrow from banks by taking loans, which would be a win-win for both the government and the PSBs. As he was told by the bankers that the borrowing of the government was handled by DEA, he wanted my views to make the new system work.

Making a quick assessment of the situation and gathering my thoughts, I told the minister that the banks lend to the government by subscribing to Government of India bonds and there were large sums thus lent by the banks to the government. Banks provide loans to specific projects and the Government of India funds its specific projects by its revenues as well as the funds borrowed by raising bonds, including from banks. I continued that it would not be advisable for the government and the PSBs to borrow and make loans, as that would create issues about fixing rates of interest on an arm's length basis as the PSBs are owned by the government.

Piyush Goyal, a pushy minister, had talked the bankers into accepting his idea. They did not have the courage to object or even raise any doubts. As I was speaking, I noticed relief on their faces. The minister, however, did not like it.

Before he could direct his energies towards me, I told him I understood why he was discussing the matter with the bankers. The bankers must have complained to him about the losses they often encountered on their bond portfolios when interest rates went up and they had to mark down their bond values on a mark-to-market basis. I told the minister that this problem was of the bankers' own making.

Indian banks, most prominently PSBs, held a vast amount of government bonds, in excess of ₹25 lakh crore at the time. However, as they were virtually passive holders of these bonds, bond prices were basically dictated by the active buying and selling decisions of FPIs, who hardly held ₹3–4 lakh crore of government securities. I told the minister that if the PSBs decided to manage their bond portfolio more actively and remained on the buy side for government bonds, they would not face losses on their portfolio.

Piyush Goyal realized the potential of active bond management by the banks and the utter inadvisability of initiating the system of banks making loans to the government. He asked for a meeting to be convened with the banks' treasury personnel while he was in Mumbai a few days later, for AIIB's annual general meeting.

With the threat of banks providing loans to the government effectively buried, I left to rejoin my meeting. Noted economist, Prof. Charan Singh, who was chairman of Punjab and Sindh Bank at that time and was present at the meeting, later told me that it was an entirely unexpected and courageous show on my part to speak the truth and state the facts after the bankers had virtually been bullied into accepting the switch to making loans to the government.

The ₹5-a-Litre Petrol Price Cut

Crude oil prices were rising when Piyush Goyal took over as finance minister in the middle of May. In his very first interaction with the officers, he indicated something would have to be done about reducing petrol and diesel prices.

The prices of petroleum products in India have been linked to the international price of crude for many years. The pre-tax ex-refinery cost of petrol and diesel is primarily dependent on the international crude price and the dollar-rupee exchange rate. The taxes imposed by the Central and state governments made up a major component of the final retail price. The petroleum companies decided and notified the retail prices every day. Except when the Ministry of Petroleum signalled the petroleum companies to exercise restraint for any reason, daily retail prices were completely formula driven. The Ministry of Finance came into the picture only when the tax structure needed tinkering. This matter was primarily handled by the Revenue Department. However, in the price reduction exercise undertaken in May–June 2018, I was asked to take the lead and present scenarios and options.

The petrol price in Delhi was hovering around ₹75 a litre in the last week of May 2018. Brent crude prices were about $74–75 a barrel in May–June 2018. While there was no benchmark to determine the price per litre that crossed the political tolerance limit, there was some informal understanding that ₹80 a litre represented that limit. Therefore, we in the Ministry of Finance were not convinced that the time was right to cut excise duties or otherwise tinker with the formula. However, Piyush Goyal was insistent.

In the first week of June 2018, I made a presentation before a group of ministers. Petroleum Minister Dharmendra Pradhan was present, besides Piyush Goyal. Nripendra Misra was also sympathetic to the idea of effecting a price cut. The search to find the complex factors that went into the formula had led me to discover some rules of thumb. For, at that time, an increase of $1 per barrel in crude oil price translated into an increase of petrol and diesel price by 54 paise and 50 paise, respectively, per litre in Delhi. Depreciation of the rupee by one rupee per dollar meant an increase of 66 paise in petrol price and 60 paise in diesel prices. Petroleum import bill went up by $1–1.25 billion when crude oil prices went up by $1.

At the ministers' meeting I was quite forthright in saying this was not the time to effect a price cut. Piyush Goyal relented to some extent when he said that I should present the mechanics and implications of a ₹5 cut in the petrol price, rather than making a case before the PM that the price cut was not required.

Accordingly, in a meeting chaired by Prime Minister Modi, I presented a scenario for reducing petrol prices by ₹5 per litre made up of a cut in the basic excise duty by ₹2.5 per litre and the oil marketing company's margin to be reduced by 50 paise per litre. The remaining ₹2 was to come by other reduction (state's VAT automatically went down by about 50 paise and the rest of the cut was to be made voluntarily by the state government). Another rule of thumb was that the Government of India's revenues went down by ₹13,500 crore for every one rupee cut for one full year.

Much discussion took place. The underlying message from the Ministry of Finance team (Adhia, Arvind Subramanian and I) was very clear: this was not the time for a price cut. The international crude oil price movements were largely on account of American policy relating to Iraq and the lack of production quota increase by OPEC. There were serious fiscal implications as well. But Piyush Goyal was unrelenting. He wanted the PM to agree to the ₹5 cut while the PM seemed unconvinced. Piyush Goyal came up with more and more arguments. After some time, the meeting narrowed to a dialogue between the PM and Piyush Goyal. By the end of the marathon meeting, Piyush Goyal had succeeded in persuading an unwilling Prime Minister to go along. We were told to take the necessary action to get the orders on file.

Arun Jaitley did not attend the meeting but called us to his residence for a briefing afterwards. We told him everything, including the difficulty the government would face if the prices were to go back to ₹80–85 per litre after the price cut. Arun Jaitley decided to speak to the PM.

Piyush Goyal followed-up insistently. The presentation was made on a Sunday. As soon as I reached home, he started calling to ask where the file was and when it would reach the PM for orders. I told him the Revenue Department was working on it. In the evening, Arun Jaitley informed me that the PM had agreed not to go ahead with the price cut at that moment. We were relieved.

The government did reduce the petrol prices by ₹5 a litre, but much later in October 2018 when crude prices had crossed $85 to a barrel.

Proposal to Take Over RBI's Debt-Issuance Function Fails to Go Through

India is one of the very few countries in the world where government borrowings are managed by the central bank, including issuing, servicing and redemption of government bonds and treasury bills. In most countries, this is the sovereign function of the government and the government treasury manages it directly or through its controlled and dedicated agencies. Such an arrangement also puts the central bank into the path of policy conflict. To manage the borrowing programmes of governments, central banks are expected to keep liquidity conditions easy and interest rates lower, whereas for monetary management and inflation control, they might need to follow tighter monetary policy and raise rates of interest.

Proposals have been formulated and taken up from time to time to remedy this awkward and unjustifiable situation. The most serious attempt in this respect was made during the 2015–16 Budget. A provision was introduced in the Finance Bill to amend the RBI Act to allow the government to take over debt management. The amendment also provided for the formation of a Public Debt Management Agency (PDMA) under the direct control of the Government of India to undertake the debt management function, including issuance, servicing and repayment of debt securities.

Raghuram Rajan, then the RBI governor, thought this proposal was brought in to curtail his authority and clip his wings. Despite probably knowing that the proposal was perfectly in order from the economic, fiscal and monetary management perspective, he opposed it. He made it a prestige issue and forced the finance minister to order the withdrawal of the proposal. However, he assured the finance minister that the Central government and RBI would work together to draw up a roadmap to equip PDMA with the ability to understand, build systems and gradually take over most of the debt management function over a period of time.

When I joined, I picked up the thread and seriously took up the work of preparing a roadmap for the complete takeover of the debt-management function by the Government of India/PDMA. I called the World Bank and IMF to provide us the technical support to build a credible and strong PDMA over a period of eighteen months. The Budget Division worked together with the World Bank team to prepare the roadmap, including the HR plan.

However, RBI did not cooperate. In fact, it started withdrawing its officers working in PDMA on deputation. These officers were also given lower performance ratings to make them leave their deputation with the Government of India. We tried to rope in expertise from public and private-sector banks.

The PDMA started doing some analytical work. But the roadmap remained stuck. The nation will have to wait for another time for the government to be considered capable enough to manage its own debt.

Interim Budget 2019–20

Fiscal Deficit Creates Friction

The budgeted fiscal deficit for 2018–19 was 3.3 per cent. The amended FRBM Act required the government to bring fiscal deficit down to 3 per cent by 2020–21. To continue with the glide path, we proposed the fiscal deficit be retained at 3.3 per cent in the revised estimates of 2018–19, and fixed it at 3.1 per cent for the financial year 2019–20 so as to peg it at 3 per cent in the year 2020–21, as envisaged in the FRBM Act. I had initially proposed attaining 3 per cent in financial year 2019–20 itself, one year ahead of the target. Finance Minister Arun Jaitley thought differently and suggested it be kept at 3.2 per cent or 3.1 per cent for 2019–20. We settled for 3.1 per cent.

Suddenly, one day, Expenditure Secretary Ajay Jha advised Arvind Srivastava, joint secretary, Budget, to keep the fiscal deficit at 3.4 per cent for financial year 2018–19 and 3.3 per cent for 2019–20. He told Arvind this was what the PMO (Nripendra Misra) desired. I found this quite strange. First, it was conveyed in such a roundabout way (why was I not told directly?) and, second, deviating fiscal deficit by 0.1 per cent in the revised estimates made no sense. It was small money but would convey a very bad message to the market about the government not being able to stick to its deficit estimates.

Arun Jaitley had left for the US by that time. I conveyed it to him. I also took the matter up with P.K. Mishra in the PMO. He, too, found the required change baffling. It seemed Nripendra Misra had spoken to the PM about it and indicated that some slippage on the fiscal deficit was necessary on account of the envisaged new PM-KISAN scheme (one instalment of ₹2,000 to ten crore farmers was roughly equal to 0.1 per cent of India's GDP). A discussion with P.K. Mishra led to the shared understanding that PM-KISAN could be managed without a fiscal-deficit slippage. He agreed that I should meet the PM and explain the fiscal numbers to him.

Prime Minister Modi heard me out and was completely clear. He wanted one instalment of PM-KISAN to be accommodated. But he also agreed that it would be better if the fiscal deficit could be maintained at the budgeted level. However, he wanted Arun Jaitley to be fully on board and advised me to take his views. I did that the next morning. Arun Jaitley agreed and I conveyed to the Budget Division to retain the fiscal deficit at 3.3 per cent for revised estimates 2018–19, and at 3.2 per cent for 2019–20.

That evening was reserved for the presentation of the draft Budget speech for the PM. All the secretaries of the Ministry of Finance were waiting in the adjoining room before the meeting. Suddenly, Nripendra Misra walked in. At his furious worst, he asked me whether I had met the PM to discuss the fiscal-deficit issue. I confirmed that I had and he blew up. Quoting statistics from the UPA era when the fiscal deficit had ballooned after the global financial crisis, he questioned the very logic of the fiscal consolidation path and the Ministry of Finance's fixation with low fiscal deficit. He bluntly said I had no business going over his head to discuss the matter directly with the PM. I listened to him without any flinching, only saying I was simply following my call of duty.

I made the presentation before Prime Minister Modi, which went reasonably well. The subject of deviating from the fiscal deficit did not come up in the discussion. Nripendra Misra also did not raise it. I took that to mean that we would stick to 3.3 per cent for the revised estimates, as agreed by Finance Minister Arun Jaitley.

After the meeting, the expenditure secretary had stayed back and waited till the taxation-related discussions were over. Apparently, he checked with Nripendra Misra on what to do about the fiscal deficit. Nripendra Misra told him (as he conveyed to me the next day) that the fiscal deficit would stay as he had originally wanted—3.4 per cent for the revised estimates and 3.3 per cent for the budgeted estimates for 2019–20. Ajay Jha also conveyed the PMO's decision to Arun Jaitley, who reluctantly agreed.

The final printed fiscal deficit numbers in the Budget were what Nripendra Misra had decided. In the Budget speech, Piyush Goyal said: 'From the high of almost 6 per cent seven years ago, the fiscal deficit has been brought down to 3.4 per cent in 2018–19 RE.'

Welfare for Ten Crore Labourers

India's workers are divided equally in two broad classes—farmers and farm labour on one side and industrial and other non-farm labour on the other. PM-KISAN was expected to take care of farmers as well as landless farm labour, as increased farming activity and a spike in farmer incomes, spurred by income-transfer under the scheme, was expected to increase farm labour wages as well.

The rest of India's labour works in the unorganized sector, including as street vendors, rickshaw pullers, construction workers, rag pickers, domestic workers, and in the handloom, leather and numerous other similar sectors. The government wanted to see to their welfare too by providing them comprehensive social security coverage. A committee was constituted under the chairmanship of Hasmukh Adhia serviced by the Ministry of Labour. I was a member of the committee. It held a number of meetings and looked at various options to improve income and social security for labour. It looked at comprehensive social security as defined by the International Labour Organization (ILO) and the gaps in the Indian situation. The package it developed, however, became somewhat complicated.

The government finally decided to improve old-age security for unorganized labour, including agricultural labour. The mega announcement was made by Piyush Goyal when he announced the Pradhan Mantri Shram-Yogi Maandhan (PM-SYM) for workers in the unorganized sector with a monthly income up to ₹15,000.

The PM-SYM pension scheme envisaged providing unorganized workers with an assured monthly pension of ₹3,000 from the age of sixty, on a small monthly contribution during their working age. In the Budget speech, it was explained that an unorganized sector worker joining the pension scheme at the age of twenty-nine would have to contribute only ₹100 per month till the age of sixty. A worker joining the scheme at eighteen years would have to contribute as little as ₹55 per month. The government promised to deposit an equal share in the pension account of the worker every month.

It was expected that at least ten crore labourers and workers in the unorganized sector would avail the benefit of PM-SYM within the next five years, making it one of the largest pension schemes in the world. Unfortunately, the long-term nature of the social security benefit and, later, the unemployment and wage reduction faced by unorganized workers owing to the Covid-19 pandemic, has resulted in lukewarm implementation of the scheme.

The scheme was launched immediately after the Budget announcement. About 27.5 lakh workers joined the scheme by 31 March 2019. Enrolments slowed down in 2019–20 and only about sixteen lakh workers joined. The year 2020–21 was literally a washout, with only 1.5 lakh workers joining the scheme. The scheme virtually stalled in 2021–22 when hardly any new enrolments took place.

Vision of a Ten-Dimensional $10-Trillion Economy

The Interim Budget 2018–19 was also an occasion to set out a long-term and medium-term vision for the country. The government felt confident that a $5 trillion economy was within its grasp in the next term and boldly stated in the Budget speech, 'We are poised to become a five trillion-dollar economy in the next five years.' Thereafter, the finance minister stated India's aspiration 'to become a 10-trillion-dollar economy in the next eight years thereafter', by 2033. The government laid out its vision to realize this aspiration by invoking the Indian ethos to 'bestow, cause, create and do good in all ten directions' and defined the ten most important dimensions of its 'Vision 2030'.

The first dimension was to build physical and social infrastructure for the $10 trillion economy and to provide ease of living by constructing next-generation infrastructure of roads, railways, seaports, airports, urban transport, gas and electric transmission and inland waterways, and to ensure every family has a roof over its head and lives in a healthy, clean and wholesome environment.

With digitalization transforming the future of the economy, the second dimension spoke of creating a Digital India, reaching every sector of the economy, every corner of the country and impacting the life of all Indians. Realizing that a good environment would be at the centre of the happiness of Indians, the finance minister envisaged making India a pollution-free nation with green 'mother earth' and 'blue skies' as the third dimension of the government's vision.

To make every Indian share the fruits of this infrastructure-rich, digital and environmentally wholesome country, the fourth dimension talked about expanding rural industrialization using modern digital technologies to generate massive employment and develop grassroots-level clusters, structures and mechanisms encompassing MSMEs, village industries and start-ups in every nook and corner of the country. To make lives better for everyone, the fifth dimension committed the government to vigorously work to make India a country of clean rivers, with safe drinking water for all Indians, sustaining and nourishing life, and the efficient use of water in irrigation using micro-irrigation techniques.

To realize the potential of India's long coastline to become an economic strength, the sixth dimension of the vision focused on exploitation of the 'Blue Economy', ensuring better standards and quality of life for the large number of people living in coastal areas. The government further committed to scale-up the Sagarmala programme and develop inland waterways faster. The seventh dimension visualized conquering the skies by developing the space programme Gaganyaan, making India a launchpad of satellites for the world and placing an Indian astronaut into space by 2022.

Making India self-sufficient in food, exporting to the world and producing food in the most organic way, was defined as the eighth dimension of Vision 2030, while the ninth dimension emphasized making India a healthy society with an environment that provided health assurance and the support of necessary health infrastructure.

This healthy India was to be built with the participation of women with equal rights and concern for their safety and empowerment.

Finally, the tenth dimension invoked Team India to deliver the vision with everyone working together with the elected government, to transform India into a 'minimum government, maximum governance' nation and making the bureaucracy proactive, responsible and people-friendly.

The government confidently asserted that the realization of this comprehensive ten-dimensional vision would create an India where poverty, malnutrition, littering and illiteracy would be a thing of the past. We would be a modern, technology-driven, high growth, equitable and transparent society.

27

Stamp Duty Imbroglio Finally Resolved

A Long-Pending Issue

AFTER A COUPLE OF WEEKS OF ASSUMING MY RESPONSIBILITIES AS SECRETARY, DEA, in July 2017, the Capital Markets Division convened a meeting to discuss amendments in the Indian Stamp Act, 1899. The Department of Revenue in the Ministry of Finance is the administrative department for the Indian Stamp Act, not DEA. The meeting was convened under my chairmanship with a joint secretary of the Department of Revenue present.

The rates of stamp duty on shares and debentures are within the domain of the Union government. Stamp duty and other taxes on transactions in stock markets are a taxation matter. The subject of stamp duty was therefore rightly allocated to the Department of Revenue. The Capital Markets Division in DEA handles issues concerning transfer of securities—shares and debentures and their derivatives—in stock exchanges. The transfer of securities attracts stamp duty. A state of anarchy prevailed in the country with respect to levying stamp duty on transfer of shares and debentures.

The stock exchanges are located in Mumbai, and Maharashtra claimed and attempted to levy stamp duty on every transaction taking place in the country. The states were taking all kinds of measures to collect stamp duty through brokers or otherwise for transactions made by shareholders and bondholders residing in their jurisdiction. Stamp duty was being levied on a multiplicity of documents. It was being levied at different rates. The division had calculated that, in actual practice, the states together were not able to collect even one-sixth of what their rates of levies would normatively indicate.

The Department of Revenue claimed it did not understand the stock markets. It also claimed there were several other reforms and amendments pending in the Stamp Act. Therefore, it wanted a comprehensive amendment to be legislated. As the pressing need was to streamline stamp duty taxation on transfer of shares and debentures, the entire amendment legislation was being processed in DEA, though quite unhappily. The matter was pending for more than four years.

I made two decisions in the first meeting. First, to separate the proposals relating to stamp duty on transfer of shares and debentures and the rest. Second, DEA would handle the entire matter relating to this part and the Department of Revenue would only be requested to formally process this on its file since the matter, as per the rules of business, was in its domain. The Department of Revenue's representative first resisted, but finally agreed.

Deconstructing the Problem

Entry 91 of the Union List empowers the Union government with respect to the 'rates of stamp duty in respect of bills of exchange, cheques, promissory notes, bills of lading, letters of credit, policies of insurance, transfer of shares, debentures, proxies and receipts'. The Union also has powers on 'taxes other than stamp duties on transactions in stock exchanges and futures markets'.

The rates of stamp duty leviable on transfer (which includes initial issuance as well) of shares, debentures and the derivatives of shares and debentures are to be decided by the Union of India. Article 268 of the Constitution of India provides that the stamp duties mentioned in the Union List shall be collected by the states within which such duties are respectively leviable. The levy, collection and appropriation of stamp duty is in the competence of respective states, where such duties are respectively leviable.

Trading in shares, debentures and their derivatives almost completely takes place on the stock exchanges: the National Stock Exchange (NSE) and Bombay Stock Exchange (BSE) in Mumbai, Maharashtra, and other exchanges like the Negotiated Dealing System (NDS), operated by RBI. The actual collection of stamp duties on shares, debentures and their derivatives takes place in the state of Maharashtra while shareholders and debenture holders are located all over the country. Likewise, brokers and other intermediaries too are located all over the country.

Stamp duty is levied on a document. In the chain of documentation relating to a trading transaction, depending upon the location of shareholders and bondholders, brokers and other intermediaries, stock exchanges and concerned banks, many documents that have a connection with the transaction get generated in different places. The states would seek to levy a duty on such a document at rates that suited them.

Different documents were sought to be taxed for stamp duty at different rates in the country. System players—stock exchanges, settlement bodies and intermediaries—were being forced by more than one state to collect stamp duty. Stock exchanges were finding it very difficult to levy stamp duty on different rates.

The result was a big mess. Everybody was hassled yet the total tax collected by all the states together was not even 20 per cent of the estimated collection at rates prescribed by the states.

Finding the Solution

A deeper diagnostic of the problem threw up the solution. Rates of stamp duty to be applied would need to be uniform across all the states. A single instrument/document in the entire chain of transaction would have to be selected and declared as the only instrument on which the duty would be payable.

A single agency would need to collect the stamp duty and distribute it among the states. Therefore, it appeared very logical and sensible that a single rate of duty to be applied on a single instrument and collected by a single agency would be the core of the solution. These basic reforms in the stamp duty system for transfer of shares and debentures presented the opportunity to resolve some other issues as well.

For some transactions in shares, stamp duty was collected only from buyers; for some, it was collected from both buyers and sellers. There was also the question of ascertaining at which specific stage of transaction, the stamp duty should be levied—under the present system, some transactions were subject to levy of stamp duty twice. Who should pay the stamp duty when the initial allotment of shares or debentures takes place? All these issues were also to be resolved.

It was felt that stamp duty should be levied and collected from buyers as it was one transaction and one document. It was also felt that in case of initial allotment, the duty would be paid by the issuer, not the buyer. For the options also, a single point was identified.

For fair distribution of stamp duty collections among states, it was felt that duty collected by the trading institution should be distributed on the basis of where the buyer or allottee resided. A few iterations of what the fair rate of stamp duty should be, led to a structure that was estimated to double the total collection of stamp duty.

We had a fair solution. We went ahead and prepared the draft amendment law. The draft Indian Stamp Act (Amendment) Bill, 2017, was ready. We wanted to introduce it in the winter session of Parliament in December 2017.

Tortuous Path to Implementing a Solution

I spoke to Revenue Secretary Hasmukh Adhia. The Department of Revenue was required to get it vetted through the Law Department and obtain formal approvals of the government to introduce the amendments. I also mentioned it to Finance Minister Arun Jaitley. Hasmukh Adhia wanted the states to be formally consulted. We circulated the draft law to the states in November–December 2017 for their comments. As expected, Maharashtra and Gujarat, two states that were undue beneficiaries of the prevailing system, raised some objections. Tamil Nadu raised a technical objection. Another state raised a minor issue. Some states actively supported the proposal. Most states had nothing to say.

The consultation process killed the opportunity to introduce the bill in the 2017 winter session. I reasoned that it was essentially a money bill and wanted to take it thereafter as part of the Finance Bill, 2018. Hasmukh Adhia was sympathetic. He advised another round of consultation with the state finance secretaries and ministers, who were due to assemble in the GST Council.

I made a presentation before the GST Council meeting with the finance secretaries of the states in January 2018. All the matters were clarified. Maharashtra also came on board. Only Gujarat had some discomfort, which was not based on any genuine rationale. We thought we had wrapped up the matter. No state GST minister opposed the proposed law at the meeting. Two or three GST ministers said they were not in charge of stamp duty law in the state.

We thought we had adequate consultations to go ahead with presenting the Stamp Duty Amendment Bill as part of the Finance Bill, 2018. Hasmukh Adhia, however, had different ideas. He felt we would have to complete formal consultations with the ministers in charge of stamp duty law in the states. The opportunity of 2018 Budget and Finance Bill was also lost.

After some time, the Indian Stamp Act (Amendment) Bill, 2018, was fully ready. It was approved by the finance minister and submitted to the cabinet secretariat for taking the cabinet's approval. The PMO advised more inter-ministerial consultation, most specifically on the constitutionality of the Bill.

The rate of stamp duty on transfer of shares and debentures was clearly in the Government of India's domain. However, actual levy, specific document to levy it on and collection of stamp duty on transfer of shares and debentures were in the domain of state governments.

The cabinet secretary convened the inter-ministerial meeting. Representatives of the Department of Legislative Affairs, which has to formally draft the law, and the Department of Legal Affairs, which has to certify the constitutionality of the proposed legislation, were present. They created doubts about the constitutionality of the proposed law. The cabinet secretary advised us to hold deeper consultations with the Ministry of Law.

A lot of correspondence took place with the Ministry of Law. A few changes were suggested in the draft law. The Department of Legislative Affairs wrote long notes on the constitutionality of the Amendment Bill.

The drafting changes were resolved in a few iterations but the differences on constitutionality persisted. We argued about the constitutionality of law. Our arguments were clear. The power to decide the rate on transfer of shares and debentures was exclusively that of the Union. As the stamp duty was applicable on the transfer, the instrument that would constitute the transfer is also exercise of this power. Therefore, the states cannot decide on the document and the rate to be applied. Further, the Stamp Duty Act was part of the Concurrent List of the Constitution and thus any amendments could also be carried out by the Parliament.

Things were less straightforward on the question of collection of duty through specific agencies of stock exchanges. We argued that as states have agreed to this arrangement and it was the most efficient way of collecting duty, it should also be legislated in the Amendment Bill. Many discussions took place on this issue.

The mechanism for revision of duty rates in the future also came in for considerable discussion. We had initially proposed to constitute and empower a GST-like body headed by the finance secretary. The Ministry of Law did not find a body of officers to be legally competent for the purpose. We proposed that the GST Council be given this jurisdiction. Owing to this protracted examination and correspondence, the consultation could not be completed in calendar year 2018.

Amendments to the Stamp Law were being discussed in the country for the past twenty years. I had separated the stamp duty related to transfer of shares and debentures about eighteen months earlier. The Parliament was to meet next only for the Budget session (Interim Budget 2019–20). The end of the government tenure was approaching in 2019. Increasingly, it appeared that stamp duty rationalization would perhaps need to wait for some more years.

Luckily, It Made Its Way into the Finance Bill, 2019

Sometime in January, I mentioned to Piyush Goyal that amendments in stamp duty provisions were extremely necessary for the smooth functioning of the stock and debt markets. I told him that we had done everything we could and we were ready with the amendment bill, but the Ministry of Law was holding up the matter on some minor issue of constitutionality. I proposed that we take up the Stamp Duty Amendment Bill as part of the Finance Bill, along with the interim Budget. Piyush Goyal, who understands the stock markets well, agreed and promised to speak to the law minister if necessary.

This gave us the authority to work to bring it in the Finance Bill. Necessary changes were made accordingly though, conventionally, almost no significant legislative business is transacted through the Finance Bill during the years when government is completing its period and presenting only an interim Budget. To strengthen our case, we dug up some precedents.

Ajay Bhushan Pandey, the new revenue secretary, had no strong views on the matter and agreed to the proposal. Piyush Goyal cleared it on file. The matter again landed up with the Ministry of Law. The Finance Bill is also formally drafted and signed by the secretary, Department of Legislative Affairs.

Again, rounds of discussions took place. The Ministry of Law rejected the proposal at least three times on file in three days. Every day mattered. The Capital Markets Division and I kept up the pressure. Finally, possibly tired of the endless examination and, in my judgement, grudgingly accepting that DEA was on stronger ground, the Ministry of Law relented. Amendment provisions were approved on file.

The Amendments to the Indian Stamp Act, 1899, formed Part I of 'Chapter IV—Miscellaneous' of the Finance Bill, 2019. After being passed by the Parliament, the bill received the assent of the President on 21 February 2019. The Finance Act 2019, with stamp duty amendments, was published in the official gazette on that day. We in DEA had a sense of relief and some achievement having pulled it through.

New Stamp Duty Regime on Capital Market Instruments

We finally got the amendment necessary to reform and streamline stamp-duty collection in the country. This had contributed to the smooth functioning of the securities markets, increasing the revenue collection for state governments, and is very fair and reasonable to the parties to the transaction.

This law introduced a regime of stamp-duty collection on transactions in shares, debentures and their derivatives that is built on an extremely efficient and smooth structure, replacing a complex web of mutually contradictory and overlapping processes.

The new law provided for the following major changes. Two unique documents—'allotment list' for allotment of fresh securities and 'clearance list' for transactions in the exchanges—have been made the basis of charge. All other documents that had any potential for misuse were deleted from the law. It was also specifically provided that no stamp duty would be charged on any other instrument. Further, specific and uniform duty rates on debenture and securities, other than debentures, were specified at reasonable rates. The need to physically stamp instruments of transfer was done away with.

A very clear provision was made that stamp duty would be collected from the buyer at the market value of securities at the time of settlement of transactions. The duty would be collected by the clearing corporation in case of a market transaction, and the depositories, in case of initial allotment of shares. Specific obligation was cast on the collecting agents to remit the collected duties to the states within three weeks, based on the residence of the buyer.

Immediately after the Indian Stamp Act (Amendment) Law was passed and notified on 21 February 2019, the task of approving the rules was initiated. The draft rules had been prepared earlier. They were soon circulated to the stock exchanges and other stakeholders concerned. The stock exchanges raised some objections. These were discussed and final implementable rules were arrived at. The stock exchanges, clearing corporations and depositories also wanted some time to adapt their processes and systems to the changes being brought in.

Lag in Notification of Rules and Bringing Them into Effect

We wanted to make the rules applicable from 1 April 2019. The general elections were declared in March 2019. Arun Jaitley had become seriously ill. The rules could not be approved in April–May when the process of elections was on. Nirmala Sitharaman took over as finance minister at the end of May 2019. We submitted the rules for her approval in June 2019. She did not think the matter was urgent and the file remained pending in her office until I demitted office on 24 July.

The Indian Stamp (Collection of Stamp-Duty through Stock Exchanges, Clearing Corporations and Depositories) Rules, 2019, were finally notified on 10 December 2019. These rules provided that the new regime of stamp-duty collection would come into effect from 9 January 2020. By way of the first amendment made in these rules, the date of rules enforcement was shifted to 1 April 2020.

Coronavirus played another spoiler. The government again amended these rules on 31 March 2020 to shift the date of commencement of rules from 1 April 2020 to 1 July 2020.

On 30 June 2020, the government issued a comprehensive press note headlined: 'Implementation of Amendments in the Indian Stamp Act, 1899, and Rules made from 1 July 2020 for Rationalized Collection Mechanism of Stamp Duty across India with respect to Securities Market Instruments'.

Finally, the system of collection of stamp duty on capital market instruments was implemented in the country from 1 July 2020. It created no disruptions. It smoothened the entire ecosystem of levy, collection and sharing of stamp duty in the country. The new system continues to work flawlessly.

28
Regular Budget 2019–20

Run-Up

Economic Situation Worries PM

THE GROWTH OF GDP HAD BEEN SLOWING DOWN IN FY2018–19. From a high of 8 per cent in the first quarter, it came down to 7 per cent in the second. The third quarter (October–December 2018) results, which were released in February 2019 (just before the announcement of the general elections), showed that growth had further slipped to 6.6 per cent. Prospects for fourth quarter growth (to be announced just about the time the new government was expected to be sworn in) were also not looking particularly bright (it was finally only 5.8 per cent).

The election campaign ended on 19 May 2019. The results were expected by 23 May. Though the votes were not counted, the BJP government was expected to return to power. Prime Minister Modi was rightly worried about the state of the economy. A meeting was convened on 20 May, at his residence. Rajiv Kumar, vice chairman, NITI Aayog, and I made separate presentations on the state of economy and what needed to be done. The PM heard us out patiently and wanted us to make the same presentation before two ministers—Piyush Goyal and Nirmala Sitharaman—the next morning.

Arun Jaitley was ailing and was expected to stay out of the government. We made our presentations before Piyush Goyal and Nirmala Sitharaman. Both of them took serious interest in the issues discussed. This meeting gave us some indication of who might succeed Arun Jaitley in North Block.

The government was sworn in on 30 May 2019. Nirmala Sitharaman was appointed finance minister and joined the next day. The Budget was due on 5 July 2019, barely five weeks later. Finalizing Budget 2019–20 was my No. 1 task.

Budget Speech Preparation Off to a Rocky Start

As I recount in the last chapter in this book, my personal and working relationship with Nirmala Sitharaman was broken from the get-go. This affected the Budget preparation. As secretary, economic affairs, I was responsible for drafting the Budget speech of the finance minister. This required an atmosphere of trust and confidence between us. Unfortunately, this was not the case.

I started working on the draft of the Budget speech very early in the month of June. I informed the minister that I would deliver the first draft to her latest by 24 June. I was included in the PM's delegation for the G-20 leaders' meeting and was due to leave on the night of 25 June.

Despite the stressful conditions, worsened by the virtual snapping of communications between us, I drafted the Budget speech and handed it over to the finance minister on 24 June. I requested her to work on my inputs and send me the first version of her draft as soon as possible. I had made all the arrangements to receive her version of the speech and update it while attending the G-20 meeting.

I did not receive her comments for the next version while I was away. I worked to further improve the draft I had submitted to her on 24 June, on the flight back on the PM's plane from Japan on 29 June. I delivered the revised version of the first draft to her on 30 June, again underlining the absolute urgency for her to work on it and finalize it to be shared with the PMO.

A Stunner from the Finance Minister

The PMO played an important and intensive role in the making of the Budget. It vetted every paragraph that went in the Budget speech. A presentation before the PM was scheduled on 2 July to finalize the basic thrust of the Budget speech.

A stunner was to follow. The forenoon of 2 July, Finance Minister Nirmala Sitharaman delivered her version of the draft speech directly to the PMO, without providing me a copy. When I asked her for a copy, she said the speech as sent by her was by and large what I had given her and that she had only added a few paragraphs.

This created an unprecedented situation. I was responsible for finalizing the speech and seeing it through print without any glitches. Further, I was also primarily responsible for defending the speech with the media and analysts. And I did not have the draft finance minister cleared.

Normally, the Budget speech is read by secretary, economic affairs, at the meeting chaired by the PM. Here, I didn't even have a copy of the speech! Anyway, I reached the PM's residence for the meeting. At the meeting, Brajendra Navnit, joint secretary in the PMO, read from the physical copy of the draft Budget speech sent by the finance minister. I only had my version of the draft speech.

She had included ten to twelve new paragraphs, had dropped a few, and left the bulk of the draft speech untouched. Over the next three hours or more, Prime Minister Modi went through the draft, accepted a few of her additions and asked for a lot of reorientation of emphasis and priorities. When the meeting finished past 9.30 p.m., I was worried about how to carry forward the process and come up with a revised draft as the PM wanted it read out before him the next day, 3 July. The Budget was to be presented on 5 July.

I asked her how to handle the matter after the meeting finished.

'I will hand over all the papers, including my draft, to you and you have to get this done tomorrow,' she responded. I could see a disaster waiting to happen.

I told her this was not the best way and that she would have to guide the process to complete the draft. I suggested we meet at 8 a.m. in her office in North Block and work together to complete the revisions. She agreed. I informed all the concerned staff to be available in her office at 8 a.m.

The Speech Gets Finalized, Somehow

I was in the office with all the concerned staff at 8 a.m. on 3 July. She did not turn up. In fact, her personal staff did not even open her office at 8 a.m. When I called her at home, I was informed that she had been working from very early in the morning on the draft and would reach the office only at 9.30 a.m.

After she reached, from 9.30 a.m. to about 4 p.m., I worked with her to put together the revised draft—she did a lot of work on it too. There were many loose ends, some paragraphs were missing, and some paragraphs that needed to be dropped, pruned or tightened still remained hanging.

I worked to improve it as much as I could until 6 p.m. The second reading of the draft speech was rescheduled for 6.30 p.m. This round again went on until 9.30 p.m. Prime Minister Modi was still not satisfied and offered a lot of new ideas to work on. However, realizing the gravity of the situation with almost no time remaining with the Budget team and the finance minister, he indicated that he did not need to see the further revised version, saying he would listen to the Budget speech only in Parliament on 5 July.

We worked together on 4 July and prepared a near final draft by 4 p.m. At this stage, I was quite relieved as a good package of capital market reforms, encouraging public private partnerships, further opening up the economy to FDI and FPI, containing the fiscal deficit and announcement of new initiatives like sovereign bonds in foreign currencies, all intended to push investment in infrastructure and manufacturing in India, which I had prepared and included in the first draft, had survived almost unscathed. Her contribution was mainly political and social messaging, that too in other parts of the speech.

After sharing it with the PMO it underwent two more iterations and I was happy that the Budget speech was sent for printing at about 9 p.m. It was delivered in Parliament on 5 July and was largely well-received.

Budget 2019–20

A Budget Speech without Any Numbers

The peculiar circumstances in which Budget 2019–20 was drafted/prepared and the kind of competing and conflicting constituencies it was meant to serve, led to an extraordinary change in the character of the Budget speech. The Budget is an occasion to present estimates of revenues and expenditures for ensuing years and the Budget speech highlights significant changes in expenditure allocations and the final Budget balance indicators: fiscal deficits, revenue deficits and the like.

As always, the PMO wanted the Budget speech to highlight the good work the government had done in the past five years, addressing every constituency with large numbers—agriculture and farmers, MSMEs and labour, rural development and rural people, urban development and people living in cities and towns, women, youth, and so on.

The stocktaking of all the good work done and highlighting it consumes a good portion of the Budget speech.

The Tax Department wanted to include every single change (small or large) made in the tax base and the rates and procedure to address the concerns of all segments of taxpayers. DEA wanted all the measures proposed to be taken to uplift economic growth and develop financial markets to be included in the Budget. The new finance minister also had certain preferences relating to the invocation of sages and wisemen and to present herself as the new champion of Indian women.

A few years earlier, the government had hit upon the idea that a good part of these must-includes, but relatively less appealing parts, be shifted to annexures to the speech. The Budget speech for 2019–20 also had annexures—thirty-four pages out of the printed sixty-six pages. Despite shifting so much material to the annexures, the thirty-two-page speech was long enough to get Finance Minister Nirmala Sitharaman completely exhausted as the speech lasted beyond two hours.

Still, the most conspicuous feature of the speech was that it had no numbers—no allocation was highlighted, no deficit numbers were stated, not even overall levels of expenditures and revenue collections mentioned. I believe that the Budget speech is a good occasion to articulate the government's economic, financial and developmental policy vision. Though there were some policy measures, the complete absence of Budget numbers, especially highly critical macroeconomic indicators, was beyond the pale.

I had given her a four- to five-line handwritten note on the morning of Budget day, before we proceeded to Rashtrapati Bhavan to brief the President and take formal leave to present the Budget. She kept this with her. As she was getting completely exhausted by the end of the speech, the Speaker of the House allowed the last few paragraphs to be taken as read. The handwritten paragraph could not have been taken as read as it was not part of the Budget speech.

The finance minister remembered the note after a minute or so. Marshalling her strength, she sought the permission of the Speaker to read those four lines. They contained the overall size of the Budget and critical fiscal deficit and revenue deficit numbers. The handwritten note was also placed on the table of the House along with her Budget speech. They were the only numbers that the 2019–20 Budget speech officially carried.

Equity Finance Corporation Failed to See the Light of Day

India was able to develop an excellent infrastructure of stock markets for equity trading. However, raising equity for new ventures was still a major problem. The first test of a functional and enterprise-friendly stock market is whether equity can be raised for new enterprises, start-ups and social ventures—the primary equity market. Secondary markets provide liquidity and trading opportunities to existing equity issued, not new equity.

There were very low levels of primary equity raised in the Indian stock markets. Total equity raised through IPOs was in the order of about ₹30,000 crore in 2016–17, which was a record. In the previous three years, the resources raised through IPOs had averaged only ₹6,500 crore.

Initial public offerings in India are also raised by companies which, after completing the construction of their plants, have been making profits for some time. However, there was no company raising equity at the start of a project—before construction work was completed. The banks provided loans at this stage of project implementation, not equity. With a complete absence of equity even for projects of established businesses, the promoters undertook numerous kinds of manipulations, such as raising debt on the holding company to provide equity to the project through subsidiaries and padding up the construction contracts to 'extract' equity.

The Government of India had established many institutions, but primarily to provide debt. There was a massive equity squeeze in the country. Against this backdrop, I worked out a proposal to establish an equity financing corporation by the government, which could raise about 50 per cent of the equity capital required from the market. This was a new-age development finance bank.

When the proposal was presented to Prime Minister Modi at the pre-Budget meeting, surprisingly, all hell broke loose. The objections were started by Principal Economic Advisor Sanjeev Sanyal, who questioned the very rationale for an equity financing institution, DIPAM Secretary Atanu Chakraborty and DFS Secretary Rajiv Kumar piled on. I stood my ground and provided explanations for every point they raised. The PM sincerely tried to understand what the fuss was all about. The slanging match went on for forty-five minutes.

At that stage, Finance Minister Nirmala Sitharaman also joined in and said some things that showed her disapproval of the way the proposal was brought in. Narendra Modi, irritated by then, asked all of us to discuss the proposal in the Ministry of Finance and make up our minds. The next day, Sanjeev Singla, PS to the PM, called me to ensure that nothing like the previous day should happen again—a presentation before the PM was not the place for finance ministry officers to blow off steam at each other, he said.

After development finance institutions (DFIs) like IFCI and IDBI in the public sector and ICICI in the private sector stopped capital financing in the mid-2000s, there were no financial institutions in the country that provided any equity financing. The LIC has also been largely a financial investor, instead of an equity provider, to new projects. The NIIF was created in 2017 to provide equity financing for infrastructure. The equity deficit for infrastructure, industrial projects and start-ups in India still remains massive. However, the proposal to establish an equity financing corporation got shelved.

Slew of Proposals to Promote Equity Financing Made It to the Budget

I had initially formulated Budget 2019–20 as a major equity financing policy transformation Budget—for both domestic and foreign equity. The lack of development of a good working relationship with the new finance minister, and the fiasco regarding the equity financing corporation, dented the framework. However, some fragments survived that were significant.

The first set of proposals related to foreign equity investment, both FDI and FPI.

Much new equity in Indian enterprises, both mature and start-ups, was coming in the form of FDI, with India registering strong inflows of $64.4 billion in 2018–19. To carry on with the mission to make India a more attractive FDI destination, the government signalled further opening up of FDI in the aviation, media (animation, visual effects, gaming and comics, or AVGC) and insurance sectors. After overcoming the protracted resistance of DFS Secretary Rajiv Kumar, the Budget finally announced 100 per cent FDI in insurance intermediaries. Mustering the courage to finally rest the ghost of insistence on local sourcing in the single-brand retail sector, like the sale of iPhones by company outlets, the Budget announced that local sourcing norms would be eased for FDI in single-brand retail.

India had gradually opened up its economy for foreign investment, both FDI and FPI. However, this opening has also been quite regulation-heavy. One irritating regulation left standing was inconsistency regarding the operationalization of sectoral limits for foreign investment for a specific company. The regulations posited a default limit of 24 per cent of the equity capital issued for FPI. If the sectoral limit were higher (for example, 74 per cent in private banking, or 49 per cent in insurance), the companies concerned in the sector were required to pass specific resolutions to allow foreign investment up to the sectoral limit.

The Budget aimed to upturn the situation. The finance minister proposed increasing the default/automatic statutory limit for FPI investment in a company from 24 per cent to the sectoral foreign investment limit. To still allow any company concerned in the sector to restrict foreign investment, the option was given to the concerned corporates to limit it to a lower threshold by passing an appropriate regulation. It was expected that most companies would go by the default regulatory limits and, therefore, the default limit for almost all companies in the sector would get aligned with the sector limit.

The second set of proposals aimed to introduce the funding of social impact projects through the Indian capital markets in India.

To take the Indian capital markets closer to the masses and meet the social welfare objective of inclusive growth, the finance minister proposed to initiate steps towards creating an electronic fundraising platform—a social stock exchange—under the regulatory ambit of SEBI for listing of social enterprises and voluntary organizations to raise capital as equity, debt or as units like a mutual fund.

The third set of proposals included transforming the architecture of equity held by the government in public-sector enterprises. Noting that the government had been following the policy of maintaining at least 51 per cent equity in non-financial PSUs (like NTPC and Indian Oil)—which acted as a constraint to further divestment of equity in many CPSEs—the finance minister announced that the government was open to dilute its equity stake below 51 per cent to an appropriate level on a case-to-case basis, still retaining management control. She further announced that in case it was considered more prudent to retain 51 per cent equity stake, the government would modify the policy of retaining a 51 per cent stake to mean a 51 per cent stake inclusive of the stake of government-controlled institutions.

Affirming clearly that the strategic disinvestment of select CPSEs continued to remain a priority of the government, Nirmala Sitharaman announced that not only would the process of strategic disinvestment of Air India be reinitiated, but more CPSEs would be offered for strategic participation by the private sector. In fact, I wanted the government to mention specifically the strategic divestment of BPCL and a few other companies in the Budget. The concerned paragraph, which remained in the draft Budget speech for quite some time, finally got diluted in the manner that no specific name was announced.

The government set an enhanced target of ₹1,05,000 crore of disinvestment receipts for FY2019–20, banking on undertaking the strategic sale of PSUs.

Finally, the government targeted increasing India's weight in the Emerging Market (EM) Equity Index. The EM index was constructed based on the free float of equity shares. Examination revealed that capping foreign investment to 20 per cent in most PSUs reduced the effective free-float. To rectify this, the finance minister announced that the foreign shareholding limits would be raised to maximum permissible sector limits for all PSU companies that were part of the EM index at the time.

However, there was a jarring announcement as well.

In the run-up to the Budget preparation, in a meeting chaired by the PM, Rajiv Kumar, vice-chairman, NITI Aayog, proposed that the minimum public shareholding should be raised from 25 per cent to 40 per cent, which he believed would bring additional public participation and help grow the equity market and culture in the country. I had explained that the proposal might not be advisable at that juncture, as many listed companies were finding it difficult to even meet the 25 per cent norm and government companies, both financial and non-financial, were the biggest culprits in this regard.

We had to grant a two-year extension to the PSBs to meet the 25 per cent shareholding norms around the same time. However, the emotional appeal of Rajiv Kumar's proposal seemed to strike a chord with the principal secretary to the PM. He said there was no harm in trying out this proposal, with the PM not clearly taking a stand either way. Aware of the likely adverse implications on the stock market, I had worded the proposal carefully. Therefore, instead of making it a directive announcement, the finance minister said in the Budget speech that she had 'asked SEBI to consider raising the current threshold of 25 per cent to 35 per cent'.

As expected, this proposal received wide backlash. To cut our losses and specifically signal that the government was not interested in going down that path, I made it clear in post-Budget conferences that SEBI would only examine this suggestion and there was hardly any likelihood of this move going any further.

Debt Package Includes Sovereign Bond Issuance

There are three major deficiencies in India's debt market. First, the corporate debt market is quite underdeveloped and has not played a legitimate role to finance debt capital. Second, the participation of FPIs in India's sovereign and corporate debt, on account of the fickle nature of their investment and unsteady policies for both sovereign and corporate debt, has been volatile. Third, retail participation in both sovereign and corporate debt is negligible. We did not have a complete package to address all the three deficiencies; yet, some weaknesses were sought to be plugged.

To make infrastructure financing, estimated to require debt investments of ₹20 lakh crore every year, a little more appealing and secure, a few measures were announced in the Budget speech.

A credit guarantee enhancement corporation had been structured by DEA to provide enhancement guarantees for debt raised by infrastructure projects. Setting up a new corporation required the approval of a committee headed by the expenditure secretary and the cabinet. The committee's approval had been obtained despite many roadblocks by DFS. RBI had also cleared the regulations as this corporation was a special kind of NBFC. The finance minister announced that the guarantee enhancement corporation would be set up in 2019–20.

In addition, she said an action plan to deepen the market for long-term bonds—including markets for corporate bond repos and credit default swaps, with a specific focus on the infrastructure sector—would be put in place during the year. Further, to deepen the corporate triparty repo (where a third party, mostly the settlement/guaranteeing entity, enters into the contract between the borrower and lender of securities) market in corporate debt securities, the finance minister announced that the government would work with regulators RBI/SEBI to enable stock exchanges to allow AA rated bonds as collateral. The user-friendliness of trading platforms for corporate bonds was also promised to be reviewed, including issues arising out of capping of the International Securities Identification Number (ISIN).

In a major move to develop corporate bond markets by means of public issue, NBFCs, which were subject to maintaining a debenture redemption reserve (DRR) and, in addition, a special reserve as required by RBI, were to be allowed to raise funds in public issues without any mandatory creation of DRR.

To nudge foreign debt investments in a direction good for the country, the finance minister proposed to permit investments made by FIIs/FPIs in debt securities issued by Infrastructure Debt Fund – Non-Bank Finance Companies (IDF–NBFCs) to be freed from the restrictions of a lock-in. These investments would be allowed to be transferred/sold to any domestic investor even within the specified lock-in period. The FPIs were also to be permitted to subscribe to listed debt securities issued by REITs and InvITs.

The Budget also included an announcement by the government on the issuance of sovereign bonds in foreign currencies. This led to a furore. I have discussed this entire episode in an earlier chapter.

India Initiates Partial Risk, First-Loss Guarantee Instrument

The NBFCs accessed low-cost, short-term funds from mutual funds by issuing a certificate of deposits, and used these for lending for the medium- and long-term. The IL&FS crisis in September–October 2018 had dried up this source of financing. The NBFCs also fund by raising loans from the banks. Some major liquidity-stressed NBFCs wanted to meet their needs by selling their assets. The PSBs were nudged indirectly by the government to buy out the good-quality assets. From October 2018 onwards, the banks, including PSBs, bought most of the AAA and AA-rated assets from stressed NBFCs.

However, the NBFCs wanted more of their assets, including lower-rated assets, to be sold to the PSBs to meet their liquidity needs. This led to the system building constant pressure on the Ministry of Finance and the PMO to help ease liquidity for the financial sector in general and NBFCs in particular. The most appropriate solution was for RBI to relax the excessively tight liquidity it maintained in the system. Old-timers remembered that in 2008, RBI had created a backstop facility to infuse liquidity by providing a refinancing facility to an SPV created for this purpose. However, RBI was unwilling to do anything like this in 2018.

The search for an alternative solution led some banks suggest to DFS that if the government were to take the first loss of a specified percentage on itself, the PSBs could be asked to buy the lower rated pool of assets from the stressed NBFCs. In fact, DFS had made a formal proposal to DEA to agree to issue such a guarantee. The proposal was routinely examined in the Budget Division, which is pathologically against issuing government guarantees for obligations that are unclear or too risky. I was travelling at the time. Without showing me the proposal, the Budget Division had raised numerous objections, including some petty ones, and rejected it. This infuriated DFS Secretary Rajeev Kumar, who in turned relayed DEA's objections to Nripendra Misra, who was also upset. For him, resolving the liquidity problem in the economy was the number one priority.

After I returned, I convened a fresh meeting with the DFS and budget team and tried to understand the proposal. The way it was drafted made it ominous, not as bad as the guarantee DEA had agreed to issue in 1990s for the Dhabol project but serious enough. Ironically, it also appeared that the proposal was largely unimplementable. I extended lukewarm support to the proposal buttressed by many additional conditionalities. However, most of DEA's objections were set aside and the new facility was announced in Budget 2019–20.

After recounting the important role played by NBFCs in sustaining consumption demand as well as capital formation in the small and medium industrial segment, the finance minister announced that the government would provide a one-time, six-month partial credit guarantee to PSBs for the first loss of up to 10 per cent to selected NBFCs—those that were fundamentally sound for purchase of their high-rated pooled assets amounting to a total of ₹1 lakh crore during the current financial year.

The DFS took some time to work out the contours of the facility. I was transferred out of the Ministry of Finance in the last week of July. I did not have to further deal with the matter.

The DFS issued a scheme on 10 August 2019 (further modified on 23 September 2019) to provide a one-time partial credit guarantee by government to PSBs for purchase of pooled assets from financially sound NBFCs/housing finance companies (HFCs). The guarantee was limited to 10 per cent of fair value of assets purchased by the banks under the scheme or ₹10,000 crore, whichever was lower. The scheme did not take off. There were no transactions until 31 October 2019, the day I left the IAS, as I had suspected.

The participants in the system wanted more relaxations. These included making NBFCs that had started defaulting even in the one-year period prior to the IL&FS crisis eligible for the PSBs to purchase their pooled assets. They also wanted to revise the minimum rating of the underlying asset pool from AA to BBB+. The cabinet agreed to cover NBFCs/HFCs which might have slipped into a financially stressed status called special mention account (SMA-0) during one year prior to 1.8.2018. This concession was announced on 11 December 2019. The scheme was extended until 30 June 2020 as well.

The scheme did not attract much coverage. It underwent massive dilution as part of the first Covid-19 stimulus package announced in May 2020. The government redesignated the scheme as the

Partial Risk Guarantee Scheme–Version 2 (PCGS 2.0) and included borrowings (bonds, etc.) of NBFCs/HPCs and also that of other micro-finance institutions (MFIs), with lower credit rating. The government covered default on their bonds, etc., increasing the first-loss guarantee to 20 per cent of the purchase cost of bonds or commercial papers (CPs) with a rating of AA and below (including unrated paper with original/initial maturity of up to one year) by the PSBs. Later, the total amount covered was increased to ₹1,00,000 crore.

There were hardly any transactions relating to the original purpose of the scheme—to take over the pooled housing and other consumer loans of NBFCs/HFCs.

₹100 Lakh Crore Infrastructure Investment Pipeline Had Roots in Budget 2019–20

There were three parallel tracks of work going on for infrastructure construction and financing in India. DEA, working with CRISIL, had carried out a comprehensive study on envisioning 'Infrastructure for India of 2030'. This had led to broad estimates of the financing requirement of ₹100 lakh crore for the envisaged infrastructure of 2030.

DEA had also initiated work on mainstreaming the monetization of infrastructure assets. After an announcement was made in Budget 2018–19 about monetizing transmission lines, gas grids and other assets, considerable momentum had been generated for sensitizing the concerned ministries and departments to initiate this work. As explained in a previous chapter, after discussions in the PMO, infrastructure asset monetization work was formally entrusted to DIPAM.

The third track represented incessant demand for a new public-funded infrastructure financing development finance institution or DFI. DFS Secretary Rajiv Kumar was pressing to include an announcement relating to the establishment of such a DFI in Budget 2019–20. I saw no merit in the demand to set up a DFI in the public sector. The experience of IDBI and IFCI earlier and IDFC and IIFCL in more recent times, inspired no confidence that such risky and long-term asset financing should be undertaken by a government-owned institution.

There was some sympathy with Rajiv Kumar's proposal in the PMO. Some Budget announcement appeared inevitable in this regard. I thought of using it to register the resolve of the government to work on preparing a grand infrastructure vision for 2030. I thought it might be good to get an expert opinion on the desirability of setting up an infrastructure DFI in the public sector. Accordingly, a carefully worded announcement was made in Budget 2019–20:

> [The] government has announced its intention to invest ₹100 lakh crore in infrastructure over the next five years. To this end, it is proposed to set up an expert committee to study the current situation relating to long-term finance and our past experience with development finance institutions, and recommend the structure and required flow of funds through development finance institutions.

After I left the Ministry of Finance, the work on translating the infrastructure vision for 2030 using private-sector initiative and financing got converted into the development of a National Infrastructure Pipeline. Unfortunately, the NIP that the government came up with was nothing more than a nominal listing of infrastructure projects that different ministries/departments and state governments were either implementing or could conceive of, without much consideration of their technoeconomic viability and financeability.

Finance Minister Nirmala Sitharaman released the Report of the Task Force on National Infrastructure Pipeline (the NIP) , with much fanfare, on 31 December 2019, for ₹102 lakh crore.

NIP became a holy book to which homage was paid from time to time. Nothing concrete, however, has emerged from it in the past two years. Later, it was merged with PM Gati-shakti programme.

The committee the government appointed to examine the desirability of a DFI went into the process perhaps with the mandate that it had to be established. The government decided to take the plunge later. Budget 2021–22 announced the government's decision to establish the National Bank for Financing Infrastructure and Development. To convey that the government meant business and infrastructure was the new big priority, the government also introduced the National Bank for Financing Infrastructure and Development Bill, 2021, in the Budget session.

The bill envisaged the National Infrastructure Financing and Development Bank (NaBFID) as a kind of developmental and refinancing institution on the lines of NABARD and the merger of IIFCL into it at some stage. It also envisaged the establishment of such banks owned by the private sector. The bill was passed in the same Budget session and notified on 28 March 2021. The NaBFID was formally established soon thereafter. K.V. Kamath was appointed its chairperson on 27 October 2021. ₹20,000 crore of equity was infused in NaBFID in February 2022. Announcements have been made from time to time that NaBFID was about to make its first loan. No loans were made until 31 March 2023. Two years have gone by and nothing really has moved.

The whole construct of the National Infrastructure Bank is poorly designed and excessively dependent on financial support from the government. Infrastructure is a difficult asset to finance. It is extremely difficult for public-sector organizations to fund infrastructure. Past experience in this regard has been terrible. This experiment is not as costly as it has not got off. A bad idea not implemented is perhaps better for the government.

Government Unnecessarily Complicates Direct Tax Structure

I was not directly concerned with the tax proposals. For Budgets 2018–19 and 2019–20 (interim), as I have explained above, my involvement in part B of the speech relating to taxation was somewhat peculiar. I was not involved in the tax proposals of 2019–20 regular Budget.

Piyush Goyal had played the popular act in Interim Budget 2019–20 by virtually making more than 80 per cent of income-tax payers free from paying any tax, by making total income up to ₹5 lakh per annum tax-free. To make up some of the lost revenue,

Nirmala Sitharaman tinkered with the income-tax slab and surcharge structure.

Noting that the government had taken several measures to alleviate the tax burden on small and medium income-earners, those with an annual income up to ₹5 lakh, she called upon those in the highest income brackets 'to contribute more to the Nation's development'. For this purpose, she proposed enhancement of surcharge on individuals with a taxable income between ₹2 crore and ₹5 crore and ₹5 crore and above to raise their effective tax rates by around 3 per cent and 7 per cent respectively. This introduced two more slabs in the income-tax structure, totalling seven slabs in all. The next year, in 2020–21, she made the structure still more complicated by giving taxpayers an option to be taxed at lower tax rates without claiming designated exemptions, which included most of the existing exemptions. The new optional regime took the number of tax slabs to more than ten.

Other complications were introduced as well. While the dividend distribution tax was rightly abolished, a tax of 20 per cent on the buyback proceeds was introduced, which impacted share-buybacks adversely.

The media does not recognize the fine allocation of responsibilities assigned to different secretaries in the Ministry of Finance relating to Budget formulation and presentation. In post-Budget conferences, besides the sovereign bonds issue, the largest number of questions thrown at me related to the introduction of tax on buyback, dividend distribution tax and additional surcharges levied on the higher income slabs. These tax proposals had unintended consequences as well, such as impacting the tax liabilities of FPIs structured as trusts. That collateral damage also invited many comments and questions.

Nirmala Sitharaman Clears North Block of Media

North Block is a favourite of the pink press and online economic news and business channels. At any point of the day, there would be, at the minimum, ten to fifteen media persons, accredited by the PIB, present in the North Block with most standing or sitting outside the finance minister's chamber or the room of the secretary, economic affairs. Whenever there was any major economic policy event, the number would swell to more than thirty-five to forty, making it difficult to move around in the corridor. The media personnel were decent, in the sense that they would not barge into the room unless an appointment had been granted. However, some of them had the habit of catching me if I stepped out of the chamber even for a short break or to go to the minister's chamber.

North Block was made completely off-limits to the media a month before the presentation of the Budget. During this period, none of the accredited or senior media persons were allowed in, except on a personal exemption basis, which was rare, if the minister or any of the secretaries wanted to speak on an important issue. During this period, armed guards stood outside the rooms marked as handling sensitive Budget work, where no one could enter without permission.

A few days after Nirmala Sitharaman took over as finance minister, she phoned me late one evening to inform me that she was considering barring the entry of media personnel in North Block permanently. She said they could be provided a place to sit under one of the covered outdoor spaces outside Gate 2 of North Block, which could also be converted into a closed room with air-conditioners installed. She wanted them to be allowed entry only when an officer or minister specifically wanted to speak to a particular media person or media persons in general. Finally, she suggested that a system of weekly briefings could be institutionalized where all the secretaries could speak to the media in a designated room.

I welcomed the idea. I also told her that not all the secretaries prefer to speak to the media and some might not have something to say every week. However, I told her that the media was unlikely to be pleased with this arrangement. They had always been scouting for news before it was officially out. They wouldn't be able to do that anymore. She said she didn't really care about what they liked. She also asked me whether I could speak to all the secretaries and inform them about the plan. I suggested that the matter be discussed the next day in the daily 11 a.m. secretaries' meeting she had started. She seemed a little unhappy at my response, but said she would talk to the secretaries then.

She must have spoken to one or two other secretaries thereafter. I raised the subject the next day in the secretaries' meeting. All the secretaries were on board, though hardly anyone was interested in speaking to the media on a weekly basis. I said I had many issues to discuss so I would hold a weekly meeting. In any case, after a week, the Budget-related media ban was coming into force. The minister implemented her decision by accordingly directing the joint secretary (personnel) in the Department of Expenditure, who was formally in charge of maintaining the North Block building, and the two DG/director-level officers from PIB posted in the Ministry of Finance.

The evening the ban was implemented, several media personnel walked up to me as soon as I stepped out of Gate 2. They were furious. One of them angrily accused me of being behind the ban. I just smiled and walked past them.

Sitharaman's Office Excludes Shereen Bhan from Post-Budget Dinner

The finance minister traditionally hosts a post-budget dinner for the senior officers of the ministry and senior media persons. DEA organizes it. The finance minister's office cleared the list of invitees and the dinner was slated for the evening of 12 July 2019 at 7 p.m. at Taj Man Singh Hotel.

At about 5 p.m. on 12 July, I received a WhatsApp message from Shereen Bhan, anchor and managing editor of CNBC-TV18, to the effect that she had not been invited to the dinner that day and that she was just letting me know.

Taken completely by surprise, I checked with my organizing team. They confirmed that Shereen was on the invitation list. They speculated that someone from the finance minister's office might have asked for her exclusion. I called Vipul Bansal, PS to Nirmala Sitharaman. He was a little cryptic but said she was invited. It was clear to me that a message had been conveyed orally to Shereen that she was not expected to attend. I told Vipul that unless the finance minister's office had a serious reservation, she should be asked to attend. Vipul confirmed there was no such reservation.

I messaged Shereen after about forty-five minutes to invite her to attend the dinner. Shereen was apologetic, saying she did not want to 'extract an invite', and wavered. I reiterated my invitation. She messaged back saying she did not want to be somewhere she was not welcome but would nonetheless come out of her regard for me.

Shereen Bhan attended the dinner. Three other senior reporters, miffed by the North Block entry ban ordered by Nirmala Sitharaman, had reached out to PIB officers to say they would boycott the dinner as a protest. I told the PIB officers to communicate to them that they should attend and let their views be known to the finance minister at the dinner. A boycott would not even be noticed. They came too.

The post-Budget dinner went off well.

SECTION V

VOLUNTARY RETIREMENT

29

Don't Think I Can't Violate You

ON 11 JUNE 2019, FINANCE MINISTER NIRMALA SITHARAMAN WAS chairing the first of the pre-Budget consultation meetings in North Block. Only twelve days had gone by since she assumed charge, including the days spent at the G-20 finance ministers' meeting in Japan. It was a Budget consultation meeting with agriculture experts and representatives. As finance secretary, I was conducting the proceedings.

Pre-Budget consultations essentially involved listening to invitees for their views and suggestions for framing the Budget. Sometimes the finance minister and secretaries do ask for some clarifications or to elaborate specific suggestions but the thinking of the government on the specific proposals is never revealed or even hinted at.

At one stage of the meeting, I routinely stated this protocol. Finance ministers take this as a matter of routine and formality. However, Nirmala Sitharaman reacted strongly. First, she said that she would abide by whatever I, as finance secretary, said. A few seconds later, she shot at me in a visible display of anger: 'What do you think, I cannot violate you? I would.'

The people in the room pretended not to take note of this unexpected blow-up. The meeting proceeded as if nothing happened. I found the episode both disconcerting and embarrassing. However, I did not react in the meeting and continued with it without any visible reaction. I had noticed her disturbed state of mind in the few days that we had worked together. I had also noted that she carried a definite bias against me.

After the meeting, I went to her chamber for a frank talk. In the room, she accused me of treating her like a *bachchi* (a child).

Perhaps I am getting ahead of the story. Let me begin from the time she was appointed finance minister.

Cold and Officious Upon Arrival

Nirmala Sitharaman joined as finance minister on 31 May 2019. She was known to be quite officious in dealing with officers, especially secretaries to the government working in her department. I was prepared for that. From day one, however, she appeared to have a strong bias against me. I did not pay attention to this initially but consciously noted it within a couple of days.

I had a few urgent files for her approval on the first day itself. These related to the Budget, which would have to be presented within the next five to six weeks, the G-20 finance ministers' meeting to be held from 7 June 2019, preceded by the meeting of the finance deputies (I was India's finance deputy) on 5–6 June, and a few other matters.

I reached her chamber with the files duly prepared for her orders. I briefed her on each matter, but she didn't seem to be paying much attention. She addressed me as 'Mr Secretary' a couple of times. While this was expected, it indicated that my relationship with her would be more officious, unlike the very open and informal relationship I had shared with Arun Jaitley.

After listening to my brief for three to four minutes, she ended the meeting abruptly and asked me to leave the files with her personal secretary. She also reminded me that she wanted all files to be routed only through her PS, as per what she believed to be the correct official procedure. Though this was a major departure from my working relationship with the earlier minister and was possibly not in the best interest of deciding important matters, I did not find this particularly objectionable, believing that every individual has their idiosyncrasies. I left the four files with Vipul Bansal, her PS.

Then next day, on 1 June, comprehensive departmental briefing presentations began. She decided to start her reviews with DEA, which I headed. I made my presentation, with the additional secretaries and joint secretaries present in the room. Minister of State for Finance Anurag Thakur was also present. I thought I made an informative and incisive presentation with a view to introduce her to all the important issues and matters in DEA. She and Anurag Thakur listened attentively. She, too, had been a minister of state earlier in the Ministry of Finance with Arun Jaitley. However, from the few questions that she asked, I sensed she was not very deeply interested in the issues of the department. As this was only her second day in the office and she had not dealt with DEA matters earlier as minister of state, I thought maybe she was hearing about most of these issues for the first time. There might have also been other matters on top of her mind.

She did not comment on any of the substantive issues. However, she chose to make the rules of engagement between us quite clear in the meeting. She announced that she would be seeking a briefing or discussing matters in the ministry with whomever she considered appropriate—this could range from the level of undersecretary to the secretary. Looking at me, she asked whether I had any objection to this arrangement. Again, knowing every minister has their own style of functioning and recalling the way of Finance Minister Chidambaram in 2004, I quickly said this was perfectly fine with me.

Her announcement did not imply any change in the order of processing and routing all DEA files through me. If she felt comfortable in understanding any matter in greater detail or granularity by discussing it with another officer in the department, that was fine with me. I would have all the freedom in the world to record my views and present the policy proposals.

I did not have any insecurities.

Stiff and Unwelcoming during G-20

I left to attend the finance deputies' meeting in Japan late evening on 4 June, reaching Tokyo in the morning on 5 June, proceeding to Fukuyama via the Shinkansen high-speed (bullet) rail and reaching in the evening.

The most significant work the finance deputies do is to negotiate the communique of the finance ministers' meeting. These negotiations are quite hard. We wanted numerous changes in the first draft presented by the Japanese presidency. Every change was hard fought. On 6 June, the first day, the negotiations went on until 11 p.m. The next day was even more strenuous. The negotiations finally closed (with substantial agreement to our satisfaction) only at 3.30 a.m. on the morning of 8 June.

The finance minister had arrived on the evening of 7 June. Her briefing was first scheduled for 8 p.m. However, as the communique negotiations were still unfinished, I suggested to her PS that Aparna Bhatia, G-20 advisor, could brief her or we could alternatively have the briefing at 8.30 a.m. on 8 June. Nirmala Sitharaman decided to have the briefing on 8 June.

The meeting of the finance ministers and central bank governors was scheduled to commence at 1 p.m. There was also a seminar on international taxation issues (base erosion and profit shifting and taxation of digital companies) at 10.30 a.m. The finance minister was a panelist in one session.

We had prepared sharply focused interventions for her for the four sessions where she was to speak. This was the first time after quite a while that the finance minister was representing India, as Arun Jaitley had not been well and I had represented India at the previous four G-20 meetings. I was able to build up a reputation for India for making significant, material and notable interventions. Using that experience and knowledge, we had prepared excellent and precise interventions for her to make her presence felt in the forum. We had also prepared a good set of interventions for her to use at the taxation seminar, fully conscious that the issues were intricate and she was new to such an event. We wanted to capitalize on her ability to make points effectively in international forums.

At 8.30 a.m. on 8 June, after a short nap, I went into her room to brief her along with two other officers. Mustering all my energy and fighting the sleep deficit, I began briefing her on the issues, beginning with the taxation seminar, and suggested the specific interventions she could make. After about fifteen to twenty minutes, she abruptly asked us to leave as she wanted to prepare in her own way. She did well in her seminar interventions and we felt good.

In the main meeting of the finance ministers and central bank governors, she chose to go by the written interventions we had given her and delivered them without any changes. During the coffee break that followed, I complimented her for speaking very effectively at the meeting. Her reaction was surprising. 'I hope I did not disappoint you,' she said. Her tone was sarcastic but I ignored it.

As there was hardly any time available between her swearing-in on 30 May and the G-20 meeting on 8 June, we could not schedule many bilateral meetings for the finance minister. Nor did she perhaps want any in her first G-20 meeting. The only bilateral meeting was with the UK's Chancellor of the Exchequer Philip Hammond, a very senior and immensely affable minister.

Philip came very well prepared and invited Nirmala Sitharaman to visit London in July for the long-pending finance dialogue between the two countries. He also graciously invited her to watch the final of the Cricket World Cup, which he hoped would be between India and England. I found her response to him a little brusque. Citing the constraints of the Budget schedule in July, she declined the offer. She also referred to some incidences from India's colonial history with the British, which I could sense left Philip Hammond a little bit embarrassed. However, he chose to ignore the same and ended the meeting reiterating his invitation to her to visit the UK at the earliest possible time at her convenience.

There is a tradition of issuing a press release every day during G-20 meetings, highlighting the finance ministers' interventions and matters raised in the G-20 and bilateral meetings. I had carefully edited and expanded the draft press release for the first day, which was prepared by Aparna the G-20 advisor, and a director accompanying us as part of the delegation.

At about 7.30 p.m. on 8 June, we handed the draft press release to Nirmala Sitharaman's PS. We were informed that she wanted to edit it further. She did not ask me or Aparna to come but summoned the director (he was actually representing the Revenue Department to assist us on taxation issues) after dinner.

He later related the sequence of events to us. First, she expressed her unhappiness at the draft. Then, she started writing alternative formulations for some portions. Subsequently, she rejected all the alternatives she had formulated. Thereafter, she dictated some paragraphs to the director, but later did not deem them good enough. Finally, after about an hour and a half, she more or less cleared the draft we had submitted to her for release and returned it.

During the G-20 meeting, I had occasion to travel in her car twice. I used the opportunity to brief her on important issues. Among other matters, I gave her a detailed account of where the discussions stood in the meetings of the expert group on the issue of RBI's ECF, and the financial implications that the recommendations of the group would have on transfer of revaluation, cash reserves and annual surpluses of RBI. I found her quite receptive on this score. She also assured me that she would speak to the RBI governor to sort out the matter.

However, by the time, the G-20 meeting concluded on 9 June and we boarded our flights back to Delhi the next afternoon, I could see visible signs of coldness in our relationship. But I was not unduly concerned.

Surprising Public Display of Anger

As mentioned above, our pre-Budget consultations began the day after our arrival from Japan. The first consultation was with the agriculture group on 11 June.

It is a tradition for the finance secretary to go to the finance minister's chamber a few minutes before the pre-Budget consultations actually begin. I went to her chamber, but was told to proceed directly to the conference room as she would join us there. It was somewhat unusual but I did not pay serious attention to it at the time. As there was only a limited time available for these consultations, we began listening to the experts as she was running late.

She came in about an hour later. She looked rather stiff when talking to me, with an unsmiling, grim face. I requested the principal speakers to highlight their suggestions again in brief, which they did. The meeting was moving towards closure. At that stage, she discussed some of the suggestions with the participants. When I was making my concluding remarks, I mentioned that all their suggestions had been duly noted. To assure the participants that the government valued their suggestions, I underlined that while we could not discuss the merits of their proposals, following the tradition, all their views and suggestions would be put up for the consideration of the finance minister for appropriate orders, after due examination.

I don't think I said anything objectionable. However, she reacted sternly when I finished my closing remarks, saying, 'I will abide by what the finance secretary says, especially a finance secretary who is much older than me in the finance ministry, and not discuss the suggestions.' Her remarks were certainly not in order but I said nothing. I simply smiled.

That said, she did not close the meeting. One secretary and another expert, believing that the finance minister was quite receptive and interested in their ideas, initiated a discussion on two more issues. I remained quiet during this discussion. While listening to them and interacting with them, she suddenly shot back at me without any rhyme and reason, saying: 'What do you think, I cannot violate you? I would.' This was the proverbial last straw on the camel's back. It was very clear that she was deeply frustrated with me over something, but I did not know exactly what it was. I remained quiet.

I went to her room immediately after this meeting to clear the air before the next meeting was to begin in the afternoon. She was livid. I offered to reshape the process of consultation as it pleased her. I also apologized if anything I had done had caused any misunderstanding. She was relentless and besides herself. She said, at one stage, that I treated her like a *bachchi*. At another moment, she said that I had gone to various people and 'bitched' about her. Both these allegations were completely false. She also threatened to bring the entire matter to the PM's notice.

Strangely, despite her diatribe, she maintained that the pre-Budget consultations must be conducted in the way I wanted, adding that she would not even open her mouth in the consultation meetings thereafter. I don't know what had got into her. It was clear, though, that we had a serious problem and that our functional relationship had broken.

I was distraught. The Budget was drawing very close. I had to see it through. With a cooler head, I decided to ignore everything that had taken place and carry on without any further breakdown to ensure the Budget went off smoothly. I decided to worry about the rest after the Budget, though soon after I started paying some attention to my post-Budget plans.

The remaining pre-Budget consultations were completed more as a formality that year than probably at any other time in the past. She did not attend some meetings and came very late for some. Whenever she did come, she mostly sat through the meetings with a glum face. I also had to miss two consultations, as there were conflicting meetings scheduled in the PMO.

The Relationship Keeps Worsening

On 15 June 2019, Prime Minister Modi called a full meeting of the NITI Aayog at Rashtrapati Bhavan's conference hall. I attended as finance secretary. Before the meeting, in the reception hall, Additional Principal Secretary P.K. Mishra took me aside and said, 'Subhash, you don't keep any tension but you cause a lot of tension to others.' I understood that he was referring to Finance Minister Nirmala Sitharaman.

Three days earlier after a meeting in the PMO, Nripendra Misra, principal secretary to the PM, had asked me to come to his chamber. He wanted to know whether everything was going on well with the finance minister. Ignoring the import of his question, I replied that I was fully focused only on completing the Budget exercise. When I asked him the reason for his question, he informed me that Injeti Srinivas, secretary, corporate affairs, had complained to him about the way the finance minister was dealing with him and his department. I told him that there were a few issues but that I would come and explain them only after the Budget. I also indicated that I would offer possible solutions to remedy the situation after the Budget.

P.K. Mishra mentioned that the finance minister had met Prime Minister Modi twice or thrice in the last few days and had been complaining bitterly against me. Looking concerned, P.K. Mishra noted that she was in great tension. He advised that I should do everything to contain the situation. I told him that I did have some problems with her where she had behaved in a very awkward manner. However, I assured him that I was completely focused on seeing the Budget through. I informed him that I hadn't complained to anyone or even discussed the matter with anyone. However, I mentioned that something would definitely have to be done, after the Budget.

Gold Policy Discussions Further Queer the Pitch

DEA had been working for quite some time on developing a policy to promote gold as a financial asset class, to substitute the revamped 2015 gold promotion policy.

Work on the policy had reached the stage of a cabinet note before the elections. The note, which was circulated before the elections after due approval of previous Finance Minister Arun Jaitley, had been referred to a committee of secretaries headed by the cabinet secretary in March 2019. The proposals were strongly supported by most departments in the meeting chaired by the cabinet secretary, but RBI and SEBI had some issues. The cabinet secretary directed us to discuss the outstanding issues with RBI and SEBI and then take the proposal to the cabinet.

These consultations were completed in the months of April–May. We were ready with the final proposals when Nirmala Sitharaman joined as finance minister. A discussion was organized with the secretaries on the evening of 10 June, chaired by Prime Minister Modi, on deliverable policy reforms as part of the first 100-days' programme of the government (which both Nirmala Sitharaman and I could attend after flying in from Tokyo in the late afternoon). This was before the day (the pre-Budget morning) when she had chosen to behave poorly with me. The finance minister was present at the

10 June meeting where I mentioned the contours of reformed policy to develop gold as a new asset class.

As the matter had been highlighted in the PM's meeting, Nripendra Misra decided to hold a meeting to finalize the matter on 13 June. Substantive discussions took place, after which he gave a go-ahead to the proposed policy. A few changes were agreed upon. We were directed to bring the matter before the cabinet soon. Nripendra Misra also directed me to make a presentation before the PM, as he had taken a keen interest in the matter.

I briefed the finance minister about these developments and put up the file two days later with the revised cabinet note for her approval. She approved the note, which was duly submitted to the cabinet secretariat for further action. The PMO scheduled the briefing with Prime Minister Modi on 21 June. It was decided to first make a presentation before the finance minister, and this was scheduled for the morning of 21 June.

Nirmala Sitharaman's demeanour was getting grimmer by the day and she was quite acerbic in tone and manner during the presentation on the gold policy. At one stage, she accused the 'stupid bureaucracy' of not respecting established procedures. It was clear that the accusation was intended for me, without saying so explicitly, possibly to express her displeasure at the gold policy matter having gone to the PMO without first being brought to her full and functional knowledge.

However, she cleared the presentation and suggested only some minor additions, which were made. In the evening, the presentation was made before Prime Minister Modi. During the presentation, she did not back up the department. The discussions went in a somewhat different direction. The PM directed that the subject be brought up only after the Budget.

The ECF Matter

I have recounted this entire matter in an earlier chapter.

On 19 June, Nirmala Sitharaman called me to discuss the file relating to RBI's ECF. After the briefing in Japan, I expected her to discuss the finer points supporting the view I had developed for the next and final meeting of the expert committee scheduled for 24 June.

Her attitude shocked me. She questioned my locus standi in the matter. She asked me whether the stand I had taken had been approved by the finance minister on file, whether I was present in the committee as a representative of the government or in an individual capacity, and similar strange questions.

I tried to focus her attention on the issues at hand, rather than the procedural matters she had raised. She refused to go into the substantive issues. In the end, she gave me two choices. If I was representing the government, I would not present any dissent note as it had not been approved formally by the government. If I was present in an individual capacity, I was free to do what I pleased. I said that I was the representative of DEA, the committee was an 'expert committee' and I was making my contribution as an expert. I decided to go by my professional judgement.

Her handling of the matter in the meeting of the informal group of ministers constituted by the PMO under Home Minister Amit Shah, especially her assessment of my role, was not only unprecedented but quite unbecoming of the stature of the finance minister of the country.

She sat through the entire presentation completely stiff, grim and glum. When she sensed my submissions were getting some traction, she said what I had presented was totally one-sided and far from the truth. However, she was unable to point out any weakness in my presentation. At that stage, she started complaining bitterly against me. She alleged that I had no authority to present a dissent note from the government, yet I was determined to do so. She claimed I did not properly brief her in the matter and that I did not treat her as the finance minister. She accused me of bypassing her in all important matters.

I denied all this and wanted to explain how she had been kept completely in the loop. When Amit Shah saw that the situation was becoming indefensible for her, he concluded the meeting. At the next meeting of the informal group of ministers headed by Amit Shah held after some time, I was able to convincingly demonstrate how damaging the committee's recommendations were.

At one of her daily meetings, Nirmala Sitharaman shouted at the team from the Central Board of Indirect Taxes and Customs (CBIC), especially at an officer of the level of additional director general (ADG), saying she would do what she pleased. She added, quite unconnectedly, that people could write what they felt like about her conduct in their memoirs.

The Message Conveyed through an Additional Secretary

It was evident that Finance Minister Nirmala Sitharaman had got totally fed up with me by the end of June.

I was away for the G-20 leaders' meeting from 27 June 2019 onward, as part of Prime Minister Modi's delegation. On 28 June, I got a long message on WhatsApp from Additional Secretary Sameer Khare, later India's executive director at ADB. Recording his understanding of what had transpired at a meeting of secretaries held on a day when he attended in my absence, and the directions he received to convey to me, he wrote:

> She observed that there is lack of coherence among the departments under the Ministry of Finance and Ministry of Corporate Affairs on many issues on Budget which is not healthy. The finance minister cannot be bypassed or kept outside the loop by the Secretaries in their direct discussions with PMO relating to MoF and MoCA in which approval of FM is required at a later stage. Though the Secretaries of various Departments in MoF and MoCA are free to have discussions with PMO, the FM would have to be kept informed of all such discussions on a day-to-day basis. The FM would not sign or approve any such proposal in which she had not been kept in the loop or she had not been informed on a day-to-day basis. In the end, FM directed representative of FS [finance secretary] i.e. AS (FB & ADB)

to bring the deliberations and directions to the notice of FS & Secretary (EA).

The cookie had crumbled. I still decided to keep my cool as seeing through the Budget was my single biggest priority for the moment.

I have written about the final presentation of Budget 2019–20 in a previous chapter.

Despite all the odds, Budget 2019–20 happened!

The Clincher: A Note from a File Is Changed

A parallel set of events during the Budget process generated more tension between us.

Principal secretary to the PM, Nripendra Misra, was very keen that a financial package be announced for NBFCs. This package was to include two kinds of measures: first, giving further regulatory and resolution jurisdiction over NBFCs to RBI; and, second, announcing a special window to provide them liquidity support.

Secretary, DFS, Rajiv Kumar proposed a package of amendments in the RBI Act, including conferring regulatory and resolution jurisdiction to RBI, to be included in the Finance Bill. I was opposed to vesting resolution authority in RBI and in favour of creating a resolution mechanism on the lines of the Financial Resolution and Deposit Insurance Bill (FRDI). Besides this principal issue, I found certain other weaknesses in the package, including the unintentional insertion of a bail-in clause and excessive penalty provisions.

During my absence from Delhi to attend the G-20 meeting, the draft amendments proposed by DFS got approved and had been vetted by the Legislative Department. I wrote a letter to the secretary, DFS, on 30 June asking for three changes to be made in the material that he had got approved for the Finance Bill. He agreed with two of these proposed changes, but disagreed with excluding conferring of resolution authority on RBI. He routed the file through me, recording his views on my letter. I recorded my reasons for not conferring this authority on RBI and submitted the file to the finance minister.

Finance Minister Nirmala Sitharaman found it difficult to clear any file where differing views were recorded. She wanted every file to be completely clean before she signed. In my short time with her, I could not find a single file where she recorded her views or decided to take a stand. She would either sign it, return it unsigned or keep it pending.

In view of the urgency to finalize the Finance Bill, she called Rajiv Kumar and I on the morning of 2 July for a discussion. I explained my reasons. I did not think she understood the difference between regulation and resolution clearly, but she seemed persuaded to agree with my opinion. She asked me to record some background and additional reasons for my line of suggestion and resubmit the file. I did so.

Rajiv brought up the matter again at the speech-reading session with the PM. There, Nripendra Misra supported Rajiv. The finance minister only commented that I had recorded a long note opposing Rajiv's proposal. The PM ordered that the view expressed by Nripendra Misra and Rajiv Kumar be accepted.

The next day, the file was returned to my office from the finance minister's office with the oral instruction: 'FS knows what is to be done'. I sent the file to the secretary, DFS, who submitted the same back, noting on a fresh page that the proposal of DFS might be approved. I signed it and sent it to the finance minister in view of the specific decision taken the previous day.

However, Nirmala Sitharaman had different ideas. She would not sign the file with the earlier notes remaining on it. Her office conveyed this clearly to Rajiv. Rajiv told me the note sheets recorded earlier would have to be taken out, destroyed and replaced with new note sheets with the same dates and numbers. Though I had never allowed such a thing in my life, I acquiesced only to ensure that the Budget process went through.

I was determined not to be party to something like this ever again.

The second part of the package for NBFCs was further fraught with risk. Somebody had suggested to Rajiv that the government should provide a partial risk guarantee to encourage banks to buy highly rated pooled assets of the NBFCs. SBI had suggested this guarantee to cover the first 5 per cent of loss.

I did not favour this idea as the concept of pooled assets has the potential to be misused for toxic assets, as happened in the US in the subprime crisis. Further, I felt that if the guaranteeing of bank loans began, it was unlikely to be confined to six months as proposed and would probably perpetuate for long. I believed that it would make banks stop their normal lending to NBFCs, as this mode was less risky and that there would be a flight to such asset-based financing. My considered view was that the government had no business to create a moral hazard by loosening the credit appraisal and risk assessment of banks by offering such comforts.

A day earlier, the finance minister had disfavoured the idea of including this announcement in the Budget speech on the grounds that the PM had not asked her to do it. However, on 4 July, when Nripendra Misra spoke to her about it, she not only agreed to include it but also raised the extent of coverage to 10 per cent, instead of Rajiv's original proposal of 5 per cent.

The inclusion of this proposal in the Budget speech convinced me that there were likely to be many compromises in the development of the financial sector and banking, which were, in my judgement, anti-reform.

These developments convinced me that my time in the government was over.

An Undercurrent of Resentment against Me

I form my opinion and views on the basis of my understanding of the facts guided by the standpoint of public interest. I express my opinions and views very clearly and specifically, aiming to get the right decision made or consensus built. I would never modulate or modify my views or opinion to suit the perceived or expressed views of my superiors. After debate and discussion, if a decision is taken, even contrary to my understanding of what is right or appropriate, I usually abide by the same. If a decision is likely to hurt the legitimate interests of the country or is severely wrong, I will make more effort to bring the facts, circumstances and implications to the notice of decision-makers. Basically, I have never aspired to win a popularity contest, but only to get my job done, always keeping in mind the public interest.

I guess quite a few people were upset at my posting as secretary, economic affairs, that too coming straight from the post of executive director, World Bank. Nothing was expressed to me overtly. For my part, I remained focused on my work and never had time to gossip or meet officers for anything other than work. Therefore, it did not matter to me if somebody was upset. But there seemed to be an undercurrent of resentment against me.

As my decisions were generally made after a lot of hard work, and my understanding of the global and Indian economic and financial system was good, it was rare that my decisions would create problems or embarrassment for the government.

I first sensed the undercurrent against me in December 2017.

As mentioned earlier in this book, the fiscal situation in 2017–18 was really difficult. The government had announced a fiscal deficit of 3.2 per cent for the financial year 2017–18. Not only were the revenues uncertain during the year thanks to the decision to shift to GST from 1 July 2017, an overestimate of at least ₹1 lakh crore had been built into non-tax revenues. As the economy had entered a phase of uncertainty, the committee on the borrowing calendar (co-chaired by secretary, economic affairs, and deputy governor, RBI) had decided to issue only a quarterly calendar (October–December 2017) in its September 2017 meeting.

A call on the borrowing amount for the last quarter (January–March 2018) was taken at a meeting held in the last week of December 2017. As it appeared by then that the government would need additional borrowing, it was jointly decided to raise additional borrowing of ₹50,000 crore in the last quarter. Although RBI team led by the deputy governor had fully agreed with the decision, the RBI governor did not like it. He telephoned P.K. Mishra, who asked me about the issue. When I explained the situation, he did not press me to change the decision. Besides the RBI governor, some other influential people probably complained to the PMO about my lack of experience in financial markets and my 'inept' handling of the situation. This episode lingered and one of the participants raised this issue at a meeting chaired by the PM on Budget discussions in January 2018.

Later, a slander campaign was launched against me by the powerful relatives of a joint secretary in DEA, whom I wanted shifted out of the department. Many false complaints were generated and circulated. However, nothing stuck as nothing wrong was done. Some officers complained against not getting high scores of 9.9 or 9.8 in their annual performance appraisal reports (APARs).

I believe Prime Minister Modi understood the real issues. He never asked me for an explanation. In fact, I sensed nothing unusual in his interactions with me; at least until November 2018.

'You Are Not in Tune with the Thinking of the Government'

Principal secretary to the PM, Nripendra Misra, was a very senior civil servant. His understanding was sharp and he was an excellent observer of matters. He was also extremely decisive. Further, he could assess the abilities, values and utility of officers very quickly.

Initially, he treated me as a kind of upstart, but very soon developed respect for my ability to work hard, my knowledge of the economic and financial system and my ability and inclination to speak effectively, clearly and decisively at meetings. He started inviting me to many meetings concerning departments/ministries where the secretary, economic affairs, was not usually invited. This was of great benefit to me professionally, as I would prepare comprehensively to attend these meetings.

However, Nripendra Misra had a certain view of economic and financial matters, much of it shaped by the licence-permit raj of the 1970s and '80s, when he had spent the bulk of his career in service. He also had a preference for a 'Mai-Baap Sarkar'(a more welfare-oriented state) and was not too enamoured with the market. I would always express my views frankly, even when they were not to his liking, and serious differences emerged between us on some matters.

He worked the system to use me wherever it suited him and kept me out where he thought my presence would be problematic.

Considering the difficult fiscal position, after several rounds of discussions at the level of the finance minister and in the PMO, it was decided to allow the fiscal deficit of 2017–18 to slip from 3.2 per cent as indicated in the Budget estimates to 3.5 per cent in the revised estimates. While Nripendra Misra did not believe in the efficacy of fiscal deficits for macroeconomic stability, he decided for some reason that the fiscal deficit should be allowed to slip only to 3.3 per cent. As there was a lot of legitimate justification (introduction of GST in the year, over-projection of non-tax revenues, etc.), I tried to persuade him to allow it to go to 3.5 per cent, which would have saved us from some unnecessary adjustments as well. But he asked Expenditure Secretary A.N. Jha to ensure it did not go beyond 3.3 per cent.

When two new programmes were taken up at a very late stage (Ayushman Bharat and raising MSPs to a minimum of 150 per cent of the cost of cultivation) and I had worked out how to accommodate the extra expenditure by raising the fiscal deficit to 3.4 per cent, Nripendra Misra ordered the expenditure secretary to ensure it stayed at 3.3 per cent.

During the Budget preparation for 2019–20, there was a preference to provide some direct support to farmers. I had also spoken several times in favour of converting input subsidies into direct cash support to farmers. I had also argued that subsidies embedded in the MSP should be directly provided to farmers. The principal secretary was never in favour of touching any existing programmes. He wanted this cash support to farmers to be additional.

I was deliberately excluded from all discussions connected with what finally emerged as PM-KISAN (Pradhan Mantri Kisan Samman Nidhi). When I shared my ideas with Finance Minister Arun Jaitley about what I thought was the right way for removing distortions from the rural economy and delivering the benefits to farmers directly, he asked me to prepare a presentation for him and the PMO. When I did so, Nripendra Misra sternly asked me to stay away from the matter.

There were a few more cases like this.

The lid finally came off with my stand on the second recapitalization of banks, which was proposed to be done by way of providing requisite funds in the second supplementary grants for 2018–19. I could not have been bypassed in this matter. I told Nripendra Misra that the recapitalization programme was excessively large and we needed to design it better rather than over-providing for it. Secretary, DFS, Rajiv Kumar was pushing for it with little care for the fiscal stability of the country. For my part, it was important to extract as much value as possible from the fiscal resources of the government.

The principal secretary took a view on how much funds were to be provided as recapitalization bonds for PSBs. Rajiv Kumar was on leave and I was holding charge of DFS as well. After studying the entire matter, I recorded a long note bringing out how the prescription was not in the best interest of the government. I suggested an alternative formulation. When this was brought to the notice of Nripendra Misra, he was livid. He spoke to the finance minister. The finance minister recorded a note overturning my recommendations and approving the earlier formulation.

Two issues—recapitalization of banks and my interference in the new programme to provide additional direct benefit to farmers— seemed to have brought matters to a head. For the first time, I was overtly told by Nripendra Misra, 'The prime minister is unhappy with you. The finance minister is unhappy with you. Subhash, you are not in tune with the thinking of the government.'

Despite this statement I decided to stay the course and continue with my work, as I thought it was in the best public interest. Principal Secretary Nripendra Misra continued to use my services for many matters and meetings. Life went on.

'Never Try to Go over My Head'

Finance Minister Arun Jaitley had to go to the US for an emergency ten days before the presentation of the Interim Budget 2019–20. For some days, there was an atmosphere of uncertainty about whether he would return to present the Budget. He remained available for all consultations and the reading of the drafts of the Budget speech sent to him through secured electronic means.

The matter of the fiscal deficit was again rearing its head. The government had amended the Fiscal Responsibility and Budget Management (FRBM) Act in February 2018 to provide for limiting the fiscal deficit to 3 per cent by 2020–21. We were preparing the Budget for 2019–20. I wanted to take it close to 3 per cent for this Budget while the finance minister wanted it at 3.2 per cent. There was also an issue of fiscal deficit in the revised Budget of 2018–19. While the fiscal position was not comfortable, there was a consensus that it should not exceed the budgeted level of 3.3 per cent. I was in favour of taking it to 3.2 per cent if possible.

Principal Secretary Nripendra Misra was separately working to provide some additional expenditure for the farmers' direct benefit programme in the revised Budget of 2018–19 itself. It was an Interim Budget. Normally, you don't launch a new programme in the Interim Budget. The PMO was working to launch the new programme by providing for it in the revised estimates of the year that was ending.

The principal secretary asked the expenditure secretary, who was also finance secretary by then, to provide for a fiscal deficit of 3.4 per cent for both the revised estimates 2018–19 and Budget estimates 2019–20. I believed this was quite damaging for the market. I feared a spike in bond yields.

I took the matter to P.K. Mishra, additional principal secretary to the PM. After he heard me out, he agreed to arrange a meeting for me with Prime Minister Modi to discuss this matter. I briefed the PM the next day. As discussed earlier, he appeared convinced about 2018–19 and wanted to ensure requisite provisions were made for the farmers' scheme. He asked me to speak to Finance Minister Arun Jaitley.

I spoke to the finance minister, who was in the US, the next morning. He also felt that 3.3 per cent for 2018–19 and 3.2 per cent for 2019–20 would be fine. When the expenditure secretary told the principal secretary this, Nripendra Misra decided to publicly confront me. The APS called me to find out whether the principal secretary had spoken to me and asked me not to tell him that he had arranged my meeting with the PM on this issue. I assured him that I would not name him.

That evening, we had a pre-Budget session with Prime Minister Modi. The Ministry of Finance team was in the waiting room. There was another meeting for which some ministers were waiting.

Principal Secretary Nripendra Misra entered the room and blew up. After asking me to confirm that I had met Prime Minister Modi the day before, which I did, he asked me never to go over his head. He questioned my judgement and dismissed all my apprehensions about higher fiscal deficits and market reaction. He argued that winning the elections was the most important thing for the government and quoted numbers about what the UPA government had done in 2008. His harangue lasted for about fifteen minutes.

I remained unruffled and dignified. I simply said I was doing what I considered to be my duty. I did not offer any apology or even acknowledge the wisdom or correctness of his arguments. I continued my interactions with him thereafter without unduly getting influenced by this episode.

A Weakening Relationship with the PM

From the beginning of 2019, I could sense that Prime Minister Modi had developed a certain coldness towards me. It was evident from his interactions with me.

Principal Secretary Nripendra Misra had informed me that Piyush Goyal, who often filled in for Finance Minister Arun Jaitley during his illness, had been incessantly complaining against me to the PM. He appreciated Piyush Goyal's efficiency but was wary of his intentions and abrasiveness. The principal secretary was aware of the tough time I'd had in Piyush Goyal's first tenure as the officiating finance minister, when we had to seek the PM's intervention to stop Goyal in his tracks. That said, there was a good chance of Piyush Goyal emerging as the new finance minister after the elections.

The increasing coldness of Prime Minister Modi and the prospects of Piyush Goyal taking over as finance minister had already got me thinking about the scenario after the elections. I was not worried about moving out of the Ministry of Finance. I also felt that it would not be really productive to work with Piyush Goyal as finance minister.

Thus, some seeds of leaving the government had already been sown in my mind before the election results were out and Nirmala Sitharaman was appointed finance minister.

Mulling the Option to Leave Government Service

All these events, exacerbated by my deteriorating relationship with Finance Minister Nirmala Sitharaman, crystallized my thinking about leaving government service during the run-up to the Budget 2019–20.

I began seriously mulling over this from the first week of July. I made up my mind around 12 July that I would prefer to take voluntary retirement as it was completely apparent to me that it would be dysfunctional for the finance minister and I to continue working together. Upon reflection, I had concluded that it would be worth my while to work outside government to realize the goal of building a $10 trillion Indian economy rather than functioning in any other government department or organization in a somewhat lame-duck manner.

P.K. Mishra called me to his office and broached the subject of transfer to me on 18 July. He said to the effect:

> Subhash, you are a brilliant, hardworking, competent and a very committed officer, but you would need to be shifted from the finance ministry. The finance minister has met the Prime Minister a few times and has continuously complained against you. We cannot change the finance minister. Therefore, you will have to make way. We are thinking of shifting you to the Ministry of Power. You can choose any other department or autonomous organization if you want.

This did not surprise me as I was expecting it to happen sooner or later. I was quite ready with my response. I thanked him for sounding me out on the transfer and offering me a job in any ministry or autonomous body. He did not offer me the cabinet secretary's job. Nor was I interested, as I wanted to continue to work in the economic space. The cabinet secretary has a rather limited jurisdiction to work in the economic space and is also completely cut off from the international economic and financial system.

I told P.K. Mishra I had already thought about the matter and, after considerable thought, had concluded that I would take voluntary retirement and set up a foundation to work for policy and other reforms required to usher in the $10 trillion economy. P.K. Mishra, an extremely nice and supportive person, requested me to reconsider. He also felt that such a move would not be viewed very favourably for the government, as it would be equated with the departures of Arvind Panagariya and Arvind Subramanian.

I reiterated my resolve and requested it be brought to the kind notice of Prime Minister Modi. I also mentioned that I was working on 100 major policy and structural reforms needed to put India in the $10 trillion economy orbit, which I would like to present before the PM. I also underlined that I would be positive and constructive and would always be happy to work with the PM as it was my considered opinion that if anyone could propel India into that orbit, it was Prime Minister Narendra Modi. I sincerely believed this at that time.

P.K. Mishra told me he would discuss the matter with the PM.

Voluntary Retirement

I drafted my application for voluntary retirement on Saturday, 20 July. I had dated it 29 July. I wanted to submit it a couple of days before 31 July and to give the required notice of three months. This would make my retirement effective from 31 October, exactly a year before my normal date of superannuation. I had expected my transfer orders to be issued around 30 or 31 July.

Somewhat unexpectedly, my transfer orders to the Ministry of Power were issued on 24 July. The orders reached me around 8.15 p.m. I was participating in the finance group secretaries' meeting in the DFS conference room at the time. We were about to get up when I saw the order on my phone. On the way to the elevator, I told Revenue Secretary Ajay Bhushan Pandey about my transfer orders. He appeared more keen to know whether he was also in the transfer list!

I came straight to my office in North Block, changed the date of the VRS letter from 29 July to 24 July and printed three copies. I signed a copy for the government of Rajasthan and addressed it to the chief secretary, Rajasthan, D.B. Gupta, who was also my batchmate. Another was addressed to the DoPT secretary. I signed the last copy as my office copy. Handing over these two letters to K. Abdulla Syed, my PPS, I left for home. I had taken a photo of my office copy on my phone. On the way home, I spoke to D.B. Gupta to inform him so that he wouldn't be unduly surprised when the letter reached him the next day. He displayed a good degree of understanding.

It was untenable to continue in the Ministry of Finance given the acrimonious relationship that had developed with the finance minister. Working anywhere else in the government would have been suboptimal. I hoped I would be more productive outside the government in rendering my services for the attainment of the $10 trillion economy goal.

Taking Leave of Nirmala Sitharaman

Finance Minister Nirmala Sitharaman has a sharp mind. She is quite articulate and can ably defend matters of importance to her. However, working for a vision like the $10 trillion economy seemed somewhat alien to her persona and preferences. She was also likely to falter at the altar of reforms in capital markets and in scaling up investments in infrastructure, digital economy and employment generation—the goals she announced in her Budget speech.

On the morning of 25 July, the day after my transfer and submission of voluntary retirement application, I went to attend the meeting of secretaries she used to hold every day. After two other secretaries had briefed her on the important issues at hand, I sought to speak.

I informed her of my decision to take voluntary retirement. I further asked to be relieved right away. However, the power secretary needed a day and Atanu Chakraborty, who was designated my successor, also wanted to take over the next day. Therefore, it was agreed that I would hand over charge on the morning of 26 July. I further added that my application for voluntary retirement had reached the Rajasthan government, my cadre controlling authority, and DoPT in the morning. Finally, I thanked her for Budget 2019–20, which I worked on with her.

She did not speak. Her expression said it all—'good riddance' I suppose she was thinking. The meeting ended and I left the room of the finance minister, in which I had attended hundreds of meetings and discussions over the preceding two years. This was my last visit to that room. I wished her well.

Departure from the Ministry of Finance

With the burden of maintaining such a tough relationship, now off my mind, I was still more at ease.

I had a 'farewell' session with the officers of DEA in the afternoon of 25 July in a very relaxed setting. However, some of the officers were tense, perhaps thinking of their future in the department. I explained briefly my reasons of seeking voluntary retirement for a more productive life ahead. I joked and tried to set them at ease.

Almost everyone in DEA came to meet me that day. Most senior officers from the sister departments of revenue and expenditure also came. There was a flood of people.

Around 4.30 p.m., I asked Atanu Chakraborty to come and take charge as I did not want to return to the office the next morning. He agreed. I bid goodbye to North Block on the evening of 25 July 2019. I have not entered North Block thereafter.

While I still had three months to spend in the Ministry of Power, my innings in the government was as good as over.

30

The Muddle Goes On in the Ministry of Power

I WENT TO THE MINISTRY OF POWER WITH THE EXPIRY DATE OF MY SHORT tenure—a little over three months—well-known. However, I had decided not to while away my time and do whatever constructive work I could in this period.

Minister of State for Power (with independent charge) Raj Kumar Singh, had served the government as an IAS officer for long, retiring as home secretary of India. Essentially a decent man, albeit with a socialist (public sector) and hierarchical mindset, he was genuinely concerned at my decision to take voluntary retirement.

On the first day of assuming charge as secretary when I called on him, he spoke at length about the inadvisability of taking such an 'impulsive' decision. He related his own experience after retirement and how he felt miserable without a proper job, which finally led him to take the plunge as a politician. He felt I should reconsider my decision, withdraw my voluntary retirement application and serve as secretary, power, which he noted was an extremely important ministry with a lot of work.

After thanking him for his concern, I told him a little about the background of my decision and explained that my decision was not impulsive but well-considered and thought-out. I agreed with him that the Ministry of Power was an extremely important infrastructure ministry and assured him that I would work for the next three months with full devotion and initiative as if I had been posted there as a regular secretary. Though he saw my resolve to stick to my decision, he still requested I give the idea of staying in service a rethink.

The Ministry of Power is not a ministry with a heavy workload. Implementation on most of the schemes takes place in the states. The PSUs, like REC and PFC, do much of the planning and monitoring work. The ministry has a large suite of strong public-sector enterprises, such as NTPC, Powergrid, PFC, REC, NHPC, and many others. These organizations have a joint secretary or additional secretary-level officer from the ministry on their board. The Ministry of Power is not supposed to concern itself with the day-to-day management of these organizations.

To signal my intent that I would work as hard and decisively in the ministry as I did elsewhere, I convened briefing meetings with the joint secretaries and directors of the Ministry of Power on 27 July (a Saturday), which was unusual. I had worked with the power sector for many years in one form or another since the 1990s. In the Ministry of Finance, too, I had participated in several important policy decisions concerning the Ministry of Power. With these comprehensive briefings, I was ready to spend my last three months in service productively.

Gearing Up to Enforce the Payment Security Mechanism

Almost the entire electricity generated in India was supplied to the distribution companies owned by the state governments under the terms and conditions of power purchase agreements signed between the generators and distributors. The PPAs and the payment security mechanism introduced in 2003 provided for the distributing companies opening up a letter of credit (LoC) in favour of the generating companies concerned, generally covering about a month of power supplied. The generating companies were empowered to enforce the payment in case the distribution companies failed to pay within the due time (generally forty-five days after the month for which the power supply was billed) by encashing the LoC.

Continuous under-recoveries by the distribution companies had created a situation where there was hardly any state that was not in default of payments due to central and private power suppliers (default in payment to state generating companies was not taken note of) in June 2019. One state was in default for more than twelve months, another for over six months and quite a few states that had overdues for more than three months. In aggregate, the state distribution companies owed more than ₹53,000 crore to central generating companies like NTPC and the private suppliers. The arrears were going up every month. In the month of June 2019, while the states were billed for ₹18,500 crore, they paid current dues of only ₹5,700 crore. While they cleared about ₹8,000 crore of older dues, on a net basis, there was an addition of over ₹6,000 crore during the month.

While the dues were piling on, payment security in the form of LoCs remained uninvoked. The Ministry of Power decided to act and issued a clear order on 28 June 2019 that the payment security mechanism be enforced. The load despatch centres (LDCs) at the national, regional and state levels are lynchpins in the power business, because they control the flow of power over transmission lines. The LDCs 'schedule' power, which allows the power generated by every specified generator to transmit it and every distribution company to receive it for final supply to customers. The ministry ensured that the LDCs would schedule power supply only to the generators that had received LoCs and only to the extent that it was covered by the LoC amount. The order was to come into effect from 1 August 2019. I assumed charge on 26 July 2019.

I was completely convinced about the strict enforcement of contractual provisions relating to receipt of electricity supply and the payment. When I was briefed about the matter by S.K.G. Rahate, additional secretary in charge of transmission, and G. Prasad, chief engineer in charge of distribution, immediately after assuming charge, I gave them my unstinted support and instructions that the system must be enforced without fail or exception. They were monitoring the LoC situation by the day and reported that there were still a couple of states that had not provided the requisite LoCs, most particularly Jammu & Kashmir (it was still a state in the last week of July 2019). I told them to convey the message unambiguously that power would be cut off on 1 August if they did not provide LoCs in time. We did try to help some states in financial difficulty by arranging finance, but no exception was to be made.

There were many apprehensions in the minds of the officers of the department about how things would turn out on 1 August. Eventually, no power cut had to be imposed. There was some short supply of power in the case of J&K and Assam but nothing highly unusual happened, and J&K also managed to provide some sort of LoC. However, the situation changed when the state was turned into two union territories on 8 August. The governor reached out to Home Minister Amit Shah for exemption from the LoC requirement.

Home Secretary Ajay Kumar Bhalla (who was power secretary when the orders were issued in June 2019) spoke to me. I asked him not to grant an exemption but make some other arrangements to provide finance. Two days later, the home minister spoke to R.K. Singh, the power minister, who reluctantly accepted the demand for exemption. I told him the enforcement system would collapse if any exception were made. However, the power minister gave orders in writing that led to J&K being treated differently. The system continued to operate somewhat satisfactorily in other states but the rigour started getting diluted.

Gradually, the bite of the payment security mechanism got completely blunted. Later, Covid-19 would upend the power arrears situation badly. The government came up with a financing facility of ₹90,000 crore (through PFC and REC) to help the state discoms clear their dues. The enforcement mechanism was completely sidestepped.

Power Minister Does Not Let REC Merge into PFC

The Rural Electrification Corporation (later REC) was established by the Government of India in the 1970s to fund rural electrification schemes and finance agricultural pump sets to increase irrigation. The Power Finance Corporation (later PFC) was formed in 1986 by the Government of India to finance power-sector generation, transmission and distribution enterprises. These two corporations primarily funded state-sector power enterprises.

After liberalization in the 1990s and the entry of the private sector in the power business, both REC and PFC started undertaking similar financing for power-sector projects, still largely for state enterprises but, to some extent, also for private-sector enterprises. Most private-sector financing ran into non-performing loans. For the past decade or so, the two power-sector public NBFCs had largely funded the capital expenditures of state power-sector utilities.

As these power-sector financing twins were doing almost the same kind of work and the government was looking for disinvestment receipts to bridge its widening fiscal deficit, it decided to sell REC to PFC, similar to the transaction the previous year when HPCL was sold to ONGC. The cabinet approved the sale in December 2018 and the transaction was finally completed in the last week of March 2019. The Government of India's 52.63 per cent stake in REC was sold to PFC for a consideration of ₹14,500 crore. REC became a subsidiary of PFC to be merged into PFC soon.

The official PIB press release issued on the day of the cabinet's decision on 6 December 2018 said that the Cabinet Committee on Economic Affairs gave in-principle approval for 'strategic sale' of the Government of India's existing 52.63 per cent of total paid-up equity shareholding in REC to PFC 'along with transfer of management control'. It also envisaged the merger of the two when the release stated that the strategic sale 'may also allow for cheaper fundraising with increase in bargaining power for the combined entity'.

Power Minister R.K. Singh did not like the idea of ceding management control to PFC and the merger of REC with PFC. After the cabinet approved the strategic sale in December 2018, he ensured that the shareholders' agreement prepared to give effect to the takeover specifically provided that the government would continue to nominate its representative on REC's board of directors besides appointing its CMD. The PFC management gave in completely and REC continued to operate as much under the direct control of the Ministry of Power as before the strategic sale. The PFC was reduced to being a mere investor with literally no say in the management of REC though 'management control' was officially transferred to PFC. The government appointed PWC as a consultant to report on the roadmap of REC's merger with PFC.

This was the state of affairs when I took over as power secretary. I had watched the transaction from the other side and was very clear that the government intended the two entities to merge. A couple of weeks into the ministry, a presentation was scheduled before me by consultant PricewaterhouseCoopers (PwC). It was shocking. The minister's staff and REC officials had worked in close coordination to 'persuade' PWC to make a report stating the grounds to support their objective that REC functions as a CPSE under the administrative control of the Ministry of Power, though PFC had taken over the entire shareholding of the Government of India.

It took about two hours to discuss all the arguments built in the report and convince the PwC consultants, the CMDs of PFC and REC and other officials that the merger was in the larger interest of the company and the nation. There were two arguments the REC team (it also had two IAS officers working as executive director and in another senior managerial position) kept making again and again—that the covenants of external loans raised by REC would be breached if PFC took over and that the ability of the two institutions to fund state power entities would get impaired in case of a merged entity.

The first argument had no leg to stand on as REC was no longer a Government of India enterprise and the impact of covenants had already got factored in. The second was technically correct as RBI regulations did not permit a single NBFC to have more than 25 per cent exposure to a single borrower, whereas together the two could have 50 per cent exposure. For financial soundness, the two entities (which were actually now one) had to limit the exposure to 25 per cent. I wanted PwC to present a roadmap listing out sequential steps and timelines for effecting the merger. After the discussion, PwC agreed to change its presentation, bringing in arguments as to why the merger would be financially sound and in the interest of the power sector.

After a few days, the revised presentation was made before the minister. The REC officers and the minister's personal staff informed him about the changed presentation before he came to the meeting. He announced even before the presentation had started that he was not going to have the merger. That created a peculiar situation. I suggested he listen to the presentation with an open mind and if there was no good case for a merger, the idea could be reconsidered. He agreed.

The power minister latched on the issue of reduced capacity of PFC and REC to fund state power-sector entities in case of a merger. He said he would not permit this under any circumstance. The argument of the financial unsoundness of a Government of India enterprise taking so much exposure to state entities, which were by and large bankrupt, did not convince him.

After the fiasco, I told the PwC team their job was done. They could give us their report and we would process the same on file for appropriate orders of the minister. The presentation came only some time before I was to leave the ministry. I wrote a detailed note making a case for the merger. The minister kept the file with him till I superannuated.

I don't know what the final orders were, but PFC and REC continue to operate as separate entities. The façade of strategic sale with transfer of management control of one Government of India entity to another continues as it is. Both REC and PFC continue to function independently under the management control of the Ministry of Power.

'Send Only Policy Files through the Secretary'

There was considerable difference between mine and the minister's worldview of the government's role in the development and management of the power sector, in particular the relationship of the government with the PSUs. I would record my views frankly and, in my judgement, persuasively on the files. R.K. Singh, a career bureaucrat, loved to impose his writ on the decision. He tried to write long notes giving reasons why he disagreed with my proposal and what his orders were. That was fine, except that I would resubmit some of these files with additional facts and arguments to request reconsideration. Very soon, the minister developed some sort of irritation towards me. In two weekly meetings, which he used to convene to take stock of the progress and implementation of his previous orders, he cryptically said that officers of my batch were his probationers. I refused to take these hints and continued in my way.

Sometime in late August, a note came from the minister ordering that the routine and administrative files needed to be quickly disposed of and, therefore, files of such nature had to be put up directly by divisional heads (special secretary/additional secretary/ joint secretary) to him, with the secretary being bothered only with policy matters. This order turned the conventional role of the minister and secretary on its head.

It is the minister who should be concerned only with policy matters, leaving all administrative and day-to-day matters to the secretary. This was what Finance Minister Arun Jaitley did with considerable success. This was what the transaction of business rules envisaged. I was also reminded of the dysfunctional situation created in the Ministry of Women and Child Development by Minister of State Krishna Tirath in 2013, when she had ordered that no files would be routed to her through the secretary.

To ensure the order did not create any unnecessary confusion in the ministry, I wrote out a detailed note by hand on the same file that came from the minister's office. It referred to business rules, the real division of work/responsibility between the minister and secretary; and the kind of problems such an order could create with respect to discharge of the secretary's responsibilities as the chief accounting authority of the ministry in ensuring expenditures were in line with the rules of procurement, answering Parliament questions and also when the secretary gave evidence before parliamentary committees as the administrative head of the department.

In the end, I noted that the administration wing might examine the minister's order keeping in consideration my observations and put up a revised allocation of business in the ministry. I specifically directed that the file be routed through me for the final orders of the minister.

Rahate, who was in the administration wing at that time, came over. He was quite indignant. I told him to examine the matter very objectively and put it up. I don't think the administration division had the intellectual gravitas to propose anything on the matter. The officers must have shown my notes to the minister and expressed their helplessness in implementing his orders. I did not hear about that file thereafter. Nor did the minister mention it again.

Awarding Solar Transmission Lines to Powergrid without Bids

The transmission sector was opened up to the private sector in 2006 through what is known as the tariff-based competitive bidding (TBCB) system. While it took some time for full policy development and implementation of the system, the TBCB system had been adopted from 2016 for all interstate transmission projects. The amendment notified in the tariff policy in 2016 mandated that all investment by transmission developers would be through competitive bids in accordance with the guidelines issued by the Central government. The policy further mandated that the Central government could give exemption from the TBCB-based award of transmission projects only in two cases: for specified projects of strategic importance and technical upgradation; and for works required to be undertaken in urgent situations on a case-to-case basis.

Quite a few large solar power projects were envisaged to be established by the Ministry of New and Renewable Energy (MNRE) from 2015 onwards. Earlier, the government had adopted a policy of socializing the transmission tariff. The policy transferred the burden of higher transmission tariffs of these solar projects to all the power consumed in the respective states. However, these solar projects were neither strategic nor urgent. In fact, the implementation of solar projects had lagged considerably and some projects were not envisaged to get implemented in the next two to three years.

The power minister, R.K. Singh, believed his views were always final and if he had ordered something, it had to be carried out. He had decided that transmission lines for four to five major solar projects—where land had been identified for development of solar parks but solar power projects had not been awarded or been only partially awarded—be given to Powergrid on a nomination basis instead of being bid-out through the TBCB system.

The transmission division was struggling to carry out R.K. Singh's order when I joined the ministry. After I understood the matter fully and concluded that these projects were not covered by the two exceptions, I asked the additional secretary, transmission, to submit the file with his views. Rahate, a conscientious officer, submitted the file with some roundabout language that indicated there were problems with awarding the contract on a nomination basis—but as the minister had approved it, it might be allowed.

I have never fought shy of unambiguously recording the correct course of action. I clearly noted that the award of these transmission lines was not covered by either exception and, therefore, they should be awarded only on the basis of TBCB.

When the file reached the minister, he called Rahate and gave him a piece of his mind. He then sent the file to the secretary, MNRE, who recorded that all these transmission lines were absolutely urgent and therefore should be awarded on a nomination basis directly to Powergrid without any loss of time. The file came back from the minister with the order that the lines be awarded. I told Rahate that urgency was not a certificate and it had to be established on a case-to-case basis and asked for a meeting to be arranged with the secretary, MNRE, to understand the nature of the urgency.

Secretary, MNRE, Anand Kumar was initially reluctant to meet me but came over after some time. We discussed each and every case. It became clear that only one and a half lines out of the five could actually be treated as urgent. Anand Kumar agreed with the assessment. I asked him to record in writing the reasons we had discussed to treat just those lines as urgent so we could submit the file to the minister for final orders. It took Anand Kumar some time but he did the needful.

The file was submitted to the minister to consider approving only those one and a half lines to be awarded on a nomination basis and the rest on the TBCB system. The minister reconsidered the entire matter. After judging one more line as urgent, he agreed to order half the transmission lines to be awarded on a nomination basis and the remaining on the TBCB system.

Suggested Reforms for the $10 Trillion Economy, Revert to the Power Ministry for Comments

I had presented a package of about 100 reforms that India needed to become a $10 trillion economy to Prime Minister Modi in early August. The PM was quite interested in pursuing these ideas further. Principal Secretary Nripendra Misra asked me to provide a few copies of the presentation (running into over 200 slides) to the PMO, which allocated the proposed reforms to the concerned ministries (these were mostly arranged sector-wise in any case). Nripendra Misra sent the proposed reforms with a demi-official (DO) letter to the secretaries of the concerned departments. I also received the reforms I had proposed for the power sector with a DO letter from him. As there was no hint as to the authorship of the suggested reforms, the Ministry of Power took it, like other ministries and departments, as a directive from the PMO to examine. I also had no reason to record or indicate that the suggested reforms flowed from my own presentation to the PM.

I placed the PMO letter before R.K. Singh for information and to tell him that the ministry would examine these suggested reforms and put up the matter for his consideration soon. R.K. Singh kept the letter with him and asked for a discussion. I presented the potential rationale for the reforms. They were quite radical in nature: privatization of the distribution sector; and replacement of electricity subsidies to farmers and residents by direct cash transfer; privatization of all the CPSEs in the power sector except NTPC, Powergrid and NHPC; replacement of the Ujjwal DISCOM

Assurance Yojana (UDAY) scheme by a more reform-oriented scheme, to provide states reduction in their power-sector debt upon carrying out reforms, and the like. R.K. Singh did not like most of it and generally indicated that the Ministry of Power should provide reasons for not undertaking the suggested reforms.

The proposed reforms were examined in the ministry by a team of officers led by Special Secretary S.N. Sahai. The ministry was steeped in public-sector tradition. The minister was completely pro-public sector. S.N. Sahai was widely expected to be appointed my successor. He submitted a response that agreed with the rationale of some of the recommended reforms but suggested more public-sector oriented solutions. I extensively recorded the rationale why the recommended reforms represented the final solution to the mess in the power sector.

The file remained with the minister until I left the ministry.

Roving Enquiry against Lavasa

Election Commissioner Ashok Lavasa had been in the power sector for quite some time as additional and special secretary. One day, DoPT Secretary C. Chandramouli came over to see me. It had nothing to do with my voluntary retirement. He handed over a fat envelope of papers and wanted the ministry's response in complete confidence within two days.

After he left, I saw the contents of the envelope. It contained a preliminary report from the Income Tax Department into allegations of misconduct on the part of Ashok Lavasa. The papers had a lot of details about the directorships his wife had got, the payments she had received from these directorships and otherwise, and his son's job and business. The expectation from DoPT, which was enquiring into the matter, was to find out whether Ashok Lavasa had used his influence as the additional secretary in the ministry and also as director in the CPSEs to get any undue favour for his wife or son's dealings.

This type of enquiry required a detailed fact check from all the divisions of the ministry and the CPSEs under its administrative control. I asked the administration division to make the requisite number of copies and send the same with a note from me to make a comprehensive fact check and provide us specific instances or actions that might be construed as exercising any influence. If there was no such case, the concerned divisions or CPSEs were to report accordingly.

The reports came from all the divisions and CPSEs within the stipulated period. All of them confirmed that they could ascertain no case of undue favour. They also provided the details of board meetings and the matters examined to corroborate that they could not find any such instance.

I provided a clean report to DoPT and affirmed that the Ministry of Power could not find any instance of undue influence exerted by Ashok Lavasa for his wife or son.

Using the Opportunity to Sort Out as Many Issues as Possible

R.V. Shahi had been secretary, power, in 2003–05 when I had worked in DEA and the Expenditure Department in the Ministry of Finance, and I interacted with him closely. Shahi remained immersed in the power sector after he retired. He was the spirit and force behind the Southeast Asia Energy Forum supported by the World Bank, which brought policymakers, regulators and managements of power utilities together. He had been in touch with me during my days as executive director in the World Bank to push these initiatives to build a network of power infrastructure in South Asia, utilizing the synergies of the immense hydro-potential of Nepal and Bhutan, burgeoning demand of power in Bangladesh and large connecting infrastructure and demand of India.

As soon as I joined the Ministry of Power, Shahi came over to discuss the state of shared power generation, infrastructure and demand in South Asia and the state of initiatives launched under bilateral cooperation forums at the secretary level between India and Bangladesh, India and Nepal, and India and Sri Lanka. He specifically drew attention to a number of issues waiting to be resolved between India and Bangladesh and India and Nepal. He was hopeful of these issues being settled if I agreed to have these two meetings scheduled during my tenure. I scheduled the bilateral meeting with Bangladesh in Dhaka and with Nepal in India to make a sincere attempt to sort out the pending issues.

The governments of India and Bangladesh had previously established transmission infrastructure to transfer 1,000 megawatt (MW) of power on the western side of Bangladesh and 130 MW on the eastern side. There was a proposal to establish a new 765 kilovolt (kV) link between Katihar–Parbatipur–Bornagar, almost parallel to the existing link, to transfer another 1,000 MW of power. The principal issue that was holding up the project was sharing the cost of constructing this link and line.

India wanted Bangladesh to bear most of the cost as the power transmitted through it was to be used by Bangladesh, whereas Bangladesh wanted the cost to be shared in the geographical land area by the respective countries. We resolved this issue by agreeing that the transmission tariff would be paid in terms of power transferred to the buyer, and the infrastructure cost was to be borne by the two countries in their respective territories. This also took care of Bangladesh's demand to export some power in surplus months. While power purchase would depend upon the decisions of the buying and selling parties, for the power transmitted through this corridor, payment of transmission charges would be paid by the respective buyer.

India and Bangladesh were building a 1,320 MW coal power project, the Maitree Project, in Khulna district of Bangladesh. The NTPC had a 50 per cent share in it and I visited the project along with its CMD. This power project was being built by BHEL. There were many issues between NTPC and BHEL. Some of these were also resolved.

The power trade, investment and cooperation between India and Nepal was far more complicated. Though the sixth meeting of the steering committee had taken place only a few months earlier in Pokhara, Nepal, at the insistence of the Nepal government and Shahi, I convened the seventh meeting on 14–15 October in Bengaluru.

The Butwal–Gorakhpur cross border transmission line was the biggest stumbling block in the bilateral power-sector relationship between the two countries. Of this 140-km transmission line, 20 km fell in Nepal and 120 km in Indian territory. Very complex implementation structures were being discussed for this line for a number of years. For the Indian portion, a jointly owned company with 50:50 partnership was envisaged and Nepal was being asked to pay 100 per cent transmission charges for power transfer. These demands were unfair and not leading anywhere.

With the formula used in Bangladesh, which was also used in an earlier transmission line project between India and Nepal, I agreed that the costs would be borne by the respective countries in their territories with the transmission tariff to be paid by the drawer of the power. This would help the Indian company to recover its investment on the transmission line as it would recover on any other transmission project. Nepal was grateful as the transmission line would now see the light of day. For Nepal, it was a historical breakthrough; for India, it was a sound commercial decision.

The Power Ministry Muddle Continues

The power sector has been perennially in crisis since the 1990s. Most of the distribution companies did not recover the cost of power despite following a system of heavy cross-subsidization, penalizing industrial and commercial use of power and massive subsidies from governments. The total power generated in India in 2018–19 amounted to 1,376 billion units. Substantial expansion of generation capacities in previous years had virtually eliminated the energy shortage—there was only 0.6 per cent of energy shortage in 2018–19, which was also on account of local problems, not power shortage.

Energy consumption in 2018–19 was, however, only 1,130 billion units with 246 billion units lost in process consumption and transmission and distribution (T&D) losses—about 18 per cent of the power generated. The average cost of power supply exceeded ₹6 per unit in 2018–19; the distribution companies recovered less than ₹4.5 per unit. At the rate of ₹1.5 per unit, the electricity distribution system of the country lost about ₹1.8 lakh crore. This was the cost of the muddle in the power sector.

The Central government made massive policy interventions in the power sector. The Electricity Act, 2003, authorized the Centre to frame electricity and electricity tariff policy for the country. Using these powers, the Central government had formulated very comprehensive and highly intrusive electricity and tariff policies. It had also formulated a complex renewable obligations policy. The Act empowered the Centre to constitute the Central Electricity Regulatory Commission (CERC) to determine interstate tariffs as well as the tariffs payable to Central electricity generation companies.

Using its financial heft, the Central government launched large investment schemes that enticed states to make the kinds of investments it desired. Two financing entities—PFC and REC—ensured that state-sector entities became completely financially dependent on them, not only for capital investments but also for financing losses. Power-generation entities controlled by the Central government produced more than 50 per cent of the power. The stranglehold of the Centre over the states and the private-sector entities was complete.

The power-sector reforms and investment financing scheme, UDAY, launched in 2015, had failed like its predecessors in reducing both T&D losses and financial losses. The government was contemplating another version of UDAY, dishing out almost the same medicine. R.K. Singh had constituted a group of officers to draft the new avatar of UDAY. I was completely convinced that our prescription—giving funds for investments on promises to improve operations to reduce T&D and financial losses—was wrong. The fact that the distribution system was operated by inefficient state utilities under the populist control of the government—which did not allow rationalization of costs and power tariffs—was the reason for the mess.

Unless these two fundamental ills were addressed—and that could only be done by cutting the umbilical cord between the government and utilities by privatization—the mess in the power sector would never be resolved. Therefore, I proposed to this group of officers that we make a clean break from the past. I suggested that, this time, the Central government should provide grant funds to states only upon their shedding ownership and management control of state utilities.

If the Central government paid 50 per cent of the accumulated losses in return for privatization, the mess in the power sector would be sorted out forever. I explained the entire mechanics of framing the scheme. The officers had a lot of questions, which I answered. They appeared convinced and promised to put the same in their report. The report was not finalized while I was in the ministry. I don't know what they finally suggested but after one and a half years, in 2021, the government announced a ₹3 lakh crore scheme—Revamped Distribution Sector Scheme (RDSS), which is substantially another version of UDAY, with extra emphasis on smart metering. RDSS has also not delivered much. Nor is it likely unless basic issues are addressed.

A national power tariff policy had been in effect since January 2016. It prescribed norms for power production, transmission, distribution and almost every other point of exchange. It prescribed debt-equity ratio, return on equity for new power-generation plants, tariffs for captive power generation and pricing of renewable power for all projects where power tariffs were not discovered on a competitive bidding basis. Distribution tariffs and principles for cross-subsidy surcharge were all dealt with in the policy. It required the electricity commissions to determine tariffs after taking into account the revenue requirements of the electricity companies and the power generated and sold.

What the tariff policy did not decide was how to control the behaviour of the state governments who owned the power-sector utilities and did not allow tariffs to be charged as approved. The tariff policy was actually a paper tiger with no ability to discipline the behaviour of state governments, power utilities and consumers.

Power Minister R.K. Singh wanted another version of the National Power Tariff Policy to be developed, with additional penalties for unscheduled cuts in power by utilities and a built-in charter of consumer rights. He wanted to remove transmission projects for renewable power from the TBCB system. All these additional impositions were unlikely to succeed on the ground and would have made the situation in the power sector worse.

The draft of the policy was ready when I joined the ministry. I tried to explain to the officers that we should actually discard the excessively detailed tariff policy and only set some principles in the policy that encourage setting tariffs on market principles. I also argued against the heavy segmentation of consumers, cross-subsidization and unnecessary interference with consumers (industrial or otherwise), impelling them to buy power only through state utilities. If we were to make the tariff policy on these principles, it would be a three-page document at best. The officers smiled. When I noted the ask on the file on tariff policy, it got stalled.

However, R.K. Singh was in a hurry. He approved the new tariff policy on almost the same lines as it was drafted by the officials. It went to the PMO. It was not approved until the time I left. According to newspaper reports in April 2020 (six months after I left), it seemed that it was still pending approval, with the minister exuding confidence that it would be done in a month's time. By the time of writing in July 2023, the tariff policy was still to be approved.

There were also amendments proposed in the Electricity Act. The nature of amendments was strange. One amendment suggested that the Central government take over the authority to appoint the chairman or a member of a state electricity regulatory commission if the state government failed to do so in a defined period of time. Another was to empower the Centre to issue directions to the regulatory commissions. The introduction of competition in distribution was not proposed in 2019, but has reportedly been suggested in the Electricity Act (Amendment) Bill 2021. De-licensing of the distribution sector is a welcome measure as it would bring in many more enterprises in the electricity supply business, which would help in the privatization of the state distribution companies. There was considerable speculation that this amendment would be introduced in the monsoon session of Parliament in 2021. However, this is still to happen.

The reform and investment schemes continue on the hackneyed model, convoluted tariff policy formulation remains under discussion and the Electricity Act amendment also hangs in the balance. The muddle continues.

Bidding Farewell to the IAS

At 5 p.m. on 31 October 2019, after serving in the IAS for over thirty-six years and one year before my normal date of superannuation, I bid farewell to the service at Shram Shakti Bhawan, where the Ministry of Power is housed. The officers gathered in the conference hall and we chit-chatted for half an hour. It was a lighthearted farewell.

I did offer my advice to pursue the bold and challenging path to completely transform the power sector in India by privatizing the entire sector, particularly the distribution segment. I knew it was too difficult an undertaking, especially with a government that talked about privatization of CPSEs but had no conviction about it and a minister who was totally steeped in the socialist mindset and saw the public sector as the essential instrument to achieve public good. Still, civil servants must continue to work for the right policies and to serve the public interest.

I released a farewell note on my Twitter and LinkedIn accounts once I reached home. It recounted the great time I had in the service despite many out-of-turn transfers and being relegated sometimes to the most unwanted jobs. I also laid my vision for India's economic future and how I would try to play a role in it. (The note is available on my Twitter account @Subhashgarg1960 and my Facebook and LinkedIn account.) I received an enormous response from people who had known me.

Leaving the IAS marked the beginning of another exciting phase in my life—the post IAS life.

I released my take on the 100 most pressing reforms India needed to build a $10 trillion economy, which I had presented to Prime Minister Modi, on my blog page subhashchandragarg.blogspot.in as well as on my Twitter and LinkedIn handles.

When I completed one year after leaving the IAS, when my cooling-off period—the rules prohibit officers from taking commercial employment for the first year after superannuation—got over, I posted a blog that recounted why I left the IAS and how meaningful and satisfying my post-service life was; this is also available on my three communication handles. This post, too, received a tremendous response.

Sometime in July 2020, Penguin approached me to write a book on the Indian economy. This culminated in my first book—*The $10 Trillion Dream: The State of Indian Economy and the Policy Reform Agenda*—published in February 2022. My interest in national budgets found expression in my next book—*Subhash Chandra Garg's Explanation and Commentary on Budget 2023–24*, published by Commercial Law Publishers in April 2023.

I write opinion editorials extensively in newspapers and magazines on important economic, financial and fiscal policy issues. My engagement with the economic policy has blossomed.

In this book, published by HarperCollins, I have recounted my participation in and encounters with economic policymaking. Not many ministers and civil servants do so in India. I hope this book breaks new ground.

There is indeed much to do for public policy and service outside the IAS. I am relishing my post-IAS life.

A Note of Thanks

Roots of my placement in the Department of Economic Affairs goes back to May 2000. Dr E.A.S. Sarma, then secretary, economic affairs, was instrumental in inducting me into DEA. He was a brilliant officer. For some reasons he was shifted to the Ministry of Coal as secretary. He was certainly miffed and thought the position of secretary, Ministry of Coal, a demotion, and took voluntary retirement from the IAS. I happened to be the next officer, after about nineteen years in the same department, to take a voluntary retirement. I thank him for being instrumental in inducting me into DEA, though my voluntary retirement was certainly not inspired by his action.

Prime Minister Narendra Modi chose me, in quite an unconventional manner, to go to the World Bank as India's executive director while I was serving in Rajasthan as principal secretary, finance. This was quite an exceptional case when an officer serving in the state government was sent to the World Bank, that too despite active opposition of the incumbent chief minister. Dr P.K. Mishra was instrumental in selecting me for this position. He was also the person who played an important role in the decision to bring me in as secretary, economic affairs. I am immensely thankful to PM Narendra Modi and additional principal secretary (currently principal secretary) Dr P.K. Mishra for choosing me for these two really important jobs.

The late Arun Jaitley was quite a remarkable finance minister and a human being. His ability to get to the nub of issues was perfectly suitable for quality policymaking. His trust in his officers to run the departments was simply extraordinary. Both these qualities provided me an unprecedented opportunity to make the best of my two-year period in the finance ministry. Finance Minister Arun Jaitley gave me free-run to manage DEA, immerse myself in economic policymaking, bring only serious policy proposals to him for his consideration, prepare two Budgets and contribute significantly to the finance minister's Budget speeches during 2017–2019. I cannot thank Arun Jaitley enough, for the great privilege of working with him and enabling me to participate in policymaking as I describe in the book.

Nirmala Sitharaman is the principal reason for making this book happen. Her unease with me in the ministry, led her to create conditions for me to take voluntary retirement from the IAS in October 2019. I could, thereafter, invest my time pursuing my interest in economic policy, particularly on building India as a $10 trillion economy. I was also able to write and publish two mega books—*The $10 Trillion Dream: The State of Indian Economy and The Policy Reform Agenda* (Penguin, February 2022) and *Subhash Chandra Garg's Explanation and Commentary on Budget 2023–24* (Commercial Law Publishers, April 2023). This would not have been possible if Nirmala Sitharaman had not shown me the path out of North Block. The present book—*We Also Make Policy*—describes my fifty-five-day journey with Nirmala Sitharaman at some length. I will always remain grateful to her for leading me to choose a path that sharply forked, taking me from my life as an administrator and government policy advisor to my present station as an independent observer, writer and speaker in the economic policy space, in wider civil society.

There are three officers whom I want to specially thank— Nripendra Misra, principal secretary to the PM; Hasmukh Adhia, secretary, revenue; and Arvind Subramanian, chief economic advisor. Nripendra Misra, one of the sharpest and most decisive officers I have come across in my service career, made the decisions happen. While sometimes I did not find these decisions palatable—as his objectives, views and tactics appeared influenced by political and other considerations—there was never a state of indecision. Most decisions were based on merits and were in the larger public interest. He initially took me to be an upstart but later entrusted me with numerous responsibilities, sometimes beyond the scope of the secretary, DEA's normal sphere of work. Hasmukh Adhia was a decent human being. He was always fully prepared and allowed liberal participation in meetings. It was only during his time that I got involved, while preparing the Budget, in tax policies and proposals as well. Arvind has always been ebullient with enormous command over language. His presentations were a joy to watch. My sincere thanks to all the three.

I have named quite a few officers at the joint secretary, additional secretary and special secretary level in DEA in the prologue section. I had a very competent and efficient team of officers and staff in DEA. I will always remain grateful to them for their work, briefs, examinations and delivery. In fact, I have also dedicated this book to them. A big thank you to all of you.

I cannot conclude this note without specifically thanking Anjali, my wife. She is a brilliant chartered accountant and was employed with IPCL when we got married in 1986. She switched her career to that of a practicing chartered accountant, to shift base to Rajasthan after our marriage. When I was appointed secretary, economic affairs, she decided to close her chartered accountant firm. Caesar's wife must be above suspicion.

I am thankful to Mitali Mukherjee for introducing me to Swati Chopra and through her to HarperCollins. Swati has been totally professional and very helpful. We agreed on a timeline. She organized everything on time to make this happen. Sashi Aiyer and Suzanne Hughe have been flawlessly meticulous with the editing and proofreading of the manuscript. Their many suggestions have helped in improving the quality, flow and consistency of the book. I thank

Swati, Sashi, Suzanne and the HarperCollins team profusely. I also thank Arati Menon, who assisted me in editing this book when I first wrote it.

I feel quite happy that HarperCollins has made this book come out so elegantly. I thank everyone at HarperCollins Publishers India.

Finally, it is the readers—you—who I thank most. I hope you found the book a truthful and engaging account of real economic policymaking in the country. Please do write to me with your feedback and suggestions at suchgarg60@gmail.com.

—Subhash Chandra Garg
13 July 2023

Abbreviations

AAI	Airports Authority of India
ACC	Appointments Committee of Cabinet
ADB	Asian Development Bank
ADF	Asian Development Fund (of ADB)
Adhia	Abu Dhabi Investment Authority
ADR	Association for Democratic Reforms
ADRs	American Depository Receipts
AG	Attorney General
AGR	adjusted gross revenue (of telecom licence companies)
AIBP	Accelerated Irrigation Benefit Programme
AIF	Alternative Investment Fund
AIIB	Asian Infrastructure Investment Bank
AoA	articles of agreement
APARs	annual performance appraisal reports
AVGC	animation, visual effects, gaming and comics (sector in media)
AY	Assessment Year
BIPA	Bilateral Investment Promotion Agreement

BIT	Bilateral Investment Treaty
BJP	Bharatiya Janata Party
BOT	build-operate-transfer
BPCL	Bharat Petroleum Corporation Ltd
BPRL	Bharat Petro Resources Ltd
BRBNMPL	Bhartiya Reserve Bank Note Mudran Pvt., Ltd
BRICS	Brazil, Russia, India, China and South Africa
BSE	Bombay Stock Exchange
BSNL	Bharat Sanchar Nigam Ltd
CACP	Commission of Agriculture Costs and Prices
CAD	current account deficit
CAG	Comptroller and Auditor General
CBDT	Central Board of Direct Taxes
CBI	Central Bureau of Investigation
CBIC	Central Board of Indirect Taxes and Customs
CCB	Committee of Central Board (RBI)
CCB	capital contingency buffer
CCD	Coins and Currency Division (DEA)
CCEA	Cabinet Committee on Economic Affairs
CEA	Chief Economic Advisor
CEC	Chief Election Commissioner
CERC	Central Electricity Regulatory Commission
CF	Contingency Fund (RBI)
CFI	Consolidated Fund of India
CFU	Climate Finance Unit
CGAM	Core Group of Secretaries on Asset Monetization
CGM	chief general manager
CONCOR	Container Corporation
CoS	Committee of Secretaries
CPI	Communist Party of India
——	consumer price inflation
CPSEs	Central public-sector enterprises
CRAR	capital to risk-weighted assets ratio
CSS	Centrally Sponsored Schemes
DBT	direct benefit transfer (system for fiscal benefit transfers)
DCC	Digital Communications Commission

DEA	Department of Economic Affairs
DFI	development finance institution
DFFT	data free flow with trust
DFS	Department of Financial Services
DG	director general
DIAL	Delhi International Airport Ltd
DIPAM	Department of Investment and Public Asset Management
DIPP	Department of Industrial Promotion and Policy
DPIDF	Dairy Processing Infrastructure Development Fund
DPIIT	Department for Promotion of Industry and Internal Trade
DO	demi-official
DoC	Department of Commerce
DoPT	Department of Personnel and Training
DoT	Department of Telecommunications
DPE	Department of Public Enterprises
DPR	detailed project report
DRR	debenture redemption reserve
DTAA	Double Tax Avoidance Agreement
EASE	Enhanced Access and Service Excellence (framework)
EBIT	earnings before interest and taxes
EC	Election Commission
ECB	European Central Bank
——	external commercial borrowing
ECF	Economic Capital Framework (ECF)
EMs	Emerging Markets
EODB	ease of doing business
EoI	expression of interest
ETF	exchange traded fund
EU	European Union
EXIM	Export-Import
FAR	fully accessible route (for foreign investment in government securities)
FATF	Financial Action Task Force
FCNR	Foreign Currency Non-Resident-B Deposit Scheme
FDI	foreign direct investment

FEMA	Foreign Exchange Management Act
XV FC	Fifteenth Finance Commission
FII	foreign institutional investor
FIFP	Foreign Investment Facilitation Portal
FIPB	Foreign Investment Promotion Board
FMC	forward markets commission
FPI	foreign portfolio investment
FPO	farmers producer organization
FRBM	Fiscal Responsibility and Budget Management
FRDI	Financial Resolution and Deposit Insurance (Bill)
FSAs	Fuel Supply Agreements
GCF	Green Climate Fund
GDP	gross domestic product
GDR	global depository receipt
GFC	global financial crisis (2008)
GIFT	Gujarat International Finance-Tec City
GoM	Group of Ministers
GST	Goods and Services Tax
HAL	Hindustan Aeronautics Ltd
HCI	Human Capital Index (developed by World Bank)
HFC	housing finance company
HPCL	Hindustan Petroleum Corporation Ltd
IAS	Indian Administrative Service
IBC	Insolvency and Bankruptcy Code
ICO	initial coin/currency offering
IEDCL	IL&FS Energy Development Company Ltd
IER	International Economic Relations (a Division in DEA)
IES	Indian Economic Service
IDF–NBFCs	Infrastructure Debt Fund–Non-Bank Finance Companies
IFC	International Finance Centre (GIFT City, Gandhinagar)
——	International Finance Corporation (of World Bank Group)
IFIN	IL&FS Financial Services Ltd
IGL	Indraprastha Gas Ltd

IGGL	Indradhanush Gas Grid Ltd
IGST	integrated GST
IIML	IL&FS Investment Managers Limited
IIP	Index of Industrial Production
ILO	International Labour Organization
IMF	International Monetary Fund
IMG	inter-ministerial group
INR	Indian Rupee
InvIT	Infrastructure Investment Trust
IOC	Indian Oil Corporation
IOSCO	International Organization of Securities Commission
IPO	Initial Public Offering
IRDA	Insurance Regulatory and Development Authority
ISB	Indian School of Business
ISDS	Investor State Dispute (Resolution) System
ISIN	International Securities Identification Number
ISSL	IL&FS Security Services Ltd
ISTSL	ISSL Settlement and Transaction Services Ltd
ITNL	IL&FS Transportation Networks Ltd
JPC	Joint Parliamentary Committee
JWP	joint work programme
KYC	know your customer
LDC	load despatch centre
LIBOR	London Inter-Bank Offered Rate
LIC	Life Insurance Corporation of India
LoC	letter of credit
LRS	Liberalized Remittances Scheme
LTCG	long-term capital gains (tax)
LTIF	Long-Term Irrigation Fund
MBRT	multi-brand retail trade
MCA	Ministry of Company Affairs
MDR	merchant discount rate
MEA	Ministry of External Affairs
MEITY	Ministry of Electronics and Information Technology
MFIs	micro-finance institutions
MHA	Ministry of Home Affairs

MIAL	Mumbai International Airport Ltd
MIF	Micro Irrigation Fund
MNRE	Ministry of New and Renewable Energy
MoCA	Ministry of Civil Aviation
MoEF	Ministry of Environment and Forests
MoHUA	Ministry of Housing and Urban Affairs
MoPNG	Ministry of Petroleum and Natural Gas
MoRTH	Ministry of Road Transport and Highways
MSME	micro, small and medium enterprises
MSP	Minimum Support Price
MTNL	Mahanagar Telephone Nigam Ltd
MW	Megawatt
NABARD	National Bank for Agriculture and Rural Development
NBFC	non-banking financial company
NCLT	National Company Law Tribunal
NDA	National Democratic Alliance
NDB	New Development Bank
NDF	Non-Deliverable Forward (market/contracts)
NDS	Negotiated Dealing System (RBI)
NIIF	National Infrastructure Investment Fund
NIP	National Infrastructure Pipeline
NIPFP	National Institute of Public Finance and Policy
NMP	National Monetization Pipeline
NPA	non-performing asset
NSA	National Security Advisor
NSDL	National Securities Depository Ltd
NSE	National Stock Exchange
NSO	National Statistical Organization
NTC	National Textiles Corporation
ODI	overseas direct investment
OECD	Organization of Economic Cooperation and Development
OFS	offer for sale
OIL	Oil India Ltd
OMDA	operation, management, development agreement (model)

ONGC	Oil and Natural Gas Corporation
OPI	overseas portfolio investment
PAB	Project Approval Board (DIPP)
PCA	Prompt Corrective Action Framework
PCF	Prompt Corrective Framework (RBI)
PCGS 2.0	Partial Risk Guarantee Scheme–Version 2
PDMA	Public Debt Management Agency
PFC	Power Finance Corporation
PIB	Press Information Bureau
PIM	preliminary information memorandum
PISA	Programme for International Student Assessment
PIB	Press Information Bureau
PM	Prime Minister
PMO	Prime Minister's Office
PM-SYM	Pradhan Mantri Shram-Yogi Maandhan
PNB	Punjab National Bank
PPA	Power Purchase Agreement
PPP	public-private partnership
PPPAC	Public Private Partnership Appraisal Committee
PRB	Payment Regulatory Board Public Sector Banks (PSBs)
PSE	public-sector enterprise
PSS	Payments and Settlement Systems Act
PwC	PricewaterhouseCoopers
RBI	Reserve Bank of India
R&D	research and development
REC	Rural Electrification Corporation
REIT	real-estate investment trust
RFP	request for proposals
RIDF	Rural Infrastructure Development Fund
RSBY	Rashtriya Swasthya Bima Yojana
RTI	Right to Information
SAARC	South Asian Association for Regional Cooperation
SBI	State Bank of India
SBRT	single-brand retail trade
SCI	Shipping Corporation of India
SCRA	Securities Contract (Regulation) Act, 1956

SEBI	Securities and Exchange Board of India
SFIO	Serious Fraud Investigation Office
SMA	special mention account
SPA	sale purchase agreement
SPAC	special purpose acquisition company
SPMCIL	Security Printing and Minting Corporation of India Ltd
SPV	special purpose vehicle
SSDP	staggered surplus distribution policy
S-VaR	stressed value at risk
SWF	sovereign wealth fund
TBCB	tariff-based competitive bidding
T&D	transmission and distribution
TDR	transferable drawing right
TDS	tax deducted at source
TIMSS	Trends in International Maths and Science Study
ToR	Terms of Reference
TOT	toll, operate and transfer
TPC	total project cost
UAE	United Arab Emirates
UDAY	Ujjwal DISCOM Assurance Yojana
UIDAI	Unique Identification Authority of India
UK	United Kingdom
UNFCCC	United Nations Framework Convention on Climate Change
UNDP	United Nations Development Programme
UPA	United Progressive Alliance
UPI	unified payment interface
US	United States
USIBC	US India Business Council
USISPF	US India Strategic Partnership Forum
UT	Union Territory
VAT	value added tax
VaR	value (of asset) at risk
VC	virtual currency
VGF	viability gap funding
VRS	Voluntary Retirement Scheme

Index

About the Author

As a member of the Indian Administrative Service for more than thirty-six years, Subhash Chandra Garg was deeply involved in public administration, execution of development programmes, managing state-level institutions, making Budgets both at state and Central government levels, and policymaking. He crafted many Budgets as secretary of Budget, as finance secretary of the government of Rajasthan, as secretary of economic affairs and as finance secretary to the Government of India. He served as secretary of economic affairs for a little over two years, from 2017 to 2019.

After taking voluntary retirement from the IAS in October 2019, he now works as a policy observer, strategist, commentator and writer on important economic and financial policy issues with a focus on Indian economic and fiscal affairs and policy.

Garg's first book, *The $10 Trillion Dream: The State of Indian Economy and The Policy Reforms Agenda,* was published in February 2022. His second book, *Subhash Chandra Garg's Explanation and Commentary on Budget 2023–23,* includes the results and outcome of Budget 2021–22 and the implementation of Budget 2022–23 and develops a national standard for analysing and commenting on Central government budgets.

He writes opinion-editorials and columns for print and online newsmagazines, and speaks to think-tanks, educational institutions and investors regularly. He appears on television channels for discussions on economy, Budget and other public-policy matters as well.

30 Years *of*

HarperCollins *Publishers* India

At HarperCollins, we believe in telling the best stories and finding the widest possible readership for our books in every format possible. We started publishing 30 years ago; a great deal has changed since then, but what has remained constant is the passion with which our authors write their books, the love with which readers receive them, and the sheer joy and excitement that we as publishers feel in being a part of the publishing process.

Over the years, we've had the pleasure of publishing some of the finest writing from the subcontinent and around the world, and some of the biggest bestsellers in India's publishing history. Our books and authors have won a phenomenal range of awards, and we ourselves have been named Publisher of the Year the greatest number of times. But nothing has meant more to us than the fact that millions of people have read the books we published, and somewhere, a book of ours might have made a difference.

As we step into our fourth decade, we go back to that one word – a word which has been a driving force for us all these years.

Read.